# The Deer
# of North America

**An Outdoor Life Book**

# The Deer
# of North America

## Leonard Lee Rue III

**OUTDOOR LIFE BOOKS**

**CROWN, NEW YORK**

Library of Congress Cataloging in Publication Data

Rue, Leonard Lee.
  The deer of North America.

  Bibliography: pp. 435-447
  Includes index.
  1. Deer—North America.   2.   Mammals—North America.
I. Title.
QL737.U55R83     599'.7357     77-26484
ISBN 0-517-53630-7

Manufactured in the United States of America

This book is dedicated to four men who
enriched my life through their friendship —
George Homer Hicks
Bill Shipley
Jess Staugaard
Joe Taylor

# Contents

Contents

# Preface

The writing of this book has been a labor of love. Even before I finished writing my book *The World of the White-tailed Deer,* back in 1962, I knew that I'd have to write this one someday.

I've often been asked how long it takes me to write a book. A lifetime! All of my life I have been preparing for this and every other book I've written or ever hope to write. All of my life I have been watching, studying, living with, and reading about wildlife, and my hope is that I can spend the rest of my life watching, studying, living with, and reading about wildlife.

I've always considered myself most fortunate to have been raised on a farm; my roots are in the soil. Even today, no matter where I travel throughout the world, I am always checking the livestock, crops, water, and soil from a farmer's point of view — and calculating how those components of the ecosystem affect wildlife.

Times were rough on the farm during the last years of the Depression, and the work was hard. The life was a good one, though, and if I had my early life to live over I wouldn't change it at all. I'm thankful that I haven't forgotten how to do hard manual work, although I'm equally thankful I don't have to work that hard physically today. Every moment that I could spare from my work (and some that I couldn't) I roamed the wooded hills and valleys and explored the streams and river. I lived for the hours I could spend in such surroundings, and I still do. Not much of a formal education ever rubbed off on me, but my thirst for knowledge about everything in the outdoors was unquenchable. It remains so today. I've looked for the beauty of God's work that surrounds us on all sides, and I find it.

I've lived among deer all my life. I've watched them, studied them, photographed them, hunted them, eaten them. For more than two decades I was Chief Gamekeeper of Coventry Hunt Club, the largest such club in New Jersey. I've seen a hundred and eighty-three deer in one night, in one hour's time, within five miles of my home. I can still see deer most days just by looking out my windows. I've crisscrossed the continent, east to west, north to south, more times than I can recall to study and photograph deer and other wildlife. I read everything I can get my hands on about deer. My personal library — my pride and joy — has over six thousand bound volumes, and I have bulging file cases of clippings and research reports.

No one could write a book like this one from personal experience alone. No one could ever live long enough to experience more than a fraction of the things I want to tell you about. I have, of course, written from my personal experiences and observations, and I've also used all the pertinent references in my library. In addition, I've carefully studied the voluminous research reports and data that most of the states so graciously supplied to me. No species of wildlife has been the subject of as much study as the deer of North America.

The question remains, am I qualified to write a book that endeavors to tell everything — all that's known — about the life and habitat of America's deer? As I intimated, no one is qualified to do so on the sole basis of his own field studies. But, as you'll note in my acknowledgments, I've had the cooperation of experts in all of the continental United States as well as authorities at independent agencies, universities, and organizations working with deer. And as you'll note in the bibliography, I've had access to an enormous number of books, monographs, reports in scientific journals, and so on. When in doubt about some detail (or some contradiction in printed sources) I consulted the experts who had most extensively investigated the question at hand. As a result, much new information has come to light, and I believe this book to be both an accurate and thorough portrayal of our deer.

In this context, the word "deer" refers to animals of the genus *Odocoileus* — those known in the vernacular as deer and commonly meant when anyone speaks of deer. Technically, the deer family, or Cervidae, includes moose, caribou, and wapiti (elk). Despite their relationship to the whitetail and the mule deer, these animals are not only larger but less plentiful, less widely distributed, and vastly different anatomically and in their ways of life. Each would require a book of its own if all the known facts about it were to be explored. The deer I'm dealing with are America's best-known group of wild animals, the animals that arouse the greatest public interest, excitement, and concern — the favorites. They are my own favorites, too.

I've worked to make this book as complete and up to date as possible. Research continues to be done, continues to pour in, yet the book must be finished. Until the day the printer receives the final corrected proofs, I'll be inserting new material; I learn something new every day.

I can only hope that you find this book as exciting to read as I did to write it. There were times when I could hardly sit still to write, there was such a wealth of information inside of me waiting to be poured out. I have tried to substantiate in photographs many of the things I have talked about. A picture is still worth a thousand words, and I want you to see the deer as I have seen and known them.

## Acknowledgments

In listing acknowledgments, there is always the danger of inadvertently leaving out some of the people who should be included. I will not take the easy way out with a blanket "thank you" to all who helped. I do thank everyone who helped me in any way whatever, but I want to single out by name all I can recall because they deserve recognition.

A substantial foundation for this book was the work done by the people listed in my bibliography. I hope you will browse through the list and perhaps have occasion to read the original books or papers for further information. My thanks to all of those authorities. I must add that I think Joseph Dixon of California did a really superb job on the natural history of the mule deer of that state, making the most extensive use of photographs of any of the biologists.

I will list the various states alphabetically, naming the people of those states who shared with me their time and research: Alabama, Carl Scardina; Alaska, Donald E. McKnight, Robert Burnett; Arizona, Bill Sizer, Robert Jantzen; Arkansas, George Purvis, Lew Johnston; California, A.H. Murphy, Mike Frey, Richard Thompson; Colorado, Harold M. Swope, Peter T. Hansson; Connecticut, Paul G. Herig; Delaware, Elizabeth T. Caulk; Florida, James T. Floyd; Georgia, Terry Kile; Illinois, Gary C. Thomas, Jack Calhoun, Glenn

Harper; Indiana, Herbert Hill; Iowa, Lee Gladfelter, Robert B. Dahlgran; Kansas, Vic McLeran; Kentucky, James Gilpin, Martha Jane Harrod; Louisiana, Bob Dennie, Roger Hunter, Jerry Farrar; Maine, William Mincher; Maryland, Eugene F. Deems, Jr.; Massachusetts, John McConough, Richard Cronin; Michigan, David A. Arnold; Minnesota, Charles Wechsler, Leroy Rutske; Mississippi, D.L. Upton; Missouri, Dean Murphy, Wayne R. Porath, James F. Keefe; Montana, Bill Schneider; Nebraska, Jon Farrar, Jim Wofford; New Hampshire, David L. White, Richard Wentz; New Jersey, Robert C. Lund, Robert Mangold; New Mexico, Walter A. Snyder; New York, Arthur Woldt, Wayne Trimm; North Carolina, Rex Gary Schmidt; North Dakota, Pershing Carlson; Ohio, Dale L. Haney, Theodore Bookhout, Robert W. Donohoe; Oklahoma, Dean G. Graham; Oregon, Jack Dugan; Pennsylvania, Bob Bell, Steve Forbes; Rhode Island, John M. Cronan, Bradford Monahan; South Carolina, John Culler; South Dakota, Warren Jackson, Chuck Post; Tennessee; L.F. Gilchrist, Phil Tidwell; Texas, Richard McCune, Charles K. Winkler; Utah, Alton Frazier; Vermont, Bob Candy, Lawrence E. Garland; Virginia, Robert H. Giles, Jr., Harry L. Gillam; Washington, Tom Knight; West Virginia, Ed Johnson; Wisconsin, Burton Lohen. I must also thank a number of people connected with institutions, associations, and private enterprises: Smithsonian Institution, Francis M. Greenwell; National Rifle Association, Boone and Crockett Records Division, William Nesbitt; Weyerhaeuser Company, George Hess, Byron Carrier; Arizona State University, Sidney Wilcox.

The following people are personal friends and family members who have helped me immeasurably: Elaine and Manny Barrone, Denise Hendershot, Marilyn Maring, my sons Tim and Jim Rue, Bill Shipley, Fred Space, Danita and Glen Wampler. Also thanks to Bob La Rose, who prints my thousands of photos; Susan Dulaney, who dries them; Mary Ann Johnston, who copies the captions for them; and Barbara Dalton, who files and refiles them.

Helen Whittemore has allowed me to have a permanent photographic blind on her land. I've spent hundreds of hours studying and photographing deer there. Helen has shared not only her deer, but her home and her friendship, and I thank her.

Amy and Joe Taylor have been my friends forever. I've probably learned more about deer from Joe than from any other person. He is more than a friend. I seek his advice not only about deer but about most things I do in life.

Irene Vandermolen is of great help to me in my photography; she is also one of the main reasons my life is so exciting and worthwhile.

A number of the photos in this book have been taken by my oldest son, Leonard Lee Rue, IV. Because most editors do not notice the difference between the III and IV, he now goes under the professional name of Len Rue, Jr. I want to make sure he gets credit for his excellent photographic work.

A special note of thanks goes to my sister, Evelyn Rue Guthrie, for the typing of this manuscript. I write my books in longhand and I don't see how she is able to read what I have written. There are many times when even I am puzzled by my handwriting. She has frequently apologized for getting words wrong; she needn't. I apologize to her for not writing more legibly. It is her supreme effort that put this manuscript into a form that could be sent to the publisher.

And I want to say that it has been a pleasure once again to work with my good friends and editors at Outdoor Life Book Club. My thanks go once again to Editor and Publisher John W. Sill, Associate Editor Neil Soderstrom, and my good friend and editor Bob Elman.

God be with all of them and you.

Leonard Lee Rue III
Blairstown, New Jersey

# I

## The Animal
## and Its Behavior

# 1

## Man's Historical Impact on Deer

Biologically as well as in their behavior, deer are exquisitely adapted creatures. Like a number of other herbivorous mammals, they are ruminants—in other words, cud-chewers—and this digestive adaptation is one of many that helps them avoid predators, as will be shown in later chapters. They are ungulates—that is, hoofed quadrupeds—and their particular type of cloven hoof structure is another aid to survival that will be explored in later pages. Members of the order Artiodactyla, family Cervidae, genus *Odocoileus*, they evolved during the Miocene, fifteen to twenty million years ago, and they have outlasted many of the related and unrelated species and genera that evolved during that period.

They have also outlasted some forms of wildlife that thrived until the advent of civilization on this continent. The history of the deer population in North America is one of the greatest success stories in conservation literature. But it cannot be credited entirely to the efforts of conservationists, because today's population level is the result primarily of the tremendous adaptability of the deer themselves.

Deer were frequent subjects in Currier and Ives lithographs and other nineteenth-century art. (Collection of the Library of Congress)

It is often said that there are more deer in North America today than there have ever been. I have made that statement myself, but my present research forces me to question its accuracy. Although I may question the population estimates, I cannot prove the point one way or the other and I don't think anyone else can.

One of my earliest heroes was Ernest Thompson Seton, an excellent naturalist who really knew the wildlife he wrote about. I've read everything he wrote that I could get my hands on. In his memorable book, *Lives of Game Animals*, Seton went out on a limb by trying to estimate the population of various game animals before the Europeans came to this continent. He based his work on the writings of the earliest explorers, naturalists, and hunters. Seton then compared this research with the reports from various game departments of all the states and provinces. He filtered all these findings through his own considerable expertise, and his calculations gave us the first major wildlife census figures. Many of his estimates have stood the test of time, having been backed up by research in recent years. But I must risk charges of sacrilege by refusing to accept his figures on the population of the deer in North America.

Seton calculated that two million square miles of whitetail country originally existed, with an average of twenty deer per square mile. That added up to forty million whitetails. He estimated that mule deer occupied two and a half million square miles, with four or five to the square mile, for a total of about ten million mule deer. He figures that blacktail deer had about three-hundred thousand square miles of territory, and allowed ten deer to the square mile—or three million blacktails.

The greatest discrepancy is in the allotment of deer range. The continental United States, including Alaska, has 3,669,209 square miles of territory. Most of Alaska should be discounted because its deer (blacktails) inhabit only a portion of the southeastern Alaskan panhandle. If we take off most of Alaska, we have 3,089,209 square miles. Of this area, Seton allowed 2,000,000 square miles for the whitetail and 2,500,000 square miles for the mule deer. The whitetail has always been found in every one of the lower 48 states, although the population is minimal in such western states as California, Oregon, Nevada, and Utah. The whitetail's main range today is the eastern two-thirds of the United States.

Seton's estimate of twenty whitetails per square mile is now considered to be about the optimum number of deer *on the best of ranges.*

With regard to whitetails, then, Seton evidently underestimated the range but drastically overestimated the population density throughout that range. The result was much too high a figure for whitetails. His figures for muleys and blacktails were not as far off the mark but they, too, were probably inflated. Certainly, if there is any truth in the claim that we now have more deer than ever (or even as many), all of Seton's estimates were fantastically magnified. It is unlikely that the continent ever had enough habitat of just the right kind to support forty million whitetails, though it might possibly have supported slightly more than the present twelve and a half million. The latest census of mule deer puts their population at just a bit over half of Seton's ten-million estimate, and the census of blacktails is a little less than half of his three-million estimate.

All three groups now total about nineteen and a half million. That is a high population for any single type of wildlife. Whether or not there were more deer before the coming of the Europeans, deer were always abundant on this continent and they were always important to man.

The whitetail was as important to the eastern woodland Indians as the bison was to the Indians of the plains. Venison was a dietary staple, their

5

"bread of life." Deer hide was made into clothing, the sinew was used to sew the skins, the bones were fashioned into splinter awls to make the holes in the leather so that the sinew could be used, the hooves provided glue and ornaments and rattles. The deer's hair was stuffed inside moccasins in the winter to act as insulation. The bones and antlers were made into tools, weapons, decorations, and religious implements. The mound-building Indians of Ohio deified the deer and made sacred headdresses adorned with antlers.

Deer were equally important to the earliest settlers, providing them with almost as many of the basic necessities of life as they did for the Indians. The settlers, in fact, hunted deer far more intensively than the Indians. There were soon more settlers than there were Indians and, moreover, the deerskins and venison became major items of trade with Europe. This situation gave rise to professional hunting. Thomas Meacham of Hopkinton, in St. Laurence County, New York, kept an exact record of the game he killed as a professional hunter. When he died in 1850 he had killed 214 wolves, 77 cougars, 219 bears, and 2,550 deer. Nathaniel Foster of Herkimer, New York, killed 76 deer in a single season. Meshach Browning, who died in 1859, was a professional hunter from Garrett County, Maryland. In 44 years he killed between 1,800 and 2,000 whitetails. There were many such hunters.

The records of His Majesty's Custom Service show that 2,601,152 pounds of deer skins from 600,000 whitetails were shipped to England from Savannah, Georgia, in the years 1755 to 1773.

A traveler named Captain Marcy told of passing through southern Texas in 1846 and seeing thousands of deer daily—as many as 100 to 200 in a single herd. If Captain Marcy were to travel now in the Llano Basin of Texas he would find the deer there as plentiful as they were in his day. Texas currently has over three million whitetails, and there are as many as 121 deer to the square mile in the Llano Basin.

Today, ill-informed people tend to condemn the professional hunters of yesterday. These men were a product of their time, a time when it was believed that the supply of game was endless. The professional hunters were heroes to the boys of that era and the envy of most of the men.

The citizens of the short-lived state of Franklin (Tennessee today) even paid their officials salaries in deer skins. After all, they had no money but they did have lots of deer skins.

According to the records of the railroads in St. Paul, Minnesota, 7,409 venison saddles and carcasses, 4,000 venison hams in boxes, and 750 pounds of venison in barrels were shipped to markets in November and December of 1877. It is estimated that about 2,000 deer were killed within 15 miles of Osakis, Minnesota, in October, November, and December of 1880 by professional hunters. The venison was shipped to markets as far away as Boston.

Records such as these abound—and would seem to support Seton's statistics. However, there are also many records such as those of Major Robert Rogers, who found deer exceedingly scarce in the Northeast. During the French and Indian Wars, Rogers led his famous company of rangers north from Massachusetts through Maine to attack the Abenaki Indians on their home ground. His men, although skilled hunters and frontiersmen, saw no game and were actually starving by the time they returned.

Most of my home state of New Jersey was originally covered with mature forests, and we know that deer are not creatures of the mature forests. Most of the eastern half of the United States was also covered with such forests and undoubtedly those woods did not have high deer populations. Although we cannot be sure how many deer were on this continent in the early days, we do know that by the last of the 1800s most of the deer, as well as many other forms of wildlife, were close to extermination.

In 1646, Rhode Island became the first colony to pass a law protecting the deer from hunting for a part of the year. Other colonies and then the states followed Rhode Island's lead in protecting the deer in some manner. Often the laws were considered just a nuisance to be ignored. After all, no law has ever prevented anyone from doing anything; laws merely punish those who are caught breaking them.

The late 1800s were the blackest period for all types of wildlife throughout the continent. As the deer herds were reduced, conservationists labored to alert the populace to the fact that this splendid game species was on the verge of being annihilated. The northeastern states were the hardest hit. By the end of the nineteenth century, New Jersey was down to less than 200 deer. In Massachusetts, New Hampshire, and Vermont deer were so scarce that just sighting the tracks of one made headlines in local newspapers.

Finally, because of the increased awareness of the general public, more rigid game laws, better enforcement of the laws, and the importation of deer from states that still had them to the areas where they had been extirpated, the pendulum started to swing back the other way. Today, that pendulum is still swinging in the direction of a population boom for whitetails, although the populations of both mule deer and blacktails have declined slightly in recent years. Much of the decline in the populations of the mule and blacktail deer stems from the competition of domestic livestock—that is, the practice of overgrazing on federal lands, the public lands, by stockmen, particularly those who own sheep.

Despite that situation, the future of deer of North America is bright. Deer thrived before the coming of man and they still thrive. Barring some new calamity, they should continue to inhabit this continent farther into the future than we can speculate.

# 2

## Varieties and Distribution of Deer

Members of the deer family range throughout most of the world, although they are not found in Antarctica and they have an exceedingly limited range in northern Africa. They have been introduced into Australia and New Zealand. There are 17 genera, 40 distinct species, and more than 190 subspecies. The North American deer family includes the elk, moose, and caribou, as well as the animals more commonly known as deer, those of the genus *Odocoileus*.

Scientifically, a deer is assigned to the phylum Chordata because it has a backbone. It belongs to the class Mammalia because the females have mammary glands and suckle their young, which are born alive rather than as egg-enclosed embryos. A mammal is also characterized by a four-chambered heart, hair covering at least a part of its body, and a homoiothermal system — meaning the animal is warm-blooded, with a fairly constant body temperature regardless of the temperature of its surroundings. The deer is in the order Artiodactyla, meaning even-toed, because it has four toes (the two hoof lobes plus the dewclaws) on each foot. It is in the suborder Ruminantia because it has a four-compartmented stomach and chews a cud. The family grouping is Cervidae.

The exclusively American genus of deer, *Odocoileus,* is generally considered to include only two species—the whitetail (*O. virginianus*) and the mule deer, or mule-deer group (*O. hemionus*). The Columbian blacktail and the Sitka blacktail are ranked as subspecies of the mule deer. For that matter, there are a good many other subspecies of both the whitetail and the muley. As will be seen, these classifications have engendered some controversy among biologists and some confusion among the rest of us.

A species is an organism that is genetically linked so that its members are sexually compatible, making reproduction possible. Occasionally, matings take place between different species but only very rarely are the resulting crosses fertile. Most members of most species look alike, having similar character-istics. Variations that evolve within a species, creating subspecies, are usually caused by geographic and physiographic conditions causing spatial isolation of one or more populations. The response by the organism to a given environ-ment affects its size, weight, body conformation, and color as the species adapts to differences in temperature, light, moisture, altitude, regional vegeta-tion, and so on.

The different subspecies of deer conform to three biological laws of natural selection. One of these, called Bergmann's Rule, states that the farther a geo-graphic race is found north or south of the equator, the larger the mass of its body will be. The larger the body, the smaller is its relative surface area, resulting in a reduced loss of body heat. Conversely, the hotter the habitat is, the smaller the body and the larger its relative surface will be, allowing for greater heat dissipation. Thus, the Key deer (*O. v. clavium*), our most southern deer, is the smallest subspecies while the northern whitetail (*O. v. borealis*) and Dakota whitetail (*O. v. dacotensis*) are our most northern deer and our largest.

The second biological law, Allen's Rule, states that among warm-blooded creatures the physical extremities—ears, tail, and legs—are shorter in the cooler part of their range than in the warmer part. This rule is borne out by the Coues whitetail (*O. v. couesi*) of southern Arizona, which has larger ears and tail (compared to its body size) than the northern deer. When hunters or other observers see the relatively mule-eared Coues deer—also known as the Arizona whitetail—at a distance, they occasionally mistake it for a muley. However, the color and shape of the tail and, in the case of a mature buck, the conformation of the antlers will usually distinguish a race of whitetail from a muley where both species are encountered. In subsequent pages I will give de-tailed descriptions to facilitate field identification.

The Florida Key deer, a subspecies of whitetail, is North America's smallest deer. Small
races of deer evolve in warm latitudes, large
ones in cold latitudes.

The third law, Gloger's Rule, states that among warm-blooded animals dark
pigments are most prevalent in warm, humid habitat. I must add that dark
coloration also tends to prevail in forested regions. Note the darkness depends
on humidity as well as temperature. Hot, *dry* habitat does not produce darker
coloration, for pigment is a survival factor and a dark deer (or other prey
species) would invite predation by standing out conspicuously against a background of desert rock and sand. Red and yellow tints tend to dominate in arid
regions, paler tones—reduced pigmentation—in colder climates. The operation
of Gloger's rule will be seen in the descriptions of the various subspecies.

There are thirty recognized subspecies of the whitetail deer. Seventeen are
found north of the Mexican border, and these are the ones I will be discussing.
There are eleven subspecies of the mule deer, and I will discuss the eight that
are found north of the Mexican border. Although the blacktail deer is scientifically classified as a subspecies of the mule deer because of close biological
links, most wildlife biologists believe that the blacktail is a nascent species—
an emerging species which in time, will evolve into a separate species. This
process would be speeded if barriers such as impassable mountain ranges, barren deserts, or great bodies of water caused spatial isolation. At present, however, the blacktails are widening their range and frequently hybridizing with
other mule-deer races. All the same, the two varieties of blacktails differ
markedly from their close relatives in some respects, and at times I will
discuss them separately, as if they already constituted a distinct species.

This northeastern buck represents one of 30 recognized whitetail subspecies, of which 17 are found north of Mexico. Like whitetails in many regions, however, the New Jersey deer shown here probably has mixed ancestry. This is because several races were introduced to bolster dwindling herds in the early 1900s.

The deer of our continent are native Americans, descended from a common ancestor of the Pliocene period of ten million years ago. This ancestor was itself evolved from Miocene types that existed perhaps twice as long ago. Deer as we know them today developed during the Pleistocene period, about one million years ago, when they spread throughout the continent and diversified into the two separate species. Geographical and physical barriers tended to isolate them while continued evolution created further differences, the bases for the subspecification.

The genus name of *Odocoileus* was bestowed on all of them by the French-American naturalist Constantine Samuel Rafinesque, a gifted but slightly eccentric and glory-hungry scientist with a mania for discovering and naming species—sometimes erroneously. For example, between 1818 and 1820 John James Audubon, who enjoyed practical jokes, tricked him into publishing descriptions of almost a dozen purely fictitious creatures. Rafinesque added sub-

**11**

stantially to nineteenth-century knowledge of American wildlife, but in his rush to claim credit he occasionally grew careless. In 1832, while exploring caves in Virginia, he found a fossilized deer tooth, the last remains of some ancestor of the whitetails browsing in Virginia's woods. From this prototype he named the genus and species. Evidently he meant to call the genus *Odontocoelus*, meaning hollow tooth or concave tooth (why, no one is certain) but Greek was not his strong suit and the result was *Odocoileus*. The error has been perpetuated because taxonomists honor the earliest recorded name for a creature. *Virginianus* was added because the fossil was discovered in Virginia, and so the whitetail deer of that region became the "type species."

It was also Rafinesque who christened the mule deer *O. hemionus*. He named it—in this instance more accurately—from a specimen taken at the mouth of the Sioux River in what is now South Dakota. *Hemionus* is another Greek word, meaning mule or part-ass, a reference to the animal's very large ears.

All living things are scientifically classified according to a system originated by the great Swedish botanist and naturalist Carolus Linnaeus, in the mid-1700s. Thanks to this system, organisms are catalogued scientifically and are given a distinctive, often descriptive, universal Latin or Greek name. The chief advantage is that scientists throughout the world, regardless of their own language, know by an organism's scientific name that they are all talking about the same genus, species, or whatever.

The classification of living things, known as taxonomy, is a complex but not always exact science. Among taxonomists there are two warring factions, the "lumpers" and the "splitters." The lumpers are those biologists who want to simplify (but sometimes oversimplify) the divisions and differences found within a single genus, species, or other classification. The splitters are those who emphasize slight (or sometimes imagined) differences. Quite often the arguments advanced by both groups seem beyond any reasoning, but they have brought order out of what would otherwise be chaos. As one side or the other prevails in a controversy, and as new discoveries are made, reclassification continues.

The original division of subspecies was based on physical differences in skull characteristics, dentition, body size, and geographical locations. Such differences are sometimes clear-cut, sometimes subtle. The little Key deer of Florida, *Odocoileus virginianus clavium*, is the smallest deer north of the Mexican border, and no one would disagree that this whitetail is a distinct subspecies. The largest whitetail, *Odocoileus virginianus borealis*, is found in the northeastern United States and Canada. Most people, including me, could not tell it from any of the other large subspecies.

The deer of my home state of New Jersey are classified as *Odocoileus virginianus borealis.* I defy any expert in taxonomy to prove this classification is correct and I'll tell you why. According to Dr. Witmer Stone, an eminent naturalist whose writings appeared at about the turn of the century, the white-tail in New Jersey had been reduced to less than 200 individuals by the end of the 1800s. In an effort to save the deer, hunting was prohibited for twenty-one years. New and stronger game laws were passed and they were more strictly enforced. Many private individuals, notably Charles C. Worthington of Pahaquarry Township, and the State of New Jersey purchased hundreds of deer from Virginia, Maine, Michigan, Wisconsin, and perhaps other states. There were no centrally kept records of the private purchases, and current information is sketchy. The deer were released or escaped into various parts of the state, breeding with the remnants of the native deer. Since the original importation, many more deer have been transplanted to many different locations throughout the state. Those imported from Maine, Michigan, and Wisconsin were the *borealis* subspecies, as were the original New Jersey deer, but those from Virginia were not. Yet the subspecies in New Jersey is still classified as *O. v. borealis.*

This has been the situation in most eastern states. Even within a single state (and within a subspecies) there are considerable variations in body size and conformation, depending on habitat and the amount, quality, and types of food available. To further complicate the issue, unless there are definite geographic features dividing the ranges of subspecies, there is always an overlapping and interbreeding, making positive identification of many races arbitrary.

Before describing the species and subspecies in more detail, it may be helpful to discuss the marks of identification that enable a naturalist, hunter, or other observer in the field to recognize whitetails, mule deer, and blacktails. The three simplest keys to field identification are geography, tails, and antlers.

East of the Mississippi River, there are no mule deer or blacktails, except for small transplanted populations such as Oregon blacktails that have been stocked in Tennessee, and these introduced herds are usually well publicized. In the East, therefore, you can generally assume that a wild deer is a whitetail. The range of the blacktail is restricted to coastal areas in California, Oregon, Washington, British Columbia, and Alaska. So, in most of the West, if a deer is not a whitetail it must be a mule deer.

Muleys tend to be larger than blacktails or whitetails but, as the chapter on weights will show, size is not a reliable criterion. The tail is. A mule deer has a relatively short, narrow, pendant-shaped tail, mostly white but tipped with black. Some subspecies also have a bit of black at the base of the tail. The blacktail has a somewhat fuller tail, but it is considerably smaller than a

## Ranges of Whitetail Subspecies

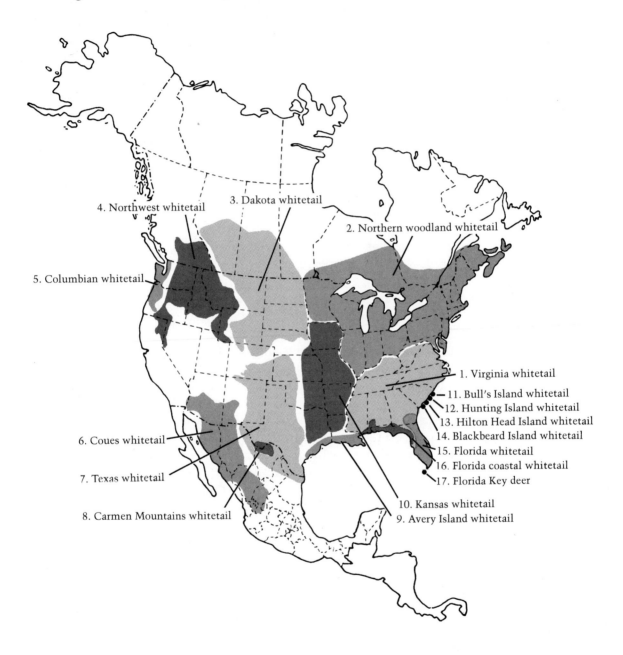

4. Northwest whitetail

3. Dakota whitetail

2. Northern woodland whitetail

5. Columbian whitetail

1. Virginia whitetail
11. Bull's Island whitetail
12. Hunting Island whitetail
13. Hilton Head Island whitetail
14. Blackbeard Island whitetail
15. Florida whitetail
16. Florida coastal whitetail
17. Florida Key deer

6. Coues whitetail

7. Texas whitetail

8. Carmen Mountains whitetail

10. Kansas whitetail
9. Avery Island whitetail

*(Based on map by Smithsonian Institution)*

whitetail's. Its dorsal (outer, or rear) surface is black or blackish from base to tip. A blacktail-muley hybrid has a black stripe (with white showing on each side) from tail base to tip. The whitetail has a longer, fuller tail, brown or with gradations of black on the dorsal surface. It is white underneath, and when the tail is raised, as in alarm, this white is very conspicuous—hence, the name of the species.

Bucks with sizable racks can usually be identified by their antler structure, as well. The points, or tines, of a whitetail's antler branch up from the two main beams. On a mule deer or blacktail, each main beam is bifurcated—that is, it forks, and then forks again. Generally, there are two such Y-forks or four points (though there may be more) on each side, plus a pair of small brow tines on a fully grown set of muley antlers. But antler conformation is less reliable in some regions than the size, shape, and color of the tail. There are occasional blacktails with antlers that look like a whitetail's, and a few whitetails grow bifurcated antlers that look like a mule deer's.

In addition to these marks of identification, the size and placement of the glands on the hind legs furnish a key to species recognition. However, you have to get a close look in order to make such use of these glands. The tails and antlers are discussed in more detail in Chapter 4, the glands in Chapter 5.

The whitetail deer, also called white-tailed deer and sometimes flagtail, is found in all of the contiguous states and in eight of the Canadian provinces. The latest estimates put the total whitetail population at over twelve and a half million. The following list enumerates some general physical characteristics and the distribution of the seventeen North American whitetail subspecies, or races.

1. The Virginia whitetail, *Odocoileus virginianus virginianus*, is the prototype of all whitetail deer. Its range includes Virginia, West Virginia, Kentucky, Tennessee, North Carolina, South Carolina, Georgia, Alabama, and Mississippi. This is a moderately large deer with fairly heavy antlers. It is hunted in all of the states it inhabits, and each state has a good deer population. It has a widely diversified habitat, varying from coastal marshes, swamplands, and pinelands to the "balds" atop the Great Smoky Mountains.

2. The northern woodland whitetail, *O. v. borealis*, is the largest and generally the darkest in coloration. It also has the largest range, being found in Maryland, Delaware, New Jersey, Pennsylvania, Ohio, Indiana, Illinois, Minnesota, Wisconsin, Michigan, New York, Connecticut, Rhode Island, Massachusetts, New Hampshire, Vermont, Maine, and the Canadian provinces of New Brunswick, Nova Scotia, Quebec, Ontario, and a portion of Manitoba. More whitetails of this subspecies are hunted than any other. Some 541,000 deer were legally taken from the region of the *borealis* subspecies in 1974.

Eight-point Virginia whitetail buck *(O. V. virginianus).*

Northern woodland whitetail buck *(O. v. borealis)*—largest and darkest of whitetails.

This area has also produced half a dozen of the top twenty record whitetail heads listed in the Boone and Crockett Club's official records book, *North American Big Game.* Founded by Theodore Roosevelt, the Boone and Crockett Club is dedicated to big-game hunting and to the study and conservation of wildlife. Since 1932, the organization has been publishing and updating a series of record books in which the most outstanding trophies are listed for thirty-two species of North American game animals. Official scoring charts and a very careful scoring system govern the measurement of these trophies. A Big Game Awards Program is now jointly administered and the records book is jointly sponsored by the Boone and Crockett Club and the National Rifle Association.

The seventh edition of *North American Big Game* was published in 1977. For the sake of dispensing information, it lists not only the outstanding animals harvested by hunters but also trophy animals of unknown origin—some killed by anonymous hunters long before the record-keeping began, some simply found and submitted because of impressive size. Unless otherwise specified, the record trophies I mention in my book will be those officially recognized by the Boone and Crockett Club.

As might be expected, the current world-record whitetail head is from the northern woodland region of *O. v. borealis.* The deer was killed in Minnesota on an unknown date by an unknown hunter. Its antlers score $206^5/_8$ in the Boone and Crockett system. Both main beams measure 30 inches (76.2 cm.) and each has five points—tines more than an inch long. Each main beam has a circumference of more than 6 inches (15.24 cm.) at the smallest place below the first point. A good many trophies have longer beams or more points, but scoring takes into account such other factors as the girth of the beams, their inside spread, and the lengths of the points. Incidentally, I am speaking here of typical heads; there is a separate classification for "non-typical antlers," which are generally asymmetric and sometimes studded with so many points that they look like stalagmite formations in a limestone cavern. Second place among typical whitetails is held by a twelve-point buck shot in 1971 in Missouri. Third place is held by a thirteen-pointer shot in 1965 in Illinois—again, prime *borealis* country.

The range of *borealis* is expanding steadily northward. In the seventeen years when I guided canoe trips into the wilderness areas of Quebec, I witnessed a northward expansion of more than 100 miles. As a lumber company cut the virgin forests of spruce for paper pulp, the network of logging roads opened up vast areas for hunters, fishermen, and tourists. Before such an onslaught of disturbances, the moose and wolves retreated northward. The cutover land sprang back with newly sprouting aspen, birch, berry bushes, and co-

Dakota whitetail buck *(O. v. dacotensis)* with antlers in summer velvet.

nifers. With the increased food and decreased competition and predation, this whitetail is enlarging both its range and its numbers.

3. The Dakota whitetail, *O. v. dacotensis,* is another very large deer, about equaling the northern whitetail in weight (see Chapter 9 for tabulations of body weights). This subspecies has produced even more of the high-ranking trophy heads than the *borealis* race. The range covers North Dakota, South Dakota, and parts of Nebraska, Kansas, Wyoming, Montana, and the Canadian provinces of Manitoba, Saskatchewan, and Alberta. Dakota bucks have heavy, fairly widespread antlers. The winter coat is a little paler than that of *borealis.* This is a deer of the breaks. Its home is in the timbered coulees, gullies, draws, and river and stream bottoms that cut through the prairies.

4. The Northwest whitetail, *O. v. ochrourus,* is also a large deer. It inhabits parts of Montana, Idaho, Washington, Oregon, California, Nevada, Utah, and

Northwest whitetail buck *(O. v. ochrourus)* shown here in velvet.

the Canadian provinces of British Columbia and Alberta. The biggest whitetail I ever saw was in Glacier National Park. It could have been either this subspecies or a Dakota. The two races intergrade in that area. This subspecies has very widespread antlers and a winter coat of relatively pale cinnamon-brown.

5. The range of the Columbian whitetail, *O. v. leucurus*, has been so greatly reduced that most of these deer are now found only on the Federal Columbian White-tailed Deer Refuge, on the Columbia River near Cathlamet, Washington. The subspecies formerly ranged along the Pacific coast in Washington and Oregon, spreading eastward to intergrade with the Northwest whitetail. The Columbian whitetail is not hunted as it is now on the endangered-animal list.

Columbian whitetail doe *(O. v. leucurus)* with numbered collar and ear tag attached by management researchers.

**19**

Coues, or Arizona, whitetail buck *(O. v. couesi)* in velvet.

The population is estimated at between five hundred animals or less. Unfortunately, of the thirteen Columbian whitetails I've seen, nine wore large numbered collars and ear tags. I fully realize the importance of research to improve our management of wildlife, but I was terribly disappointed to find most of the Columbians wearing tags. They are large deer with high but narrow-spreading antlers.

6. The Coues (pronounced "cows"), or Arizona whitetail, *O. v. couesi,* is a small variety. At one time it was thought to be a distinct species but more recent research has relegated it to the status of subspecies. It has larger ears and tail in relation to its body size than most whitetails, but I found that the ears and tail were not as large as I had been led to believe. This deer is found

Large six-point Texas whitetail buck *(O. v. texanus).*

in the dry, desert regions of southeastern California, southern Arizona, southwestern New Mexico, and on down into Old Mexico. The Coues is apparently isolated from areas where it could intergrade with the Texas whitetail but in the southern part of its range it probably intergrades with several Mexican subspecies. Even in Arizona the Coues whitetails are more or less isolated in the mountainous areas that rise above the desert, such as the Chiricahua and Huachuca Mountains. Arizona estimates it has about 25,000 Coues deer but does not give any harvest figures. New Mexico has a hunting season for this deer but gives neither a population estimate nor the hunters' take. The Coues deer has its own classification in the Boone and Crockett Club, dating back to when it was considered a distinct species. From the hunter's point of view, the

Carmen Mountains whitetail spike buck *(O. v. carminis)* in velvet.

separate classification remains legitimate since the little Coues deer has a light "rack," or antlers. A trophy that is outstanding by Coues standards could hardly compete with a trophy northern or Dakota whitetail.

7. The Texas whitetail, *O. v. texanus*, is found in western Texas, Oklahoma, Kansas, southeastern Colorado, eastern New Mexico, and the northern portion of Old Mexico. Everything about Texas is big, even its population of whitetail deer. It has an estimated three and a half million of them, more than any other state. The annual harvest usually goes over 350,000. Texas has four whitetail subspecies, of which the most abundant is the Texas whitetail. Its body is much smaller than that of the more northerly deer but it is the largest of the southern forms. The antlers are slender but widespread and there are several record heads among the top twenty-five.

8. The Carmen Mountains whitetail, *O. v. carminis*, is a small deer found in the Big Bend region of Texas. Its range is limited to the Carmen Mountains on both sides of the Rio Grande. Not many of these deer are hunted because most of their range falls within the boundaries of Big Bend National Park, where hunting is prohibited. Here is a good example of isolation. A buffer strip of semi-desert, inhabited by mule deer, separates this subspecies from the Texas whitetail and prevents intergrading.

9. The range of the Avery Island whitetail, *O. v. mcilhennyi*, stretches along the Gulf Coast in Texas and Louisiana. This is the deer of the Texas Big Thicket Country. It is a large one with a dark, brownish winter coat, and it intergrades with the white-tail subspecies found to the west, north, and east.

Kansas whitetail doe *(O. v. macrourus)*.

10. The Kansas whitetail, *O. v. macrourus*, is the fourth subspecies occurring in Texas. Found in eastern Texas, Oklahoma, Kansas, Nebraska, Iowa, Missouri, Arkansas, and Louisiana, it is a large deer with heavy main antler beams and short tines. Several deer of this type are listed among the top 25 heads.

11. The Bull's Island whitetail, *O. v. taurinsulae*, is an isolated and very limited race of whitetail deer, found only on Bull's Island, South Carolina.

12. The Hunting Island whitetail, *O. v. venatorius*, is another of South Carolina's minor variations, found only on Hunting Island.

13. The Hilton Head Island whitetail, *O. v. hiltonensis*, is still another South Carolinian variation, limited to Hilton Head Island.

14. The Blackbeard Island whitetail, *O. v. nigribarbis*, is found only on the Georgian Islands of Blackbeard and Sapelo.

All of those last four subspecies are medium-sized deer with fairly small antlers that are heavily ridged or wrinkled at the base. The islands they inhabit are far enough out in the ocean to prevent intergrading with mainland subspecies or with one another. I believe that hunting is currently allowed on all of these islands.

15. The Florida whitetail, *O. v. seminolus*, is a good-sized deer with a good rack. Some of the Florida deer that I photographed in Okefenokee Swamp in Georgia were every bit as large as those I have photographed back home in New Jersey. Some had antlers as impressive as the *borealis* though the spread was not as wide. The race is the deer of the Everglades.

Florida whitetail buck *(O. v. seminolus)* in velvet.

16. The Florida coastal whitetail, *O. v. osceola,* is found in the Florida panhandle, southern Alabama, and Mississippi. It is not as large as the Florida or the Virginia whitetail but it intergrades with both.

17. The diminutive Florida Key deer, *O. v. clavium,* is the smallest of our native deer. No hunting is allowed for this subspecies, which is on the endangered-animal list. By 1949, the Key deer population had plummeted to an all-time low of thirty individuals. This reduction was brought about mainly by habitat destruction, fires, hurricanes, automobile kills, and hunting. The Key Deer National Wildlife Refuge was established in 1953. With the protection thus provided, the deer population has crept back up to about three hundred. Today the automobile is the number-one killer, as the highway linking the Florida Keys passes through the center of the range. Additional land should be added to the refuge to assure this deer's future.

The mule deer, also known as the muley, inhabits the mountains, deserts, coast, and high plains of the western half of the United States and Canada. The latest figures for the mule deer are estimated to be about five and a half million. The blacktail deer is generally regarded as a coastal variety, but in California blacktails are found as far east as the mountains of Yosemite Na-

Florida coastal whitetail buck *(O. v. osceola)* in velvet. (Photo by Len Rue, Jr.)

Six-point Florida Key buck *(O. v. clavium).*

## Ranges of Mule Deer Subspecies

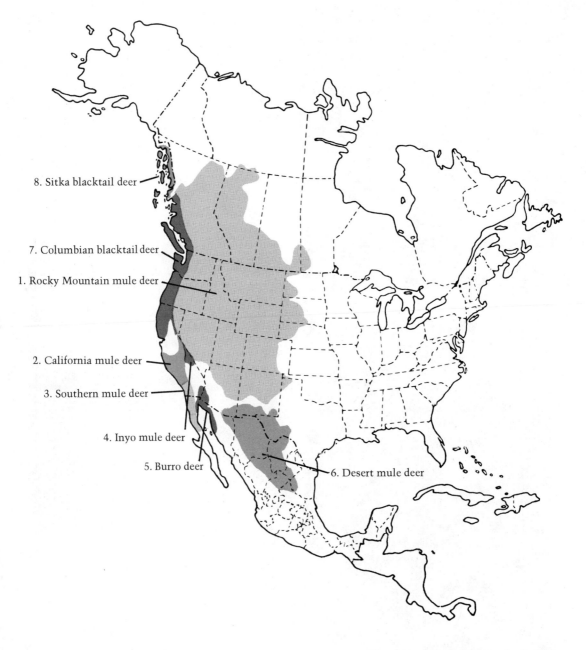

8. Sitka blacktail deer

7. Columbian blacktail deer

1. Rocky Mountain mule deer

2. California mule deer

3. Southern mule deer

4. Inyo mule deer

5. Burro deer

6. Desert mule deer

*(Based on map by Smithsonian Institution)*

tional Park. The total blacktail population is estimated to be 1,430,000. The following list enumerates the eight subspecies of mule deer, including the two races of blacktails.

1. Rocky Mountain mule deer, *Odocoileus hemionus hemionus,* is the prototype. It has a larger range than any other subspecies of mule deer or whitetail. This race is the northernmost of the mule deer, the largest, heaviest, and darkest in coloration. (In view of its northerly distribution, you might expect it to be paler, but much of its habitat is forested, whereas some other races— most notably the desert muley—have a paler coloration that blends best with their surroundings.) The Rocky Mountain race is found in the Canadian provinces of British Columbia, Alberta, Saskatchewan, Manitoba, and the Northwest Territories, as well as in Washington, Idaho, Montana, North Dakota, Minnesota, South Dakota, Nebraska, Wyoming, Oregon, California, Nevada, Utah, Colorado, Oklahoma, New Mexico, and Arizona. And I have recently received reports indicating it has spread its range to Iowa.

Large Rocky Mountain mule deer buck *(O. h. hemionus)* in velvet.

The average mule deer is larger than the average whitetail, and superlatives are needed to describe this particular subspecies. All of the top twenty-five mule-deer trophies in the Boone and Crockett records are of this subspecies. At the western fringe of its range the Rocky Mountain muley intergrades with the Columbian blacktail.

2. The California mule deer, *O. h. californicus*, is found only in California, from the Sierras to the Pacific. It intergrades with the Columbian blacktail along the northern border of its range. It is smaller than the Rocky Mountain mule deer and also has a smaller white rump patch.

3. The southern mule deer, *O. h. fuliginatus*, is found along California's coast, from the vicinity of Los Angeles south into Mexico's Baja California Peninsula. It is a very dark subspecies, of about the same size as the California mule deer.

4. The Inyo mule deer, *O. h. inyoensis*, has only a small range in and around Inyo County, California. In size and color, it is intermediate between the Rocky Mountain mule deer to the east and the California mule deer to the west. Its white rump patch is also intermediate. The black on its tail goes far-

California mule deer buck *(O. h. californicus)* in velvet.

Desert mule deer bucks *(O. h. crooki)* — one spike, one mature deer, both in velvet.

ther up the dorsal surface than does that of the Rocky Mountain deer, but not quite as far as that of the California mule deer.

5. The burro deer, *O. h. eremicus*, is found in the extreme southeastern portion of California and from southwestern Arizona down into Mexico. This subspecies is smaller than the Rocky Mountain mule deer and much lighter in coloration.

6. The desert mule deer, *O. h. crooki*, has the second largest distribution of any of the mule deer. Its range includes southeastern Arizona, southern New Mexico, western Texas, and it extends hundreds of miles south into Old Mexico. This is a good-sized deer — large-boned, that is — and it would probably be heavier if more forage were available. However, the scantiness of desert vegetation may be only one of two factors limiting this muley's weight. In the hotter parts of its range, Bergmann's Rule may also apply; that is, if the animal's mass were greater relative to its surface area, it could not dissipate heat as efficiently.

The desert mule deer copes with some of the harshest conditions imaginable for a deer. Much of its habitat is so arid that forage is relatively meager and water is scarce during much of the year. In much of its habitat there is also intense heat — and intense cold, as well. And most of its range is open country, with relatively little cover in which to hide from enemies. Yet a desert muley not only can sustain itself in seemingly impoverished habitat but can make itself almost invisible when it beds down in a little clump of vegetation or even a small depression in the terrain, blending with its background.

Ten-point Columbian blacktail buck *(O. h. columbianus).* (Photo by Len Rue, Jr.)

The desert muley is the palest of mule deer—a very light tannish-gray. It has a very small rump patch and a dark stripe running partway down the tail.

7. The Columbian blacktailed deer, *O. h. columbianus,* is found in California, Washington, Oregon, and British Columbia. It manages to thrive in the mountains, in dry chaparral, and in the densest, wettest forests on the North American continent. Although both of the blacktail races—the Columbian and the Sitka—occasionally exhibit very respectable weights, these two subspecies usually are smaller than their closest relatives, the other varieties of mule deer. They are, in fact, smaller than the average whitetail. The Columbian blacktail has a redder coat than the mule deer with which it interbreeds. Its tail top is all black and its ears are intermediate in length—shorter than the muley's, longer than the whitetail's.

8. The Sitka blacktail deer, *O. h. sitkensis,* has a cinnamon-brown coat and is smaller on the average than the Columbian. This would seem to be a refutation of Bergmann's Rule, but in this case the size is more directly connected to food (or lack of it) than to latitude. Forage becomes meager in the winter. When deep snows occur, this deer is forced down to the beaches to subsist on a marginal or starvation diet.

Sitka blacktail button buck *(O. h. sitkensis).*
(Photo by Len Rue, Jr.)

There are parts of the Sitka range where deep snows are seldom a problem, but in those more temperate pockets of habitat severe cold is seldom a problem, either. Therefore, a large body mass relative to the deer's surface area is not needed to conserve body heat, and the Sitka's size does not refute Bergmann's Rule, after all. The Sitka blacktail is an animal of the coastal rain forests. Originally, its range extended only from the Queen Charlotte Islands, off British Columbia, northward through the islands and mainland of the southeastern Alaska Panhandle. Beginning in 1916, herds were successfully introduced to several islands in Prince William Sound near Cordova, and later to Kodiak Island and the Yakutat area.

Harsh conditions are the limiting factor in this subspecies' northern range expansion. The Sitka blacktail is very important to the hunters of the areas it inhabits because no other members of the deer family live there.

# 3

## In the Tracks
## of Our Deer

We read almost daily about the depletion of our wildlife resources, as one creature or another is being relentlessly pushed down the road to extinction. Each time it happens, no matter what creature is involved, the world is poorer. The fact that most of us have never heard of some of the threatened species does not lessen the tragedy when existence ends for some variety of wildlife. However, our perspective may be a little clearer if we bear in mind that more species have already disappeared from the face of the earth than are in existence today. The vast majority of those evolutionary failures occurred before the coming of man.

There are approximately forty-five hundred species of mammals alive today. Some, such as the opossum, are from very ancient orders. Some, such as the deer, are of rather recent origin. All of the mammals that are alive today share many characteristics, but perhaps the most significant one is that they have evolved to survive under specialized conditions. The geological features of the world have been shaped by the stresses of continental drift, disturbances of the earth's crust, climatic conditions, and erosion. The creatures of the world have also been shaped so that they can obtain the necessities to support life and can withstand their adversaries.

The deer we know today are beautiful, alert, graceful, intelligent creatures because in the past all inferior deer were weeded out by predators, disease, competition for food, and all the rigors of their environment. The whitetail, in particular, has the widest range and is found in the greatest variety of habitats. It is primarily a deer of the woodlands, frequenting the edges and openings that have been created by natural conditions, fire, or man. It is also at home in the swamps of the South, the river bottoms of the prairies, and the forest edges of the high country. The mule deer is a deer of the rough, broken, tumbled, mountainous country, though it is also found on deserts and prairies. Its primary habitat is more open than that of other deer. The blacktail is equally at home in the dense, dark, tangled rain forests of the coastal areas and the dry, hot, brush-covered chaparral regions. Each of the deer has been altered—and strengthened—by its environment.

Although the deer is not a long-distance runner, it depends primarily on speed to escape its enemies. The ancestors of our modern deer had five toes on each foot, an adaptation to living in the forested areas that dominated much of the world at that time. As the climate of the earth changed, many of the forested areas gave way to savannas and grassland. The need for more sustained speed in these open spaces called for a sacrifice in the number of toes so that those remaining could be enlarged and strengthened. The deer lost its thumb or great toe completely. It raised up on its two center toes, and the digits that correspond to our "pinky" and index finger became vestigial bone splints that moved to the rear and are known as dewclaws. The toenails lengthened, hardened, and evolved into the deer's cloven hooves.

Hooves are composed of keratin, the same type of substance as our fingernails. Keratin is actually a type of solidified hair. On a deer's hooves, the outer rim is much harder than the central portion. Usually the central portion retracts somewhat in the winter so that the hoof has a concave appearance.

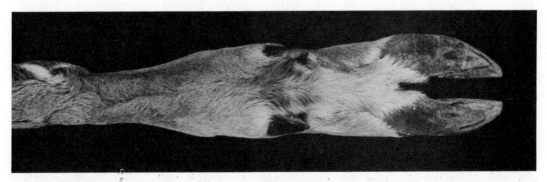

This typical underside of a deer's foot shows hoof lobes and dewclaws—the nails of four toes.

After running out on the ice and falling, this deer cannot rise.

   With this slight retraction, only the hard outer rim makes contact with the ground. This provides good traction on a rough surface but is treacherous on any smooth surface such as ice or an oiled black-top road. When snow is on the ground, deer often run out on ice to escape from dogs or other predators. If these deer slip, they are doomed because they seldom can regain their footing on ice. Usually they dislocate their hind legs or strain the muscles in the front legs. I have seen a number of deer that fell on ice and had to be killed. They could not rise again, and their legs would not function when they were taken off the ice. Of course, every rule about deer seems to have its exceptions. My friend Joe Taylor, who owns a deer preserve, has reported observing three whitetails walking on very smooth ice. They had learned to keep their front legs rigid and slide with their front hooves flat on the ice, while they splayed their hind feet and pushed forward with the tips of their rear hooves.
   Discounting such exceptions, it can be stated that the deer's hoof structure is of little help on ice, and when predators chase deer out onto a frozen lake disaster generally ensues. Under most circumstances, however, the hoof structure helps a deer move about sure-footedly, find forage, and escape enemies. It is an evolutionary adaptation to general conditions—far more an advantage than a disadvantage.
   Most of the year, the central portion of the hoof is almost convex, swelling outward to provide the foot with a spongy surface similar to that of wild goats and sheep. The hoof substance grows continuously throughout the deer's life but is kept worn down by the abrasion of rock and hard soil. The hooves of

"Swamp" deer develop exceptionally long hooves and dewclaws.

deer that live in swampy areas wear down at a much slower rate than those of deer that live on hard ground. Their hooves often become elongated, providing a much greater support area that prevents their sinking into the mud.

The front hooves of most animals are larger than those on the hind feet. My most recent measurements involved a whitetail buck that had a live weight of 151 pounds (68.5 kg.). One of its foot hooves measured 3¼ inches (82 mm.) in overall length and 2 inches (51 mm.) in width. The hind foot hoof

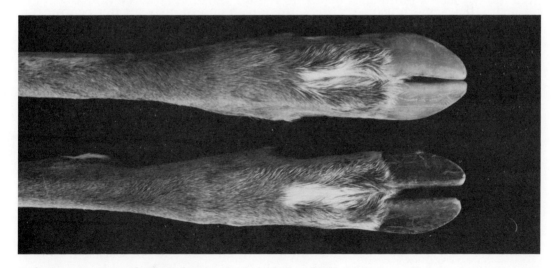

At bottom is a normal, black deer hoof. The colorless hoof on top is rare.

measured 2¾ inches (70 mm.) in overall length by 1¾ inches (44 mm.) in width. On a hard surface, a deer does not walk on the overall length of its hooves because they slope upward at the rear. The front hoof of this deer had a *bearing surface* that measured 2¼ inches (57 mm.) in length, then angled upward at 38° for another inch (25 mm.). Rarely are the two toes on a hoof of equal length. Usually the outside toe is about ¼ inch (6 mm.) longer.

When the ground is soft, the entire hoof surface comes into bearing. When the ground is very soft or muddy, the dewclaws are also used. On the buck I measured, the front foot's overall length, including the dewclaws, was 4½ inches (114 mm.) by 2⅜ inches (56 mm.) in width. The slightly greater width is because the dewclaws spread out a fraction wider than the hoof. The advantages of being able to splay the hooves and to use the dewclaws are apparent. When this deer was walking on hard ground, it had about 5 square inches (32 sq. cm.) of bearing surface per hoof or 20 square inches (128 sq. cm.) altogether. This works out to a body-weight ratio of only 7½ pounds (3.6 kg.) per square inch of bearing surface. When the deer was on muddy ground, with hooves and dewclaws splayed out, it effectively doubled its bearing surface, having about 40 square inches (256 sq. cm.) and a ratio of only 3¾ pounds (1.8 kg.) of body weight per square inch. The hooves of a blacktail deer are about the same size as the whitetail's. A mule deer's hooves are slightly larger because it is a slightly larger animal.

Regardless of species, the feet are a marvel of adaptation. If you have ever watched a deer browse its way gracefully through the woods, you will agree that the feet look delicate—and delicate they must be to pick their way through tangles and brush—yet they provide an enormously greater bearing surface than their appearance suggests. And they provide the best possible traction under the most common conditions. Moreover, when a deer must sprint for safety, the hooves are shaped to dig in powerfully, forming perfect bases for a fast run or sudden bolt.

Many hunters claim they can often tell a deer's sex by looking at its tracks. They say a buck's hooves are broader, longer, and have more rounded tips because a mature buck weighs more than a mature doe. The greater weight creates more wear on the toe tips, blunting them. This argument might hold water if the tracks were found in a national park where no hunting was permitted. In most regions, all of these supposed buck signs more often indicate a doe's track. In my own state, New Jersey—which is fairly typical—very few bucks ever live beyond 2½ years. They are usually harvested when they are 1½ or 2½ years old. Like many states, New Jersey now has an annual "antlerless" harvest, but it is much more limited than the buck season. Consequently, most does have the chance to become much older and larger than the bucks.

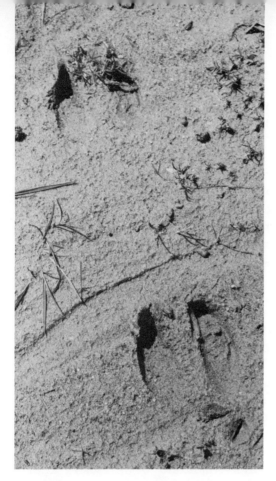

Imprints of dewclaws show behind hoof marks in these tracks because the deer was heavy and the ground soft.

Only one type of track reliably indicates sex: It is only the bucks that leave a hoof-dragging mark in shallow snow.

Biologists have proved that a buck's hooves, measured a third of the way back from the tip, average 5 percent wider than those of a doe. Fine, but I defy anyone to detect the difference when looking at tracks in the wild.

The fact that the dewclaws show in the tracks does not indicate the deer's sex, either. What it does indicate is that the ground was soft when the animal left the tracks.

Some hunters claim that a buck's tracks angle out more from a central axis or, in other words, "toe out" more. There is a degree of truth in this, but the degree of splaying can be pretty subtle.

The only reliable sex-indicating track that I know can be found after a snow of one inch (25 mm.) or less. A buck's feet produce a drag mark in the track because, like most males, he doesn't lift his feet any higher than he has to. The doe, being daintier, like most females, picks her feet clear and leaves just the track of the hoof imprint.

When there is more than an inch of snow on the ground, all deer leave drag marks. During the rutting season, bucks drag their feet even more than they ordinarily do, producing continuous drag marks in shallow snow. As to why, we can only speculate. Perhaps the bucks are conserving energy, or perhaps the shuffling walk is a means of leaving more glandular scent on the ground.

This test for drag marks also works on sand or any other surface where the deer sinks in about an inch. Under other conditions I, personally, cannot tell the sex of a deer by its tracks, though I have been studying and living with deer for more than thirty-five years. The so-called experts would stop claiming they could do so if they ever managed to see most of the deer that made the tracks.

The drag marks are made by the tips of the toes as they begin to straighten up so that their bearing surface is brought horizontal to the ground just before the next step is made. As the deer continues to walk, the front of the toes leave just a slight forward indentation in the snow as they leave the track to take the next step.

"Reading" tracks and other wildlife signs—that is, recognizing and interpreting them—is one of the most exciting and rewarding of outdoor activities, whether you do it for its own sake or in connection with hunting. If deer tracks cannot often reveal sex, they can give you a great deal of other information. They can tell you the number of deer that went by and they do tell you which direction they took. And if you find more than one set of tracks you may, after all, learn the sex of one of the deer even without snow or sand. When you find the tracks of one large deer accompanied by two smaller ones, it is safe to assume you are looking at the trail of a doe with her two fawns.

Depending on recent weather, you may even be able to date the tracks. A hard rain washes nature's blackboard clean, and even a moderate rain dims it somewhat. Sharp-edged tracks are fresh. They were made after the rainfall. Rounded edges mean the tracks were made prior to the rain.

If the tracks are in dirt or sand, the edges will tend to soften as wind brushes them. And if debris has blown into the tracks, you can date them to the last strong wind. Where cold keeps the snow powder-dry, tracks often can be dated to the last snowfall. Or the last heavy wind. Powder snow drifts easily, and in a wind it will fill or partially fill the tracks. In many areas the wind blows all day but dies down at night and this, too, may help in dating tracks.

In my area, what begins as powder snow often takes on a glaze of ice as it melts and then freezes again with fluctuating temperatures. If the snow is powdery, I date the tracks back to the snowfall. If the tracks are glazed slightly (and they will glaze before the crust of the snow because they are punched into the surface and are protected from the wind), you can figure they

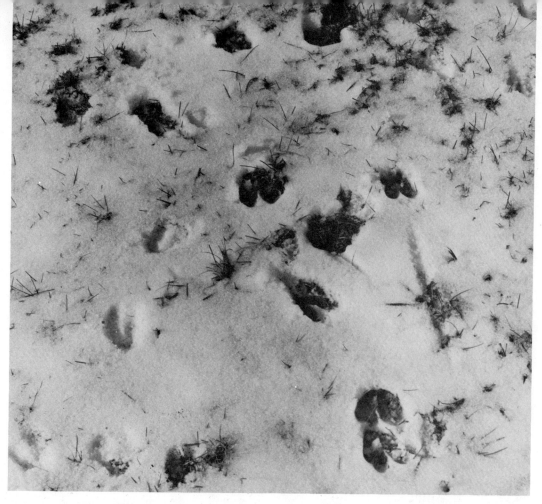

In snow like this, old tracks have a melted look. Crystals show in the fresher tracks.

were made the day following the snow. If they are punched through the glaze of the snow, they will have crumbly pieces of snow in them. In that event, they were made after the last warm day following the snow.

Moderating weather often fools an inexperienced tracker. The prints of little deer spread out in the melting snow, becoming larger as the trail grows old, and the prints of larger deer look as if they were left by monsters. The amount of melting can also help to date the tracks.

I love to go out after a fresh fall of slightly moist snow, a good tracking snow that is not too deep to obliterate what made the tracks. It's like reading a gossip column. You can tell who went where, when, with whom, and what they did there. That is, you can tell all this if you can read tracks.

The average adult deer—whitetail, mule deer, or blacktail—has a hind foot about 19 inches (48.26 cm.) long, the ankle being the portion we refer to as the tarsal joint, or hock. A deer's legs are long and heavily muscled to provide the power needed to run and jump.

Whitetail deer walk, trot, and gallop. Blacktails and muleys walk, trot, gallop, and bound. When a deer walks, it starts off by moving one of its hind feet forward. This pushes the weight of the body forward, allowing the other three legs to act as a weight-supporting tripod. After the left hind leg is halfway through the forward motion, the front leg on the same side starts forward. As the left hind leg touches the ground, the right hind leg starts forward, followed a half step afterward by the right front leg. This is the basic pattern of walking for most land mammals. A feeding deer may use its feet in other sequences but it usually has three feet on the ground at the same time.

When a deer walks, the hind feet are placed in almost the exact spot just vacated by the front feet. With young deer, the hind foot usually overshoots the track made by the front foot by a little so that a portion of the front track is visible sticking out behind. Larger, heavier deer usually have a slightly shorter stride for their size, so the front foot toe tips show in the front part of the track made by the hind foot. In walking, a whitetail deer's normal stride, the distance measured from toe tip to toe tip, is about 18 to 19 inches (46 to 48 cm.). A blacktail's stride is comparable. A mule deer's stride is about 20 to 23 inches (51 to 58 cm.).

Deer seldom run without cause. They usually walk or trot from one place to another because then they can use all of their senses to be alert for danger. They tend to walk rather slowly, perhaps feeding as they go. When walking steadily, they move a little faster than a man—about 3½ to 4 miles per hour (5.63 to 6.43 kilom.).

When a deer trots, the left hind foot is teamed with the right front foot. The left hind foot starts forward and, when it is halfway through the step, the right front foot starts forward. As the left hind foot touches the ground, the right hind foot starts forward. When the right hind foot is halfway through the step, the left front foot starts forward. Deer trot if they are definitely going somewhere, whether they are just in a hurry to get to their feeding area or, in the case of the blacktail and muley, they are migrating. They can trot hour after hour at a speed of about 10 to 12 (16 to 19 km.) miles per hour. I have clocked deer trotting, and the speeds vary considerably, depending on the urgency that the animals feel.

When a deer trots, its stride lengthens to about 30 to 36 inches (76 to 92 cm.). Because of the greater speed, the feet fall almost directly under the body, giving the track more of the appearance of a dotted line. When a deer trots, you will see the track of each foot individually.

The whitetail has a variation of its trot that I call "single-footing." Usually done when the animal is nervous, it is an exceedingly graceful motion. It appears that the deer is about to stamp its foot but then changes its mind and starts to trot off. The raised front foot is held parallel to the ground while the other forefoot makes two steps. Then the first front foot makes two steps while the alternate front foot is held up. It is a beautiful dainty motion that looks almost like a gesture of impatience or uncertainty—as if the animal were eager to trot off but could not quite make up its mind to do so.

Galloping deer use what is called a rotatory pattern. It entails an eight step sequence in which all four feet are off the ground during two different steps. Some animals, such as the horse, use the transverse gallop and have all four feet off the ground during only one step. When deer gallop, the right front foot contacts the earth first. Then the left front foot hits the ground a little distance ahead of where the right foot touched down. Now the deer's body bunches up as the hind legs come forward and the right front foot leaves the

(Text continues on page 44)

This whitetail buck exhibits the typical walking gait.

### Gaits of Deer

A whitetail trots in this manner.

A blacktail doe is pictured in a very fast trot.

The step sequence changes for a gallop.

Running at full speed, this buck has only one foot touching ground.

All four feet are off the ground twice during the eight-step sequence of a gallop. In this phase the deer seems to float, leaving enormous spans between tracks.

A jump of this height is easy for deer.

ground. The momentum propels the body forward and all four feet are off the ground. The right hind foot touches the ground first, followed by the left hind foot. The hind feet land ahead of where the front feet touched down. Now the body lengthens out like an uncoiling strip of spring steel. The right hind foot and then the left hind foot thrust mightily and again the body is launched forward to complete and repeat the entire cycle.

A whitetail deer's top speed is about 35 to 40 miles per hour (56 to 64 kilom.). A blacktail's top speed is about 30 to 35 miles per hour (48 to 56 kilom.). A mule deer can match the whitetail for a short distance but it soon slows down. Ordinarily, whitetails run at speeds of 20 to 25 miles per hour (32 to 40 kilom.) and can maintain these speeds for a long period. Mule deer can do about 20 miles per hour for considerable distances.

Donald McLean tested the speed of mule deer by herding them with his car on Mosquito Lake Flats in Modoc County, California. The highest speed was 38 miles per hour (61 kilom.) and that only for a short distance. The deer then slowed down to about 23 miles per hour (37 kilom.) and were badly winded in less than a mile.

When a whitetail really gets into high gear, it appears almost to float over the terrain with its tremendous ground-eating gallop. The longest span between tracks that I have personally measured was a little over 26 feet (8 m.). C. W. Severinghaus, of New York State, measured the distance between the tracks of a deer running down a slight grade. The deer had to leap over a 7½-foot (2.3 m.) windfall and it still cleared 29 feet (8.8 m.) horizontally.

One of the most dramatic examples of the jumping ability of the whitetail was displayed for me a number of years ago. At that time the Hercules Powder Company owned a large tract of land outside Belvidere, New Jersey, my hometown area. When the deer inside the enclosure became too numerous, it was decided to take down a wide section of the chain-link fence and drive the deer out through the hole.

The local hunting club and all interested local people, including me, turned out to participate in the deer drive. When the string of men began to encounter the deer, pandemonium broke loose. A very important lesson was learned that day. You don't really drive deer (even if you organize a group of hunters who are experienced in conducting deer drives). All you do is stir them up and they go where they want to. Most of the deer ran in front of the drivers, some ran between the drivers, and a couple ran right over the drivers. No one was seriously injured but I am sure that the deer, in their panic, never saw the drivers. Most of the deer never saw the hole in the fence, either; they simply jumped over the fence, which was 8 feet (2.2 m.) high and topped by three strands of barbed wire, raising the total height to a little over 9 feet (2.3

This blacktail doe crawls under a fence she could easily vault. Though deer can jump high, they avoid exerting themselves more than necessary.

m.). I saw numerous deer jump the fence from both the running and standing positions. Many of the panicky deer also ran into it. One doe broke her lower jaw. The next day several of the deer were seen leaping over the fence to get back inside.

Although deer can easily jump such a fence, they don't exert themselves any more than they have to. Many times I have seen a doe, followed by her two fawns, come to a standard 4-foot (1.2 m.) three-strand barbed wire fence. Sometimes the doe would jump over while the fawns jumped through the strands. Sometimes she, too, would go between the strands. Does and fawns can jump through strands of barbed wire that are 10 to 12 inches (25 to 31 cm.) apart at the speed of a gallop and not touch the wire. But frequently they will stop and crawl under the wire. There are times when deer will jump over blowdowns and other times when they will worm their way underneath. There is no predicting what wild creatures will do; they are all individuals.

Both the mule deer and the blacktail have another unique gait. They bound. All four legs are used simultaneously, thrusting down and backward, powerfully propelling the body up and forward. Although a bounding deer appears awkward, the gait is very functional. It must have evolved as an adaptation to the rough, broken, and steep country that these deer inhabit. The bound not only lets deer jump easily over rocks and brush, it allows them to gain elevation quickly when scrambling up a mountainside.

Naturally, the longest bounds are made when going downhill. Donald McLean, recording the jumps of two mule deer on level ground, found that they measured 19½ feet (6 m.) and 23¼ feet (7 m.). But on a 7° downward slope, one bound measured 28 feet 7 inches (8.7 m.).

I have never seen a blacktail bound more than about 10 times before it settled down into a stiff-legged gallop. The muley can bound for a longer period of time but the gait is very tiring. After about 500 feet (152 m.) the deer's mouth will be wide open and the tongue lolling out. A mule deer can bound about 8 feet (2.4 m.) high and can cover 26 feet (8 m.) horizontally. When winded by bounding, the muley then gallops like a whitetail.

Because a mule deer is usually a larger, heavier, more chunky-bodied animal than a whitetail, it does not move quite as gracefully. But a blacktail can slip through the most impenetrable tangles of underbrush as easily as the whitetail.

The oddest example of deer locomotion I ever heard of was related to me in a letter by Mrs. Paul Warnich of Williamsport, Pennsylvania. The incident was witnessed by five people. In July of 1967, the group had been out looking for deer when their trip was cut short by heavy rain. On the way home they saw two deer in a field of high weeds. Suddenly one of the deer raised both of his hind feet in the air, as if it were doing a handstand, balancing and walking on its forefeet. They thought the deer was injured and had to walk that way, but then the second deer did the same thing. Both deer walked on just their front legs for a distance of about 75 feet to where they could no longer be seen. I have never seen anything like this nor can I find any records of similar behavior. I have included the incident here because I feel that it warrants recording. We are constantly learning new things about deer. Moreover, this incident demonstrates their marvelous coordination and balance. Perhaps it also demonstrates their adaptability to circumstances. Just as our own species engages in play, most of the highly evolved animals seem to indulge in some antics just for fun, but more often there is a serious reason for what they do. It may well be that walking on forelegs had a definite though undetected value to those deer.

When deer are startled, they dash off as if they were late for an appointment in the next county. This headlong flight is just long enough for the deer to

All deer possess excellent swimming ability. (Photo by Len Rue, Jr.)

reach protective cover. The mule deer almost always stops to look back just before it reaches heavy cover, and the whitetail does so quite often. Deer are skulkers; they prefer to sneak away from danger rather than expose themselves by flight. A running deer is at a tremendous disadvantage because it has no way of checking for danger ahead, and the deer knows it. A deer will not run when it can walk and will not walk away from danger if it believes it can escape detection by remaining motionless. I want to stress this because it explains why so few deer are actually seen even in areas where their population is high. Hunters walk past far more deer than they see. I always say that for every ten creatures we see in the woods, a hundred see us and either remain hidden or slip away undetected.

Deer often take to water to elude their enemies. In the summertime, especially in the north woods, they spend a great amount of time in the water feeding, cooling off, or just seeking relief from the stinging and biting insects that plague the woods in warm weather. Sometimes they enter the water just to play and splash about. I have seen fawns get as much enjoyment as a human child would get by splashing with one of its feet. Does frequently swim out to islands before giving birth to their fawns, thus gaining the protection of a water barrier.

Deer swim well, fast, and for long distances. Walter P. Taylor reports one man who was able to check the speed of a swimming whitetail doe by using the tachometer on his powerboat. The doe was frightened at first and swam about a quarter of a mile (402 m.) at 13 miles per hour (20.91 kilom.). When the deer found she was in no real danger from the boat, she settled down to an easily maintained speed of 10 miles per hour (16.09 kilom.). Whitetails have been seen swimming out in the Atlantic Ocean five miles (8.05 kilom.) from Cape Cod, Massachusetts.

47

## Routine Rise

**1.** A doe at rest decides to rise.

**2.** She heaves up onto her front knees.

**3.** She then raises her hindquarters.

**4.** Next she lifts a front leg foreward.

**5.** She fully extends one leg.

**6.** And, once up, she stetches luxuriously.

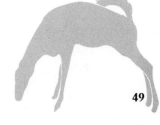

49

## Startled Rise

**1.** When startled, a deer rises fast.

**2.** All four legs are used to catapult the body upward.

**3.** And the deer is instantly running at full speed.

A Millbridge, Maine, lobsterman did more than clock the speed of a swimming deer—he gave it a ride. When hunters chased a spike buck into the ocean off Millbridge, the deer started to swim to an island a mile offshore. The lobsterman ran his boat alongside the deer, caught it by the antlers, and swung it aboard. He ran his boat over to the island and put the deer back in the water where it waded ashore to safety.

Sanford D. Schemnitz, in a deer study done in Maine, saw an adult doe swim from Isle Au Haut to Vinalhaven Island, a distance of 6.8 miles (10.94 kilom.).

Blacktail deer often swim from island to island in the Pacific Ocean off the coast of British Columbia. Arthur Einarsen tells of one Sitka blacktail buck that swam 14 miles (22.52 kilom.) during the breeding season from one island to another along Alaska's southeastern coast. What especially intrigued me about this record was that the deer could not have seen another island 14 miles away. What guided that deer? Could it have been scent?

For many years I lived along the Delaware River. The deer-hunting season in Pennsylvania always opened one week in advance of the New Jersey season. Every year when the guns started banging and the drives commenced in Pennsylvania, the deer—sometimes more than a dozen at a time—would swim across the river to the Jersey side. A week later, when the New Jersey deer season opened, the Pennsylvania side of the river was comparatively quiet even though the season was still open, and the deer would then swim back to Pennsylvania.

Different types of animals have different ways of using their legs to lie down and to get up. When a deer or other cloven-hoofed animal lies down, it lowers itself to both knees of its front legs, then lowers its hindquarters to the ground. The deer generally lies with one side of its body touching the ground, the legs on that side tucked underneath. Only rarely will a deer lie down with all four legs beneath the body. In fact, this position usually indicates that the deer suspects danger and is ready to jump up fast. Ordinarily, when the deer arises it reverses the normal lowering procedure, throwing its weight forward and rising up on its front knees. In that same motion, the animal raises its hindquarters and extends its hind legs. Then the deer extends one front leg, which raises the forepart of the body so that the other foreleg can be extended. Usually the deer then takes a long, leisurely stretch before walking off. But when a deer is startled, it rolls its body off the ground so that all four legs are beneath the body and, chiefly using the hind legs, it literally explodes into action and is away.

# 4

## Heads and Tails

Tails alone would serve to distinguish the three types of deer. The whitetail deer's tail is the largest, performs the most functions, and is frequently conspicuously displayed. The size of the tail, of course, depends to a great extent on the size of the subspecies. Most of my work has been done on *borealis,* the largest of the whitetail deer. I have found that the average tail length from the rump to the bone tip is 9 to 10 inches (23 to 25.4 cm.). From the rump to the hair tip is 11 to 13 inches (28 to 33 cm.). The longest tail that I can find record of was 14 inches (35.5 cm.). The hairs on the tail can be erected and flared out to the sides for a maximum width of 10 to 11 inches (25.4 to 28 cm.).

The top, or dorsal, surface is brown, but the tips of the top hairs may be black. There is a great variation in the amount of black; on some tails it is entirely lacking, on others it may be a third to half of the top surface. The deer gets its name from the white underside of the tail, which is seen when the tail is elevated. The white hairs always extend beyond the dark hairs of the top so that the tail is bordered with white.

Tail size and coloration help identify the three types of deer. From left, the tails in this photo typify whitetail, mule deer, and blacktail.

This tail is another marvel of evolutionary adaptation. Anyone who has stalked (or tried to stalk) whitetail deer, whether to hunt them, photograph them, or just get a close look at wildlife in its habitat, will have no doubt whatever that the tail is an efficient mechanism for communication. An alarmed whitetail deer raises, or flags, its tail to signal to other deer in the vicinity. When they see the danger signal (which operates simultaneously with other, more subtle means of communication) their own flags are raised and all the deer in the group make a hasty departure. There is also a theory that the suddenly raised tail conveys a message to a predator—that it has been discovered and its prey is too alert for a successful sneak attack. The chapter on communication will include further details regarding these functions.

The tail of the blacktail deer, from the rump to the bone tip, averages about 5½ to 6 inches (14 to 15.4 cm.) long. From the rump to the hair tips, it averages about 9 to 9½ inches (22.8 to 24.2 cm.). The dorsal hair is dark brownish-black, and some of the dark hairs extend all the way to the tail tip. The hair on the underside is white, and there is a slight white bordering on the lower third of the tail. The hairs do not flare out and the tail is not used for signaling. When the deer is running, the tail may droop or may be carried almost horizontal to the ground, elevated almost vertically, or tilted forward toward the head.

The muley's tail is a pendant, wide at the top, tapering to a narrow middle, then sloping outward slightly near the tip. This tapering is caused by the hairs breaking off. The upper portion of the dorsal surface is brown, the central portion white, the tip black. The underside is white except for the black tip. The hairs cannot be flared and the tail is not used for signaling, nor is it elevated when the deer runs. The tail length from the rump to the bone tip is 7 to 8 inches (17.8 to 20.4 cm.). From the rump to the hair tips it is 10½ to 11½ inches (26.7 to 29.2 cm.).

Where the blacktail and muley interbreed, hybrids are most readily identified by the body size and the coloration of the tail. A hybrid's tail is not much different in size from the tail of one parent or the other, but it has a black stripe, of variable width, running down the length of the top.

Now let us look more closely at the opposite end of our subjects. A deer's tail may be of some interest anatomically (and behaviorally in the case of the whitetail) but it lacks the romantic fascination of the antlers. The sweeping rack of a big buck has come to symbolize the majesty of the wilds for most people.

The words "horns" and "antlers" are often used interchangeably, as if they were one and the same thing, which they are not. Horns are found on sheep, goats, cattle, bison, and antelope. Horns are never shed. They grow continuously throughout the animal's life, but if they are broken off they do not grow back. Horns have a porous core and a hard, strong, outer surface composed of keratin, the same substance as your fingernails. Horns are nourished by internal blood vessels and grow from the inside out. Usually, both the male and female of America's horned species have horns. The pronghorn is the only horned animal in the world that annually sheds a part of its horns. The outside layer, called the casque, is pushed off each fall by a new horn growing un-

This deer is a cross between a California mule deer and a Columbian blacktail. Such hybrids are characterized by a black streak down the center of the tail.

derneath. The pronghorn is also the only animal in the world whose horns branch, creating the prong for which it was named.

Antlers are found on the Cervidae family—deer, elk, caribou, and moose. Under normal conditions, antlers are shed each year. The caribou (and its European equivalent, the reindeer) is the only antlered species whose females *normally* have antlers. However, the female roe deer of Europe frequently have small antlers and female whitetail, blacktail, and mule deer occasionally have antlers. The Chinese water deer and the marsh deer of Asia are the only two deer that do not have antlers. These two Asian species have tusks that are actually elongated canine teeth, projecting downward from the upper jaw for use in fighting and protection.

Both horns and antlers are actually extended growths of the frontal skull plate. The core of the horn is a part of this frontal bone. The pedicel of an antler is also a part of this bone but provides only the base from which the

A buck fawn has small, dark swirls of hair on his forehead (between the ears and eyes) where the pedicels of his antlers will develop.

antler grows. Antlers are true bone, composed of calcium and phosphorus. But unlike most mammal bones, they are solid and without marrow.

When a buck is born, he has two swirls of hair on his forehead, showing where the antlers will form as he gets older. At two or three months of age, bony knobs, the pedicels, start to form on the buck's frontal skull plate. Without these bases no antlers can grow. If a young buck is castrated before the pedicels have formed, he will never produce antlers.

Abnormalities such as a third antler are uncommon but not really rare. Joseph Dixon recorded two muley bucks in Yosemite National Park, California, in 1927 and 1929, each of which had an extra pedicel base growing on the nasal bone in the middle of the head instead of on the skull. The extra antler on the first buck grew to be 2⅛ inches (54 mm.) high. This was a real antler. While it grew it was covered with velvet; it hardened and the velvet peeled off, and the antler was later dropped when the buck's normal antlers dropped off. This buck died in the winter of 1928. The following year another buck was seen with a third antler growing in the same spot, indicating that this characteristic was an inherited one.

In Colorado in 1964, Duwayne Statzer of California shot a four-point muledeer buck that had a 6¾-inch antler growing beneath its left eye. The normal antlers were polished but the freak growth was still in velvet. There is also a

This is a three-antlered whitetail buck. The small third antler is in front of the right main beam.

These deer show typical whitetail antler development—from spike to forkhorn to six-point rack and eight-point rack.

record of a buck that had a small antler below his right eye. Prehistoric animals often had antlers growing from different parts of their heads. That this characteristic was not perpetuated through evolution proves that it was not advantageous.

In 1972, I photographed an eight-point whitetail buck in Hunterdon County, New Jersey, that had a third antler growing out of the frontal skull about an inch (25 mm.) below the right main beam. The extra antler was only about 1/2-inch (13 mm.) long but was polished. In 1973 the buck had a more massive body, and although he was still an eight-pointer it was a large rack. The third antler was now over 3 inches (75 mm.) long, ridged and polished, a perfect little spike. Unfortunately, the buck was shot that year so my investigation was ended. There have been occasional reports of three-antlered bucks from other parts of the country.

At five to six months of age, the pedicels are about 3/4 to 1 inch (19 mm. to 25 mm.) long and have raised the skin up so that they are quite noticeable. A deer at this stage is known as a "button" buck because of the knobs. Usually, no further antler growth occurs until the following spring when the buck will be about 10 months old.

The size and the shape of the antlers depend on sex, food, age, and heredity. You are what you eat, and so is the deer. A diet containing high protein, the proper amounts of fats and carbohydrates, and adequate minerals such as calcium and phosphorus will produce large antlers. Many people, even today, think they can tell a deer's age by counting the number of points, or tines, on the antlers. It just isn't that simple. A buck does not reach his full physical growth until he is 4 1/2 years old. From birth until he is 2 1/2, the first demand on the food he consumes is for sustenance and body growth. After he has obtained his maximum body size, then all nutrition not used for body sustenance can go to antler development.

The number of points, or tines, on a buck's antlers may vary in number, depending on the food the deer eats that year. The diameter of the antlers, usually measured an inch above the burr, increases each year but not at a constant rate. Furthermore, not all deer start out with antlers of the same diameter. *New Jersey Deer Report Number Three* gave the averages of the 1 1/2-year-old bucks taken in the state in 1975. The antlers of bucks on the poorest soil in the Pines region averaged 7/16-inch (11.5 mm.) in diameter. The bucks from the rich farmlands had antlers averaging 7/8-inch (22.4 mm.). A buck of the same age, taken in 1966 from the best of Pennsylvania's farm country, had 14-point antlers with a diameter of one inch (25 mm.).

In a Michigan study of two hundred sixty whitetail skulls, the beam diameter was taken 1/2-inch (13 mm.) above the burr. The 1 1/2-year-old bucks

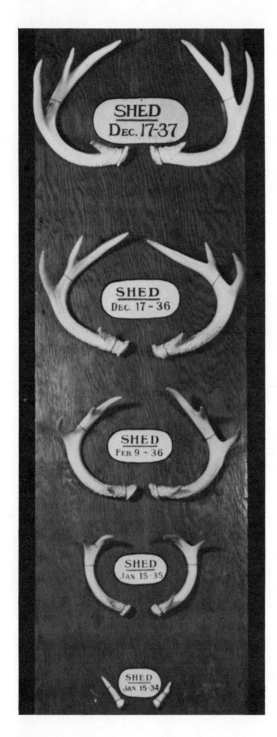

SHED
DEC. 17-37

SHED
DEC. 17 ~ 36

SHED
FEB. 9 ~ 36

SHED
JAN. 15 - 35

SHED
JAN. 15 - 34

Here is a five-year collection of antlers from a single whitetail buck, showing antler development and dates of shedding.

A seven-month whitetail is usually only a button buck, but this one has tiny spikes showing.

had antlers averaging below $^{13}/_{16}$-inch (21 mm.). The 2½-year-old bucks averaged between $^{13}/_{16}$- and 1$^{1}/_{16}$ inches (21 to 27 mm.). The 3½- to 4½-year-olds averaged between 1$^{1}/_{8}$ and 1$^{3}/_{8}$ inches (28 to 35 mm.) and the 5½-year and older bucks averaged above 1$^{7}/_{16}$ inches (36 mm.).

Heredity is also important. The most recent research indicates that the shape and number of points may depend chiefly on heredity, while the size of the antlers is the result of diet. A five-month-old buck usually develops just the buttons I mentioned. Most biologists claim that it is extremely unusual for a five-month-old buck to develop anything more, but I disagree. It is not a common occurrence but I think it is far more common than suspected. The antlers on a five-month-old buck are nothing to brag about but they can be antlers, not just buttons.

I do a lot of my deer photography in Hunterdon County, New Jersey. This is exceedingly rich farmland and the soil has a high calcium content from limestone. Some of the largest deer in my state come from this region. I have seen a number of five- to six-month-old bucks sporting polished spikes ½-inch to 1 inch (12 to 25 mm.) long.

In my home area, northwestern New Jersey, the antlers begin to develop about the first of April. The start of antler growth is a response to photoperiodism. With the winter solstice in December, the number of daylight hours gradually increases. At the base of the deer's brain is a tiny endocrine gland, the pituitary. The activity of this gland is lowest in January and February. The animal's eye functions rather like a photoelectric cell, transmitting messages about light received. As the hours of daylight increase, the eye is exposed to more light, and this stimulates the pituitary. The gland becomes activated in March and April, producing a somatotropic hormone that governs body, bone, and tissue growth. It is this hormone that starts the antlers growing. Although a deer can live if its pituitary gland is removed, it cannot grow antlers even though the pedicels are formed.

In a test of photoperiodism, control deer were subjected to the normal ten to twelve hours of winter daylight, while the tested deer were kept in sixteen hours of light by the use of electric bulbs in their pens. The deer exposed to more light were three to four weeks ahead of the control deer in all cycles of their life. Their antlers started to grow earlier, they shed their winter coats earlier, their antlers were fully developed and polished earlier.

In another study, at the University of British Columbia, Ian McTaggart Cowan subjected mule deer to twelve daily hours of light and twelve daily hours of darkness the year round. These bucks were unable to shed their antlers and grow new ones. Other bucks, kept in continuous light, grew and lost three sets of antlers in two years.

Triggered by the growth hormone, bone salts are deposited on the pedicel by a network of blood vessels beneath the skin. The skin covering the growing antlers is called velvet because it looks and feels exactly like velvet cloth. Antler growth is one of the fastest known forms of tissue growth. The antlers may grow as much as $1/2$-inch (12.5 mm.) per day. This rapid growth puts a tremendous drain on the buck's body as calcium salts are withdrawn from the deer's skeleton and also pulled from currently ingested nutrients. Some biologists believe it takes as much out of a buck's body to produce a large set of antlers as for a doe to produce a pair of fawns.

While a buck's antlers are growing, they are hot to the touch because of the blood vessels lying just beneath the surface of the velvet. Deer do not like to have their antlers touched while they are growing because the bone is still soft, tender, and easily damaged or broken. During this growing period, bucks become recluses, withdrawing to areas where they will not be bothered and do not have to move about much.

Within a month after the antlers have started to grow, the first fork or tine will start to appear. Three to four weeks more will produce the second tine on

The antlers on this New Jersey whitetail buck in spring are just beginning to grow.

This whitetail buck in summer has a second tine forming on each main beam.

a whitetail and the second fork on a muley or blacktail. These tines grow longer as new ones are being formed. On a whitetail, the second tine formed is usually the longest. In four months, the antlers are fully developed and the burr starts to form.

In the generally accepted method of trophy measurement, for a point to be counted it must be at least an inch (25 mm.) long, and it must be longer than the base from which it grows. Antlers are usually symmetrical, bearing the same number of tines of roughly equal length on each side of the head. Asymmetrical antlers are also quite common. A fairly symmetrical head that has an extra point or two — or even three — on one side is considered "typical" for the purpose of trophy scoring, but differences between the left and right sides will lower its score.

Truly abnormal racks, those having oddly shaped or located points, are sometimes fairly symmetrical, sometimes extremely asymmetrical, and are classified separately in the record book *North American Big Game*. Antlers in this "non-typical" category often have a great many more points than the typical trophies, and such abnormalities would dominate the records if they were not classified separately. The world-record non-typical whitetail, shot in Texas in 1892, had twenty-three tines on the right side and twenty-six on the left. The top-ranking non-typical muley, killed in Alberta in 1926, was a forty-three-pointer. Non-typical blacktail records have not been kept, evidently because few non-typical blacktails have been sufficiently impressive.

There are second forks developing on the main beams of this blacktail buck in summer.

Freak antlers can result from injury during growth, but large non-typical racks bearing a great many tines are usually congenital oddities. I will examine the causes and characteristics of various abnormalities later—after discussing normal antler development. Although non-typical antlers are interesting and desirable trophies, symmetrical racks are considered to epitomize what a deer's antlers should be.

When a hunter in the eastern United States speaks of taking a four-point buck, he means it has a total of four tines—presumably two on each side. For

This young, healthy whitetail buck has exceptionally long spikes.

many years, hunters in the West used one side only (the side with the larger number of tines if there was a difference) in giving the count. By "western count," a four-point buck had four tines on one side, and he might or might not be an eight-point buck by eastern count. The old western system obviously lacks clarity. Fortunately, it is now losing favor.

A typical whitetail buck has main beams that project backward, then sweep out to the side, going upward, forward, and in some cases curving inward again. The first tines on either side are usually short and are known as eye-guard or brow tines. The second points on the inside are usually the longest, and each succeeding tine is usually a little shorter. The tips of the main beam are also considered tines.

In a whitetail buck's second summer of life, if his diet is adequate, he usually grows single, unbranched main beams known as "spikes." These spikes are usually 3 to 6 inches (76 to 152 mm.) long and project straight up from the head. My brother-in-law, Dave Markle, shot a spike buck that had long, gracefully curved spikes 14 inches (36 cm.) long. James Hartman of Elverson, Pennsylvania, shot a buck that had 16-inch (41 cm.) inwardly curving spikes. And I

The rack on this rutting whitetail buck has the typical structure but is long-tined and massive. (Photo by Irene Vandermolen)

have photographed spikes varying tremendously in length and curvature. Most of these deer were of the same approximate age, the variations having resulted from heredity or diet or both.

When each of a whitetail's main beams has just one tine branching from it, the deer is called a forkhorn, four-pointer, Y-buck, pronghorn, or crotch-buck. A deer with more than four points is called a rack buck. Eight points is considered average for a whitetail but there may be ten, twelve, fourteen, or even sixteen points. Or there may be odd numbers. Some racks are large but have few points, some are small but have more points. The combinations of sizes and shapes seem almost infinite.

A muley or blacktail buck at six months has just the skin-covered pedicels. I have never seen a mule deer or blacktail of that age with the little polished antlers I have seen on young whitetails, nor have I read of one in any of the literature.

When a mule-deer buck is eighteen months old, it is usually a forkhorn. Each beam now has two tines, giving it almost a Y shape. A blacktail at that age usually has just spikes. At thirty months, a muley buck's main beams usually divide, or fork, again. The rear fork now has the two points while the

This blacktail has eight-point antlers, consisting of small brow tines and three main tines on each side. At a glance this buck would be hard to identify because his rack looks much like a whitetail's.

forward section is still a single tine. A smaller brow tine may or may not be present. The blacktail at this time may be a forkhorn or it may have three tines on each beam. While it is usually easy to tell the antlers of a mule deer from a whitetail's because of the double forking of the main beams, this is not true of the blacktail. Often a blacktail, when it has three main points on each side, not counting the brow tine, has antlers indistinguishable from that of a whitetail. The main beam does not clearly divide and the three points appear to rise from the single main beam. To further confuse the matter of identification, western whitetail deer occasionally have antlers that appear to divide like those of the muley and blacktail. The mature mule deer's main beams generally fork and then fork again into roughly equal tines, looking like four good slingshots above the brow tines. This pattern is also considered ideal for a blacktail trophy but it is attained far less often.

With all of the deer, age, heredity, and food determine antler size. With a 16 to 18 percent protein diet and adequate calcium and phosphorus, bucks will

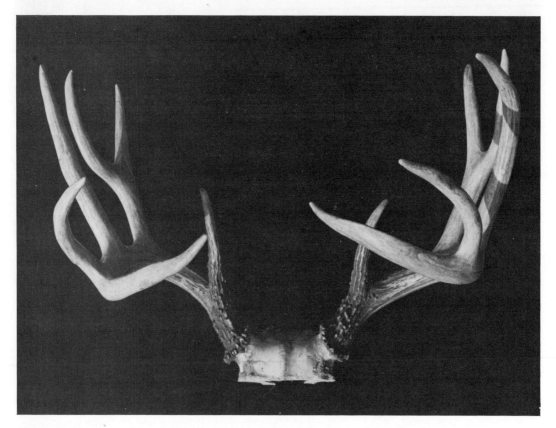

The forked tines on this whitetail rack look almost like those of a muley.

develop from button bucks at six months to large, heavy rack bucks at eighteen months. This is a generalization, of course. Nutrition makes the difference with most deer but, as indicated in a recent Texas study, some bucks may fail to grow large antlers because they are genetically deficient. When genetically small-antlered bucks are put on the same diet as more impressive bucks, they still fail to grow comparably impressive racks.

When a buck gets old, its antlers may regress. It may retain a large, spreading rack while the number of points decreases. The rack will probably be smaller in the last years of life. A buck may then regress to being a forkhorn or spike, or he may not grow any antlers at all. This is caused by poor teeth, which prevent him from getting an adequate diet, and by dwindling hormones.

The pituitary gland, having started antler growth in the spring, stops it in the fall and causes the bone to solidify. Bucks are not capable of breeding during the spring and summer months. A hormone from the pituitary affects the

This is an old muley buck, indicated by the wide spread of the rack and the few short tines. Often, antlers on old bucks show these regressive, short-tined characteristics. Note that this rack is in the late velvet stage, almost ready for peeling.

testicles and, beginning in August, the testicles begin to enlarge and descend from the body. The scrotum now becomes visible. As the testicles enlarge, the male hormone testosterone is produced and this puts an end to antler growth. Increased calcium goes into the connective tissue of the antlers and the burr grows outward. This diminishes the flow of blood and then shuts it off. The velvet dries and the antlers harden. The longitudinal grooves at the base of the antlers were made by the blood vessels that nourished them.

From personal observation, I believe that the drying of the velvet is irritating. Deer are anxious to get rid of it. I would liken it to our peeling off dead skin after a sunburn. Usually the velvet is peeled off within twenty-four hours. Yet I have seen one captive buck peel all velvet from his antlers in just ten minutes. I have seen bucks, however, that had dried velvet shreds on their antlers for several weeks. One buck I was photographing had short strings of velvet

Velvet can be seen peeling from the rack of the young whitetail buck in the foreground.

that he could not get off the bases of his antlers. Sometimes deer will eat velvet as it comes off. It is not completely dry; it is usually quite flexible and the strands are bloody on the inside. Sometimes you can actually see where blood has run down an antler as the velvet was peeled off. It is this blood that colors the antlers brown. Sometimes there is some staining from the vegetation that the bucks rub against but the brown color is chiefly from the blood. With the velvet peeled off, the antlers immediately start to bleach white from exposure to sun and rain.

Bucks peel their velvet off by rubbing their antlers against small, resilient saplings and bushes. Resilience is the key characteristic of the saplings and bushes they use. They want something with give, something that pushes back. Many people have the impression that all buck rubs are made by bucks rubbing the velvet off. This is only the beginning of rub marks. Before a boxer fights, he exercises to tone up his muscles and build his strength. This is what deer are doing as they *fight*, not rub, their antlers against vegetation all fall.

Here is a whitetail buck rubbing his antlers during the rutting season.

Joe Taylor measures a 4-inch cedar, an unusually large tree to be used for rubbing.

Most buck rubs are on saplings an inch or two (25 to 50 mm.) thick, but many are on 3-inch (75 mm.) trunks and occasionally on small trees 4 inches (102 mm.) or larger. I have found a definite correlation between the size of the buck and the size of the sapling or tree he pushes against. The larger or heavier the buck, the larger the diameter of the trees he uses.

Bucks not only fight with the trunks of saplings, they also hook their antlers into branches. They even raise up on their hind feet to tangle with the higher branches. There is one record of a buck that actually entangled his antlers in overhead branches, became hung up, and died.

I don't know whether this action developed from food gathering or from jousting. I have seen both deer and elk stand on their hind legs, slash their antlers into the overhead branches, and then feed on the pieces that they broke off.

During the rutting season, a buck's neck swells as evidenced on this big whitetail.

As the testicles enlarge and the level of testosterone skyrockets, sperm is formed. By the time the velvet has peeled, the bucks are capable of breeding.

During spring and summer, an average whitetail buck's neck measuring 6 inches (15 cm.) thick behind the ears is about 16 to 17 inches (41 to 43 cm.) in circumference. A blacktail buck's neck is about the same size, a mule deer's about 17 to 18 inches (43 to 46 cm.) around. After the velvet has peeled, the constant battling with saplings and bushes strengthens and enlarges the neck muscles, making it easier for bucks to carry their antlers. The increased level of testosterone causes the blood vessels in the neck to enlarge so that they become engorged with blood, greatly swelling the neck. This engorgement acts as a shock absorber, cushioning the deer's neck and body from the tremendous impact of fighting. The 151-pound (68 kg.) buck whose measurements I have been using, had a neck circumference of 21½ inches (55 cm.). The largest buck's neck I have ever measured was a little over 28 inches (71 cm.). I have seen larger necks, including one that looked as big around as my waist, 34 inches (86 cm.). The two largest neck records I can find were of a mule deer and a whitetail, each with a 37-inch (94 cm.) circumference.

After breeding season, the testosterone level drops markedly. This is caused by the expulsion of testosterone in the semen and the diminishing activity of the pituitary gland due to decreased number of daylight hours. These combined factors cause the antlers to drop off. When the testosterone level drops, a layer of cells at the base of the antlers granulates and the antlers drop away at the pedicel. The largest, strongest bucks do most of the breeding, and these bucks drop their antlers the earliest. I have seen this happen year after year among both captive bucks and those in the wild. The breeding bucks use up their testosterone fast and their antlers fall off. Large, strong bucks kept in captivity without a chance to breed will keep their antlers for a month or two longer than deer in the wild. The younger bucks, those with spikes or small racks, are kept from breeding by the mature bucks, and they, too, keep their antlers one or two months longer. This also holds true for elk.

The granulation process is fast. One day the buck's antlers are so solid they could not be broken off if you hit them with a pipe. The next day, after granulation sets in, one or both antlers may drop off by themselves. A friend of mine, Fred Space, had a captive buck that had not had a chance to breed, and therefore kept his antlers—and his aggression—on into March. One day Fred decided to knock the rack off to tame the buck down and he hit the antlers with a piece of pipe. The blow knocked the buck off his feet but the antlers remained intact. A couple of days later the antlers dropped off of their own accord.

The loss of antlers causes the buck no pain, it is like the leaves falling from a tree. Both antlers may drop off simultaneously or one antler may drop off one day and the other the next day, the next week, or even the next month.

A dropped antler has a convex base of about ⅛-inch (4 mm.). This leaves a corresponding pit on the deer's head down to the top of the pedicel. After the antler falls, the pedicel is slightly bloody and has a faint odor of decay. It looks as if the scab of a wound had been pulled away. This pit dries up in a few days and within two weeks a hairless layer of skin grows from the outer edges to the center of the pit, covering it. This covering remains as it is until spring, when a new surging of hormones transforms it into the start of the velvet that will form the new antler underneath.

Antlers are not for protection from predators. This is proved by the fact that they usually drop off before the period of deep snow. When the snow is deep, deer are most vulnerable to predation and to harassment by dogs. At such times, a deer protects itself by rearing up and slashing out with its front feet, and that is also how deer usually fight among themselves at all times of the year.

This young buck has just shed one antler.

At the National Bison Range in Montana in August of 1967, I was photographing a young pronghorn antelope in a large enclosure when a muley buck approached. He presented the "ears-back-and-tucked-chin" sign of aggression but I was not too concerned because he was in velvet. Bucks are seldom very aggressive while their antlers are soft and vulnerable to injury. I was caught off guard when the buck reared up and slashed at me with his front feet. I scrambled out of his way, alert now for trouble. Again the buck reared up but I turned out of the way and pushed him off balance. Before he could rear up again I was over the fence. That buck wasn't about to use his soft antlers but he was far from being defenseless.

When a buck's antlers drop, he usually becomes less belligerent. The breeding season has tired him. He has to eat as much as possible in an attempt to gain back the weight he lost in the previous month of chasing and breeding the does.

Bucks are capable of breeding before the does are ready to receive them. In the wild, a doe can run away from a buck, but in captivity she is often cornered. A lusting buck is not a gentle lover, particularly when he is constantly being thwarted. Under the influence of his surging hormones, he may fly into a murderous rage and vent his fury on the nearest living object. If there are no other bucks to fight, he frequently kills the does he is penned with by goring them.

At the Pennsylvania research stations where many of the basic deer studies have been made, the men carry shields of ¼-inch (5 mm.) plywood when entering the pens of bucks during the rut. On several occasions, bucks have attacked the men with enough fury and strength to pierce the plywood with their antlers.

Often, when a captive buck attacks or kills a doe or is exceedingly dangerous to his handlers, he is knocked out with tranquilizers and his antlers are sawed off. Without his antlers, he usually becomes as docile as any of the does. No researcher has yet found the reason. The buck's testicles are still functioning, the male hormones are still in his blood stream, the pituitary is not affected to any degree, but all belligerency usually dissolves. In fact, the buck may not even attempt to breed. Losing his antlers seems to be an insurmountable psychological shock. But all rules have exceptions. Biologist Harry Laramie of New Hampshire removed the antlers of a 1½- and a 5½-year-old-buck that had become very aggressive to their handlers. Both bucks were just as aggressive after they lost their antlers. Both bucks were later used for breeding and the does produced fawns.

Hilbert Siegler, also of New Hampshire, reported a 3½-year-old buck that had his antlers sawed off after the velvet peeled. At first this buck became docile with humans and with younger bucks kept in the same pen. But after two weeks he again asserted his dominance over the other bucks, became very aggressive to his handlers, and was successful in breeding two does in one day.

Antlers have a social significance. In most cases, the larger the buck's antlers are, the higher that buck is on the dominance scale. Antlered animals fight far less than is commonly supposed. Many writers portray the males as doing constant battle. There are fights, and some individuals fight a lot more than others, but they do a lot more posturing and bluffing than fighting. This is true of most antlered or horned species. Buck deer in their threat activity often shake, or toss, their heads at rivals. Big bull moose tilt their chins in, turning their antler palms upright. Then they slowly rock their heads in wide arcs, from side to side, so that the rival can see how big their antlers are. Elk, caribou, deer, and wild sheep all tuck their chins in as a sign of aggression and project their antlers or horns forward. The antlers or horns are now in position for fighting but they also *show* to their greatest advantage. The larger the antlers or horns, the more dominant the animal is and the less chance that a fight will take place.

Deer throughout the United States all go through the stages of antler growth that I have described, but they don't all do it at the same time. The breeding seasons for all creatures in the world's temperate zones are keyed to a master plan. All wild mammals have definite breeding seasons to insure that the

The massive ten-point rack on this whitetail buck is the result of heredity, food, and age. Such bucks are dominant over those with less impressive antlers.

young are born during a period that will allow for the greatest survival rate. In the United States, most animals breed so that the young are born in the spring to take advantage of warm weather, an abundance of food, and a lessening of predation. Some animals, such as wolverines and other members of the weasel family, often breed whenever they chance to encounter a mate, and conception takes place but there is delayed implantation so that the fertilized egg does not become implanted into the wall of the uterus until the development will allow for the proper birthing time.

Breeding, birth, and antler development are all inextricably tied together. The timetables for these happenings vary according to the latitude. In the Northeast, my home area, bucks usually start to grow antlers during April.

The fawns are born in the latter part of May and in June. Antler development is completed in the last part of August. By about September 5 most of the bucks will have the velvet peeled. The peak of the breeding season occurs between November 10 and December 15. The antlers usually drop off from late December to the end of January.

On November 21, 1975, while at my blind in Hunterdon, I saw a magnificent buck that had shed one antler. He shed the other two days later. This is the earliest dropping of antlers I have personally witnessed. The hunting season in New Jersey usually starts the second week in December. During our bucks-only season, a legally harvestable buck must have antlers at least 3 inches long. On several occasions I have seen big bucks that had shed their antlers prior to the season and could not be hunted. Pennsylvania's hunting season usually opens around the first of December. In a study conducted during the antlerless seasons there, it was found that on the average .8 percent of all bucks lost their racks before the opening of the bucks-only season. This .8 percent had to come out of the trophy bucks because the big fellows shed their antlers first.

This pattern is almost universal for whitetails in most of their range north of Georgia and east of Iowa. According to Arnold Haugen's study of deer in Iowa, the whitetails there breed just a little later, and therefore shed their antlers a little later.

Records in Illinois show that whitetail bucks there carry their antlers a little longer than other deer in the northern part of the country. The antlers usually drop off from January 15 to February 15, with some bucks carrying their antlers until April 15. Illinois has extremely rich soil with a good limestone content. The deer of that state are farmland animals. They may inhabit the forested areas but most of them feed in the fields. In Illinois you find no overbrowsing, no browse lines, no starvation. It has been proved that bucks fed an especially good, high-protein diet retain their breeding vigor for extended periods after the peak of the breeding season has passed. The bucks of Illinois have such a diet, and as long as the supply of testosterone stays high, the antlers stay on.

J. W. Farrar, a deer-study leader in Louisiana, has written to me that the whitetail breeding season starts in late September and peaks in the second week in November over most of the state. That is an earlier start than in other sections of the country, but the most interesting fact is that the deer of the Louisiana lowlands and the delta peak in the middle of December, with the season extending into late January or February. This means that most fawns of the delta will be born in July and August. Among delta deer, the bucks' antlers follow the same cycle, dropping off in February and March and

The Florida whitetails here were photographed in June. In antler development, these warm-latitude bucks are about one month ahead of those in northern states.

starting to grow in May. The delta deer polish their antlers in October and November.

Deer that I photographed in June in northern Florida had nicely developed racks but the antlers were not fully grown. These Florida deer were about one month further advanced than the deer in my home state of New Jersey. They would polish their antlers in early August, which would throw the breeding-season peak into October, with the fawns being born in the middle of April and the beginning of May.

I have not had the opportunity to photograph whitetail deer in the Everglades or most other portions of southern Florida. Charles Loveless, in his study of Everglades deer, found that the peak breeding season was in September, with the fawns being born in March. Antlers usually dropped off in November and new ones started to develop in February. By mid-July the antlers were completely developed and the velvet was rubbed off in August.

The Key deer of Florida live under tropical conditions, in a continuously warm climate. Such animals have no regular breeding seasons, although they, too, have peak seasons. There is one record of a Key buck shedding one of his antlers in September, but this was considered abnormal. Most of them shed their antlers in March and April. The new ones start to develop in May and the velvet is shed in late September. This would throw the breeding season back to the middle of December, with the fawns being dropped in July and August. From the records, it appears that most fawns are born in August, although spotted fawns have been seen in every month of the year. A beautiful 6-point buck that I photographed on January 15, 1977, on Big Pine Key was still in the rut, for his neck was swollen and his antlers were still brown.

The Coues whitetails of Arizona's deserts drop their antlers in May and June. New ones begin to grow in July. This is a later date than for any other whitetail subspecies. The antlers are fully developed in November, and in December the velvet is cleaned off. The peak of breeding occurs in mid-January, and fawns are dropped in August and September. This later birthing coincides with the second rainy season of the year, between August 7 and September 4 in southern Arizona. The period of moisture produces the needed vegetation for the doe to be able to nurse her young.

In 1967 I made my first trip to the Southwest to photograph wildlife. For about a week I was a guest at the Gage Holland ranch at Marathon, just outside Big Bend National Park in Texas. That region is considered semidesert, averaging 12 to 13 inches (30 to 33 cm.) of rain per year. There is an old saying about that section of Texas: "Everything stings, stinks, or bites." Cactus was all about. The plant life was the most inhospitable-looking I have ever seen— everything had thorns, stickers, spikes, or cutting edges. And I took care not to walk too close to the stalk-shrouded bases of the yuccas, because the rattle-snakes hid there in the daytime.

I arrived during a terrific desert rain storm that broke a drought, plummeted the temperature, and brought the desert to life. Never had I seen so much wildlife in what appeared to be barren wasteland. There were flocks of quail, jackrabbits beyond counting, antelope, javelinas, and deer. I counted eighty mule deer.

I was amazed that such habitat could support any deer, let alone so many. It was the first time I ever saw small herds of bucks. Whitetail bucks often form little bachelor groups of three or occasionally four. The muley bucks were far more sociable, foraging in groups of six to twelve, with eight being the average. This was in the last week of July and I was also amazed to see that the antlers on these deer were two months behind our northern deer in development. I learned, too, that the fawns were about to be dropped. This was my first experience with wildlife cycles geared to moisture rather than cold. The rain storm that greeted me was the start of the region's vegetative growing season. The deer had adapted so that there would be enough vegetation and moisture to allow the does to nurse their fawns. This was the factor on which everything in the cycle pivoted. The bucks' antlers were polished in October, the breeding season peaked in January and February, the antlers were dropped in February and March, and the new growth began in May.

The mule deer and blacktails of California breed in December and January, with a peak from December 20 to January 15. The fawns are born in mid-July. The bucks' antlers are dropped in January and February, and new growth starts in April and May. The antlers are full-grown in September and are being polished during late September and the first part of October. The bucks start running the does in late November.

The mule deer of the northern Rocky Mountains and the Sitka blacktail deer of Alaska follow the same schedule as northern whitetails. Antlers start to grow in April, and fawns are born in May and June. The antlers are full-grown in August. Polishing begins in late August or early September. The breeding season peaks between November 15 and December 15. The antlers drop off in December and January.

There may be slight local differences in the schedules of the various deer, but the dates I've given encompass the time pattern for deer in all parts of the United States and Canada.

Although antlers are usually symmetrical, abnormal shapes are quite commonly produced by mutations, injuries, metabolic or hormonal deficiencies, or heredity. I have found that injuries to the antlers are much more frequent among whitetails than mule deer. Perhaps this is because whitetails inhabit

The velvet-sheathed antlers on this muley in August are fully developed.

regions with more vegetation to bang into. Conversely, I have found more genetic deformities among mule deer, and I don't know of a theory to explain this.

When a deer's antlers are growing, they are so soft that they are easily bent or broken. I have seen whitetail bucks smash into fences and bend their antlers. As a rule, the antlers do not break off but are knocked out of shape. A buck shot in 1955 in Sullivan County, New York, had the right antler badly bent. The antler had continued to grow after the injury and it came to rest against the buck's mouth. The left antler had three points, polished and sharp, while the injured antler was still in velvet.

A six-point buck that was shot near Huntingdon, Pennsylvania, had well-developed, polished antlers. The right one was normal while the left one had been bent so that its tip pressed tight against the deer's upper jaw.

A buck mule deer killed near Laramie, Wyoming, had both antlers bent down toward its nose. The antlers then curved under the jaw, preventing the deer from opening its mouth more than ½-inch (13 mm.). The antlers were

On this young whitetail buck the left antler is normal, but the right one was broken while it was growing.

still in velvet. Still growing. Although the deer was in good condition when shot, it probably would have starved to death as further antler development would have prevented its mouth from opening.

A forkhorn whitetail killed by an automobile in 1966 in Steuben County, New York, had a small but normal and polished left antler while the right one was bent down over the forehead and was in velvet. The Y of this antler fitted over the deer's nose and the right side of his face.

All of these deer were in good condition, indicating that the abnormality was caused by an injury to the antler, not to the body of the deer. I could enumerate many more such cases. If an antler is injured only slightly, it may harden and be polished as quickly as its normal mate. My friend Bob Elman showed me a typical example, the frontal skull plate of a spike buck shot in the Catskills in 1974. The left antler was normal, curving out, back, and up to a fairly sharp point. It measured 6½ inches (16.51 cm.) long. The right antler curved in the opposite direction—forward and down to a blunt tip over the snout—and it measured 5½ inches (13.97 cm.). In 1977 in Pennsylvania, an acquaintance of Bob's shot a buck with a fairly long, straight spike on one side and a forkhorn on the other. At the base of the fork was a large hole, clear through the bone. Again, both antlers were hard and polished.

Here is a whitetail skull with freak antlers that show massive multiple beams and thirteen tines.

The oddest antler formation in my personal collection was given to me by my friend Joe Taylor. The buck was killed in Warren County, New Jersey, by an automobile in early September. Most of the velvet had been peeled from the rack, although some shreds remained. The deer was in excellent condition. The pedicel was normal for a large buck, but that's where all normality ended. The pedicel on the left antler was 1¼ inches (32 mm.) across but the antler was 3¼ inches (83 mm.) across. The seven main beams have thirteen tines that point in all directions. The accompanying photograph of this head shows the deformity better than I can describe it.

Another oddity was a deer I photographed in Pennsylvania. The left beam split at the base to form two main beams. Usually this type of formation is genetic, occurring year after year. Unfortunately, I could not prove this with the two deer just described because neither lived beyond the year when I saw it. I did see a big bull elk in Yellowstone that had such a formation for three consecutive years. The elk's second brow tine formed another, unbranched main beam that was as large as the original main beam.

Most deer that are kept in captivity injure their antlers on the fence. This usually results in split antler tips. Bucks that are captured or have to be

The left antler on this Pennsylvania whitetail has split to form a double main beam.

This captive whitetail buck deformed his antler tips by rubbing them against wire fence.

transported to live-trap carrying cages almost always knock their antlers into grotesque shapes.

There are many records of deer that have misshapen antlers due to bodily injuries. Usually, if a deer is injured on the right side of the body, particularly on the hindquarters, its left antler will be the one showing the damage, and vice versa. One theory is that the deer, in trying to lick the injury, is apt to bang its outside antler against vegetation. My own theory is that because the left part of the brain controls the right side of the body, and vice versa, damage done to one side is reflected by damage to the antler on the other side. One deer that I photographed in Hunterdon County, New Jersey, had a badly injured left hind leg that left it with a permanent limp. This buck grew a normal antler on the left side but the right side had only a small, misshapen antler.

Some deformities are caused by unusual circumstances in which a buck's

Note the injured left hind leg and stunted right antler on this New Jersey whitetail. Injury to one side of the body often causes antler deformity on the opposite side.

food supply is drastically reduced or no minerals are available. Sometimes injury to internal organs prevents a buck from properly utilizing or metabolizing its food, and this will be reflected in his antlers.

Like the previously mentioned bucks of Yosemite that grew freak antlers on their nasal bones, some deer have antler deformities as a result of heredity. For a number of years I had made two or three annual trips to Yellowstone National Park at different seasons for photography. I got to know many of the animals individually by their outstanding characteristics. One huge nontypical muley buck had the widest rack I have ever seen on a deer. Another not only had a widespread set of antlers, it always had a down-turned tine on its left antler. Both of these deer had the same characteristics each year, indicating that the antler structure was inherited.

Palmation of antlers is another odd genetic characteristic. In some instances, the antlers are merely much wider than normal. Once this trait appears in a given area, many bucks in succeeding years will have antlers of this

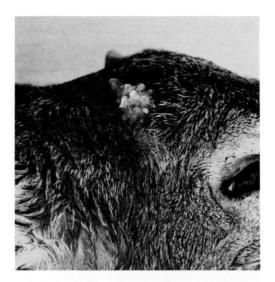

Another abnormality, this drastically stunted "rosebud," or "rosette," antler barely shows above the pedicel.

Here is a magnificent muley buck with non-typical antlers—and the widest rack the author has ever encountered.

This non-typical muley was shot by Harold Throop in Oregon in 1935. Palmation makes the rack look like that of a moose. (Photo by Michael Cooley)

type. Occasionally the palmation is so extensive that the antlers look like those of a moose. Harold Throop of Odell, Oregon, shot a mule deer like that in 1935. The antlers spread over 30 inches (76 cm.) across and had 35 points, but the most interesting feature was the 14-inch (36 cm.) palmations.

Leslie Robinette reports on 14 mule deer that had genetic antler deformities, all from the Oak Creek drainage of central Utah. Some of these bucks had no antlers or pedicels at all. Some had nothing at all on one side of the head and an exceedingly large antler on the other side.

A large mule deer buck killed by Ennes Aldredge of Ogden, Utah, was eight years old and weighed 204 pounds (92.4 kg.) hog-dressed. The left antler was 25½ inches (65 cm.) long, had a 1½-inch (38 mm.) beam diameter and seven points. The antler on the right side was a mere bony protuberance ½-inch (13 mm.) long.

Louis Matthews poses with the "cactus buck" he shot in Wyoming in 1971. (Photo courtesy of Missourian Publishing Co.)

Occasionally, deer have antlers that don't even look like antlers but resemble a mass of coral brought up from the ocean floor. Such deer are called "cactus bucks." Instead of having beams and points, they have a mass of knobs. Louis Matthews of New Haven, Missouri, shot such a mule deer in September, 1971, near Dixon, Wyoming. It had 69 knobs on its head. Such "cactus" formations are caused by atrophied testicles, and the antlers are usually retained for the rest of the animal's life.

Buck fawns that are castrated, either deliberately or accidentally, never develop antlers at all. If they are castrated while their antlers are growing and in velvet, the velvet never dries, nor are the antlers shed. However, these soft antlers are usually lost because the moisture in them freezes in the winter and the frozen pieces break off. Bucks that are castrated after the antlers are fully developed, solidified, and with the velvet peeled off, will shed these antlers within two or three weeks. Such bucks may grow another set of antlers the following year but the antlers do not harden and are lost through freezing. If a castrated buck lives in an area that is not subject to freezing, the antlers will grow larger but they do not solidify and the velvet will not be lost. Pieces of the soft antler will continue to break off.

A great deal of research is currently being done on antlered does. At one time, Pennsylvania estimated that one out of every 18,000 antlered deer killed in that state was a doe. Recently it has been found that the percentage is much higher. As more states concentrate on this type of research, the ratio is constantly being lowered. C. W. Severinghaus, head of New York's deer-research work, has found that in his state the ratio of antlered does to antlered bucks is one in 2,500 to 2,700. In 1959, J. Kenneth Doutt and John C. Donaldson of the Carnegie Museum in Pittsburgh, Pennsylvania, found that of 38,270 antlered deer killed, 17 were antlered does, producing a ratio of 1/2251, or close to the New York figures. Doutt and Donaldson continued their studies and in 1961 reported that out of 173,038 antlered deer killed in Pennsylvania in the previous four years, 43 were does—a ratio of 1/4,024. In checking through the records I find that in the Pennsylvania study no single area is producing a majority of these deer. The antlered does are randomly scattered throughout the state.

Antlered does fall into three categories. In the most common type, the antlers never harden, nor does the velvet ever come off. Does usually lose most or all of these antlers through freezing. Such a doe can breed and produce milk to feed her young. She is a true female, but her female hormones are usually not produced in sufficient quantity to suppress the somatotrophic growth hormones of the pituitary glands. The antlers are formed under the stimulation of the pituitary but the doe, lacking testicles, does not produce the male hormone testosterone needed to harden these antlers and complete the cycle. Her neck does not swell as a buck's neck would, nor are the hock hairs stained as darkly.

A four-year-old whitetail doe killed near Mercer, Pennsylvania, on April 19, 1967, was just starting to grow a new set of antlers. That this doe was definitely a female was proved by the triplets she was carrying.

The second type of antlered "doe" is basically a male, but its sex organs are abnormal. Usually such a deer has both penis and vagina, but the scrotum is not visible because the testicles are up inside the body cavity. An animal of this sort never bears young. The antlers are like a typical male's, often well developed with tines. They harden and the velvet is peeled off. But the neck does not become swollen as a normal buck's neck would.

The third condition is very rare. It occurs when a tumor in the doe secretes male hormones. Both male and female organs may be present, and the antlers may or may not complete their development. A hunter who shoots any antlered doe should immediately contact his game department so that the deer and its reproductive organs can be saved and studied. It is hoped that in time, if enough specimens can be examined, our knowledge of deer with characteristics of both sexes (hermaphroditism) can be greatly increased and perhaps help can be given to humans afflicted with this condition.

I am often asked why, if a deer's antlers always fall off, few of the antlers are ever found. One reason is that there aren't that many bucks in any given area, and a great amount of ground per antler would have to be searched. However, the chance of finding dropped antlers is greatly increased if you know the local wintering area of the deer and concentrate your search there. Most antlers are dropped during the winter concentration.

When a buck is carrying his antlers, they look impressive, but without the skull to provide the base and the arch, an antler lying on the ground doesn't stick up very high and is soon covered by leaves and other vegetation.

Of course, the main reason why antlers aren't found is that they are eaten. It is amazing how wildlife finds trace elements or minerals. Animals feed on vegetation grown on the richest soil whenever possible. They instinctively know what is best for them. It is almost impossible to find a bone or an antler out in the forest that has not been gnawed. And we don't often find such bones or antlers at all because they are soon consumed. Mice, squirrels, hares, porcupines, chipmunks, foxes, etc., all gnaw on bones for the calcium and phosphorus contained in them. Even the deer themselves chew on dropped antlers. I have seen deer chew on a buck's rack while he still had it on his head. The other deer needed those minerals and they were not about to wait until the antlers dropped off. As antlers or other bones are exposed to the elements, they become softer and are more easily consumed.

Once I brought an old moose skull down from Canada one summer and fastened it up on the garage roof. That garage became a Mecca for all the squirrels in the area. They chomped through the antlers as if they were eating soft ice cream. In a little over two years they had eaten all of the points and most of the palms from that very large set of antlers.

# 5

# External Glands

Three primary external characteristics—tail, antlers, and glands—identify each of three basic types of deer. All of the deer have four major external sets of glands: preorbital (tear-duct), interdigital (between the toes), tarsal (on the inner sides of the hocks), and metatarsal (on the feet). Two other glandular areas are the forehead and the tail. As identifying characteristics, the metatarsal glands are very important and—unlike antlers—they are present on all three deer at all times, regardless of age or sex. But to the deer themselves, of course, all the glands are important, and all are interesting to the student of nature.

The preorbital, or lacrymal, gland is the tear duct located in front of the deer's eye. This gland was a difficult problem for old-time taxidermists because, after the head was mounted, it would dry, shrink, and leave a big hole that was neither lifelike nor attractive. Modern taxidermy has overcome this problem. On the whitetail deer, the preorbital gland is about 7/8-inch (22 mm.) long, on the blacktail about 1¼ inches (32 mm.), and on the mule deer 1⁹/₁₆ inches (40 mm.).

The preorbital gland is a "trench" of almost bare skin in front of a deer's eye. In this photo, its waxy secretion is visible.

The preorbital gland is a trench-like slit of almost bare skin, dark blue to black. Frequently there is a residue in the bottom of the opening, formed by particles of hair and plant material held together by secretions from the eye. There are some sebaceous glands and sudoriferous glands located in the lip of this gland.

Sebaceous, or sweat, glands produce sebum, a fatty substance that lubricates the hair and skin to keep them from drying out and becoming brittle. Sudoriferous, or epocrine, glands produce scent. These glands secrete a substance known as pheromone through the hair follicles, causing a body odor. The word "pheromone" was coined from two Greek words—*pherin*, meaning "to carry," and *hormon*, meaning "to excite." Pheromones are essentially, although not exclusively, sexually stimulating scents.

Biologists claim that the preorbital gland is not an important producer of scent. I wonder. On numerous occasions, I have seen whitetail bucks rub this

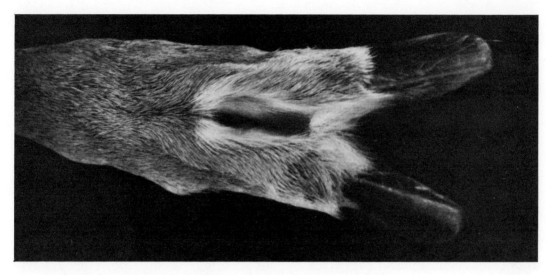

Here a whitetail's interdigital gland is visible between the spread toes.

gland against branches and other vegetation. They did not rub with the vigor that would be used if the spot were merely itchy. They rubbed carefully, as if they were marking the twig with scent. I have photographs of an African antelope species, the dik-dik, marking the edges of its territory with this gland. The rubbing perhaps explains how residue of plant material happens to be found inside the gland opening. Although the scent is not strong, this gland does emit a distinctive odor of ammonia.

I have not seen whitetail deer raise the hair surrounding the preorbital glands, but when muleys and blacktails are startled or frightened, the hairs around these glands are erected and laid outward, making a large, very noticeable rosette. With the hairs erected, the trench opens and the gland becomes very visible. I do not know if scent is given off at this particular moment but it would be logical to assume that the reason the gland opens is to release scent.

The interdigital gland is located between the two center toes—the hoof lobes—of each of the deer's feet. The gland is usually overlooked because of the long hair that comes down over the hooves. If the toes are spread apart and the hair separated, an opening will be found into which a match stick or twig could be inserted. A closer examination will show hairs inside the gland. These act as wicks for the yellow, waxy secretion that is constantly discharged from the many sudoriferous glands located under the skin. The hole, or sac, of the gland is much larger in the whitetail than in the muley or blacktail. Every time the deer puts its foot down, some of this scent rubs off on the ground or vegetation. The odor is strong (though I do not find it as offensive as some people claim it is). Predators that hunt by scent have such a keen sense of smell that they could detect or track prey even if there were no glandular odor, so the scent given off by this and other glands is no disadvantage to the deer. On the contrary, it is an aid to reproduction and to the protection and rearing of the young.

This gland plays an important role by helping deer to track one another. Each deer must have its own personal scent-gland odor, which allows it to be identified. Individuality is acquired through variations in the chemical components of the scent. It is the means by which the doe locates her fawn if the little one wanders away from the spot where it was bedded when the doe left it. A doe never tracks down another doe's fawn, she follows only her own.

I have often watched a buck tracking a doe during the rutting season by the use of this scent. Bucks never track by "air-scenting," as dogs do. They always track with their noses held just a few inches above the ground. The bucks doing this are sexually stimulated and usually hold their tails straight up in the air as they walk.

Perhaps some clarification is needed for the assertion that there is more survival value in leaving a trail-marking scent than in not leaving it. In the United States today, the cougar is probably the greatest predator of the blacktail and mule deer. Other members of the cat family—occasionally the bobcat and, in Canada, the lynx—also prey upon deer of all types. But since cats hunt primarily by sight, a trail-marking scent is no great help to them. Canine predators, on the other hand, usually hunt by scent until they locate their prey, but the glandular scent is only one component of the game odor they can detect. Once their prey is started, the canines either keep it in sight or trail it by body odor that hangs in the air and clings to vegetation. Though interdigital scent might help predators, they do not really need it. Deer do need it because they are primarily scent-oriented creatures.

The tarsal gland is the most important scent gland. We are only beginning to understand just how important this gland is to deer and the role it plays in communication.

The tarsal gland is the large, tufted, discolored patch found on the insides of the hind legs on what is actually the deer's ankles. This patch of hair is about 3 to 4 inches (76 mm. to 102 mm.) across in the whitetail deer and 2 to 2¼ inches (51 mm. to 57 mm.) across in the mule and blacktail deer. Actually, the metatarsal is not a gland in the true sense, as there is no opening or duct. Beneath the skin are sebaceous glands and sudoriferous glands connected to hair follicles that act as ducts to bring the secretions to the surface.

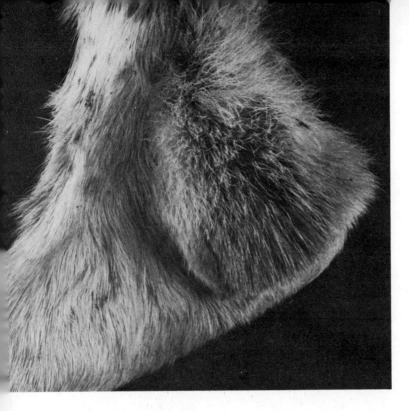

The tarsal gland is a tufted patch inside each hind leg.

Also beneath the skin are little muscles that control the long hairs of the tuft. Under normal conditions, the hairs are turned inward from the periphery of the gland. When a deer is alarmed or frightened, the hairs are made to stand on end or are flared out. This action is very conspicuous, a visible signal to other deer.

The tarsal gland has pheromones but it is primarily a depository for urine. All deer of all ages urinate on these hair tufts. The buck's penis sheath hangs loose instead of running along the belly as on domestic cattle. Under ordinary conditions, the unstimulated penis hangs down. To urinate on its hocks, a deer supports most of its body weight on the front feet and twists its hind legs inward so that they appear to be "knock-kneed." Frequently, a deer will rub its tarsal glands against each other while urinating on them. All three types of deer urinate on their hocks. Frequency varies widely among individuals. The more dominant a deer is, the more important urinating on the hocks seems to be. It has also been proved that the more dominant deer have larger, more active tarsal and metatarsal glands than do subordinate deer.

Everyone has seen animals checking the identification of others of its own species. We see this most commonly with dogs. Usually most animals smell the anal, vaginal, or penis region. When deer meet, they check each other's hocks by smelling them, and they frequently lick each other's hocks. Deer show a great interest in their own hocks and often lick the tufts immediately after depositing urine on them.

A young whitetail buck here urinates on his hocks. In this way the tarsal glands become the primary depositories for urine scent.

A whitetail sniffs the tarsal glands of another.

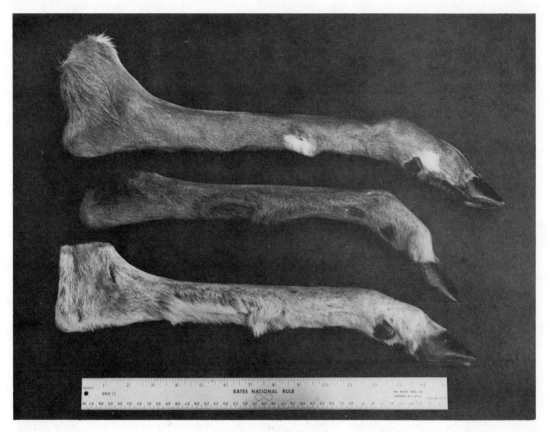

The metatarsal gland — about midway between hock and hoof — is small on a whitetail (top), somewhat larger on a blacktail (center), and considerably larger and extending farther up on a mule deer (shown at bottom).

The frequent urinating on the tarsal glands stains the hair tufts a deep, dark brown, and they reek with the odor of urine. Old-time hunters, and some modern ones, believe that the tarsal glands should be cut off as soon as a deer is shot to prevent tainting the meat. This is nonsense, because if the glands have not tainted the meat while the deer was alive, there is no chance of their doing so after the deer is dead. What can happen is that if the hunter, when he is dressing or skinning the deer, carelessly touches the glands and then handles the meat, the meat can be tainted. I always hang my deer by the head. When I am ready to skin it, I first saw off the hind legs several inches above the tarsal glands. Then there is no chance to contaminate the meat.

The metatarsal glands are an important means of species identification among the three deer. In the whitetail, each of these glands, including the hair tuft, is about an inch (25 mm.) long and is found on the lower half of the deer's hind foot. The blacktail's metatarsal gland is about 2½ to 3 inches (60 to 76 mm.) in length and is about midway down the foot. The muley's metatarsal is about 5 inches (125 mm.) in length, starting well above and extending down to the middle of the foot. Interbreeding between mule deer and blacktails produces intermediate glands. Research has shown that although these glands are present in all whitetail deer in the United States and Canada, the metatarsals are smaller or sometimes lacking among whitetails south of our border.

Again, the metatarsals are not true glands. The two main features of each metatarsal gland are the hard, cornified, or keratinized, hairless ridge in the center and the tufts of hair surrounding this ridge. Both sebaceous and sudoriferous glands are found in the ring of skin supporting the circlet of tufted hair. I believe the metatarsals play a minimal role as scent glands because I have not been able to detect any scent nor have I ever found any secretion from the hair follicles.

Some researchers have suggested that deer leave scent on the ground from these glands while lying down. (The glands are then in contact with the earth.) It has also been suggested that perhaps deer can pick up vibrations from the earth through these glands while lying down. I cannot verify or challenge either of these theories. No one really knows what use the metatarsals are to the deer.

# 6

## The Teeth and Eyes Reveal the Age

The age of a deer is of great interest to hunters and is crucial information to biologists if they are to properly manage the deer herds. When it was proved that antlers were no accurate indicator of age, the biologists took a cue from the old horse traders and began checking on the teeth of deer. The saying, "don't look a gift horse in the mouth," derives from the fact that the older a horse is, the more worn down its teeth have become.

Using the idea of tooth wear and replacement, C. W. Severinghaus and Jack Tanck of the New York Game Department worked up the system in 1949 that became the standard method of aging deer. Burton L Dahlberg and Ralph C. Guettinger of Wisconsin refined the method in 1956.

An adult deer has thirty-two teeth. There are no upper teeth in the front of the mouth, but there are six premolars and six molars, three of each on each side. The lower jaw has six incisors, two modified canines, six premolars, and six molars, a total of twenty teeth—ten on each side. There are records of four Michigan deer having eight molars each. The canine teeth of deer are not the meat-piercing canines of the dog family. A deer's canines so closely resemble the incisor teeth that they are often classed and counted as such.

In rare instances, deer have what are known as maxillary canine teeth in the upper jaw. These are rudimentary and serve no purpose since there are no opposing teeth. Many times these teeth do not erupt through the gums and most people would be unaware of their presence. Biologists locate unruptured canines by scraping the upper jaw.

C. W. Severinghaus found only twenty-three upper canine teeth in 18,000 whitetail deer he examined, a ratio of 0.1 percent. The farther south one goes, the more canine teeth are found in deer. Charles M. Loveless and Richard F. Harlow found four canine teeth in an examination of ninety-five deer in Florida for a ratio of 4.2 percent. At the Wilder Wildlife Refuge in Texas, a hundred and sixty-two whitetail skulls disclosed forty-nine canine teeth in twenty-nine of the animals. Some of the skulls had only one tooth, some had both. Twenty-six of the teeth are rudimentary and did not protrude through the gums. Among females, 18 percent had upper canines; among males, 17 percent had them. In Venezuela, E. Boelioni found four large canine teeth in ten deer that he examined, or 40 percent. As previously mentioned, the musk deer and the Chinese water deer have greatly elongated, functional, stabbing, maxillary canine teeth — or tusks — and no antlers. The muntjacs, or "barking" deer, of southeastern Asia have both tusks and antlers. Biologists believe that the canine teeth diminished in prehistoric deer with the evolution of antlers. Some other members of the deer family, such as the caribou, also have canine teeth. Elk usually have well developed maxillary canines, and thousands of elk were once killed so that these teeth could be worn as decorations by Indians and by members of the fraternal Order of Elks.

Mule deer, blacktails, and whitetails are born with eight front teeth in the lower jaw. The six center teeth are incisors while the two "corner" teeth are the modified canines that look like incisors and are used and classified as such. The two central incisors are larger than the others and are referred to as pincer teeth. All of these eight teeth are milk, or "baby," teeth. Between the fifth and sixth month, the milk pincers are lost and replaced by permanent pincers which are much larger and very noticeable. Between the tenth and the eleventh month, the other incisors are lost and replaced by permanent teeth. Incisors are accurate indicators of age up to one year and then are no longer used.

At birth, deer also have six premolars, three to a side, top and bottom. These, too, are milk teeth and will be replaced. At six months of age the first molar is fully erupted. By the ninth month the second molar is usually fully erupted. At twelve months the third molar is usually partially erupted. When

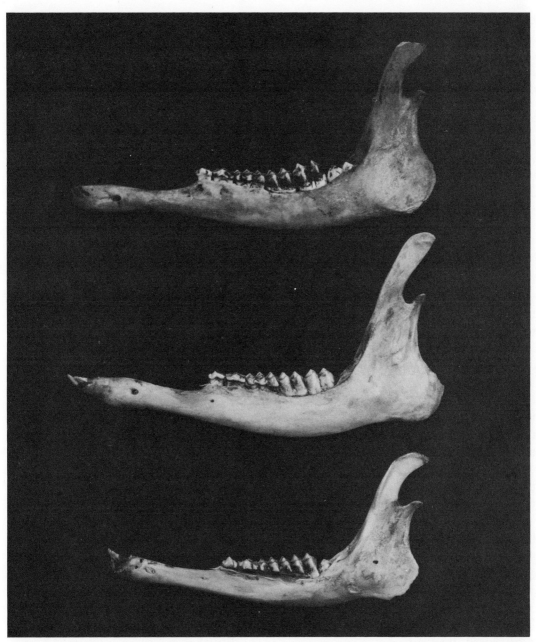

At six months (bottom), a fawn's first molar is fully erupted. At nine months (center), the fawn has a second molar. The jaw of a year-old deer (top) has a third molar partially erupted. For the first eighteen months—until adult teeth are fully developed—teeth provide an easy, accurate way to determine age.

first erupted, these teeth are deeply ridged and have sharp points known as the lingual crest. The first and second molars are bicuspid (two-pointed) and the third is tricuspid. At birth the three premolars also have sharp points, but these teeth are soft and wear rapidly. At birth the first premolar has a single cusp, the second premolar has two, and the third has three.

At seventeen months of age, the worn-down premolars are about to be replaced by permanent ones. While I was doing the research for my first deer book, a friend of mine arrived with a six-point buck he had taken in Maine. He told me his guide had stated that the deer was 6½ years old. That guide may have been a good woodsman but he really didn't know much about deer as he was still counting antler points for years of age. A quick examination of the deer's teeth showed that the buck was exactly seventeen months old. All of the premolar teeth were about to be shed and the third premolar still had the tricuspid cap in place.

At eighteen months the deciduous premolars are lost, and the third premolar thereafter has only two cusps. Up to this point, tooth replacement is a very accurate means of aging. From eighteen months on, telling the age by the teeth becomes more difficult because now age is determined by the wear on the teeth, and many variables enter into the picture.

Severinghaus and Tanck worked out their method using tagged, known-age deer living in the wild. Pen-raised deer could not be used because their diet would differ from that of wild deer. Here is where the variables started to creep in. As a deer ages, the teeth are worn down by the constant chewing of the cud. By the time a deer is eleven to twelve years old, its teeth are practically worn out—but then so is the deer's life expectancy. With age, the crests of the teeth are ground away and more dentine becomes visible. To determine the animal's age, the teeth are measured above the gum line. The variables that lower the accuracy of this method are heredity, availability of food, access to minerals, and grit.

Just as some humans have better teeth than others, so do some deer. And better teeth can often be traced to no other factor but heredity. Also very important is the availability of high-quality food. A deer getting an adequate diet of nutritious food is apt to be a healthy deer with good teeth. Perhaps of the greatest importance is the availability of minerals. Deer on good limestone soil have larger antlers, stronger bones, and strong, long-wearing teeth. Another major factor is the amount of dust, sand, or other grit material ingested with food. Hard substances cause greater tooth wear.

In a few instances, an oddity of jaw structure might also have some effect. I cannot substantiate this, but I can attest to the fact that deer vary in their jaw structure just as humans do. Right after I wrote *The World of the White-*

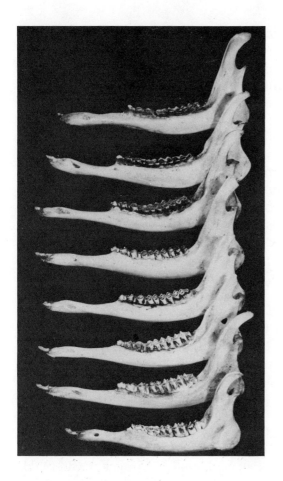

These jawbones were taken from deer 1½ years old (bottom), 2½, 3½, 4½, 6½, 7½, 9½, and 11½ (top). Note the progressive wearing down of teeth as deer grow older. Tooth wear above the gum line can be used by hunters and field naturalists to judge age (as explained in the text) though this is less accurate than laboratory methods in which the lens of the eye is weighed or in which annual "growth rings" inside the tooth are counted.

*Tailed Deer*, I was bombarded with fascinating discoveries and observations made by interested readers. I received word, for example, of a deer that looked as if it needed the services of an orthodontist. It was a buck killed by William Robbins, Jr., in Delaware County, New York. It was brought to my home so that I could examine and photograph it. The lower jaw was about two inches shorter than normal. The incisors, instead of nipping off twigs against the top mouth pad, had to function against the roof of the mouth. Apparently this was no handicap, as the buck was in good condition. There were no reports of similar deer from that area, but a short time later I received reports about a number of short-jawed deer taken during a period of several years in the area around Scranton, Pennsylvania. The condition is probably a genetic characteristic, as it seemed to be increasing in that region. Surely a severe case would alter the rate of tooth wear.

The great discrepancy in the wearing down of the teeth of the deer in South Jersey and in my area of northwestern New Jersey demonstrates the uncertainty of using teeth to measure age. South Jersey is very sandy, and along the coast there is a great deal of wind. At times the leaves of all vegetation are coated with dust particles—fine sand. Deer eating this vegetation ingest the sand, and the wearing down of their teeth is greatly accelerated. It has also been found that a buck's teeth wear out slightly faster than a doe's because the male is larger and consumes more food, producing more wear. Continued research has shown that the tooth-wear method is only about 43 percent accurate. Other, more accurate methods are currently being used, but the Severinghaus-Tanck method is still the only one that can be used in the field or by the average layman. Charts for the purpose, published by New York's Department of Environmental Conservation, are a must for anyone interested in aging by this method. They are available free from the New York State Department of Environmental Conservation, 50 Wolf Road, Albany, New York 12233.

The next aging method to be developed was the weighing of the lens of the eye. Rexford Lord, working on cottontail rabbits, and other researchers found that eye lenses, including those of humans, thicken consistently with age. This method was definitely a laboratory technique because the lenses had to be dried in a special oven at a specified temperature for a specified time. Then, using a very fine scientific scale, the lens could be weighed and the age determined.

The most recent method again involves the teeth. The technique is to extract one of the incisors, slice it, and count the layers of cementum inside. This method was discovered by two Canadian biologists, E. Sergeant and D. H. Pimlott, in 1959, and was used on other game species such as moose. Only recently has it become the standard technique for aging deer.

The procedure is based on the fact that deer (and most other types of animal and plant life) are subjected to a period of diminished growth during each winter. The diminished growth is what puts the dark annual ring on a fish scale, the tight series of rings on goat and sheep horns, the annual rings in a tree trunk. To age any of these, you merely count the dark annual rings. To age deer, you count the dark rings between the layers of cementum in the root portion of the primary incisors. To make the rings more easily visible, the tooth is decalcified and then sliced or ground lengthwise. The sections of the teeth are then stained with various solutions to make the rings more conspicuous. The sections are mounted on glass slides and viewed through a microscope.

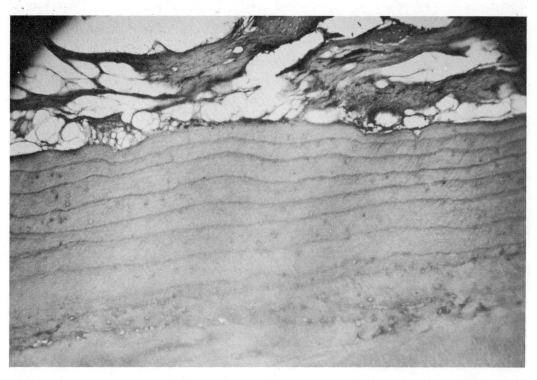

The latest scientific method of aging deer is to section a tooth, view a section through a microscope, and count cementum layers. The tooth section in this microphotograph shows the deer to be 8½ years old.

There are many advantages besides accuracy in using the incisor tooth sections. The main one is cost. Kansas found that when all hunters were required to bring their deer to checking stations, it cost the state $12 per deer to check the teeth by the older method, for a total cost in 1969 of $20,000. In 1971, the state asked all hunters to send in the two center or pincer incisors. The total cost that year was only $1,115. The work on aging the deer was accomplished in about 400 man-hours, compared to the 3,200 to 5,700 man-hours it had taken to operate checking stations.

The hunters were happy to cooperate because it meant they no longer had to haul their deer 30 to 60 miles for checking, nor did they have to worry about ruining trophies. To examine a deer's teeth for wear, the usual procedure is to slit the checks back to the massiter muscles (jawbone muscles). This is fine for the biologist, but any hunter who wants to have his deer's head mounted will not allow such mutilation.

# 7

## Life Span

$\mathrm{F}$ew deer ever live out their potential life span of eleven or twelve years. Very few bucks even reach their prime of 4½ years. Many states have a "bucks-only" season with a special doe day or season in addition. Only a few states allow the hunting of either sex on a regular basis. In the first two instances, the preponderance of does over bucks will be great. Even where either sex can be shot, more bucks are taken because they are desirable trophies and because some hunters still cannot bring themselves to shoot a doe. Consequently, in almost every state the females make up the bulk of the population and they have the greater chance of living out their life span.

In New Jersey, very few bucks live beyond 2½ years. Most are killed the first year that they bear legal antlers—at the age of 1½ years. In 1975 in one of New Jersey's management zones, 91.8 percent of the bucks killed were 1½ years old. C. W. Severinghaus figured that the average life expectancy for bucks in New York's western counties to be 1.2 years, in the Catskills about 1.6 years, in the Adirondacks about 2.0 years. The records of Pennsylvania's

Game Research Division show that 67 percent of the bucks killed are 1½ years old, 20 percent are 2½ years old, 9 percent are 3½ years old, 2 percent are 4½ years old, 2 percent are 5½ years old.

Does reach a greater age in the wild and also fare much better in captivity. In 1931, extensive studies on the life span of deer indicated that they have specific longevities of eight to twelve years and potential longevities up to twenty-three years, almost twice the age cited by most authorities. The larger species of deer have the longer life span. Averaging the life span of 200 deer researchers came up with ten years, four months, nine days for bucks and ten years, ten months, twenty-seven days for the does. According to the records of friends of mine who have deer preserves, does live quite a bit longer than bucks. Females of almost all species of mammals, including humans, just live longer. The males of most species are usually 20 percent larger than the females. Perhaps males are worn out sooner by this extra weight and the extra food that has to be eaten and processed to achieve and maintain this weight.

The greatest longevity recorded for a deer was that of a blacktail doe on Gambier Island, British Columbia. In the fall of 1918, this doe and a single fawn became tame and would come to feed at a farm. The blacktails of that area do not usually breed as fawns and usually have a single fawn at their first birthing, so it was concluded that this doe was a little over two years old when she first appeared. She stayed on the farm until she died in the winter of 1938-1939 at over twenty-two years of age.

The oldest whitetail deer that I can find a record of was a captive doe called Lady, owned by R. B. Howard of Putney, Vermont. She was born in captivity on June 8, 1932, and died on December 7, 1951, when she broke her neck jumping out of her pen. She had stayed in good health up through her nineteenth year, with no sign of feebleness, and her weight was normal, her appetite good. Her teeth were worn out, however. They had lasted as long as they did because most of her life she had been fed soft, easily chewed, commercial feed. Her health started to fail during the last four months of her life, her coat becoming rough and patchy, and she was beginning to stiffen up. There is another claim of a doe in Wisconsin that lived to be 19½ years old, but no data is available. C. W. Severinghaus and J. Tanck have a set of teeth in their collection that came from a doe that lived to be 16½ years old but, again, I have no further information.

R. S. Palmer reported a semi-tame whitetail doe called Diana at Tomhegan Camps in Maine. She was killed by a rutting buck on November 13, 1952, when she was 18½ years old. I will talk more about this remarkable doe in the chapter on birth and fawns.

Several semi-tame blacktails that lived in the wild but came to farms to

Joe Taylor poses with his ancient whitetail doe. She was over sixteen years old when photo was taken — over eighteen and still fertile and healthy as this book went to press.

feed on Hardy Island, in British Columbia, reached ages of fifteen or sixteen years. A captive blacktail buck owned by R. O. Ramport of Ukiah, California, was sixteen years old when it died. Note that this is the only impressive longevity record for a buck.

My friend Joe Taylor, of Columbia, New Jersey, has a doe on his preserve that is now over seventeen years old. This doe's coat looked pretty poor last spring and she was limping quite badly, but the limp was from a leg injury of years ago that was probably aggravated by old age. Joe turned the doe out for the early summer to wander at will over his property. She gave birth to a fawn that died in a rainstorm. The access to all of the good, natural browse and forbs rejuvenated her, and her winter coat is sleek and most of the stiffness is gone from her walk.

In 1969, John Ozoga of Michigan reported some very interesting longevity records of wild whitetail does living under natural conditions. These deer had been tagged as fawns and were retrapped later. One doe was fourteen years, nine months old and a second was fourteen years, seven months when trapped and released. Both were in good health, although they are undoubtedly dead by now. It is too bad their tags were not recovered to complete the record.

Undoubtedly, where deer are subjected to little or no predation or hunting pressure and the food supply is good, quite a few of them live out their potential lifespan of twelve years. With the greatly improved accuracy of counting the cementum rings to determine the age of deer, more longevity records probably will be set.

# 8

## Calculating Live and Dressed Weights— and Conserving Venison

Either a deer's size is mighty deceptive or else most hunters (honest though they may be in other respects) are fishermen at heart. When a hunter tells about a big one that got away, he usually holds a hand out, shoulder-high, to show how big the deer really was. A hunter who holds his hand that high ought to be describing an elk, not a whitetail or mule deer. A hand held out about belt-high would be just about on target to indicate the shoulder height or to pat a typical adult whitetail on the back. It would be held only a trifle higher even for a husky Rocky Mountain mule deer. The next chapter will deal more specifically and in some detail with weights and measures for various types of American deer. Meanwhile, I will make a valid generalization regarding size. A good whitetail buck in most regions of the country stands only a little over three feet high at the shoulder, and a good muley stands only a couple of inches higher.

Whether or not a hunter is after a trophy, he is likely to be interested in how handsome a pair of antlers a buck has. Next, he is most interested in how big the deer is. For that matter, anyone who is curious about wildlife would surely like to know the weight of a typical deer or a specific deer that has been harvested. Weights, like shoulder heights, tend to be grossly exaggerated. This is understandable, because few people have sufficient biological knowledge to judge an animal's weight simply by looking at it. And equally few know how to weigh an animal or estimate its weight.

The job of weighing a deer is complicated. Deer are seldom shot where they can be conveniently and accurately weighed. If the deer is actually a huge one, the hunter usually has no way of getting it to a scale so that its live weight can be recorded. If the deer is average, the hunter would like to know the weight but he isn't going to drag the deer out whole. So most deer are eviscerated and then taken out.

Few hunters have the opportunity to handle and weigh enough deer to become proficient at estimating live weight. It has been found that they usually overestimate the weight of their deer by 20 to 25 percent. I have found that deer seem to gain weight in direct proportion to the time, distance, and difficulty involved in getting the carcass out of the woods.

There is a substantial difference between a deer's live weight and its weight after field-dressing or hog-dressing. Therefore, before delving into the problem of weighing a deer—or estimating its weight—I had better explain the procedures involved in dressing and caring for the venison once the deer has been harvested. In reading the weight records, you will often notice those terms "hog-dressed" and "field-dressed." Frequently, the terms are used interchangeably, but they mean two different things.

If a deer is field-dressed, the skin on its belly is opened and its paunch, intestines, and reproductive organs are taken out. The liver, heart, and lungs are left in until the hunter reaches his camp or home, and the diaphragm is left intact to help hold the organs in place and keep the chest area clean. Hunters who plan to drag their deer out of the woods often do this.

When a deer is hog-dressed, the carcass is usually split open from the throat or upper sternum to the pelvic arch. The windpipe is cut off as high as possible and the heart, lungs, diaphragm walls, liver, paunch, intestines, and reproductive organs are all taken out. Probably 95 percent of the deer taken are dressed in this fashion. In both cases, the feet are left on, and in both cases the blood drains out.

I always hog-dress my deer and can do the job in about seven minutes. I cut around the anus first, then roll the deer on its back and straddle the chest, facing to the rear. Pulling up on the belly skin, I insert my knife below the breastbone. By pulling up on the skin, I avoid cutting into the paunch or intestines. I then cut the belly skin down to the pelvic arch. I always carry a six-inch Randall knife that is heavy enough to allow me to slice through the ribs,

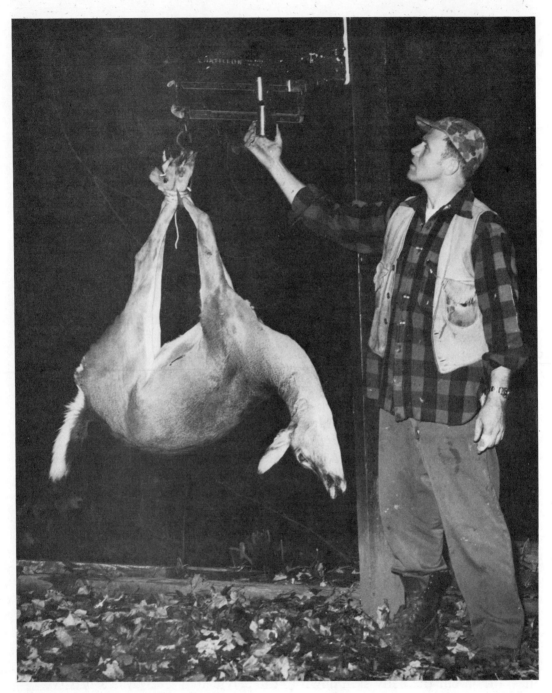

The author weighs a hog-dressed whitetail.

where they join the sternum, up to the neck. After severing the windpipe, I cut out the diaphragm walls, pull out the entrails and pull the anus in through the pelvic arch. I then roll the deer up on its belly with its legs spread wide to drain out all the blood.

Then, if I have to carry or drag the deer, I do something that few hunters bother about. I sew up the body opening with a burlap-bag sewing needle and heavy cord to keep it clean. As soon as I get the deer to my destination, I hang it up by the head and prop the body cavity open with a stick in the rib cage.

Many hunters leave their deer hanging to "age" the meat. Meat will age properly only at temperatures between 36° F. and 38° F. (3° Celsius). If the temperature gets above 40° F., the meat will start to spoil. Most deer carcasses are hung out in cold weather and freeze solid. When meat freezes, it is not aging and the hunter is wasting his time. If the deer cannot be butchered promptly, freezing keeps it from spoiling, but no one should believe the meat is aging.

In warm weather the carcass should be covered with a cheesecloth deer bag to prevent flies from laying eggs on the meat. If no such bag is available, a liberal application of black pepper will help to keep the flies off the meat. But when I can't age my venison properly, I butcher the carcass as soon as the body heat is out of it. A deer's body temperature is about 104°F. (40 ° Celsius).

Hunters are always interested in what their deer weighed, and biologists are even more interested because the body weights are the key to the condition of the deer herd and its habitat.

The easiest method of "weighing" a deer in the woods is to use a tape measure. I carry a 10-foot (3 m.), ¼-inch (6 mm.) tape measure in my pocket. When I go afield, I am always finding something of interest that I just have to measure. That tape has helped with a lot of the data in this book. Take your tape and measure the deer's heart girth—just behind the front legs. That figure can be used to give you both the approximate live and dressed weights of your deer.

For many years it has been known that there is a definite correlation between heart girth and body weight. The agricultural colleges worked out a formula that has long been standard in giving approximate weights of domestic cattle. I had a tape measure marked with the equivalents—made especially for deer by a company in Massachusetts. Unfortunately, I misplaced both the tape and the address of the maker. However, Charles Smart, Robert Giles, Jr., and David Gwynn, all of the Division of Forestry and Wildlife Resources at Virginia Polytechnic Institute and State University at Blacksburg, developed a chart which they have permitted me to include here. I now carry a copy of the chart in my wallet. All you have to do is measure the deer's heart girth and

# Weights and Heart Girth

| Heart girth inches (cm) | Hog-dressed weight Fawns pounds (kg) | Adults pounds (kg) | Live weight Fawns pounds (kg) | Adults pounds (kg) |
|---|---|---|---|---|
| 20 ( 50.8) | 27 (12.2) | | 36 (16.3) | |
| 21 ( 53.3) | 30 (13.6) | | 40 (18.1) | |
| 22 ( 55.9) | 33 (15.0) | | 44 (20.0) | |
| 23 ( 58.4) | 37 (16.8) | | 48 (21.8) | |
| 24 ( 61.0) | 40 (18.1) | | 52 (23.6) | |
| 25 ( 63.5) | 43 (19.5) | | 57 (25.8) | |
| 26 ( 66.0) | 46 (20.9) | 46 (20.9) | 61 (27.7) | 60 (27.2) |
| 27 ( 68.6) | 50 (22.7) | 52 (23.6) | 65 (29.5) | 68 (30.8) |
| 28 ( 71.1) | 53 (24.0) | 58 (26.3) | 69 (31.3) | 75 (34.0) |
| 29 ( 73.7) | 56 (25.4) | 64 (29.0) | 73 (33.1) | 83 (37.6) |
| 30 ( 76.2) | 59 (26.8) | 70 (31.8) | 77 (34.9) | 90 (40.8) |
| 31 ( 78.7) | 63 (28.6) | 76 (34.5) | 81 (36.7) | 98 (44.5) |
| 32 ( 81.3) | 66 (29.9) | 82 (37.2) | 85 (38.6) | 106 (48.1) |
| 33 ( 83.8) | 69 (31.3) | 88 (39.9) | 89 (40.4) | 113 (51.3) |
| 34 ( 86.4) | 73 (33.1) | 94 (42.6) | 93 (42.2) | 121 (54.9) |
| 35 ( 88.9) | | 101 (45.8) | | 128 (58.1) |
| 36 ( 91.4) | | 107 (48.5) | | 136 (61.7) |
| 37 ( 94.0) | | 113 (51.3) | | 144 (65.3) |
| 38 ( 96.5) | | 119 (54.0) | | 151 (68.5) |
| 39 ( 99.1) | | 125 (56.7) | | 159 (72.1) |
| 40 (101.6) | | 131 (59.2) | | 166 (75.3) |
| 41 (104.1) | | 137 (62.1) | | 174 (78.9) |
| 42 (106.7) | | 143 (64.9) | | 182 (82.6) |
| 43 (109.2) | | 149 (67.6) | | 190 (86.2) |
| 44 (111.8) | | 155 (70.3) | | 197 (89.4) |
| 45 (114.3) | | 161 (73.0) | | 205 (93.0) |

To calculate live or hog-dressed weight, first measure heart girth—the circumference of body just behind the front legs. Then consult this chart to convert girth into a close estimate of weight.

that figure will allow you to read the hog-dressed and live weights from the table.

I have found that this table also works out pretty closely on men. I have a 42-inch (107 cm.) chest and, according to the chart, I should weigh 182 pounds (82.6 kg.). Actually I weigh about 186 pounds (84.4 kg.). But some of my chest seems to have slipped down around my middle. So I checked the chart out on some friends and it came very close to their scale weight.

Of course, nothing really takes the place of scales if you want accuracy for your weights. If you finally get your deer to a scale, you will have either the field- or hog-dressed weight, depending on how you dressed your deer. In the next chapter, dealing with average weights and record weights, I will include some estimates of live weights. You will have to allow for slight inconsistencies in some instances because there was no way to ascertain in every case how a deer was dressed out before it was weighed. Most reports stipulate "hog-dressed," but some use the term "field-dressed" or—confusingly—just "dressed."

To calculate the live weight of a deer when you have the hog-dressed weight, you can use a dependable formula. Divide the hog-dressed weight by four, then add that quarter to the hog-dressed weight to come up with the live weight. If you know the live weight of your deer and want to know the hog-dressed weight, divide the scale weight by five and subtract that fifth.

If you want to use a simple mathematical formula instead of dividing and adding, just multiply the hog-dressed weight of your deer by 1.25. Some state game departments and some biologists multiply the dressed weights by 1.275 or 1.30. If you check some of the weight records in the next chapter, you will see that these higher figures were used—why, I'm not sure. Using any of these figures is only an educated guess. Personally, I feel that a figure slightly lower than 1.25 should be used on big deer, because a small deer has more "innards" in relationship to its total body weight than the great big fellows do.

At any rate, a deer's blood and entrails account for roughly a fifth of its total weight. The average weight for an adult deer's heart, liver, and lungs is 10 pounds (4.5 kg.) The heart weighs about 2 pounds (0.9 kg.), the liver 5 pounds (2.27 kg.) and the lungs 3 pounds (1.36 kg.).

The next question that most hunters ask is, how much edible meat will they get from a deer? A lot depends on where the deer was hit, what damage the bullet did, and how good a butcher the hunter is.

Some years ago I did a photographic step-by-step series on butchering deer for *Outdoor Life* Magazine. Evidently it was useful, as it was reprinted three times. I called the article "A Deer in a Dishpan." When I butcher a deer, I remove all fat, tissue, and bone, leaving nothing but pure meat. This reduces an average deer—125 pounds (56.7 kg.) live weight—to about 46 or 48 pounds (20.9 to 21.8 kg.) of pure meat. At that rate, you can carry your deer meat in a large dishpan.

A rough formula often given for finding how much meat you will get from a deer is, again, to divide your deer's hog-dressed weight by four. Subtract that quarter or multiply the hog-dressed weight by .75. According to this formula, if your deer weighed 120 pounds (54.5 kg.) hog-dressed, you should end up with 90 pounds (40.9 kg.) of meat. But these figures include the bone in a number of cuts—just as bone is included in store-bought beef cuts. It includes such items as spare ribs and shoulder roast with the bone in. On a 125-pound (56.7 kg.) live-weight deer, the skin weighs about 10 to 12 pounds (4.5 to 5.4 kg.). The feet weigh 6 to 8 pounds (2.7 to 3.6 kg.), depending on where you cut them off. The head weighs another 6 to 8 pounds (2.7 to 3.6 kg.), and the bones weigh 16 to 20 pounds (7.26 to 9.1 kg.). I usually figure that just about

50 percent of the deer's hog-dressed weight will be pure meat—or roughly 40 percent of the deer's live weight. But as I said, a lot depends on the butcher. I have a friend who uses the entire neck—not for stew but for a roast, with all those bones left in it. He happens to be a fine chef, and his dinner guests describe his neck roast as a gourmet's feast. Or so he claims.

# 9

## Lightweights, Middleweights, Heavyweights

As I noted in the last chapter, the shoulder of adult deer (the highest part along the back) would be only about belt high on an average man. To some people, that seems incredibly small. So to support that claim, here are some figures based on a consensus of sources ranging from the studies by Seton to the game-department reports and my own measurements and weighings. As you consider these measurements, bear in mind that does usually are substantially smaller and lighter than bucks.

Adult Key deer seldom stand more than about 28 inches (71 cm.) high or weigh more than about 80 pounds (36.3 kg.). Often they are much smaller. Among the little Coues deer, or Arizona whitetails, a buck is apt to stand 31 inches (79 cm.) at the shoulder and weigh perhaps 98 pounds (44.5 kg.). A northeastern whitetail buck generally stands less than 40 inches (102 cm.) high and weighs less than 160 pounds (72.6 kg.), although some bucks and even some does become much heavier under favorable conditions. The Columbian blacktail is slightly smaller than the whitetail. After studying the blacktails in Washington's Olympic Mountains, Seton concluded that the bucks seldom weigh over 150 pounds (80 kg.). According to the latest reports, the average is closer to 100 pounds (45.4 kg.). My own measurements of an admittedly rather small Columbian doe showed her to stand only 29 inches (74 cm.) high, and she weighed only 83 pounds (37.6 kg.). Don McKnight, a research chief with Alaska's Department of Fish and Game, has described Sitka blacktails as a trifle smaller and shorter-legged than Columbian blacktails. Their weight is about the same. Even a mature muley buck of the Rocky Mountain variety—the largest subspecies—is apt to stand no higher at the shoulder than about 42 inches (106.7 cm.) and weigh no more than about 200 pounds (90.7 kg.). Of course, some record muleys—and whitetails, for that matter—have weighed more than twice as much, but a very large mule deer is likely to have a shoulder height of no more than 44 inches (112 cm.).

The averages just given do not take regional differences into account, and even within a single subspecies, or a single herd, some deer are far more massive than others. How big can a deer grow? That depends on species, subspecies, geographic location, age, sex, and the amount and quality of food available in the area. Individuals vary greatly in body and limb size and general conformation. One hears about long-legged "ridge deer" and short-legged "swamp deer." Some people must think that running up mountains stretches a deer's legs. I'm always tempted to say that I thought it would wear the animal down and make it short-legged. Some deer are long and lean, others blocky, some have short muzzles, some have long muzzles, some have rounded "Roman noses." Apart from the record sizes and weights, compilations of statistics are merely averages. I will list the significant findings of specific studies to provide a clearer and more detailed concept of deer sizes, and I will also give the record sizes and weights—some of which are downright astonishing.

Before examining some figures from different parts of the country, let's clarify the picture by discussing body growth and the factors that affect it. Those factors are in operation even before a deer is born—that is, during gestation. The gestation period for American deer is usually 200 to 205 days (6$\frac{2}{3}$ months). The length of the gestation period is determined primarily by the food available to the mother. Records for gestation run from 187 to 212 days. Does that drop their fawns in the shorter range of the time are those that have received adequate food. Does on an inadequate diet carry their fawns for a longer period because this is nature's way of trying to get all fawns off to the best start possible. A longer gestation period allows the fawn more time for total development before birth. Most interestingly, except in cases of severe malnutrition, most fawns are born weighing in at about the average for their subspecies, regardless of the physical condition of the doe.

If food is plentiful, the doe gets sustenance plus the nutrients needed to feed the developing fetus. Under normal conditions an adult doe usually has twins. If there is a severe shortage of food, she will produce only one fawn, or if two fawns have been conceived, one will die during gestation and be reabsorbed. An extended period of starvation will cause the second fawn to die. The fetus may simply be aborted or it may be reabsorbed back into the doe's body so that she can utilize the nutrients. At this stage, nature is more concerned with saving the life of the mother, than the life of the young.

As pregnancy advances, this situation is reversed. After the fourth or the fifth month, the needs of the fetus are met first. If food is scarce in the early spring, the needs of the fetus are filled and whatever is left over goes to sustenance of the doe. If the doe has no body reserves left, her own body is catabolized, with the nutrients being drawn from her own tissues. The doe may be emaciated but her fawn or fawns will be about normal in weight and size for her subspecies in her particular area.

Male fawns weigh about 20 percent more than females at birth, and they maintain this ratio (or more) for the rest of their lives. Whitetail fawns in my area of New Jersey weigh between 5 and 6 pounds (2.3 to 2.7 kg.) at birth. Last spring I had a chance to weigh two full-term buck fawns taken from a doe that had been killed on the highway. These little bucks were identical in size and weight. At 7³/₄ pounds (3.5 kg.) each, they were the heaviest fawns I have ever personally weighed. The deer in my area are not as large as they should be because our herd population exceeds its food supply. They measured 29 inches (74 cm.) in overall length from nose tip to tail tip, the tail being 4 inches (10 cm.) long. They stood 18¹/₂ inches (47 cm.) high at the shoulder, had an ear length of 3¹/₂ inches (9 cm.), a crown-to-nose length of 6 inches (15.2 cm.) and a heart girth of 12 inches (30.5 cm.).

In 1950 Arnold Haugen and L. Davenport published the birth weights and measurements of twenty-nine fawns from upper Michigan. The males averaged 7 pounds, 7 ounces (3.4 kg.) and the females averaged 5 pounds, 11¹/₂ ounces (2.6 kg.). The minimum male weight was 4¹/₂ pounds (2 kg.) and the maximum was 14¹/₂ pounds (6.6 kg.). This last is the heaviest whitetail fawn that I can find on record. The minimum female weight was 3¹/₄ pounds (1.5 kg.) and the maximum was 8¹/₄ pounds (3.7 kg.). C. W. Severinghaus reported a female whitetail fawn in New York that weighed 10 pounds (4.5 kg.), which is the heaviest record I can find for a female.

Raymond Hall gave the measurements of a California muley fawn: a total

A whitetail fawn, at six months, is already two-thirds the size of its mother.

length of 23¼ inches (59 cm.), a tail length of 4⅓ inches (11 cm.), a hind-foot length of 11¼ inches (28 cm.), and an ear length of 4¾ inches (12 cm.). Paul Hudson and Ludvig G. Browman gave the weight and measurements of a mule deer thought to be about seven days old. The overall length was 30½ inches (78 cm.), hind-foot length 11 inches (28 cm.), ear length 4½ inches (11.4 cm.) and weight 15¼ pounds (7 kg.).

Fawns grow extremely fast. They double their birth weight in fifteen days and double that total again in another fifteen days or so. In six months their weight increases tenfold. Skeletal growth is very rapid up to the age of seven months, when it stops for the winter. Suspended growth is nature's way of allowing the food intake to be converted to the fat reserves needed for winter survival. At six to seven months of age the fawns are about two-thirds the size of their mothers, whom they accompany.

Joseph Dixon gave the measurements of a five-month-old muley fawn: total overall length was 39 inches (99 cm.), tail five inches (13 cm.), hind-foot length 14 inches (36 cm.), ear length 6½ inches (16.5 cm.), and height at the shoulder 25 inches (63 cm.). Unfortunately, he did not give the weight, but it would be in the vicinity of 60 pounds (27.2 kg.).

A five- to six-month-old whitetail buck that I measured in New Jersey yielded the following data: overall length 43 inches (108 cm.), height at shoulder 27 inches (68 cm.), ear length 5½ inches (14 cm.), hind-foot length 15 inches (38 cm.), and a heart girth of 26 inches (66 cm.), which would figure out to about 60 pounds (27 kg.) live weight.

The New Jersey Division of Fish and Game has done considerable deer research and it is from their *Deer Report #3* that I have taken the following material. In New Jersey we have an estimated deer population of 75,000. Our habitat for deer runs from very poor, in some of the Pine Barrens area, to good in the northwestern section and excellent in the southwestern and west-central sections. The habitat determines the deer's weight. In our poorest Pines Section #21, the average live weight for a five- to six-month-old whitetail buck is 45 pounds (20.4 kg.), and the average for does is the same. The rich farmland of Salem County has just emerged as our top deer-producing area, edging out Hunterdon and Mercer counties. In Salem County the average live weight of a five- to six-month-old whitetail buck is 93 pounds (42.2 kg.) and the does average 64½ pounds (29 kg.).

It cannot be stressed too often that deer are what they eat. Illinois has no overbrowsing. There is a superabundance of food from some of the richest soil in our nation and the results show. In their book, *Prairie Whitetails,* John Calhoun and Forrest Loomis tell of four records of giant Illinois whitetail buck fawns. The largest, five to six months old, weighed 176 pounds (80 kg.) and was shot in Mason County in 1966. The second-largest weighed 170 pounds (77 kg.), the third weighed 166 pounds (75 kg.), and the fourth weighed 164 pounds (74.4 kg.). All are live weights. These fawns were exceptional even in Illinois, where the average buck fawn of comparable age weighs 90 to 100 pounds (40.8-45.4 kg.).

The importance of food is also shown in the statistics compiled by Nebraska, which has populations of both whitetail and mule deer. As a rule, mule deer average quite a bit larger than whitetails but this is not so in Nebraska. There, the record muley outweighed the record whitetail, but an average Nebraska whitetail of a given age actually outweighs an average Nebraska mule deer of the same age. The heaviest mule deer ever recorded in Nebraska was a buck shot in Garden County in 1957. It had a scale-weight of 310 pounds (141 kg.) hog-dressed, and its live weight was estimated to be about 380 pounds (173 kg.). This record muley weight is only a little greater than that of Nebraska's record whitetail buck, killed in Cherry County in 1957. It weighed 287 pounds (130 kg.) hog-dressed, which meant it had a live weight of over 350 pounds (159 kg.). Nebraska's statistics are very interesting because they include the average weights for the whitetail and the mule deer by age class, as shown in the following table.

### Average Weights of Nebraska Whitetails

| AGE CLASS | MALE | | FEMALE | |
|---|---|---|---|---|
| | lbs. | kg. | lbs. | kg. |
| 6 months | 87 | 39.4 | 81 | 36.6 |
| 1½ years | 156 | 70.6 | 128 | 57.9 |
| 2½ years | 192 | 86.9 | 137 | 62.0 |
| 3½ years | 217 | 98.3 | 144 | 65.2 |
| 4½ years | 238 | 107.8 | 151 | 68.4 |

### Average Weights of Nebraska Mule Deer

| AGE CLASS | MALE | | FEMALE | |
|---|---|---|---|---|
| | lbs. | kg. | lbs. | kg. |
| 6 months | 75 | 33.9 | 70 | 31.7 |
| 1½ years | 135 | 61.1 | 113 | 51.1 |
| 2½ years | 173 | 78.3 | 122 | 55.2 |
| 3½ years | 201 | 91.0 | 128 | 57.9 |
| 4½ years | 213 | 96.4 | 126 | 57.0 |

The surprising discrepancies between the whitetails and mule deer in the Nebraska statistics are due solely to food. The whitetails inhabit the rich bottomlands, the farmlands, while the mule deer are found in the rougher, poor-soil areas of the state.

Pennsylvania also has discrepancies between the deer harvested on the rich farmlands and those taken in the poor woods areas of the north-central portion of the state. The statewide averages are considerably smaller than those of Nebraska's whitetails. At six months, both male and female fawns in Pennsylvania average 54 pounds (24.4 kg.). At 1½ years the bucks average 102 pounds (46.2 kg.), the does 92 pounds (41.6 kg.). At 2½ years the bucks average 117 pounds (53 kg.), the does 100 pounds (45.3 kg.). And at 3½ years the bucks average 127 pounds (57.5 kg.), while the does still average 100 pounds (45.3 kg.).

For years a really big buck in Pennsylvania was called a Michigan buck because in the early 1900's Pennsylvania imported deer from that state. The imported deer were slightly larger than those in Pennsylvania at the time. However, Pennsylvania habitat was then a deer's heaven. The deer population was low and thousands upon thousands of acres of forest were growing back into sprouts and other nutritious deer food. The whitetails responded by in-

The product of rich soil—a fine buck going into the rut in excellent condition. Both body size and rack indicate good habitat. (Photo by Irene Vandermolen)

creasing in numbers, weight, and body size. Today, the really big-racked, heavy bucks from Pennsylvania's rich farmland are Pennsylvania deer, and so are those in Pennsylvania's northern wooded areas where they are getting progressively smaller and developing ever smaller antlers. Deer, as I mentioned, are what they eat.

As for Michigan deer, many years of poor forestry management in parts of that state wrought havoc on the whitetails, but management practices have undergone some change and it is possible that Michigan will again produce sizable numbers of sizable deer. Several other states, such as Missouri and Illinois, have fine habitat and big whitetails. Still other states, from California to the crests of the Rockies, produce big muleys, though the herds have declined in recent years. I will give record figures for both whitetails and mule deer after showing that rich habitat largely determines average size.

In New Jersey, 1½-year-old bucks on the best land average 115.3 pounds (52 kg.) while those on the poorest land average 70 (31.7 kg.). Females of the same age on the best land average 116 pounds (52.5 kg.) while those on the poorest land average 60.5 pounds (27.4 kg.). Two figures really stand out here. The most important is that the does living on good soil weigh almost *twice* the weight of does inhabiting the poor regions. The underweight herd in those poor areas will continue to drop in population as well as size until corrective measures are taken. Does on the poor areas will not breed as fawns and, if they do breed at 1½ years of age, they will drop one fawn instead of two—for a net loss of two potential deer from each doe in two years. We know the problems and we know the answers, but much of the time the public living in the poor deer areas will not allow our game managers to manage the game, to correct the existing problems. The New Jersey "game doctors" recognize the sickness and have written out the prescription but the public won't take the medicine. Deer herds must be managed to keep the population in balance with the food available, either by a heavier harvest of the deer or by sufficient expenditures on habitat improvement to provide more food. I will discuss these problems more fully in the chapters on wildlife management.

The second statistic that stands out is that on our best land the 1½-year-old does actually outweigh 1½-year-old bucks. This is most unusual and can only be attributed to food. Of course, the bucks do eventually outgrow the does. They definitely pull away from the does in both size and weight with each passing year.

New Hampshire has done considerable work on the weights of the whitetail deer of different age classes. The state's biologists also take cognizance of the weight loss sustained by deer during the hunting and breeding seasons. They have prepared charts showing the average weights for bucks and does in the five major age classes during each week of November and December. I will summarize the data here because no other state, to my knowledge, has attempted to prove this significant weight loss.

### Average Weight — and Weight Loss — of New Hampshire Whitetails During Breeding and Hunting Season

| AGE CLASS | WEIGHT AT BEGINNING OF NOVEMBER | | WEIGHT AT END OF DECEMBER | |
|---|---|---|---|---|
| *Male:* | lbs. | kg. | lbs. | kg. |
| 6 months | 80 | 36.2 | 75 | 33.9 |
| 1½ years | 141 | 63.8 | 120 | 54.3 |
| 2½ years | 195 | 88.3 | 166 | 75.1 |
| 3½ years | 235 | 106.4 | 177 | 80.1 |
| 4½ years and older | 245 | 110.9 | 186 | 84.2 |
| *Female:* | | | | |
| 6 months | 70 | 31.7 | 65 | 29.4 |
| 1½ years | 125 | 56.6 | 100 | 45.3 |
| 2½ years | 138 | 62.5 | 125 | 56.6 |
| 3½ years | 150 | 67.9 | 137 | 62.0 |
| 4½ years and older | 145 | 65.6 | 131 | 59.3 |

In giving average age-class weights, the New Hampshire study shows the yearly increase in weight of the bucks. Of even greater importance is the weight loss during the rut. It was generally thought that whitetail bucks lost about 20 percent of their body weight because of the breeding season. This study proves that the weight loss is at least 25 percent for bucks 3½ years old or more. Those are the bucks that do most of the breeding. The actual weight loss is even greater than indicated here because bucks taper off their food consumption for about a month prior to the main breeding season. The bucks undoubtedly weighed more at the beginning of October than they did on the first of November, but before the hunting season opened there were not enough bucks available for weighing to make a sampling.

Data from the Arizona State Game Department includes average weights for the Coues whitetail deer taken in the 1974 buck season. The 1½-year-old bucks average 68 pounds (30.8 kg.); 2½-year-olds averaged 79 pounds (35.7 kg.); 3½-year-olds averaged 100 pounds (45.3 kg.); 4½-year-olds averaged 107 pounds (48.4 kg.), as did the even older bucks.

The Coues is one of our smallest deer. Jerome Pratt kept some very interesting records while he was wildlife manager at Fort Huachuca, Arizona. The 881 Coues bucks harvested at the Fort between 1958 and 1963 averaged 98 pounds (44.3 kg.) and the does averaged 72 pounds (32.6 kg.). Coues fawns generally weigh 3½ pounds (1.5 kg.) at birth and 31 pounds (14 kg.) at three months. At that age they stand 23 inches (58 cm.) high at the shoulder. Average bucks stand 31 inches (79 cm.) at the shoulder.

In 1963 Charles Walker killed a Coues buck that weighed 132 pounds (59.7 kg.) at Fort Huachuca. The following year, William Culbertson killed one that weighed 137 pounds (62 kg.), and three weeks later Mrs. Diane Walton broke all records with a buck that weighed 145 pounds (65.6 kg.) field-dressed—for an estimated live weight of 181 pounds (81.9 kg.). However, it is thought that her heavyweight trophy was a descendant of a cross between the Coues deer and a mule deer. Two known crosses had been previously released in the area where the Walton buck was taken.

Key deer are even smaller than the Coues. John Dickson, in his study of Florida Key deer, states that adults measure 26 to 28 inches (66 to 71 cm.) high at the shoulder and weigh 35 to 80 pounds (15.8 to 36.2 kg.). The average weight for adult bucks is about 45 pounds (20.3 kg.).

Ellsworth Brown of Washington State gives some age-class weights for Columbian blacktails, and Don Robinson of British Columbia's Game Department has recorded some for the Columbian blacktails on Vancouver Island. The accompanying table shows the averages compiled for those two areas. The samplings from Washington include older deer than those sampled on Vancouver Island, and it is interesting to note that the Washington does lost weight slightly but consistently after reaching 5½ years of age. The Washington bucks lost weight at 6½ years but then regained it and continued to gain. Their 6½-year dip may have reflected a very poor forage year when the samples were taken. It is also interesting to note that the Vancouver blacktails are much lighter in weight than those in Washington (and, I should add, those in Oregon). This, again, is a matter of forage. Blacktails of the California chaparral are even lighter than Vancouver's deer.

### Average Weights of Columbian Blacktails in Washington

| AGE CLASS | MALE | | FEMALE | |
|---|---|---|---|---|
| | *lbs.* | *kg.* | *lbs.* | *kg.* |
| 6 months | 57 | 25.9 | 55 | 24.9 |
| 1½ years | 107 | 48.4 | 95 | 43.0 |
| 2½ years | 137 | 62.0 | 110 | 49.8 |
| 3½ years | 161 | 72.9 | 117 | 53.0 |
| 4½ years | 165 | 74.7 | 118 | 53.4 |
| 5½ years | 207 | 93.7 | 129 | 58.4 |
| 6½ years | 192 | 86.9 | 127 | 57.5 |
| 7½ years | 211 | 95.5 | 124 | 56.1 |
| 8½ years | 232 | 105.0 | 124 | 56.1 |

### Average Weights of Columbian Blacktails on Vancouver Island

| AGE CLASS | MALE | | FEMALE | |
|---|---|---|---|---|
| | *lbs.* | *kg.* | *lbs.* | *kg.* |
| 1½ years | 78 | 35.3 | 75 | 33.9 |
| 2½ years | 93 | 42.1 | 84 | 38.0 |
| 3½ years | 111 | 50.4 | 86 | 38.9 |
| 4½ years | 135 | 61.1 | 92 | 41.6 |
| 5½ years | 161 | 72.9 | 99 | 44.8 |

Richard D. Taber and Raymond F. Dasmann, in a study of Columbian black-tails in California, were unable to compile weight averages for 5½- and 6½-year-old bucks but, with those exceptions, they recorded the weights of both sexes from 1½ to 7½ years. California's blacktails are very light, and the does, like those in Washington, lose weight after their prime years. Another weight table summarizes the findings.

### Average Weights of Columbian Blacktails in California Chaparral

| AGE CLASS | MALE | | FEMALE | |
|---|---|---|---|---|
| | *lbs.* | *kg.* | *lbs.* | *kg.* |
| 6 months | 33 | 14.9 | 26 | 11.7 |
| 1½ years | 62 | 28.0 | 57 | 25.8 |
| 2½ years | 95 | 43.0 | 80 | 36.2 |
| 3½ years | 101 | 45.7 | 79 | 35.7 |
| 4½ years | 127 | 57.5 | 88 | 39.8 |
| 5½ years | — | — | 79 | 35.7 |
| 6½ years | — | — | 79 | 35.7 |
| 7½ years | 144 | 65.2 | 78 | 35.3 |

The weights and sizes of Columbian blacktails in the California chaparral closely parallel the weights and sizes of Sitka blacktails in most areas. The *Alaska News* states that, in October, Sitka blacktail bucks average about 150 pounds (67.9 kg.), the does 100 pounds (45.5 kg.), but other studies indicate weights as low as those for the California deer. Of course, much depends on such factors as the forage in a study area and whether the deer are studied before, during, or after the rut.

A. Starker Leopold, Thane Riney, Randal McCain, and Lloyd Tevis, in a study of the California mule deer in the Jawbone herd, summarized some of the weights. At 6 months, buck fawns average 49 pounds (22.1 kg.), does 47

pounds (21.2 kg.); 1½-year-old bucks average 85 pounds (38.5 kg.), does 77
pounds (34.8 kg.); 2½- to 5½-year-old bucks average 135 pounds (61.1 kg.),
does 102 pounds (46.2 kg.); bucks 6½ years and older average 140 pounds (63.4
kg.), does 101 pounds (45.7 kg.). Again the records prove that bucks continue
to gain weight until they reach extreme old age while the does lose weight
after 4½ or 5½ years. This decline was also borne out by C. W. Severinghaus
in a study of whitetails in New York's Adirondacks.

Some does become sexually mature at seven months of age if they have a
nutritious diet. Far more whitetails than mule deer breed as fawns. Most 1½-
year-old does are sexually mature but, again, whitetails at this age produce
more fawns per doe than do the mule deer. Some blacktail does do not become
sexually mature until they are 2½ years old. Most does attain their maximum
growth at 2½ years, although they gain a little more weight with additional
age.

Among all three types of deer, most bucks reach sexual maturity at 1½
years, though most of them are prevented from breeding at that age by the
older bucks. They do not reach their full skeletal size until they are 4½ to 5½
years old. They continue to gain weight after that until they are about 8½
years old, when their weight and antler development usually begins to decline.

I have measured and weighed many deer. A whitetail (*O. v. borealis*) buck
that I recently worked on was about average for the northeastern states. The
buck weighed 151 pounds (68.5 kg.), live weight. It measured 68 inches (173
cm.) from nose tip to tail tip and stood 39 inches (99 cm.) high at the shoulder. Most whitetail does of this area are 34 to 36 inches (86 to 91 cm.) high at
the shoulder, most bucks 38 to 40 inches (96 to 102 cm.).

Ernest Thompson Seton recorded the measurements and weights of quite a
few outstanding whitetail bucks, and some of his figures merit inclusion here.
For example, he reported that a buck shot by John Denny in 1877 in New
York's Adirondacks weighed 286 pounds (129.5 kg.) hog-dressed, which would
give it a live weight of 357 pounds (161.7 kg.). John W. Titcomb recorded a
buck killed in Vermont in 1898 that weighed 370 pounds (167.6 kg.) live
weight. In Warren County, New Jersey, in 1895, Warren S. Potter killed one
that weighed 318 pounds (144 kg.) hog-dressed, or 400 pounds (181.2 kg.) live
weight.

Seton's statistics get better as they go on. Henry Ordway killed a *giant* buck
near Mud Lake in New York's Adirondack Mountains in 1890. It was scale-
weighed before dressing at 388 pounds (175.7 kg.). The deer had been bled and
had probably lost at least 12 pounds, so its live weight was calculated to be
400 pounds (181.2 kg.). Even more remarkable were the deer's measurements:
overall length from nose tip to tail tip, 115 inches (292 cm.); height at shoul-

Dean Coffman poses with the 440-pound (199.3 kg.) Iowa buck he shot in 1962.

der, 51 inches (130 cm.); neck circumference behind the ears, 37 inches (94 cm.). There are no measurements anywhere for whitetail deer that come close to this record. The buck had nine tines on one beam, ten on the other side. The longest tine was 13 inches (33 cm.).

However, the world-record weight for the whitetail was held for years by a buck killed by Albert Tippett in 1919 near Trout Creek in Michigan's Upper Peninsula. Railroad scales showed it to weigh 354 pounds (160.3 kg.) hog-dressed. The estimated live weight was 425 pounds (192.5 kg.). The weighing was witnessed by a number of people.

Otis Bersing, in his book *A Century of Wisconsin Deer*, described two whitetails that top the Tippett buck, but neither is considered an official record because the weighings were not officially witnessed. In 1924 Robert Hogue shot a buck in Sawyer County, Wisconsin, that had a dressed scale weight of 386 pounds (174.8 kg.) and an estimated live weight of 491 pounds (222.4 kg.). In 1941 in Iron County, Wisconsin, Arnold Peter shot one that had a dressed scale weight of 378 pounds (171.2 kg.) and an estimated live weight of 481 pounds (217.8 kg.).

Lest anyone get the impression that all the big whitetail bucks have disappeared since the "good old days," let me cite some more recent reports. In 1962, Dean Coffman and his friend John Ryan were hunting near Blencoe,

Iowa. Using a pump shotgun (because only shotguns were legal in Monona County that year), Coffman dropped a very big buck with a rifled slug. The deer was scale-weighed before witnesses. Bill Welker, a biologist with the Iowa State Conservation Commission, verified the live weight at 440 pounds (199.3 kg.). The buck was 4½ years old and had six points on each main beam. It was the largest ever taken in Iowa, where whitetails weighing 250 pounds (113.2 kg.) are common.

On a rainy day in November, 1955, Horace Hinkley and his wife, Olive, were hunting on the Kennebec River near Bingham, Maine. It was a good hunting day because a hunter could move through the woods silently and there was only a light breeze to move scent around. Mr. and Mrs. Hinkley took stands on opposite sides of a ridge. At about 9:20 that morning, Hinkley fired at a buck but missed. A few minutes later, Olive Hinkley's rifle cracked, and after a few moments she shouted that she had downed a big buck. Hinkley, certain that there were more deer in a thicket of scrub beech where he had missed the first one, remained where he was and did not respond. Suddenly a huge buck came crashing out of the brush toward him. Hinkley dropped the animal with one shot. It was so heavy that the Hinkleys had to get help to haul it out.

The buck was not officially weighed until three days later. The weighing was performed by Forrest Brown, an official state sealer of weights and measures, and there were two witnesses. Hog-dressed, and after three days of drying out, it still scaled 355 pounds (160.8 kg.). Bob Elliot, of Maine's Department of Game, calculated the live weight to be at least 450 pounds (203.8 kg.) and more probably 480 pounds (217 kg.). The buck's rack was excellent, but not in keeping with its body size. There were eight points on each side, with a spread of 21 inches (53 cm.) and a beam length of 24½ inches (63 cm.).

Minnesota, however, has had a claim to the all-time record weight since a bitterly cold November day in 1926, when Carl J. Lenander, Jr., went hunting with his father near Tofte. Lenander had been on his stand only a short time when he saw a monstrous buck walking into range. He dropped it with a single shot. Field-dressed, it scaled 402 pounds (182.1 kg.). The Conservation Department calculated its live weight to be 511 pounds (231.4 kg.). Minnesota officially recognizes the Lenander buck as the largest whitetail ever killed in the state. For that matter, no larger one has ever been officially recorded in North America.

Maine has held an annual Big Bucks Contest for the past couple of decades. One of the largest whitetails killed there was taken in 1964 by Lovell Barnes of Hiram. Field-dressed, it had a scale weight of 312 pounds (141.3 kg.), and the live weight was estimated at 406 pounds (183.9 kg.). Two other bucks weighing over 400 pounds (181.4 kg.) have been taken in the state in the last two decades but the reports lacked details.

In Illinois, another state that has a healthy population of good-sized white-tails, an archer took the largest recorded buck. Killed in 1970 in Carroll County, it had a live weight of 370 pounds (167.6 kg.).

Although the average size of whitetails tends to be largest in more northerly latitudes, Missouri is another state known for big bucks. Missouri's official weight record is held by a buck killed by Clifford Davis in 1954 in Livingston County. Its live weight, confirmed by scale, was 369 pounds (167.15 kg.). A bigger one was killed in 1970 by Dwain Perrige of Edina, Missouri, but no game-department officer was on hand to supervise the weighing and make it official (though the scales were carefully checked and witnesses were present). Six men were needed to haul this monster out of the woods to a vehicle. Field-dressed, but with the heart, lungs, and liver left in the carcass, it scaled 361 pounds (164.8 kg.). Wayne Porath, a deer biologist with the Missouri Game Department, later estimated its live weight at 423 pounds (191.6 kg.). In recent years, several other gigantic bucks—weighing well over 350 pounds (158.8 kg.)—have been registered by Missouri's Show-Me-Big-Bucks Club.

Even a state as far south as Louisiana has produced some massive white-tails. The biggest, killed in 1964 in the Russel Sage Wildlife Management Area, had a live weight of 321 pounds (145.4 kg.). And at the Thistlethwaite Wildlife Management Area, a buck killed in 1968 weighed 314 pounds (142.2 kg.) and one taken in 1969 weighed 312 pounds (141.3 kg.).

Still another huge southern whitetail was taken in Worth County, Georgia, in 1972 by Boyd Jones. Hog-dressed, it weighed 355 pounds (160.8 kg.). The estimated live weight was 443 pounds (200.6 kg.).

Mule deer tend to be larger than whitetails, and this is especially true of Rocky Mountain mule deer (*O. h. hemionus*), so it is hardly surprising that records of very heavy Rocky Mountain muleys have come to light. Dr. Ian Mc-Taggart Cowan, writing in *Safari* Magazine in 1975, commented on their size:

"The Rocky Mountain mule deer is the largest of its species. I have known autumn bucks to have a live weight of 475 pounds (215 kg.)—but this would be most unusual. Only 2 percent of 360 Madoc County, California, bucks weighed over 250 pounds (113.4 kg.) dressed and only 1 percent over 300 pounds (136 kg.).

"This is also the deer with the great difference in size between the sexes. Adult does on good range probably average about 140-150 pounds (63.5-68 kg.). This size difference appears to be related to winter cold together with the poor energy status of the bucks as they enter the winter. The larger animal is more efficient in conserving heat than the smaller one of similar shape. Thus there has been a selection pressure for bigger bucks ... whereas in the more southerly ranging races of mule deer the bucks are considerably smaller and the bucks and does more nearly the same size."

In the 1930s, the following measurements for a Rocky Mountain buck were reported by Joseph Dixon of the California Fish and Game Commission: overall length, 70 inches (178 cm.); tail, 8 inches (20 cm.); height at shoulder, 44 inches (113 cm.); ear from crown, 9 inches (23 cm.); hind foot, 20 inches (51 cm.). His measurements for an adult doe were as follows: overall length, 61 inches (155 cm.); tail, 7 inches (18 cm.); height at shoulder, 32 inches (81 cm.); ear from crown, 8½ inches (22 cm.); hind foot, 19 inches (48 cm.). He did not give the weights for these deer but quoted the records of a co-worker, J. S. Hunter, who reported in the January, 1924, issue of *California Fish and Game* that a Dr. Trusman of Adin could vouch for a Rocky Mountain muley buck from Modoc County that weighed 380 pounds (172.1 kg.) hog-dressed. The live weight estimate was 456 pounds (206.5 kg.). Another hog-dressed buck weighed 350 pounds (158.5 kg.) for an estimated live weight of 420 pounds (190.2 kg.).

The largest Rocky Mountain mule deer that Dixon could personally verify was shot on September 30, 1930, by Arthur Oliver in Shasta County, California. This buck weighed 308 pounds (139.5 kg.) dressed, for an estimated live weight of nearly 400 pounds (181.2 kg.).

John Russo recorded that the heaviest muley buck from the Kaibab Plateau in Arizona in 1963 weighed 225 pounds (101.9 kg.) hog-dressed, for an estimated live weight of 281 pounds (127.2 kg.). Obviously, the biggest, heaviest mule deer are generally found farther north, even though some record-book antlers have come from Arizona and New Mexico.

Paradoxically, the Sitka blacktails up in Alaska tend to be smaller and lighter than other mule deer. This, as I indicated earlier, is chiefly a result of their forage and habitat, but the heredity of the race also has an effect. If Sitka blacktails were transplanted to very lush habitat, genetics probably would still prevent them from growing to the size of a big Rocky Mountain muley. The record Sitka blacktail, killed on one of the islands of Prince William Sound, weighed 212 pounds (96 kg.) field-dressed. That would be an estimated 253 pounds (114.6 kg.) live weight. Columbian blacktails occasionally grow a bit larger, given ideal forage.

In 1939 a severe forest fire in Tillamook County, Oregon, burned over 305,000 acres of land inhabited by Columbian blacktails. The entire area grew back with sprouts, berry bushes, ferns, forbs, and other excellent deer food. This area was closed to hunting for four years because the Oregon Game Commission had found that four years will allow the food to grow back and will also allow the deer to reach their greatest individual and population potential.

A blacktail buck fattens himself on rich summer browse that sprouted after a forest fire in Tillamook County, Oregon. The Tillamook burn produced record-size blacktails.

Before the burn, the deer harvest averaged two deer per section, with an average live weight of about 120 pounds (54.3 kg.). Four years after the burn, when the season was opened, there were fourteen deer per section and their weight had increased 30 to 50 percent. Only seven deer weighed less than 180 pounds (81.5 kg.). Twenty-four deer weighed 180 to 200 pounds (81.5 to 90.6 kg.), nineteen weighed over 200 pounds, and one buck weighed 310 pounds (140.4 kg.). This last weight is the heaviest record I can find for a Columbian blacktail.

# 10

## The Digestive System

Deer are ruminants, equipped with a four-chambered stomach. Ruminants — that is, the deer family, the giraffe, the antelopes, sheep, goats, and cattle — are cud-chewers. A four-chambered stomach is needed to process the large quantities of low-nutrient food that these animals eat. The ruminant's stomach is also a very important survival feature, as it allows the animal to gather and swallow a lot of food in the shortest possible time and then chew it later, at its leisure, while relaxing in a safe place.

When a deer is feeding, it is at a tremendous disadvantage because it is concentrating on locating and obtaining food, rather than concentrating totally on avoiding predators. The nose and the eyes are used in locating the food. Moreover, the gathering of the food makes considerable noise through conduction via jaw bones to the auditory nerves. So engrossed, deer are vulnerable to predation, and they know it. This is one of the reasons why deer prefer to feed facing into the wind; the scent of danger ahead of them will be borne down to them. It is also one of the reasons why cud-chewers do not feed steadily in one spot. Deer take a bite of food and then take a couple of steps and nibble

A muley buck browses in winter. While eating, a prey species is most vulnerable to predators. Deer therefore move about as they eat, and afterward seek a place of relative safety where they rest and chew their cud.

again. This prevents overutilization of the food plant while it also keeps them moving away from any stalking predator. Deer lack the reasoning ability to calculate where safety lies, but natural selection favors protective behavioral patterns, establishing and reinforcing these patterns through evolution. Almost all predators hunt into the wind, whether they hunt by sight or scent, so that their own scent will not be carried to their intended prey. Any predator stalking a feeding deer has to make a longer stalk because the deer are constantly moving away into the wind. The longer the stalk, the more chance there is for the predator to accidentally betray its presence.

Depending on the type and abundance of the food that the deer is eating, it can fill its paunch in one or two hours. Naturally, if food is scarce, it takes much longer, or the deer may not even be able to fill its paunch. Deer are

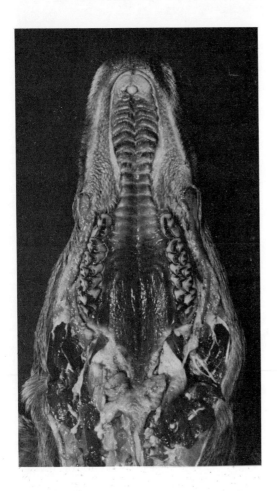

This is the roof of a deer's mouth, seen from below. Note that there are grinding teeth but no incisors. Lacking upper front teeth, a deer uses the tough pad at the front of its mouth. Twigs are nipped off by lower incisors bearing against the upper pad.

primarily browsers, feeding on the tips of twigs, branches, and shoots. In many areas, due to a lack of browse, the deer also obtain much of their food by grazing on grasses, forbs, and similar types of vegetation.

When a deer is feeding on browse, it prefers the tenderest, newest shoots and tips. Such tips are more palatable, more flavorful, easiest to bite off, and most nutritious. Tips of twigs up to about the size of a wooden kitchen match are nipped off by the deer's front lower incisors against the pad in the front of the top of its mouth. Lacking upper front teeth, the deer has to tear the twigs loose, always leaving a ragged edge. Where deer and hares or rabbits are competing for low-growing vegetation, it is easy to tell which twigs were eaten by deer. Hares and rabbits use their upper and lower incisors to clip twigs off as if with pruning shears.

Hunters and field naturalists can easily tell whether low vegetation has been browsed by deer or rabbits. Rabbits clip twigs neatly. Deer rip them, leaving ragged edges, as shown in this photo.

When deer are feeding on larger twigs, up to the size of a pencil—which they do only in times of food shortage—they take the twigs in the side of their mouths and bite them off, using the third premolars and first molars. That is why the greatest amount of wear is shown on these teeth.

When deer are grazing, they use their lips to maneuver the grass into their mouths, hold it with their incisor teeth against the mouth pads and tear it loose by moving their heads forward. I have never seen deer use their tongues to tear grass loose as cattle and bison often do.

The food is moved by the tongue to the back of the mouth, where it is chewed just three or four times before being swallowed. The food passes down the gullet into the first part of the stomach.

The four sections of a deer's stomach are the rumen, the reticulum, the omasum, and the abomasum. The food initially goes into the rumen, which can hold 8 to 9 quarts (7.57 to 8.51 liters) and has the combined functions of storing the unchewed food and acting as a fermentation vat.

To break down the fibers, cellulose, and other basic plant components, and convert them to materials that can be assimilated and used by the body's metabolic system, the deer depends on a symbiotic relationship with billions upon billions of microorganisms that live in its stomach. Among these microorga-

**137**

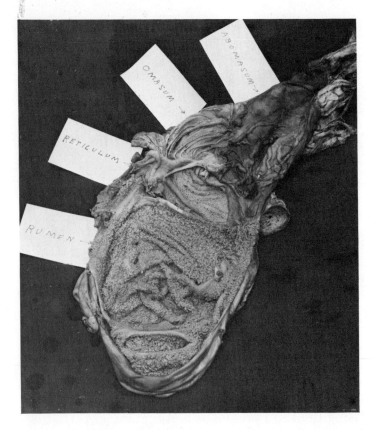

Labels alongside this deer's stomach indicate the positions of the four digestive compartments.

nisms are ciliate bacteria, and bacillis, cocci, and spirillia. Through digestion by these organisms and by fermentation, the food produces metabolites known as short-chain volatile fatty acids, such as acetic, propionic, valeric, and butyric acids. The lining of the rumen has small spaghetti-like papillae, varying in length from ³/₈- to ¹/₂-inch (10 mm. to 14 mm.). There are 1600 of these papillae to the square inch, and I know because I have counted them. Over 40 percent of a deer's essential energy is derived from the acids absorbed through the papillae and the walls of the rumen. Minimal digestion starts to take place in the deer's mouth, but it is the organisms, acids, and heat of the stomach that really do the job.

After the deer has filled its paunch, it retires to some spot of comparative safety to chew its cud. A deer may chew its cud while standing up but it usually lies down. The deer can rest or even doze while doing this but the head is held upright. Cud-chewing is almost automatic, progressing without the deer consciously starting it, but if the deer becomes alarmed or alerted the process is stopped instantly.

A whitetail doe chews her cud in secluded cover. The bulge in her left jaw is the cud.

The cud is vegetative material which is regurgitated from the rumen and comes back up the gullet. It is about the size of a big lemon, and its passage up to the mouth can easily be seen. In masticating its cud, the deer chews with a sideward motion of the lower jaw. A whitetail gives it an average of 40 chews before reswallowing it. Muleys and blacktails give it an average of 56 chews. I know how thoroughly they have to chew the cud not just from reading biological monographs but from personal observation. In the course of taking over twenty-five thousand photos of deer, I have often had to wait for an animal to come within camera range, or to get up, or to just stop chewing its cud. With not much else to do at the moment, I have counted the number of chews.

As the food is reswallowed, it does not make a noticeable lump. It goes down into the rumen again but is passed on to the second portion of the stomach, the reticulum. The reticulum has a lining that looks like a honeycomb, with hexagonal ridges about ⅜-inch (10 mm.) apart. Each ridge is about ¹/₁₆-inch (2 mm.) high. The reticulum can hold foodstuffs up to about the size of a standard softball. Some digestion takes place in the reticulum but one of its main functions is to filter out foreign material.

Like other ruminants, small children, and Indian fakirs, deer habitually swallow indigestible material. I have found stones, a .22-caliber cartridge case, and even a piece of melted glass in the deer stomachs I have examined.

Occasionally a "hair ball" forms in the stomach. Deer frequently lick themselves to help remove their old coats when they are shedding, and they often lick hair from one another. Usually this hair passes through with the food being digested. Sometimes a mass of it does not pass through. The action of the stomach, combined with food material, puts a coating on the hair mass, creating a ball which then lodges in the stomach if it becomes too large to be passed on.

On very rare occasions a "bezoar stone" is found in a deer's stomach. I have never seen one, though I have seen a photograph of one. A bezoar—also called a calculus or madstone—is formed by layers of calcium or resinous material, built up around a nucleus of some indigestible object in much the same way that a pearl is formed in an oyster. Some of these bezoar stones have reached a length of more than two inches (50 mm.). At one time they were highly treasured, as they were supposed to neutralize poison. These foreign objects are usually found in the reticulum.

There is a lapse of fourteen to eighteen hours from the time a deer's food is eaten until it has been passed up again as cud, chewed, reswallowed, and passed through the reticulum. The food then goes into the omasum, where intensive digestion and absorption take place. The omasum's lining has forty flaps of varying heights, from ⅛-inch (4 mm.) to 1⅛ inch (28 mm.) high.

The last compartment, the abomasum, has a very smooth, slippery lining with about a dozen elongated folds. It is interesting to carefully open a deer's stomach and observe how digestion has progressed in each of the four compartments. From the jumbled mass of recognizable vegetation in the rumen, the food becomes finer, more liquefied, and less identifiable as it goes on. It enters the rumen as a coarse mass and passes through the abomasum as a liquid slurry, or soup. The deer's rumen holds about 80 percent of the stomach contents, the reticulum 5 percent, the omasum 7 to 8 percent, and the abomasum 7 to 8 percent.

Passing on through 67 feet (20.4 m.) of intestines, most of the liquid is ab-

Characteristics of droppings reveal which animal left them and, sometimes, what it had been eating. Pellets at the upper left were dropped by a deer after eating browse. Pellets at upper right are from a rabbit. Masses at the lower left were dropped by a deer that had been foraging in a grassy area. Pellets at the lower right are from a porcupine.

sorbed, leaving an impacted mass of undigested particles. This mass is, of course, passed out as excrement. A deer defecates on the average of 13 times every 24 hours. The type of food eaten determines the shape and consistency of the excrement. This can be of interest not only to biologists but to hunters, since there are times when it can furnish a clue to where deer have been browsing or grazing.

If a deer has been feeding on grasses, forbs, or fruit, its feces are usually a loose, formless mass. When the deer is eating drier material or feeding on browse, the feces will form elongated pellets. There should be no confusing a deer's feces with a rabbit's because the deer's pellets are always elongated, sometimes misshapen, and often pointed, while a rabbit's or hare's feces are round. There may be anywhere from just a few pellets to well over three hundred in one defecation. Ordinarily, from ingestion to expulsion, food will pass through the deer in 26 to 30 hours. Very rough, fibrous food may take a bit longer.

Food utilization depends on the food that is eaten, the age of the deer, and the condition of its teeth. Averaging out these variables, biologists figure that of every hundred pounds of food, 65 percent will be utilized by the animal's body for maintenance, growth, and heat production. Five percent is lost as methane gas, five percent as urine, and 25 percent as feces.

Deer and some of the other herbivores lack a gall bladder. (The musk deer of Asia is the only deer with a gall bladder.) Acorns are a very high-fat food, yet they are easily assimilated by the deer without the help of gall, a digestive fluid that aids other animals to neutralize acids and emulsify fats. It is thought that the lack of gall is what enables a deer to eat the leaves of the rhododendron, which are poisonous to sheep and cattle.

# 11

## Deer Hair— from Summer Red to Winter Blue

$A$ deer's color changes somewhat from summer to winter. To describe this difference in appearance, hunters and naturalists sometimes refer to deer as being in their "red" (summer) coats or "blue" (winter) coats. There are two complete hair molts per year. The exact time of the molt depends on the altitude, latitude, subspecies, physical condition, and age of the deer. Deer in the North shed their winter coats later and their summer coats earlier than deer in the South. Adult deer shed their coats before the young ones do, and those in good physical condition shed earlier than those in poor shape.

My friend Manny Barrone, of Lincoln Park, New Jersey, is a taxidermist who constantly supplies me with bits of information and specimens that he encounters. His wife Elaine has also been of enormous help to me. On the night of December 15, 1976, Elaine did not get to bed until 4:00 a.m. because she sat up counting the number of hairs in a square inch of a deer's summer coat and on a square inch of winter coat for me. To my knowledge, no one has published such figures, and her findings were amazing.

On a single square inch (6.45 sq. cm.) of skin from the top of the neck of an adult buck, taken in late November, there were 2,664 hairs. These hairs were 2 to 2¼ inches (5.1–5.7 cm.) long and had a diameter of .007 inch (.1778 mm.).

An average-size adult deer has about 1,200 square inches (7,740 sq. cm.) of skin covering. Using the above figures, we find that the deer has about 3,196,800 hairs in its winter coat. By applying the same calculations to Elaine's count of hairs on skin taken from a buck "in the red," killed in late August, I discovered that the summer coat actually has almost twice as many — 5,176 hairs to the square inch — or about 6,211,200 hairs. These counts explain why so many birds' nests are lined with deer hair. There must be gobs of it in any woods with a good deer population.

The winter hairs are kinky, brittle, hollow, filled with air, and can easily be pulled out of the skin. Beneath these long guard hairs is a very soft, fine, kinky undercoat like cashmere wool. Elaine tried to count these undercoat hairs also but found it impossible. It is very difficult to see the undercoat, and when the wool was pulled out, it was so buoyant that it practically floated away. The long, hollow hairs, combined with the undercoat, give the deer terrific insulation, protection against the cold. Because the guard hairs are hollow, a deer in its winter coat floats much higher in water than it does in its summer coat. I have often seen a deer bedded down during a snowstorm, with several inches of snow covering its body. None of the snow would melt because so little body heat was lost.

Many hunters like to have a deerskin tanned with the hair on it, for use as a rug or throwpiece. This is a waste of time and money unless the skin is to be used only as a wall hanging. Because the winter hairs are hollow, they are very brittle. If they are walked on, they soon break off.

There is one record of a Pennsylvania doe that had no guard hairs on her coat at all. Her entire body was covered with just the silky undercoat, although the undercoat hairs were longer than on a normal deer. This doe undoubtedly would not have survived the winter because the undercoat is not waterproof as the guard hairs are. In a freezing rain, this doe's hair would have become soaked, matted, and frozen.

There are records of three deer from Pennsylvania, New York, and Michigan that had their long winter guard hairs but also had unusually thick, dense undercoats. Now there is a fourth record. Manny Barrone has sent me such a hide from a deer taken in New Jersey. These deer must have been exceptionally warm with all that insulation. However, it is obvious that such additional dense coats are not needed or nature would have provided them for all deer.

Generally speaking and regardless of species, the deer's winter hair is a grayish-brown at the tip. The base of the hair is gray, shading to almost black.

These swatches of deer hair show, from left, the short but dense summer coat; the long, hollow, insulating hairs of the winter coat; and rare, a woolly-based winter coat.

The deer of the Far North have the darkest coats while those in the South are quite a bit lighter. Deer of the desert or open areas are the palest of all. The difference in the color between the winter and summer coats is much more noticeable in the North than in the South.

Because a deer's winter coat is so much heavier, I always assumed that it contained more hairs, so Elaine's count was a great surprise. The "red" of the summer coat extends about 80 percent of the hair length, while the basal 20 percent is grayish. The summer hair is about an inch (25 mm.) long and only .003 inch (.0762 mm.) in diameter. The hairs are thin, straight, solid, and without an undercoat. A summer deerskin can be used for a rug because the solid hairs are not brittle. Being solid, they provide little insulation, but they offer another kind of protection. The increased number of hairs shields a deer somewhat against biting insects.

Hairs grow through the skin. If they have not grown out to their full length, part of their dark roots show on the inside of the skin when it is removed from the animal. The roots make the inside of the skin dark, and the skin is then said to be "blue," or unprime. Once the hairs have grown all the way through, the inside of the skin is pale, and when tanned it is creamy white.

A whitetail deer has whitish circles around its eyes, white inside its ears, a white band around its muzzle and chin, and a white throat patch. It has a

This whitetail doe is acquiring her summer coat while shedding her winter coat (visible as rough-looking patches).

Hair on a deer's brisket points forward — in the opposite direction from hair on the remainder of the body.

Mule deer have less white on their underparts than do whitetails but they have a pronounced white rump patch. (Photo by Len Rue, Jr.)

white belly, a narrow white rump, white beneath its tail, and white running down the inside of each leg.

It is interesting to note that, for unknown reasons, the hair on the brisket, or chest, of all deer points forward while all the other hair points to the rear or downward.

Mule deer and blacktail deer have white over the nose, a gray face, white inside the ears, and a white throat patch. Mule deer have a very heavy patch of dark, coarse hair on their foreheads that comes down the face beyond the eyes. Both types of deer have much less white on their bellies than a whitetail, and a smaller amount of white on the inside upper portion of the legs. They have big white circular rump patches, the size depending on the subspecies. And, of course, the top of a blacktail's tail is black, while a mule deer's is white.

Whether the deer is in its dark winter coat or its reddish summer coat, the color tends to fade in the sun. The winter coat is more subject to bleaching because it is worn for a much longer period—seven to eight months—and it is exposed to the sun more. In the winter, deer lie in the sun for warmth. They also feed more in the daylight hours, and with the leaves off the trees, the sun penetrates to the forest floor.

In the spring, while a deer is shedding its winter coat, it has a ragged, moth-eaten appearance. The hair sloughs off in patches. The old hair evidently itches, because the deer spend quite a bit of time licking away swatches of it. Or two deer may team up and, through mutual grooming, remove the hair from each other's coats. It is chiefly this licking of the long winter hair that forms the hairballs sometimes found in a deer's stomach.

The summer coat is worn for a little over four months, and at that time of the year the deer feed usually in the late evening, at night, or in the early morning. When the temperature gets about 65° F. (18 C.), deer seek shade. Even in early winter or early spring, when the sun gets too warm the deer will move into shade.

People often report seeing "albino" deer. Of course, some deer are albinos, but most of the white deer seen are not true albinos, they are mutations. These mutations are becoming more prevalent with the help of man. When

This mutant whitetail fawn has nearly an all-white coat. Unlike true albinos, this deer has dark eyes, a dark nose, a reddish-brown forehead and a mottled body.

the wildlife population was controlled by natural predators, any deer that had the deficient genes to result in a white coat would have been killed because it was so easily seen. Ordinarily, the other deer will shun the mutations, even going so far as to drive them away.

I have also found that these white deer usually have poor hearing. During the many years when I was Chief Gamekeeper for the Coventry Hunt Club, we had a number of them from time to time on our club lands. They were almost always "loners" and they were easy to creep up on because they could not hear well. All of the white deer on our club lands were females, although this type of mutation can occur in either sex. These deer were on our club before New Jersey ever allowed does to be hunted. With the large predators gone and man protecting the mutant does by law, the deficient genes were passed on, so white deer are more common today than ever before.

Around 1928, when white deer were a rarity, they suddenly became very common near Mifflinburg, Pennsylvania. It was thought that overcrowding had something to do with the prevalance of this condition, but even today we do not know the cause.

True albinism is due to lack of pigment. Ordinarily the production of pigment is controlled by the pituitary gland. In human beings, albinism is caused by the absence of the enzyme tyrosine, which is needed to produce the darker pigments. A true albino deer will have all white hair, grayish hooves, and pink eyes. The eyes appear pink because, in the absence of pigment, the blood can be seen coursing through the blood vessels.

The Seneca Army Depot in New York State has an entire herd of albino deer. The first albino fawns were seen in 1956, born to a normal brown doe. The commanding officer issued orders for protection of the white deer and the boom began. In 1958 one white fawn was born, in 1959 two white fawns were born, and in 1960 two more white fawns were born. The white herd increased from seven deer in 1960 to a hundred and fifty-five in 1968. Today there are four or five hundred at the depot.

The New York State Department of Conservation has conducted breeding studies with these deer. The biologists have found that, contrary to the usual laws of genetics, in this case the white is dominant instead of black. Except for being albinos, the white deer are as hearty in all ways as the other deer at the Army base.

Albino whitetails are much more common than albino mule deer or blacktails. In October of 1963, Pete Peterson shot an albino muley doe in Ekalaka, Montana. It was a very rare specimen, for biologists feel that albinism in mule deer may be as rare as one in 500,000 deer.

Occasionally a melanistic deer will be seen—one that is totally black. This is a rarer occurrence than albinism, but it has been reported in a number of regions. It is caused by overproduction of the pigment melanin.

Archibald Rutledge, the late dean of South Carolina outdoor writers, reported two melanistic deer. One was a small black buck killed near Georgetown, South Carolina. Rutledge did not see this animal but the reports were reliable. The second was described as "a huge melanistic buck—as black as coal." He saw this deer on four occasions. It had the most magnificent rack of any buck he had ever seen in the Santee River area of South Carolina.

In 1965 Frances Arens of Lansing, Michigan, shot a black spike buck near Roscommon. On the opening day of California's deer season in 1965, Barney Patten shot a melanistic forkhorn mule deer in Modoc County. The same county produced another melanistic mule deer on opening day in 1966—a four-point buck shot by Kim Sigler. It is most unusual for two such deer to be taken in two years in one area.

Yet another oddity of coat was displayed by a whitetail buck killed in 1967 in Dutchess County, New York. This buck, shot by Rudy Selvaggio, was normal in all respects except that it had a short, stiff mane of hair running from its forehead back and down the top of its neck to the shoulders. The ridge of hair looked just like the short-clipped mane of a showhorse.

# 12

## The Five Senses

Constant vigilance is the payment for life. Wild creatures are always alert, always monitoring the air for particles of scent, listening for the slightest unnatural sound, watching for the movements of anything within their range of vision. Adult woodchucks, for example, stand upright on an average of seven times per minute just to watch for danger over the tops of the vegetation they are feeding on.

All of a deer's five senses are important to its survival, but by far the most important is its sense of smell. A world of odors enriches and informs most of the creatures that share this earth with us. It is a world we can only guess at, occasionally venture into, and never fully know—not even with the artificial "noses," or scent-detecting devices that men are now devising. Birds are the exception, in that few of them have a well-developed sense of smell.

The sense of smell is the response to chemoreception by the limbic system, found on the base of the cerebrum, the front portion of the brain. Most odors in the natural world are of organic compounds and are released as molecules of gas. For gases to be smelled, they must be mixed or dissolved with mois-

This buck is tense and suspicious as he searches the air for scent, but he is not fully alarmed.

ture. With the exception of moose and caribou, all members of the deer family have moist, hairless muzzles. The moisture both inside and outside of the nostrils traps scent particles. Deer frequently lick their muzzles, and this provides additional moisture.

The nostrils are lined by the epithelium, containing mucous membranes and sensory nerve endings. Scent molecules are inhaled and dissolved on the moist surface of the epithelium. Responses to the chemical action are carried by the sensory nerves to one of the two olfactory bulbs. A deer's olfactory bulbs are much larger than a man's. The olfactory bulb in turn sends electrical impulses to the brain stem, where the odor is classified. This area of the brain also controls appetite, digestion, and emotions, linking the sense of smell closely to all three.

The average human being can detect skunk odor, mercaptan, when it is dissolved to 1/25,000,000 part of one milligram. Most of us can identify hundreds of odors, and professional perfumers have committed thousands to memory.

What the most sensitive human nose can do pales beside the achievements of dogs. Bloodhounds can, under ideal conditions, follow a track that is two weeks old. But then, dogs have far more epithelium than humans have. A dog's epithelium equals $1/80$ of its surface skin area while a man's equals about $1/8000$. A deer's epithelium covers a much larger area than a man's and may be equal to a dog's. Unfortunately, it is exceedingly difficult to test animals such as deer for their ability to detect odors because deer cannot be trained to respond as dogs do.

Many variables, including wind, temperature, and moisture, affect scent. The reception and perception of olfactory stimulation is heightened by a fairly warm, moist, still atmosphere. But there is a limit to the amount of humidity that is beneficial. Both rain and falling snow carry the molecules of scent to the earth and dilute and dissipate them. Light mist or heavy fog also blocks scent from traveling great distances. High humidity — that is, 50 to 70 percent — is about ideal for scenting purposes. High humidity makes deer very nervous because more scent is carried to them and they become doubly alert.

On November 18, 1976, I attempted to photograph deer from a permanent blind that I have on a large estate. The humidity was high and there was not a breath of air to dissipate my scent, which slowly suffused to a large circle around the blind. The blind is located where the deer are accustomed to feed, and they were hungry, yet they would not venture into my circle of scent.

Low humidity — 10 to 20 percent — works against wildlife because the nasal passages have a tendency to dry out and this hampers the ability to capture and register the scent molecules.

High temperatures cause air convection, and the rising thermals carry the scent molecules upward before they can reach a deer. In the Southwest, on a hot day, I have been able to approach a deer very closely, even with the wind behind me. Extremely low temperatures also handicap a deer because the scent molecules are usually pushed downward.

Air movements play a big role in the deer's ability to use its sense of smell. In most regions, breezes usually move at 3 to 15 miles per hour. Ideal scenting conditions would mean a humidity of 20 to 80 percent, with temperatures ranging from 40° to 90° F., coupled with breezes up to 15 or 20 miles per hour. Personal observations lead me to believe that under such circumstances a deer might detect danger half a mile away and perhaps farther.

However, human scent can be masked so that deer are not alarmed by it. As a farm boy, I always rode my horse bareback. I would often bend forward, lie along my horse's neck, and ride very close to groups of deer without their being alarmed. Some of the commercial deer scents on the market today are effective in attracting deer and also in masking human odor.

Deer have pawed through snow here to reach food that they located by scent.

Deer use their sense of smell not only to locate danger but also to locate other deer. Deer cannot recognize their own fawns by sight but depend upon scent. This can be seen in late summer, when the does and their spotted fawns mingle in groups as they feed. A fawn will try to nurse from any doe. But a doe will turn and smell the fawn. Her own fawns will be allowed to nurse. Any other fawn is usually driven away with hard kicks.

During the rutting season, bucks will track a doe with all the skill of a hound following a game trail. As I noted in the chapter on external glands, deer leave a glandular musk wherever they walk, and other deer recognize the odor.

The sense of smell is also important to deer in locating food. Some foods are rejected because of their odors. Deer can locate such foods as apples, acorns, and corn under a foot or more of snow if there is no crust to lock the scent beneath the surface.

The winter of 1960-61 was an extremely hard one in northwestern New Jersey, and we had deep snow on the ground. In February, when we had our first thaw, the deer came out of the mountains in droves. On Coventry Hunt Club

154

lands we had planted many game-food patches, and the patches for deer had a lot of rape, a relative of the cabbage plant. The fields were covered with 24 inches (60.96 cm.) of snow, and the deer had to leap to get around at first. They came out of the woods to feed on the rape. They located it under the snow and dug down for it. Within a few days, deer trails crisscrossed all of the patches, and within weeks every rape plant had been located and consumed.

Deer have a well developed sense of taste, as shown by their decided food preferences. They may also acquire a taste for food to which they do not ordinarily have access. Humans (and perhaps deer, as well) can only taste things which are sweet, sour, bitter, or salty. Our sense of smell is ten thousand times more discerning than our sense of taste. Most of what we *think* we taste we actually smell. Food flavors depend on a combination of taste and smell. There is no evidence that deer are endowed with any more tasting ability than we have, so undoubtedly their "taste" for foods also depends on their sense of smell. In northwestern New Jersey, there are more than six hundred and fifty foods that deer will eat, but there are also many that they will not touch. In different parts of the country, at certain times of year, mushrooms are important deer foods. The deer do not eat the poisonous ones, such as the amanitas, and no one has yet discovered how they can distinguish between them. Smell is the logical explanation.

Deer also have an extremely keen sense of hearing. Like radar antennae, their large ears are constantly being swept back and forth, turning, twisting, swiveling to locate the source of the slightest sound. No sound is too slight to deserve their attention.

Sound is a form of energy that reaches the ear as cyclic vibrations. With low-pitched sounds, the waves are fairly shallow and wide-spaced. High-pitched sounds compress the width of the waves, forcing them to high peaks, or frequencies. The adult human ear can hear in the range of 40 to 16,000 cycles per second. For some people, this range is extended on either end—as low as 20 or up to 20,000. Children can hear much higher frequencies but they lose this ability with age.

Personal observations lead me to believe that deer have an upper range extending to 30,000 cycles and perhaps beyond. I carry a "silent" dog whistle that I often use to get an animal's attention. The human ear cannot hear this very high-pitched whistle but dogs and deer respond to it readily.

The external ear of the deer, the pinna, is a skin-covered flap of cartilage and muscles. The ear on an average whitetail is about 7 inches (17.8 cm.) long and about three inches (7.62 cm.) across. It has a cupped structure. The actual surface, if flattened out, is 4½ inches (11.5 cm) across at its widest. This gives the whitetail approximately 24 square inches (154.8 sq. cm.) of reflective sur-

This whitetail doe listens for danger as she chews her cud.

face per ear. The length I have given is from the skull to the ear tip. This measurement should not be confused with the scientific measurement of the deer's ear, which is taken from the tip to the notch near the base on the inside of the ear. A whitetail's ear is a complete tube for the first inch, so the scientific measurement states the ear to be only 6 inches (15.3 cm.) long. Naturally, the various subspecies of the whitetail have different body sizes and correspondingly different ear sizes, but the figures given are an average for the species.

The mule deer got its name from its exceedingly long ears. Particularly on a fawn, the ears seem enormous. The average mule deer's ear measures nine inches (22.9 cm.) long and 6½ inches (16.5 cm.) at the widest point when the ear is flattened out. Cupped, the ear is about 4½ inches (11.5 cm.) across. A

An alterted muley doe tries to catch sounds from all directions. Note that one of her huge ears is swiveled rearward.

muley's ear measures out to about 42 square inches (270.9 sq. cm.) of reflective surface. The average mule deer is larger than the average whitetail, but the ears are disproportionately large. This is because the mule deer inhabits more open country where the need to hear danger at a great distance is more important due to the scarcity of cover.

The exceptionally large ears of the muley may also be a thermoregulator, as on some of the other large-eared mammals. In the summer, the hair on the deer's ears is exceptionally short and thin. If the ear is viewed with the sun behind it, the blood vessels can usually be seen. Even in the desert where the sun temperature may be high, the shade areas where the deer bed are much cooler and there is almost always a breeze blowing. The warm blood, after passing through the deer's ears, would be cooler than its body temperature and would thus help to cool the animal. Conversely, in winter the ears are amply protected with a thick coat of hair.

The average blacktail deer is slightly smaller than the average whitetail but it has the characteristic ears of the mule deer. The measurements fall about halfway between those of the whitetail and the mule deer. They average 6¾ to 7 inches (17.2 to 17.8 cm.) in length and 5½ inches (14 cm.) in width, with the ear flattened, giving an average reflective surface of 32 to 33 square inches (206.4 to 212.9 sq. cm.).

These sizes seem all the more impressive when compared to a man's ear, which has only about 3½ square inches (22.6 sq. cm.) of reflective surface and cannot be swiveled about in the manner of a deer's ear. It is no wonder that deer can catch very small sounds at great distances.

Regardless of the ear's external size, all three deer, and humans as well, have an auditory-canal opening about ⅓-inch (1 cm.) in diameter. Sound waves entering the auditory canal are compressed and directed to the tympanic membrane — the eardrum — causing the membrane to vibrate. The vibrations activate the three tiny bones of the inner ear, which in turn amplify the incoming sound as much as ninety times. These vibrations cause the hairs in a fluid called endolymph to be stimulated, activating impulses of the auditory nerve. The nerve impulses go to the temporal lobe of the brain, which deciphers what is heard.

(The inner ear is also important because it helps to establish equilibrium, allowing animals to stand erect without falling over.)

Hearing in deer also seems to lead to the "bump of curiosity." A deer becomes curious about the origin of any unidentified sound, though a strange sight or odor seldom makes it yearn to investigate. Times without number, I have watched deer catch a sound and then cautiously advance, trying to locate and identify its sources. When deer do this, they are extremely nervous and alert. They stalk forward stiff-legged, with head outstretched and usually lowered to or below the level of their backs, and their big ears are held straight out at right angles to the head. Sometimes the deer advance silently, at others times they stamp each forefoot as it steps. I believe this stamping warns other deer of suspected danger and is also done in an effort to startle whatever made the original sound into betraying its presence. If the deer cannot identify the source of the sound, it usually makes a circle so that eventually it will catch the scent of the source of danger.

The brain has a file of stored sounds to which it has become accustomed. Deer are not panicked by common sounds that bombard them constantly. They recognize the scampering of a squirrel in dry leaves, the hopping of a rabbit, the rubbing of one wind-tossed branch against another, the sound of falling fruits and nuts. And they are not alarmed. But they associate danger with the crunching of a human's heavy footfall or the whisper of twigs rubbing against clothing.

Deer also pay close attention to the warning signals made by the birds and animals in their area. The raucous alarm call of the crow, the strident screaming of the jay, the whirring take-off of a grouse, the chattering scolding of the squirrel, the slap of a beaver's tail against the water are all sounds with a purpose. Something or somebody caused these alarm signals to be given. Sometimes the greatest clue to danger is the total *lack* of sound. When all the wild

This whitetail doe nervously stamps as she advances. Stamping may warn other deer of suspected danger and may also startle a predator into revealing its presence.

creatures stop eating, stop moving, become silent, they are listening and watching and smelling for danger. They have detected something that worries them, and their silence is a danger signal to all animals in the vicinity, deer included.

Deer can become accustomed to almost any sounds. When they make a habit of feeding along a highway, they seldom lift their heads no matter how much noise the traffic makes. Deer populations are often high on military reservations that have vast areas of good habitat on which there is no hunting. If these reservations are used for artillery practice, the deer become accustomed to the booming of the big guns and pay scant attention to the noise. Similarly, they may become accustomed to the noise of a power saw at a rural home site or a lumber camp, and have been known to approach rather closely to investigate that sound. Yet they remain alert to other alien sounds, which may portend danger.

Deer do not associate the sound of a rifle shot with danger. The sharp report of a gun may startle them, but because of the short duration of the sound, they may be unable to locate its source. Because of this, many deer that have been shot at and missed may stand long enough to allow the hunter to get off a second shot. Deer almost always try to locate the source of danger before running off. They instinctively know that to run blindly may cause them to blunder right into danger.

High winds make deer extremely nervous, because the crashing of the wind-lashed trees and branches covers almost all sounds and the eddying and reversal of air currents makes scenting almost impossible. With the whole world in motion, deer are almost panicked. To attempt to hunt in a high wind is a waste of time.

A deer's vision is geared to detect motion. No movement, including the blinking of an eye, seems to be too slight to be noticed. But motionless objects, even if they do not blend with their surroundings, are seldom seen and if seen are seldom recognized. Many times I have been caught out in the open by deer but I escaped detection by remaining absolutely motionless. I am convinced that a deer—unlike a fox or a wolf—does not recognize a man as a man, if it cannot detect motion or scent. I am not suggesting that a hunter should allow himself to be silhouetted. Skittish deer may become alarmed just because something new and strange is in their area, even though they do not recognize that something as a person. And I am firmly convinced that deer know their areas so intimately that they are instantly aware when something new has been added. For this reason, anyone photographing or hunting deer will be wise to blend into whatever bushes, trees or big rocks are in the area.

Man and the other primates and some diurnal squirrels are the only mammals capable of seeing color. Tests have proved that most mammals, including deer, see the world in shades of gray. Deer do not see the brilliance of the blaze-orange that hunters are now required to wear in most states. The use of blaze-orange has reduced hunting fatalities because it reduces the chance that a hunter will be mistaken for a deer. Although deer cannot see blaze-orange as a bright color, it is a light shade of gray and the deer can see it more easily than the blended shades of camouflage cloth. Moreover, a blaze-orange jacket or jump-suit is a large expanse of one smooth, solid, uninterrupted shade, unlike almost anything else in the woods, and it therefore looks suspicious. A hunter or photographer wearing such clothing is well advised to pick his stand where vegetation or rocks will break up the expanse of his silhouette or stand where he will be well above a deer's normal line of sight. The difference between blaze-orange and camouflage is almost nullified if the wearer remains motionless, but how many people can remain motionless?

It is important to remember that when you have been spotted by a deer and are trying to remain motionless, the deer will do everything in its power to get a better look at you or to startle you into motion. Most commonly, the deer

The large size and pronounced bulge of a deer's eyes are clearly shown in this portrait. Eye placement permits binocular vision plus a wide arc of view. (Photo by Len Rue, Jr.)

will keep its eyes on you but will move its head as far as it can to one side of its body and then to the opposite side. This increases dimensional perception, so that an object stands out from its surroundings. Flying squirrels do this to gauge distance before launching themselves from one tree to another.

If a distant deer spots you, do not try to get out of that deer's sight. If you drop to the ground or disappear down a hollow, when you look again for the deer it will be gone. Almost all animals feel extremely threatened when an object seen suddenly disappears. They feel they are being stalked and they will not stay around to find out if the assumption is correct.

A deer's eyes are located on the sides of the skull but are angled at about 25 degrees toward the nose. Eye placement on the side of the skull is typical of most creatures that are preyed upon. This gives them primarily monocular vision but allows them to see a much greater portion of a full circle so that they can perceive danger from all sides. Most prey animals also have big, bulging eyes to increase their ability to see behind the head. A deer's eyes protrude about ¼-inch (.6 cm.) beyond the skull. The deer cannot see completely behind its head, but it can view at least a 310-degree arc of its surroundings— and probably more due to the eye bulge and curvature. Also important is the fact that the deer's eye placement also allows it to have 50 degrees of binocular vision, which makes three-dimensional perception possible.

An alarmed deer constantly flicks its ears back and forth, often laying one ear back along its neck. Perhaps it is not only trying to locate the sound of whatever has alarmed it, but also getting an ear out of the way for a better view of any danger to the rear.

Ordinarily, it is safe to move closer to a deer when its head is down because then the deer is focused on feeding. You can tell when to "freeze" because all deer invariably jerk their tails before bringing their heads up. However, a deer that is particularly wary may only pretend to feed. The deer will put its head down and then almost immediately jerk it back up to see if the object it was studying has moved. Or the deer may put its head down and pretend to feed but will keep its eye on you. There is no way you can tell when this is taking place beforehand; you will know it only as the deer wheels around and dashes off.

Basically, a deer's eye is like that of a human in that light passes through the cornea and the amount of light admitted to the lens is controlled by the opening or closing of the oblong pupil. The image is then projected onto the retina, which is connected to the optic nerve. There the nerve impulses are transmitted to the occipital lobe of the brain. In humans, more of the total area of the brain is devoted to seeing. Ours is a world of sight, while in the deer's world sounds and smells dominate.

In proportion to body size, deer have much larger eyes than humans have, and deer can see very well at night. The retina, the receptive surface at the back of the eye, is composed of rods and cones. Sharpness of vision and sensitivity to color depend on the numbers of cones in the retina. The fovea of a man's eye is a small circle of the retina directly in line with the center of the eye's lens. The sharpness of sight depends on the number of cones in the fovea —150,000 per square millimeter in the human fovea.

Surrounding the fovea are the rod cells, which are used primarily in night vision and register sight in black and white. That is why in extremely poor light a human can see objects better by looking above, below or to either side of the object being viewed. This brings into play the rods which are ordinarily used for peripheral vision.

The deer's retina is composed almost entirely of rods. This is why the deer cannot see color, has poor vision except for movement, but is able to see at

Though little is known about tactile communication among deer, it is evident that licking—mutual grooming—strengthens the bond between doe and fawn.

night. The rods also act as a mirror, reflecting and doubling the amount of light available. At night some light is always present, although the amount may be too small to be recorded by the human eye. With mammals and birds that have good night vision, the available light goes through the eye and registers on the retina, then strikes the cones and is bounced back through the retina—thus doubling impulses received. This is why a deer's eyes shine when a bright light is directed at them at night. If the deer is looking directly at the light, the eyeshine is a silvery-white. If the deer is not looking directly at the light, the eye acts as a prism and the reflective color may be red, orange, yellow, or green. In the daytime, a deer's pupil is usually a dark bluish-brown. About half an hour after death, the pupil turns green.

Deer do not usually look for danger lurking above them. Mule deer and blacktails tend to look up more than whitetails because they are hunted by the cougar. A mountain lion may be in a tree or on a rocky ledge above them. Whitetails seldom look up, and do not even seem to notice motion if it is made slowly. Hunters have been quick to take advantage of this trait, and I have found that if a tree stand is at least 10 feet (3 m.) above the deer's line of sight, the hunter will not be noticed. A tree stand also keeps the hunter's scent above the deer; under most conditions, thermals are rising and carrying the scent away completely. But the slightest sound will instantly get the deer's attention, and then it will look up.

Relatively little has been written about the fifth sense—touch. We are only beginning to realize how important the sense of touch is to deer. From the moment of birth, a deer is exposed to tactile stimulations. The fawn is licked clean by its mother's tongue, and it is touch, coupled with sight and scent, that helps to imprint the fawn on the doe's brain, linking the two to each other. The bond is continuously strengthened as the fawn and the doe touch noses or lick each other in gestures of affection. I make no apologies for using the anthropomorphic term "affection." Sexual stimulation is increased prior to mating when the buck and doe rub against each other, and when the buck licks the doe's vulva. I will show in the next chapter how deer use a combination of senses—including touch—to communicate with one another.

# 13

# Communication, Instinct, and Intelligence

I noted earlier that when a deer becomes alarmed but cannot identify the object of its suspicion it stamps a forefoot. It may stand in one spot and repeatedly stamp while doing all it can to discover what alarmed it by using its nose, ears, and eyes. Or the deer may advance cautiously, stamping one forefoot and then the other. The tremors set up by the stamping travel a long way through the ground, alerting all deer in the area. Some of the deer may be feeding or screened by vegetation from the alerted deer, and they cannot see a visual signal. But even if they cannot hear the stamping, they can feel the ground tremors. Communication has been achieved through the sense of touch.

An olfactory warning may also be involved. Each time the deer stamps, there is a probability that scent from the interdigital gland is placed on the ground. I have often noticed that deer invariably put their nose down to smell the spot where a previous deer has stamped its foot. They do not seem unduly alarmed, but they take note of it.

This buck stands tensely while repeatedly stamping. It is possible that, even beyond hearing range, other deer can feel ground vibrations produced by stamping. (Photo by Irene Vandermolen)

Alarmed, the buck sprints away with flag up and rump hair flared. Unlike a doe, a buck may lower his tail after giving the initial warning signal. (Photo by Irene Vandermolen)

Here is a blacktail buck trotting with his tail held in characteristic, almost horizontal position.

Caribou definitely use the scent of the interdigital gland as a warning, and it is heeded. When caribou are moving along and one is alarmed, it rears up on its hind feet, whirls about, and dashes off. Dr. William Pruitt, Jr., an Alaskan researcher, calls this the "excitation jump." When a caribou does this, scent from the interdigital gland is deposited on the ground. I have witnessed this jump many times while photographing caribou, and I know that every caribou that comes to the spot will sniff the scent. In my experience, every caribou then became excited and none ever advanced beyond that marked spot. It was as effective as if a fence had been erected.

A deer that is alarmed often stands with its body tensed and rigid, leaning forward. The head and neck are extended and held below the level of the back, and the head is bobbed up and down. This behavior instantly alerts every deer witnessing it of potential danger. It is an effective visual signal.

The best-known visual signal is the flashing tail of whitetail deer. Mule deer do not raise their tails when they run, nor do they signal with them. Blacktail deer usually run with their tails held below the horizontal line of their backs. When they raise the tail above the horizontal, I have noticed that it is most often canted forward much more than the whitetail is able to do. The blacktail deer does not wag its tail when it runs, nor does it flare the hairs of its tail.

A whitetail buck may run full-speed with tail clamped down—something does seldom do.

Both the whitetail's tail and the white hairs of its rump are used for signaling. The pronghorn antelope is often called the "heliographer" because it is able to erect outwardly its big white rump patch. This large rosette reflects a lot of light, and the raising and lowering of the hair causes flashes. On the open plains, home to the pronghorn, reflected light can be seen at a distance where the unaided human eye cannot see the animal. And so can the light reflected from a whitetail's rump and tail.

Most artists portray a whitetail buck running with its tail held jauntily aloft. That bucks often do run like this can be proved by many photographs. However, I have found that bucks will run with their tails down more often than up. Does almost always run with their tails up, and they usually wag them loosely from side to side. I believe that the doe's bouncing white tail is to guide her fawns as they follow her.

In the chapter that described the tails of the three types of American deer, I mentioned that behaviorists have recently come up with the theory that the whitetail's "flagging" is also a message to a predator that its whereabouts has

Mildly alarmed deer would rather hide than run. This whitetail buck has pressed his tail down and turned his rump hair inward.

When hiding seems futile, a whitetail buck signals by flaring his tail hair. This young buck is ready to "hightail" away.

been discovered. Predators that stalk to get close to their prey before attempting to capture it will frequently abandon a hunt if they find they are discovered. The chance of success is then too poor. So the whitetail's flashing tail may not only warn other deer but also inform the predator that all of the deer in the area know about the predator.

When a whitetail is in hiding, the white hair on its rump is turned inward and the tail is pressed down so that only the dorsal brown hairs are visible. This almost completely covers the white that is usually seen when a deer is viewed from the rear.

The most widely known sound of all three deer is their explosive, blasting snort. They make this snort with their mouths closed, expelling air forcefully through the nasal passageway and thus causing the closed nostrils to flutter. Deer frequently snort when they are surprised or startled. And their snorting has probably surprised or startled everyone who has ever spent any time in deer areas.

When a deer snorts, all the other deer take instant notice and most of them prepare to flee the area. Deer have another, higher-pitched, whistling snort that is made with the mouth open and is combined with a vocal sound. Upon hearing this higher snort, any deer in the area explode into action. There is no hesitancy. That snort means danger, and in seconds the deer are all gone.

The commercial deer calls that are sold to hunters imitate the raspy, low-pitched, blatting call of the bucks. Using these calls, I have been able to lure both bucks and does within range of my cameras. Such a call must be used sparingly, and the factors of wind and concealment must also be right, but the deer will come to investigate the sound. The doe's blatting call is higher-pitched than the buck's but the buck call is equally effective in attracting both. Anyone who has heard an old domestic ram blat will know exactly what a buck sounds like.

The doe makes a very soft, catlike, mewing sound when she calls to a hidden fawn. I first heard this sound while I was in a blind I had placed in the woods so I could photograph red-eyed vireos. I did not know a fawn was in the area. The fawn responded immediately by jumping to its feet and going to the doe to nurse.

Fawns bleat, making a sound more like that of a calf than a lamb. It is higher-pitched than the sound a calf makes and lacks the volume. It does not vibrate the way a lamb's call does. Fawns and young deer that have been injured just bawl loudly in terror.

I feel that the means of communication I have just described are only the most easily detected ones. We have not yet begun to know the means of animal communication. The communicators I've mentioned are the obvious ones, the ones I have seen, heard, or smelled. There must be many less obvious signs and factors that I am missing. I am sure we have far more to learn about wildlife communication.

One often hears about the sixth sense of wildlife, a feeling that warns animals of impending danger without any of the obvious clues. This exists. I have experienced it myself, though I cannot fully explain what it is. I have a hearing impairment, and even with a hearing aid I miss some of the sounds in the outdoors. While photographing wildlife I am often exposed to potential danger. At such times, with no sound to warn me, my body evidently sets up some kind of electrical field that is sensitive to vibrations in the area around me. My body hair stands on end and I tingle. I feel more "alive" than at any other time. A number of other people have reported similar sensations when exposed to danger that they could not have detected by ordinary means.

I have seen sleeping cats awaken when a mouse showed itself in our barn. I watched a fox, sleeping in a washed-out gully in Alaska, awaken because a wolf trotted over the horizon a third of a mile away. The fox could not see over the gully, the wind was quartering so that the wolf's scent was being blown away, the distance made it impossible to hear the wolf move on the soft tundra or to feel any vibrations. Yet the fox awoke like a spring uncoiling, and was gone before it could ever verify the wolf's presence. That fox was warned, it heeded the warning and lived.

Many tests, particularly in Russia, have indicated that animals have some psychic means of perception and communication. Does this sound incredible? New fields of knowledge usually do. I am convinced that as our knowledge of psychic phenomena increases, our knowledge of wildlife communication will also increase. We must learn more about the fabled sixth sense, intuition.

When confronted with danger, wildlife usually has five options. It may hide or remain hidden. It may flee. It may cry out as a warning to others of its kind or to let the "danger" know it has been detected. If young are involved, a parent may either try to lead the enemy away or perform a distraction display. Or it may threaten and bluff or actually attack.

Considerable research has been done on "flight distance" and "attack distance," especially with the larger, dangerous animals such as bears, lions, and tigers. A person can approach a dangerous animal to a specified distance before that animal feels acutely threatened. Up to that distance, the animal feels instinctively that it still has the option of running away. When the distance is shortened, the animal feels it can no longer count on flight to save itself. It feels "cornered," even if it is out on an open plain. That is when the animal attacks.

Deer seldom attack, but they do have a flight distance that depends on the pressure the individual deer has been subjected to. Most hunters and all wildlife photographers become very aware of the flight distance of animals. I can "feel" when I've approached as close to a creature as it will allow. Most wild animals have become so used to automobiles that it is possible to get closer in a car than on foot. The animals don't feel threatened by the car.

Argument goes on endlessly as to whether all of a deer's actions are instinctive responses to situations. It is the argument of "purposive actions" versus "reflexive actions." Behaviorists have found deer to be very poor subjects in a laboratory. The deer are too wild to cooperate, and they are not interested in being rewarded for something they accomplish. Removing a deer from its natural environment to the artificiality of the testing laboratory just hasn't worked. Conclusions about the mental processes of deer must be made from observations in the wild.

From the thousands upon thousands of hours that I have spent working with deer, studying, observing, and photographing them, I believe they often show a response to new situations that is akin to reasoning. Of course, most of their actions are instinctive. However, I have often seen deer react to an unusual situation by coming up with a solution that could not be instinctive. Deer do have memories: they can remember exactly where a hole in a fence is; they can remember a new source of food; they can remember many things. Memory is stored data, retained for future use by means of mental processes. And a good memory must indicate some degree of intelligence. I have seen deer do smart things and I have seen them do many "dumb" things, but then I've done "dumb" things myself. I would not claim that deer are as intelligent as many of the other creatures. I feel that the coyote is the "smartest" animal in North America today. A deer's intelligence does not begin to compare to a coyote's. But I also feel that some deer have more reasoning ability than we give them credit for.

# II

## How the Year Goes

# 14

## Life in Spring

The foregoing chapters have made it obvious that each of the three types of American deer differs from the others in many ways, and even local populations of a single subspecies may have their own peculiarities. But—with exceptions that I will note—all have roughly the same habits and life histories. So in this part of the book, I will deal with all types of deer simultaneously, singling out a particular species or subspecies as appropriate. I will divide the complex story not by race or region but by the four seasons that govern their lives, allotting April, May, and June for spring; July, August, and September for summer; October, November, and December for fall; and January, February, and March for winter.

As Ecclesiastes tells us, for everything there is a season, and a time for every purpose. The characteristics of the seasons dictate the annual events in the life cycle. It is true that these events do not occur for all deer in all regions at the same time. But in previous chapters I have enumerated the times of several major events for all types of deer in all regions—the time of the rut, of birthing, of growing antlers, peeling the velvet, and shedding the antlers. Those earlier chapters will enable you to adjust the timing of the happenings I describe hereafter to the deer in your region. I will discuss additional events, and their times, as they occur in their seasons. I will also explain differences in food and habitat from region to region and from one variety of deer to another, so the simultaneous treatment of their life histories should cause no confusion.

Let us begin with spring, the time of the vernal equinox, when the sun crosses the equator and when day and night are of equal length. In the South and in desert areas, the temperature is high. In the North, the sun's rays are still weak, but stronger than they have been, with enough warmth to make the snow compact. The warming is the key that unlocks the small streams from winter's bondage. The streams gather strength with each passing day, although their activities are curtailed each night. Bare banks are beginning to be seen, and they are bare only momentarily because vegetation quickly surges into growth. It is along the stream beds that the deer find the first green shoots of spring. For many deer, in many areas, spring cannot come too soon and for many deer it comes too late. Their decomposing corpses are often found along the stream banks where their body nutrients, that were plants in previous years, are leaching back into the soil to produce the plants of tomorrow.

As soon as the snow has settled enough to allow the whitetail deer of the North to move, those that have "yarded up" leave the yards—the relatively protected pockets where they gather in winter—not to return until they are forced to do so by the rigors of the following winter.

## Migration
Mule deer and blacktails move to the lowlands rather than yarding up in winter. Now, at a leisurely pace, they begin to wend their way back to the mountains. Whereas their winter migration had been sudden, direct, and hurried, their spring migration is accomplished in easy steps. The does and their yearling fawns are the first to leave the wintering areas. The bucks act as if they are reluctant to go, as if they know their journey will be longer because they move to higher elevations. Most of these deer wintered at elevations of 1,000 to 3,000 feet (304.8 to 914.4 m.) above sea level but will spend the summer at elevations from 4,000 to 12,000 feet (1,219.2 to 3,657.6 m.). The journey may take weeks because some of the deer migrate as far as 100 miles (160.9

Whitetail buck

Whitetail fawn, one week old

Whitetail buck

Whitetail buck and doe

Whitetail buck in rutting season

Whitetails

Whitetail doe and fawn

Blacktail buck

Blacktail buck

Mule deer buck (photo by Len Rue, Jr.)

Blacktail buck and doe in rutting season (photo by Len Rue, Jr.)

Mule deer doe

Young mule deer buck

Here a mule deer nibbles on broad-leafed forbs (left), and a whitetail feeds on spring grasses.

km.). The rate of travel is determined by how fast the snow melts at the higher elevations and the availability of food. The migration is usually under way by the middle of April.

This is no forced march. The deer feed as they make their way upward. Those that have lost the most weight in the winter are the ones to gain weight most rapidly in the spring when food is again available.

## Foods

The new-sprouting vegetation has more nutrition in it than it will have at any other time of year. The protein content of this new vegetation soars. Deer throughout the continent just about forsake all browse and hungrily turn to grasses and forbs, although the new shoots on the browse species are also highly nutritious. For a list of the common foods preferred by the three types of deer during the spring, see Appendix I.

In my home area of New Jersey, alfalfa plays a very important part in the diet of whitetails. They can be found feeding in the fields at various times of

Blacktail buck (photo by Len Rue, Jr.)

day or night. In Iowa, whitetail deer can usually be found at night in the alfalfa fields but alfalfa represents only one percent of their diet. In Iowa, deer have difficulty finding escape cover and rest habitat because man has made increasing use of the rich soil in most of the state's forest lands and the wooded streamsides. Standing corn makes good shelter for deer, but when the corn is picked miles and miles of cover disappear. The deer in Iowa feed primarily on cultivated crops and use the alfalfa fields as bedding areas because the low cover allows them to watch for danger in all directions.

The size of the home range for the different species of deer depends on the available food. Under ordinary circumstances, the does of all three types have a spring home range of .75 to 3 square miles (1.94 to 7.77 sq. km.) while the buck will have a slightly larger range, from 2 to 5 square miles (5.18 sq. km. to 12.95 sq. km.).

## Habits and Behavior Patterns

The habits of the deer change drastically with the season in response to the availability of food and the temperature.

Bucks of all three varieties, in all parts of the country at all times of the year, bed down earlier in the morning, seek heavier cover, are generally less active in the daytime, come out to feed later in the evening, and are more active after dark than the does and fawns. Bucks are almost always more wary and suspicious than the does, even where both sexes are hunted.

In the springtime, whitetail bucks are often solitary, or sometimes a big buck is followed by several younger bucks. Occasionally there may be a small group of mixed-age bucks, but the largest such whitetail group I have ever seen consisted of five bucks.

The grouping of blacktail bucks is very similar to that of whitetails; whereas muley bucks, being more sociable all year long, will often be found in larger concentrations. The largest such mule deer grouping I have found consisted of eleven bucks. Some of the really big muleys are found by themselves. This is a trait found among many mammals. With advanced age, the males tend to be loners. Most frequently this is by choice, although occasionally they are driven out by the younger, dominant males that have supplanted them in the hierarchy. Either way, the exile of the aged has survival value to the general population. The presence of the old and infirm would attract predators to the herd.

The bucks are active for two or three hours before dawn and they seek a sheltered vantage point within an hour after dawn. The whitetail bucks usually bed up on the tops of ridges. When possible, muleys like to bed up against some rim rock, and blacktails slink off into impenetrable thickets. If the

Whitetail bucks tend to be solitary and reclusive in spring.

bucks have to bed down on level ground, they usually walk with the wind for some distance before bedding. Then, when they lie down, they can watch downwind with their eyes, and their noses will tell them if anything is following their trail.

As their antlers are growing rapidly at this time, and are soft and tender, the bucks take great care not to hit anything with them. The bucks are gaining weight rapidly now on the new, nutritious food.

They may feed again for an hour or so after noon and then lie still again until about an hour before dark. The evening feeding is the heaviest of the day. They feed for three to four hours and will probably lie down in the field or open areas to rest until 1:00 a.m., when they usually feed for another hour or two. They are again active before dawn. By the time it is light, they will be back into heavy cover for the day.

"Bachelor" groups of mule deer are common in spring.

A doe's daily pattern is quite different. Does usually feed from dawn until about 9:00 or 10:00 a.m. I have found that, starting in late winter and on through the spring, does do a lot of feeding in the morning. The demands made on the doe's body by the developing fetus and by the fawns after their birth require longer feeding periods to cram in all the food possible. Although the new grasses, forbs, and browse are high in nutrition, they are also high in water content and more pounds must be eaten to meet the demands on a doe. Between 10:00 and 11:00 a.m., the does usually bed down at the edges of fields and clearings where they have been feeding. They usually feed again for an hour, beginning about 1:00 p.m. By 4:00 p.m., the does are again feeding and will continue to do so until dark. They feed again at about 1:00 a.m. and then bed down until dawn. At night they usually bed out in the middle of clearings. When they have their fawns, they usually nurse them before each of their own feeding periods. In the springtime the does are probably dispersed more widely and uniformly over the deer's range than at any other time of year.

At this time, deer throughout this continent have changed their daily habits because they themselves are being changed. As automatically as plants respond to the increased sun's light, the autonomic nervous system of the deer also responds. The pituitary gland, which has been functioning at a greatly reduced rate since December, becomes more active in late March under the stimulus of the increased sunlight. The pituitary, in addition to releasing the somatotrophic hormones that start the buck's antlers developing, also stimulates the adrenal and thyroid glands. The activated endocrine system provides the impetus for greatly increased growth of the fetuses the does are carrying.

The does were bred in the late fall or early winter, during the 24 to 28 hours when they were in estrus. In the pro-estrus period, the new ovarian follicles grew, then burst, to discharge the fully developed egg into the fallopian tubes. Countless thousands of motile sperm from the semen of the male swam up the fallopian tube where one penetrated the egg, impregnating the doe. The fertilized egg, or blastocyst, then dropped into the uterus where it became

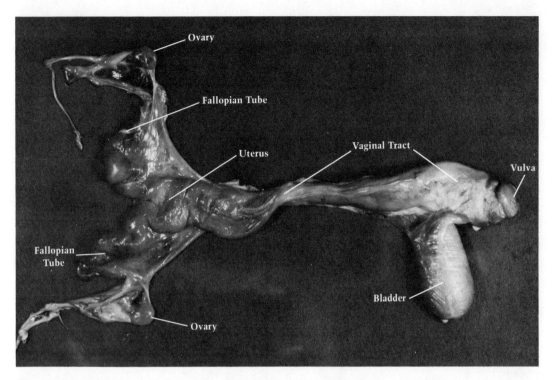

This reproductive tract of a doe shows (from left) two ovaries, Fallopian tubes, uterus, vaginal tract, bladder, and vulva. In many states, hunters are asked to remove this tract and send it to the game department for study.

implanted in the uterine wall and began to develop. The development and the multiplication of the egg cells is a phenomenal mathematical progression. It is not until 37 days after implantation of the blastocyst that the embryo is considered to be a fetus.

In deer, as in humans, identical twins result when a fertilized egg splits and produces two fetuses. Identical twins are always of the same sex. When two different eggs are fertilized, the resulting fetuses are known as fraternal twins, and they may be of one or both sexes. Triplets or quadruplets are produced in the same manner. Fraternal twins are more common than identical twins, and they are also much more common than triplets or quadruplets.

E. L. Cheatum, G. H. Morton, and R. A. Armstrong did the work that forms the basis for the following material. Their specimens were does killed on the highway or shot illegally. These does were examined at New York's Delmar Laboratory.

The researchers worked up tables that allow the age of the fetus to be deter-

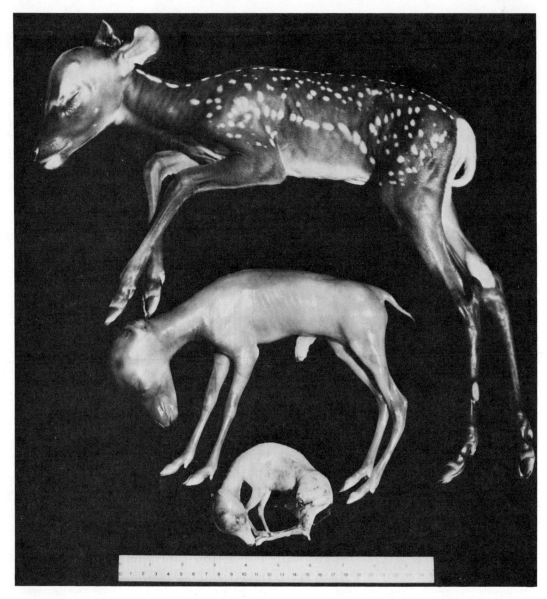

These whitetail fetuses show typical development at about 80 days, 130 days, and 180 days.

mined by measurements, which are made by two methods. Everyone is aware of the term "fetal position," a position in which a human, or any mammal, lies on its side, curls the body and head forward, and draws the legs up toward the chest.

The deer's fetus is curled into such a position until the 48th day, and until then measurements are taken in a straight line, not following the curve of the body, from the crown of the head to the rump. No attempt is made to straighten out the curvature of the fetus. At 37 days the crown-rump measurement is about $^{11}/_{16}$-inch (17 mm.) and the fetus weighs $^{1}/_{2}$-gram. At 48 days the fetus is 1$^{1}/_{2}$ inches (37.8 mm.) in length and weighs 2.2 grams.

After that, the fetus begins to straighten out and the measurements are then taken from the fetus's forehead to its rump at the base of the tail. At about 65 days the fetus will have a forehead-rump measurement of 3$^{5}/_{16}$ inches (83 mm.) and weight of about $^{1}/_{2}$ ounce (14.9 g.). The eyelids are formed, the mouth is closed, and the vibrissae follicles are present that will develop as the whiskers of the eyebrow, mouth, and chin.

### The Question of a Doe Harvest

I well remember the hysteria that arose when New Jersey first proposed having a doe day. The anti-hunters and many hunters joined forces to denounce the state's actions, and they obtained court orders to stop the proposed harvest. The hunt was planned for December but was delayed by court action and finally took place in February.

The hue and cry against the hunt was that does are mothers. Of course they are. Many hunters loudly proclaimed that they would never shoot a pregnant doe—a doe "heavy with young." The fetuses at that time of year average 60 to 90 days in development. At 90 days a deer fetus measures 6$^{1}/_{2}$ inches (165 mm.) in length and weighs about 90 grams, or roughly three ounces. At that time, I took pride in having excellent eyesight and I couldn't detect that the does were carrying those fetuses. As I was also working as Chief Gamekeeper at Coventry Hunt Club, I gathered many of our does' reproductive tracts, and in not one instance did I find twin fawns, though twins would have been normal if the food supply had not been depleted. New Jersey, like an increasing number of other states, now has a doe season, for a doe harvest is a legitimate tool of herd management. The number of does to be taken during this season is based on the estimated deer population in each of the state's management zones.

At about 120 days, the fetus weighs 22 ounces (624 g.) and measures 10$^{1}/_{2}$ inches (268 mm.). At this stage it has incomplete hair covering with some pigmentation showing in the hair, although the spots are clear. The tops of the hooves are dark with white tips.

At 125 days the fetus weighs 24.2 ounces (687.2 g.) and at 135 days it weighs 36.3 ounces (1029.3 g.). This 50 percent spurt in growth in just 10 days is followed by a gain of more than 100 percent in the next 10 days. Initially slow development, changing to greatly accelerated growth, is nature's way of

A newborn fawn is short-muzzled and long-legged.

preventing an undue drain on the doe during the period of food shortages. The doe's metabolism slows down each winter, and the fawn develops very slowly during the first four months. Then the development spurts ahead so that the young will be born at the optimal time of year.

From 180 days on, the fetus is considered full-term. Almost completely developed, it has a length of about 18 inches (450 mm.) and weighs about 2,600 grams, or 5¾ pounds. I provided detailed birth weights in an earlier chapter, so it suffices here to say that the fawns of all three types of deer average 5 to 8 pounds (2.26-3.62 kg.) at birth, after a gestation period of 187 to 212 days. (A period of 200 to 210 days is considered normal.)

## Birth of Fawns

When a fawn is born, its dimensions are far out of proportion to those it will have as an adult. The legs are much longer at birth in relation to the body than they will be later in life. A newborn fawn seems to be all legs, with none of them steady. This is true of many large herbivores, including horses, gazelles, and so on. The long legs soon become steady, for they are needed so that the young can be moved from the place of birth—a place to which predators may be attracted.

The fawn's muzzle is short, the length from eyes to nose being somewhat out of proportion to the section from the eyes to the back of the skull. The jaws gradually grow longer for almost a year to provide room for the permanent teeth. The short muzzle is particularly apparent when the fawn has its first winter coat. The long hair makes the muzzle look even shorter. The fawn's body will also lengthen proportionately with age.

At birth, the pupils of the fawn's eyes are brown and the surrounding area is bluish-gray. After nine or ten days the blue portion of the eyes begins to turn light brown like that of the adult.

As birthing time approaches, the doe wants solitude. Her fawns of last year are puzzled by her behavior. For almost a year, almost every minute of every day, the doe's main concern was for the yearlings she now seeks to elude. She may even drive them off by striking at them with her front feet. Although puzzled, at last the yearlings leave or are left. In the case of a young buck, this separation may be permanent. The young does will almost surely rejoin their mother within days or a week.

If the young does are pregnant, they are also seeking the same solitude as the older doe. Often the yearling does and their fawns will rejoin the matriarchal doe within a month or two. Sometimes the little family unit is broken up only long enough for the doe to give birth to her new fawns.

It becomes very obvious when a doe is in the last stages of pregnancy. Her swollen abdomen emphasizes her condition and so do her actions. Being heavy, she does not run and bounce around as she usually does; her manner is that of a sedate matron.

This is particularly noticeable with blacktail deer. Blacktails often run with what appears to be a very stiff, bone-jolting gait, particularly when they are nervous or frightened. This gait is abandoned by the blacktail does in the last month of their pregnancy.

Another indication of imminent birth is the swelling of the doe's udder. About two weeks prior to giving birth, her udder swells noticeably and the skin there turns pinkish with body heat. This swelling and coloration can be seen on wild deer if you check them from the rear. We have found with captive deer that within 24 to 30 hours after milk can be stripped from a doe's teats, she will give birth.

Ordinarily, a doe does not seem to look for any special spot for birthing, other than seeking a little privacy and some sheltering cover. In most cases, the young seem to be dropped almost anywhere when it is time for them to be born. Sometimes, however, a doe makes her way to an island where she drops her fawns, using the water as a protective barrier. Where predation is heavy, does seem to take more care in selecting a spot for birthing.

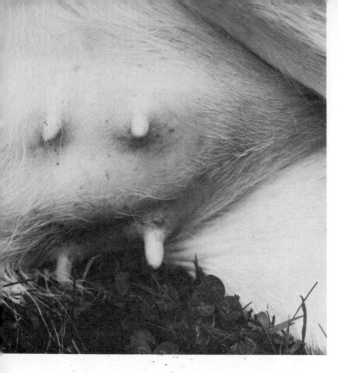

About two weeks before a doe gives birth, her udder swells noticeably as it fills with milk.

I have been most fortunate in being able to witness the birth of fawns on two different occasions. Both does were semi-tame, living on a deer preserve owned by Joe Taylor. The first occasion was in 1960 while I was gathering data for my book on whitetail deer. Joe's deer at that time had the run of an entire mountain. Their only link with man was the feed that was regularly put out for them. I was building up a series of photographs on antler development. While walking through Joe's woods looking for the bucks, I located a doe that had part of her water bag, the amniotic sac, protruding from her vaginal tract. I forgot about the bucks. Although I had seen many newborn fawns, I had never witnessed a birth, and not many other people had, either.

The doe was standing when I first discovered her. When she was sure I had seen her, she walked several hundred feet up a hillside and went into a fairly open thicket of alders. Apparently, the doe had been in labor. As I did not want her to abort the young by moving any farther, I did not immediately follow her. She lay down, and in a few minutes I could see the feet of the fawn protrude from her vagina, then the head and then foreshoulders.

At this point, the doe stood up and the fawn slipped out of her body. Knowing that the doe was now anchored to this spot by the birth of that first fawn, I cautiously approached. She showed absolutely no concern about my presence; her only interest was in licking her new baby dry. The little fellow (for I soon afterward had a chance to examine it and found it was a buck) attempted to get on his feet in less than five minutes and could stagger a few steps in less than ten minutes. His attempts to get on his feet were not helped at all by the doe's licking. Her washing of the fawn was so vigorous that she often

186

A seven-minute-old buck fawn begins nursing as his mother vigorously washes him.

knocked him over, and he kept getting tangled in part of the placental sac. At one time he became completely enveloped in the sac. He nursed when he was eight minutes old, while the doe was lying down. All the while, she continued to wash him.

After about twenty minutes, she stopped her ministrations and began to strain—a strain that sent a rippling shudder through her body. She strained and pressed and was rewarded by the protrusion of the feet of her second fawn. The straining continued until about two-thirds of the fawn's body protruded. Then she stood up and the little one slid out as easily as a diver knifing into the water. The fawn was in a diving position with its head stretched out between its forelegs. I do not know how long the doe may have been in labor before I first saw her, but I do not think it was long, considering the ease with which the fawns were born and the short time that had elapsed. This doe had given birth twice before. Those births had stretched her reproductive tract. Thus, her tract was considerably larger than that of a doe that had never had young.

While she was giving birth to the second fawn, a little doe, her first fawn lay curled up beside her. Shortly after giving birth to her new fawns, the doe's yearling buck came over to investigate. The doe paid no attention to him, just as she paid no attention to me. The second little fawn was washed and licked

This doe has dropped one fawn and will soon give birth to a second, while her yearling (button buck in background) approaches to investigate. She will tolerate but ignore the yearling at this stage.

dry until the hair on its coat stood on end. The actions and timing of the second fawn closely paralleled that of the first.

About twenty minutes after the second fawn was born, the doe commenced to eat the afterbirth, or placental sac. Most of the sac had come out of her body with the two fawns, and she pulled the remaining string out of her body with her teeth.

Almost all wild animals and most domestic ones eat the afterbirth as soon as they can. The primary reason, I believe, is to get rid of it so that it will not attract predators. Consuming it is a defensive instinct. Canine scavengers throughout the world are attracted to herd animals when they give birth, for the placental sacs provide an easily scavenged feast. No doubt, another reason why the mother consumes the afterbirth is that pregnancy and birthing have

This fawn is still entangled in the placental sac, which the doe is pulling away and eating.

drained her of substantial nutrients. Eating the sac returns some of these nutrients to her system. A doe giving birth loses from 14 to 25 pounds (6.3 to 11.3 kg.) in overall weight, depending on the weight of her fawns. It has also been suggested that eating the afterbirth is a stimulus to lactation, although I can find no research reports on this.

After the doe had eaten the afterbirth and had nursed both fawns, she was evidently exhausted. For a while she was content to lie still and rest. The fawns had curled up alongside their mother. The doe, being comparatively tame, had accepted my presence and was not concerned as I cautiously moved about taking photographs from different angles. The fawns struggled to their feet and tottered over to me. I gently put them back beside the doe but they instinctively came right back to me because I was moving. It would have been very easy for me to imprint these fawns—that is, have them accept me as their mother. This was something I wanted to avoid, so I put them both back beside the doe and quickly withdrew from the immediate area. They were then content to lie there, snuggled against their mother.

The fawns had been attracted by my moving because, in the wild, all the hoofed mammals move their offspring from the place of birth as soon as they are able to walk. Although the doe has eaten the afterbirth, her lost body fluids have seeped into the earth and that odor can attract danger.

I had not hesitated to touch these fawns because the doe was accustomed to human beings and she would not be alarmed by my odor. I never touched any of the wild fawns that I located in the woods and fields.

Every year the game departments across the country are deluged with reports of and by people who have picked up "orphan" fawns. Unless the doe has been killed, these fawns are not orphans, but if a fawn is touched and petted, there is a chance that it may become an orphan. It may be rejected by its mother if she is afraid of human scent. At one time it was thought that touching a fawn practically guaranteed its abandonment.

Research at the Wilder Wildlife Refuge, near Sinton, Texas, where fawn-tagging has been carried on for many years, has proved that in only about 5 percent of the cases will the doe abandon her fawn because of the human scent. These statistics have been substantiated by the New Jersey Game Department, which has also been doing a lot of fawn-tagging. However, I still constantly stress to everyone: *Don't touch the fawns.* The fawns you touch may be among that 5 percent, and no one should ever deliberately cause a fawn's abandonment.

In New Jersey, the middle of May brings dogwood blossoms, Mother's Day, and rattlesnakes. The second birthing I photographed took place on a day when Joe Taylor and I were coming off the mountain after hunting for rattlesnakes. It was about May 15, a week to ten days early for deer to drop their fawns in our area.

The doe, a tame one on Joe's preserve, was a yearling that had not been bred as a fawn. This was her first parturition and it was a hard, long period of labor for her. Her inexperience made it even more difficult.

We first saw the doe about 10 a.m. and she was in the throes of hard labor. This was evident because of the large area that she had trampled and cut up in her pain. Biologists recognize that most does thrash around and trample quite an area while giving birth. On fawn-tagging expeditions, they look for such areas in the grasslands, hay fields, and woodlands that pregnant does are known to frequent.

The doe moaned and groaned piteously and strained mightily but to little avail. She had not dilated sufficiently to allow for the fawn's passage. There is also no doubt that her body was feverish. Several times she got up and walked over to the spot that was wet from a small seepage. She would lie on the damp earth for a while, strain some more, then rise to go back to the spot where we had found her originally. When she strained, she put her whole body into the effort. She kicked out with her hind legs, thrashed around with her front legs, and twisted and turned her head and neck from side to side. Her eyes were closed, her mouth open. After about an hour, her vagina gradually dilated and the fawn's front feet emerged, wrapped in a placental sac.

Now was when the doe's inexperience multiplied her problems. If her actions had not caused her pain, the situation would have been humorous. She strained until it seemed as if her body would be split asunder. The fawn's front feet would emerge a little farther with each effort, but after every massive push the doe climbed stiffly to her feet and turned around to search the area for her fawn. Every time she got to her feet, the fawn would slide back into her body and the feet would disappear from view. When the doe could find no fawn, she would lie down again until the next spasm drove her to greater exertions. Now the water bag burst and the amniotic fluid poured out. Six times she got up to see if the fawn was born and six times the fawn slid back into her body. Her vagina was dilating now and at each subsequent spasm the fawn slid back out much more easily than before.

We were happy to see that the fawn's head was in the proper position between its front legs. When the labor was so difficult we thought that perhaps the fawn's head was turned back over its shoulder. This can happen, and when it does the fawn is not in the streamlined, least-resistance position needed for a natural birth. Fawns that are turned that way sometimes die in the birth process, and occasionally they may cause the death of the doe. These complications are similar to the breech-births of human babies, except that in the case of wild animals there is no attending doctor to turn the infant to the proper position.

Finally the fawn's head and shoulders were out. The doe's labor was still intense and she still thrashed and moaned. Fortunately, she did not get up again. With more effort, the fawn was pushed out a little farther. When it was half way out, the doe rested; the worst was over. A little more effort and the fawn was almost completely expelled. The doe then lay quietly for a while with the fawn's hind feet still inside her body. The fawn shook its head and moved its floppy, sopping ears. Noticing the movement behind her, the doe immediately turned and started to clean the fawn with her tongue.

In four minutes the fawn started to crawl up between the doe's hind leg and nuzzled her udder and nipples. It continued to crawl forward while she continued to wash it vigorously. Between six and seven minutes after emerging, the fawn turned around and again searched down along the doe's belly for her

## Birthing

**1.** A whitetail doe lies down during the throes of labor.

**2.** As the doe strains, the fawn's front feet emerge.

**3.** After additional spasms from the doe, the fawn's head appears.

**4.** With the fawn almost completely expelled, the doe rests.

**5.** As the fawn moves toward the udder, the doe begins cleaning her new arrival.

**6.** The doe thoroughly cleans the nursing fawn.

**7.** Thirteen minutes after birth, this fawn tries to stand.

**8.** The eighteen-minute-old fawn takes its first wobbly steps.

nipples. The fawn had difficulty getting a nipple into its mouth but it instinctively knew what to do and it kept on trying. The fawn was successful in
nursing when it was ten minutes old. It nursed for two minutes, then turned
around again, lying against the doe's front legs. The doe lovingly lavished all
of her attention on her new baby. She missed no part of the fawn in her cleaning efforts. It was as if she had decided to give it a thorough examination and
was pleased with what she found.

At thirteen minutes of age, the fawn heaved up onto its front knees, raised
its hind quarters into the air, and attempted to stand. This was a tremendous
effort, and the fawn trembled violently with the exertion. It fell. It tried again.
It continued to fall or to be pushed over by its mother's ministrations, but it
went on trying.

When the fawn was just eighteen minutes old, it took its first few wobbly,
spraddling steps. Then, thoroughly tired, it sank to the earth and curled up
into a ball. But it had walked.

I imagine that most does have more trouble giving birth for the first time
than they have with subsequent births. Whether this was an exceptionally
hard labor, I cannot say. The total time elapsed for this birthing is not known
because I did not see the very start of the doe's labor, but I was there for over
two hours before the fawn was born. At the other extreme was a birthing
described by Edwin Michael at the Wilder Wildlife Refuge.

Doing fawn research early one morning, Michael was watching a doe when
he suddenly realized she was about to drop a fawn. And here the word "drop"
is most appropriate because the doe did not lie down. In fact, she acted as if
she were not aware of what was taking place. The doe was walking along
browsing on little tidbits here and there. At 8:25 a.m. the fawn's feet were protruding from the doe's vagina, but she leisurely continued with her feeding. At
8:55 a.m. the fawn was almost halfway out of the doe's body but she still
showed no concern. She went on feeding and at no time did she even turn
around to see what was happening. About 9:00 a.m., Michael lost sight of the
doe when she entered high grass where she must have dropped her fawn.
Michael measured the distance and found that the doe had walked about 275
yards (250 m.) in the period that he watched her.

C. W. Severinghaus reported a birthing that took a long time but he did not
say whether the labor was a difficult one. A whitetail doe that was in captivity at New York's Delmar Wildlife Research Laboratory gave birth to a normal, brown fawn during the night of July 7, 1968. It was the first of two, but
its twin did not appear until early on the morning of July 9. The second fawn
was a white one.

When fawns are born, the bottoms and tips of their hooves are covered with a soft, gelatinlike substance about ⅛-inch (3 mm.) thick. It is similar to the cartilage on the tip of the breast bone of a young frying chicken. The padding prevents the hooves from puncturing the placental sac while the fawns are being carried. This soft material is usually worn off or shredded the first day or two of life. The hooves are dark gray at birth and get darker as they harden in a couple of days.

The placental, or navel, cord usually tears loose when the fawn is born. The portion attached to the fawn dries up after the third day. Usually the dried cord drops off in about two weeks and a scab forms over the spot.

A doe giving birth for the first time usually has a single fawn whether she is bred as a six- to seven-month-old fawn or at 1½ years of age. Thereafter, if she has access to an ample supply of nutritious food, she will usually have twins. We frequently hear about barren does. If the forage is so poor that a doe is starving, she may fail to conceive because her body is not functioning properly or because she herself needs all the nutrients that would be consumed by the embryos. However, old age very rarely renders a doe barren.

A study of 1,322 mule deer does in five states showed an average fetal rate of 1.44 fawns per doe. That is a good average because 1.44 fawns per doe means a herd increase of about 50 percent per year. The does examined were all at least eighteen months old at the time of breeding. A single fawn was being carried by 29 percent of them; 56 percent carried twins, and 1 percent had triplets. Those thirteen sets of triplets had to come from areas where the does had a superabundance of food. Fourteen of the does were barren.

Some of the fourteen may have been 1½-year-old does that were not yet sexually mature. Quite frequently, blacktail does on poor land do not breed until they are 2½ years old. Some of them could also have been suffering from some ailment or physical impairment that was not primarily sexual. The study showed that the fertilization rate for the 1,322 does was about 95 percent. Rarely do herds achieve a better average than that.

Most mammals produce more males than females, and deer are no exception. Individual states, and individual areas within a state, may vary but nationwide the ratio for all three types of deer is 106 males for each 100 females. As with many mammals, this ratio soon changes because postnatal mortality is higher among males than females. Since males are just as strong and healthy as females, the reason is hard to pin down. Probably it is because males tend to be more active, aggressive, and independent, and get into more trouble than the females. At any rate, within a week there are more females than males—and the ratio continues to widen with age. When deer are on a poor diet, the gestation period is usually four to six days longer than usual, and the does produce an even higher percentage of males than normal. No one knows why more males are produced in times of poor forage. As to the length of gestation, this may be due solely to the poor diet or perhaps a male fetus takes longer to develop. In human pregnancy, a male is usually carried longer than a female. Among both sexes, fawn mortality is high. Studies have shown that 6 to 7 percent of all whitetail fawns born in the wild die within the first forty-eight hours.

A Colorado study of whitetail fawns investigated the relationship of nutrition and postnatal mortality. Forty-two of the fawns that were kept on a 7 percent protein diet died. Twenty-seven that were on an 11 percent protein diet also died. But there was no mortality at all among fawns on a 13 percent protein diet.

Colorado conducted another study in which muley does were given increased protein in order to find the effects on birth and fawn mortality. The does were fed a diet that was in the vicinity of 16 to 18 percent protein. The hundred and seventy-two fawns born to these does during the program had an average weight of 8.13 pounds (3.68 kg.), which is substantially higher than the average weight of wild-born fawns. Usually, when only a single fawn is born, it weighs more than either of twin fawns, but twins may also be large if the mother has been well fed.

The does on this high-protein diet came into rut five to seven days earlier than did the control deer. They also dropped their fawns earlier; their fawns were above average in weight, and fawn mortality dropped.

Four sets of triplets were born during this research program. Again and again research proves that food is the key controlling most facets of life (and not only for deer).

Some interesting figures appeared in a New Jersey study of multiple births from 1952 to 1962. On some of the best land in central New Jersey, three does that bred at six to seven months of age produced twins. The national breeding rate for six- to seven-month-old fawns on good land runs between 40 and 60 percent. Those that do breed usually have just one fawn but these three, because of their good diet, produced twins. In that study thirty does had triplets and one had quadruplets.

In 1968 the New Jersey Game Department collected a large number of bucks and does from estates near Harbourton. This is rich land with a superabundance of food. The hundred and thirty-eight adult does that were collected were carrying, in addition to the expected sets of twins, eight sets of triplets, three sets of quadruplets, and one set of quintuplets. That is what adequate nutrition will do.

A doe killed on a highway near Espanola, Ontario, in June, 1961, evidently had access to good food. She contained four full-term fetuses—three bucks that weighed 7.9 pounds (3.58 kg.), 5.8 pounds (2.63 kg.), and 5.3 pounds (2.4

kg.) plus a doe that weighed 4 pounds (1.81 kg.). That's a total fawn weight of 23 pounds (10.4 kg.). Another doe, killed by a car in Cambria County, Pennsylvania, in 1958, was carrying full-term quadruplets—three does and a buck. In addition to the New Jersey quintuplets I mentioned, there have been other records of quintuplets but I have not been able to ascertain whether the fawns lived.

When it comes to records, a semi-tame doe by the name of Diana set a number of them. Diana lived in the woods near the Tomhegan Camps in Maine. She produced thirty-one fawns in fourteen years. She had six sets of twins and five sets of triplets. And she produced one of those sets of triplets when she was fifteen years old. From the age of twelve on, she became very docile and even her offspring "bossed" her around, but she never became barren. She was killed by an overly amorous buck just before the rutting season when she was 18½ years old.

A whitetail doe that is in a commercial herd at Hamburg, Pennsylvania, has also set some kind of a record. This doe has given birth to triplets on Memorial Day for four consecutive years. I think it would be interesting if more research were done on the punctuality of the birthing of deer. Mink breed on the same day and give birth on the same day year after year, and this precise timing is passed along to the daughters of each female.

One other fawn record of interest involved a doe injured by dogs at Higgins Lake, Michigan, on February 25, 1957. The doe, because of her injuries, was killed by a game warden. When her reproductive tract was checked, it was found that she was carrying twin fawns. One was normal, but the other had two heads that were joined at the ear. This fawn had two outside ears but only one in the center at the joint.

Albert Strausbaugh of McSherrystown, Pennsylvania, shot an odd-looking deer during Pennsylvania's 1962 antlerless deer season. It was a six-month-old fawn with three eyes, one on the right side and two on the left. It also had two noses, one where it belonged and another a third of the way between that nose and the eyes on the left side. Everyone has read of two-headed calves, five-legged sheep, and similar anomalies. They are rare, but there is nothing especially strange about their occurrence in any mammalian species, including deer. It is rather strange, however, that a three-eyed, two-nosed fawn lived for six months, because few such unusual youngsters survive for long.

### Nursing

The milk that the fawns get for the first couple of days is a particularly thick, rich, sticky, yellow milk known as colostrum. It is vitally important to the fawns because it contains immunoproteins—antibodies against disease.

The fawns grow rapidly on their mother's rich milk. A good Jersey cow has

A fawn greedily butts the doe's udder while gulping fat-rich milk.

about 5 to 6 percent butterfat in her milk, but a deer's milk is 11 to 12 percent butterfat. The fawns gain about 10 percent of their birth weight per day for the first week and then slow down to about a 5 percent weight gain per week. The doe's butterfat content drops down to about 8 percent after the first three weeks. Her diet will affect the *amount* of milk she can give but it has little effect on the *quality*.

A fawn's basic coat at birth is the bright-reddish color typical of the summer coat of all of the deer. There are two rows of white spots, one on either side of the spine, from the fawn's neck to the base of its tail. There are usually sixty to eighty spots in these two rows. On either side of the body, about a hundred or more irregularly sized white spots are scattered rather randomly. The hairs of these spots are not white to their roots but are only terminal white tufts on regular reddish-brown hair. As the fawn grows older, the white is gradually worn away so that the fawn begins to lose its spots before it molts its summer hair for its winter coat.

The spotted coat provides excellent camouflage when the fawn is lying among the brown leaves and forest litter. The sunlight filtering through the leaves of the trees casts a dappled shadow pattern that matches the fawn's coat and masks its presence.

When the fawn lies curled amid forest debris, its spotted coat is good camouflage. At a distance, the fawn looks like dappled sunlight and shadows on fallen leaves.

For the first three or four days, fawns usually lie curled in a small circle with their heads resting on their legs or on their bodies. If frightened, the fawn may stay in this position or, more frequently, it will lie almost straightened out because it can get its head lower in this position. The fawn holds its ears backward and flattened out along its neck.

The camouflage coat works in the woods but is of little value when the fawn lies in the grassland. More and more whitetail fawns are being dropped in grassy areas as increasingly more of the does spend more time grazing than browsing. This unfortunate situation stems from the fact that man's incursions continue to diminish our forested areas.

After washing her fawns thoroughly, thus removing odor, the doe soon leads them away from the birthing spot. She does not bed twin fawns together but hides them in different locations, sometimes within 25 feet (7.6 m.) of each other, sometimes as much as 250 feet (76.2 m.) apart. Then she deliberately stays out of the immediate area.

The fact that a doe does not stay with her fawns, and often is not seen if the fawns are discovered, is the reason so many fawns are thought to be orphans. The doe never goes far from her fawns, and she always knows about where they are. She instinctively stays away from them so that her body odor will not attract predators to the young.

While nursing, the doe consumes any excrement her fawn voids. Her licking stimulates the fawn to defecate and also removes scent that could attract predators.

I have often seen dogs run unaware right past fawns that were curled up in the forest. Many biologists in their reports have claimed that there is no discernible odor to very young fawns. One reason is that they do not move around much during the first week. Without movement, there is little odor. Another, probably more important, reason is that there is no excrement.

While a doe nurses a fawn she licks it continuously, and she concentrates on the anal region more than anywhere else. This constant licking stimulates the fawn's bowels, and the doe consumes the excrement as it is voided. A captive fawn that is not having regular bowel movements should have its anus rubbed with a warm, moist rag.

People trying to raise fawns seldom have as much trouble with constipation as with scours or diarrhea. At the first sign of runny excrement, the milk should be heated almost to boiling before it is fed to the fawns. That is a simple old remedy that works for man or beast. Today, there is medicine available that will stop this looseness of the bowels.

Getting enough of the proper nutrition into a captive fawn is another problem. I don't know how the practice started, but frequently a fawn is fed ordinary cow's milk cut with water. This mix is less than one-fourth as rich in butterfat and protein as a doe's milk, so the fawn is literally starving to death. Evaporated milk is better, as it has about twice the nutrition of whole milk with at least 7 percent butterfat. Today, calf-starters are being used with good success as the fat content is about 10 percent, the protein content is about 22 percent. However, nothing can take the place of the doe. There is no way to improve on the care provided by the natural mother, and there are only two exceptions to the rule that a fawn should never be taken out of the wild. One is in the event of a definitely known emergency—that is, when there is absolutely no doubt that the fawn is orphaned. The other is when fawns are needed for scientific research, either as fawns or later in life. Fawns reared by their mothers are always wilder and more unmanageable than those that are bottle-fed. This is true of all wild animals. If they are taken from the mother, bottle-fed, and handled frequently, they become tame. In the absence of this handling, it is as if they take in wildness with their mother's milk.

A doe usually nurses her fawns about four to six times in twenty-four hours, although some does nurse more frequently. Fawns at first need about two to four ounces of milk every four hours. At one week of age, they are taking about thirty ounces a day. At three weeks they will take a little more, but then they are already starting to eat green vegetation. Young does with their first fawns cannot produce as much milk as older does. Researchers, by milking tame does and by calculating how much bottle-fed fawns consume, figure that most does produce 1½ to 2 quarts of milk per day.

Deer are like cows in that not all of them give the same amount of milk, and as the quantity of milk diminishes, the butterfat content goes up. The doe's milk has 18 percent butterfat just before the fawns are completely weaned at five months of age.

In the beginning, the doe probably nurses the fawn as much because of the discomfort of her swollen udder as from maternal instinct. Because newborn fawns do not empty the udder at each nursing, the udder is swollen and often hot to the touch. Since the udder is not emptied, it fills up again soon, and the sooner the udder is filled, the more often the doe is prompted to feed the fawns. As their intake increases, the pressure on the udder lessens and there is a longer time span between feedings.

For the first week or so, the fawn is content to drop to the ground and sleep as soon as it has finished nursing. Up to four days, fawns will lie still if discovered. Between five and six days, at least half the fawns will run off, and at this age it is almost impossible for a man to catch one. It is very difficult to hold a five- or six-day-old whitetail fawn because it kicks, jumps, and

Upon hearing their mother's mewing call, week-old twin fawns have run up to nurse.

thrashes, bawling all the while at the top of its voice. A mule deer or blacktail fawn at this age is still docile.

At seven days of age, almost all fawns will run if they feel they are discovered. And at this age, fawns often get up and wander about by themselves while the mother is away. Often if a fawn is in an area that becomes too warm, it will move into the shade. When the doe comes back to nurse the fawn, she may have to hunt for it. The doe usually goes to the precise spot where she left it after the last nursing. If she cannot find it there, she will try to track it by the odor left by its hooves. If the scent is too weak to follow, she will then call—uttering a soft, mewing, catlike sound as she searches. Upon hearing this sound, the fawn immediately jumps to its feet and runs to the mother. Quite frequently both fawns hear this sound and run to her. She then nurses both at the same time. As she has four nipples, they generally have no difficulty in finding and reaching one.

The fawns may nurse from the side or the rear. If the doe lies down, they will nurse her in that position. Usually, after the first three or four days, the doe stands up while the fawns nurse.

Occasionally, if a doe is killed, another doe will adopt one or both of the orphans. More frequently, a wild doe will allow only her own fawns to nurse, but does in captivity often allow others to nurse. The actions of deer in captivity should not be interpreted as normal behavior. In captivity, deer are forced to be in one another's company constantly; they are deprived of the spatial requirements that would be normal and desirable for them in the wild.

Joe Taylor has one doe that is an excellent mother and produces a lot of milk. Whenever her fawns run up to nurse, it is as if someone had sounded a dinner gong. All the fawns in the pen run over and start to nurse, too. Of course, as the doe has only four nipples, only four fawns can nurse at a time. She welcomes them all. When young hoofed mammals nurse they pull on the nipples and then butt upward into the bag with considerable force. There have been times when four good-sized fawns were nursing this doe and they actually lifted her hind quarters off the ground as they all butted and pushed.

The fawns nurse from four to ten minutes at a time. While they are nursing, a milky froth appears around their mouths. Either the fawns will lick this milk off their muzzles or the doe will do it.

Between the first and second week, the doe begins to have a problem leaving her fawn after nursing it. By now the fawn is strong enough to travel and wants to stay with its mother. The doe usually does not want the fawn to accompany her yet and she will make the fawn lie down. Usually she does this by pushing the fawn down with her head—or with a foot, if necessary.

Years ago, I had a bird blind in the woods where I was photographing the eggs and young of the red-eyed vireo. I had entered the blind very early in the morning and made no noise because the action at the nest was very slow. The blind was made of burlap and canvas over a wooden frame. I could see out through the burlap mesh but nothing could see me sitting on the inside. I was unaware that a whitetail fawn was curled up about 75 feet from my blind until a doe came into sight, calling softly. The little fawn bounced to its feet, ran over, and began to nurse while the mother licked it thoroughly. After about six minutes, the fawn had finished nursing and the doe turned to leave but the fawn followed. Using her head, the doe pushed the little one back, but it persisted in tagging along. Finally, the doe lifted her forefoot, placed it on the fawn's back, and pushed the fawn to the ground. This time the fawn got the message. It lay still and the doe left the area.

If a predator ventures into the area where the fawn is hidden, the doe may bolt for safety while the fawn drops to the earth and remains hidden. The doe's running off may divert the predator so that it focuses all of its attention on her. At times the doe will remain hidden with her fawn, hoping the predator will not discover either of them. And on rare occasions a doe will actually attack a smaller predator.

**Predators**

The coyote probably kills more deer than any other wild predator — simply because there are more coyotes than any other predators. Today coyotes are found almost as commonly across the continent as the deer are.

Research at the Wilder Wildlife Refuge in Texas shows that in some years the fawn mortality is as high as 70 percent of the entire crop by the time the fawns are a month old. Predation by coyotes counts for half of all the fawns killed. The coyotes usually kill by biting through a fawn's head, neck, or spine.

The eastern coyote is now established in my home area of New Jersey. For years I thought that the wolf was the smartest animal in North America. But the coyote is smarter, more adaptable, and can thrive next to man while the wolf cannot. Since 1975 the coyote has been on New Jersey's list of completely protected wildlife, along with the bear, otter, bobcat, and wild turkey. I am not proposing that it be taken off, but where the coyote is established here the number of fawns seen per doe sighted is dropping. Other eastern states are also having coyote problems. Many reports are coming out of Maine and New York about coyotes killing adult deer in winter.

The records of predation by coyotes in the research literature is voluminous, and the predation is by no means just of the fawns. Coyotes are smart enough to team up and sometimes hunt in packs. But usually all it takes is a pair of coyotes. A single coyote can kill an adult deer. However, coyotes like to team up on such large prey.

Joseph Dixon reported how a pair of coyotes hunted a mule deer that had returned to the mountains in the early spring. There was bare ground except over the mountain crests where the snow had drifted to considerable depths. The coyotes did not try to catch the doe on the bare ground but teamed up to drive her up over the crests, where she floundered in the soft snow and was killed.

Dixon also reported a muley doe that drove a single coyote out of the area where she had a newborn fawn. When first sighted, the doe was chasing the coyote and lashing out at it with her front feet each time she got close. When the coyote crossed the road, the doe had to stop to avoid hitting Dixon's car.

The doe ran around the car and continued her pursuit of the coyote, which sought shelter under a pile of brush. Undaunted, the doe jumped high into the air and came down on the bush heap, holding all four feet close together. She did this repeatedly until the coyote finally dashed away again and this time made its escape.

Jean M. Linsdale and P. Quentin Tomich report a number of instances in which adult blacktail deer were chased by coyotes and several occasions when the deer chased the coyotes. They did not report seeing any deer killed by coyotes. Deer hair was found in 10 percent of all coyote scats checked on the Hasting Reservation in California but the coyote is a noted scavenger, so finding hair in the scats is no proof of a kill.

On December 23, 1976, I received a telephone call from my friend Charlie Summers, who lives in Denver, Colorado. Charlie and his photography partner, Joe Branney, had been in Yellowstone National Park right after Thanksgiving. They had gone there to photograph wild sheep and mule deer, and one incident had so impressed them that Charlie wanted to tell me about it.

They had been watching a small group of mule deer feeding on a hill when they noticed two groups of coyotes that were also interested in the deer. Unfortunately, the distance was too great for them to take any pictures so all Charlie and Joe could do was sit and watch the tableau unfold.

The coyotes had their strategy worked out in advance. The group that was below the deer carefully stalked within striking distance, keeping concealed from the deer by high grasses, sagebrush, and other vegetation. The coyotes that were to be the drivers made no attempt to conceal themselves but trotted openly along the skyline, diverting the deer's attention from their cohorts.

When the coyotes at the bottom were in position, those on the ridge charged down at the deer. The deer bounded to the bottom of the ravine—right into the coyotes waiting there. When the melee was over, a buck was thrashing around on the ground. All of the coyotes shared in the bounty of the hunt.

In a study of mule deer wintering along the Green River in Utah, researchers found concentrations of 81 to 135 deer per square mile. In the course of the study, 89 dead deer were found, of which 19, or 21 percent had been killed by coyotes.

The study showed that in this area the cougar was the chief predator of deer. Twenty-six of the eighty-nine dead deer, or 29 percent, had been killed by cougars. Cougar kills are usually easy to identify because in most cases the neck has been broken or the deer has been killed by being bitten through the throat. The cougar, which takes its prey by stalking, will eat its fill of a deer and then cover the carcass by scraping dirt, grass, leaves, sticks, or snow over

A cougar stands over a deer it has killed.

it. This caching practice is puzzling because the job is never complete; at least a part of the deer remains visible. Usually, the mound covering the carcass is so conspicuous that it attracts attention to the kill instead of concealing it. The cougar usually returns to the kill until it has consumed all of the meat. Stanley P. Young and Edward A. Goldman, in a famous study of the cougar, found that one of these big cats will typically kill fifty or more deer per year. Frank C. Hibben, in a study of the predation of mule deer in New Mexico, agreed with these figures but pointed out that most of the deer killed were old, sick, or infirm. The theory that predators kill defective prey exclusively or chiefly is widely accepted by the public but is being closely questioned today by biologists. J. Burton Lauckhart, in a study of blacktail deer in northwestern Washington, found that most of those killed by cougars were adult bucks in their prime. Ian McTaggart Cowan suggested that the reason for this might be that the adult bucks range higher in the mountains than the does range and so are more likely to be encountered by the cougar. Lauckhart found that the mountain lion in that region killed about thirty-five deer per year. Cowan's research on blacktail deer on Vancouver Island in British Columbia substantiates that figure as well as the fact that adult bucks are the deer most frequently taken.

The cougar has been nearly extirpated over most of the range of the white-tail deer, so lion predation on this species is almost nil. However, in the past couple of years the cougar has re-established itself in some of the eastern states. New Brunswick, Canada, has always had a small resident population of cougars and the big cats have now been reported in Maine, New Hampshire, and Vermont. If these sightings are reliable, there is a good chance that the cougar could re-establish itself in the Adirondack Mountains. Alex McKay photographed what looks to me like a cougar in New York State in the summer of 1972. Because of the high grass, the body and long tail do not show in the photograph and I can understand why authorities cannot accept the photo as proof of the cougar's return. According to New York authorities, there are no cougars in that state today. A cougar killed in Pennsylvania in 1967 had undoubtedly escaped from captivity. It was a young cat and very much underweight. Evidently it was having a hard time running in the wild on its own. In Florida, the cougar is on the endangered list and the population is steadily declining. The cougar has re-established itself in the Great Smoky Mountains of North Carolina and probably Tennessee and West Virginia. A number of authenticated sightings have been made in North Carolina.

Dr. Maurice Hornocker of Idaho has conducted what is probably the most thorough recent study of the cougar's predation on deer. His findings are that a healthy cougar kills a deer every seven to ten days—that's thirty-five to fifty deer a year, substantiating the work of earlier researchers. Hornocker found that the cougar was only taking 4 percent of the deer available to it. He noted that the cougar was successful in 37 of 45 attacks on mule deer and elk, for an 82.2 percent success ratio. This proves that the cougar is a very efficient predator.

A famous study of the Jawbone herd of mule deer, on the western slope of California's Sierra Nevada Mountains, showed the annual increase in the herd population to be 32 percent. But, because of tremendous overbrowsing by the deer, the habitat could not stand any increase in deer numbers. The study showed that 23 percent of the herd died of starvation each year, 7 percent were harvested by hunters, and 2 percent were taken by predators.

This is where the cougar plays an important role. In many areas that are too rough to be hunted, the cougar effectively fills the role for which it was designed—helping to keep the deer's population in proper relation to the food supply.

Wolves at one time played an important role in the control of the deer population in the United States. This is no longer true today except for parts of Minnesota.

In a recent study of wolves in Ontario, G. B. Kolenosky showed that the wolf needs about six pounds (2.71 kg.) of meat per day. Eight wolves hunting as a pack were successful in 46 percent of thirty-six chases. The wolves killed twenty-nine deer in sixty-three days, for a ratio of one deer for eight wolves every 2.2 days. In the time that the wolves hunted in this area, they removed 10 percent of the deer herd. That figure should not be taken to mean that the wolves were reducing the total deer population by 10 percent, because they were hunting in the winter, at a time when many deer die of starvation. A number of the deer that the wolves killed would have been part of the annual herd surplus that would have died of starvation if they had not been killed.

I can personally attest to the fact that wolves can limit the expansion of the deer. Years ago, when I started guiding wilderness canoe trips in Quebec, there were no deer to be found north of the Barrier Dam area of Verendrye Provincial Park. As the lumber companies opened up the country, the wolves' howling disappeared from the night and their tracks from the beaches. In a short time, with wolves gone, deer tracks were seen on the same beaches that formerly showed only wolf tracks.

Research in Alaska shows that where there are no wolves the blacktail deer are subject to heavy winter mortality because the habitat is usually heavily overbrowsed. Where wolves are present, their predation keeps the herd in better balance with their habitat so there is more winter food, less winter mortality, and the deer therefore have a much higher reproduction rate.

The bobcat and lynx have been known to kill both adult deer and fawns of all three species but most of their predation is on fawns. Minnesota reported twelve authenticated records of adult deer being killed by bobcats. New Hampshire reports forty deer killed by bobcats in seven years but acknowledges that most of the kills were fawns. During periods of deep snow, when the deer are yarded or have bogged down, they are much more vulnerable. People should not be surprised that the bobcat and lynx can kill a deer. These cats weigh up to 40 pounds (18.1 kg.), as much as the largest coyotes. Under these same snow conditions, the fisher and wolverine have also been known to kill deer. Sometimes, however, a deer is more than a match for a predator. Linsdale and Tomaich tell of several instances in which mule deer does chased and treed bobcats that happened to be in the area where the does had their fawns hidden.

Deer hair is frequently found in fox scats because the fox is one of the chief scavengers of dead deer. In winter, every fox trail will sooner or later lead to the carcass of a deer that has died of starvation, or been wounded during the hunting season but died later, or been killed by an automobile.

When foxes are caring for their kits in the spring, they carry their kill or their scavengings back to their dens. In a short time the area around the den is littered with scraps of fur, feathers, and bones. When Joe Taylor was one of New Jersey's predator-control men, he found a den that had the feet and

Here is a deer leg at the entrance of a fox den. In spring, foxes bring their scavengings to the den to feed their kits.

hooves of whitetail fawns. This might lead one to think that the fox had killed the fawns, but in this instance Joe knew the fawns had died of starvation because he had removed a nursing doe from a nearby highway after it had been killed by an automobile. The orphaned fawns had died and the fox retrieved the carcasses as carrion.

Both red and gray foxes probably do kill fawns on rare occasions. In the early summer of 1975, John Powless of Carlisle, Pennsylvania, was at his cabin in the Seven Mountains in Mifflin County, Pennsylvania. As he sat drinking a morning cup of coffee on the cabin porch, he heard a loud bleating. He was amazed to see a whitetail fawn running toward the cabin, pursued by a gray fox. He ran out and chased the fox away. The fawn was exhausted and stood trembling with its mouth wide open and its tongue hanging out. After the fawn got its breath back, it ran back into the woods. The doe had evidently been away feeding at the time or the fox never would have dared chase the fawn.

Black bears will kill an adult deer if they can get one at disadvantage. Under ordinary circumstances, a bear is too slow to catch a deer. Black bears methodically search western mountain meadows for the young of both deer and elk.

There are several records of golden and bald eagles attacking both fawns and adult deer. These instances are so rare that they are only mentioned because of their oddity. Bald eagles often feed on deer that have been killed, particularly on the ice of lakes and rivers. I have seen this on a number of occasions. Michigan has a sizable wintering population of bald eagles, and the birds make good use of some of the deer that are killed on highways but are unfit for human consumption. These deer are placed out on the ice as feed for the eagles at the Seney National Wildlife Refuge.

In my experience, the oddest case of predation on deer was a case of mistaken identity, I am sure. In June of 1975, one of my neighbors phoned and asked me to rush over with my camera.

This neighbor and his son had been driving a tractor and a wagon in one of their fields about 10 a.m. on a clear, sunny day. Suddenly they noticed a great horned owl dive out of a tree and plunge onto something hidden in the high grass at the edge of the field. As the owl dived into the grass, a whitetail doe dashed out of the woods and attacked it, striking out with her forefeet. The bird had dived at the doe's fawn. The owl turned from its attack on the fawn to fight the doe but it stood no chance against the slashing hooves of the mother. The owl was knocked into the grass away from the fawn. The fawn, uninjured, scrambled to its feet, and both deer retreated into the woods. Then the neighbor called me.

I caught the owl without effort, as it was in no condition to put up any fight. The left wing, though not broken, must have been dislocated because it hung down and could not be used. Or the breast muscles may have been badly bruised. The doe's hooves had knocked clumps of feathers from the breast. There is no doubt that if the doe had continued her attack the owl would have been killed. My theory is that the owl mistook the back of the fawn for a cottontail rabbit.

Dogs probably take a greater toll of deer than all of the other predators combined. Many of the culprits are wild dogs that have been abandoned or have strayed and reverted to living in the wild. Some, however, are well-fed pets that chase and kill deer, following an innate desire for the hunt. Healthy adult deer can usually outrun healthy adult dogs when there is no snow or ice on the ground. It is during the time of deep snow or during the birthing period that the deer are most vulnerable.

I remember my first experience with wild dogs. It occurred in 1939 or 1940. The pack consisted of a huge Airedale, a German shepherd, a big, black mongrel, and two smaller, nondescript mongrels. The deer herd was just reviving after the decline in my area of New Jersey at that time, and the dogs wiped out the nucleus. They then turned their attention to sheep and cattle. The situation reached the point where the farmers feared for their families, and everyone kept a gun handy. After the dogs were finally killed, it took the deer two more years to repopulate the area.

In parts of the Deep South and parts of Canada, swamps are so extensive and the vegetation so thick that dogs are used for hunting deer. There is no other way to get the deer out of those areas, and the use of dogs does not guarantee anyone a deer. Hunters from other sections of the country should not condemn the use of dogs in the areas where they are being used legally, because terrain and vegetation enter the equation.

A wild dog feeds on a deer it killed.

John Sweeney, Larry Marchinton, and James Sweeney of the School of Forest Resources, University of Georgia, conducted extensive tests on radio-monitored deer to find the deer's reactions to being chased by dogs. This gives important insight into the behavior of deer, but three things must be stressed. The dogs used were the same type most commonly used by hunters in the South. They were dogs trained for tracking deer, not dogs trying to kill deer. They were well-fed dogs that did not depend on killing deer for food. Moreover, the conditions were favorable to the deer; they were not on a starvation diet, and there was no snow or ice.

These deer had all been trapped earlier and had radios attached to their collars. The researchers then radio-monitored each of the deer till they knew the animal's range, habits, and constant whereabouts. Then the dogs were turned loose on the deer repeatedly, and none of the deer was ever caught or injured by the dogs. I found the report fascinating because these researchers determined actions and reactions that had only been conjectural before radio transmitters were employed.

The escape-behavior of the deer was catalogued in five divisions: holding, long-distance running, circuitous zigzag running, separating from the group, and using escape habitat.

The dogs chased the deer for an average run of 33 minutes and covered 2.4 miles (3.86 kilom.). The longest run recorded was 13.4 miles (21.56 kilom.) for a time of 155 minutes. Where the deer population was high, the runs were short because the dogs kept switching to new deer as they encountered them.

Deer will take to water to elude pursuing predators.

Where water was available the deer used it, as it almost always stopped the chase. Although the deer could be chased out of their home ranges, they came back in a day or less.

In another study, conducted in California, Raymond Dasmann and Richard D. Taber found that the holding pattern of blacktails differed. Mature blacktail bucks in heavy cover would stand and fight off the dogs, whereas whitetails did not. They would lie still until they were sure the dogs were on their trail, then they ran.

When the deer ran in circles or mazes, it was found that they were usually does and fawns that were reluctant to leave their home areas. Bucks were more likely to take off at high speed and run in a more or less straight line. During the rutting season, bucks have a much larger range, so although the bucks may have been leaving the area they usually frequented, they were not really venturing into new territories.

A tired and panicked doe gulps air as she flees pursuers.

In running in circles, deer often crossed their old tracks or encountered other deer that laid down new tracks also. This pattern was very confusing to the dogs and threw them off the trail. It was found that when the pressure was taken off the deer for just a few minutes, they would stop and rest. They would run again only when they had to.

Studies of this type were also conducted in Virginia and in Arkansas. The report from Arkansas had this opening statement:

"The domestic dog, *Canis familiaris,* is the most abundant and widespread predator, or potential predator, of the white-tailed deer, *Odocoileus virginianus,* in North America."

Yet these studies, like those in Virginia, confirmed the finding of the earlier study done in Georgia that—in terms of actual effect on the deer population—the dog is *not* a major predator of deer. This is not as contradictory as it seems. The apparent acquittal of dogs as serious predators of deer applies only to certain regions and under special conditions, as will be seen in a moment.

Using radio-tracking and harassing the deer with packs of trained dogs, the Arkansas researchers found that the dogs were able to catch only 1.1 percent of the deer chased. They found that pregnant deer does did not abort their fawns after being chased. They also found that deer did not suffer ill effects from taking to cold water to escape the dogs after being heated up by running. It had often been stated that such deer were likely to get pneumonia. Not so, claim the researchers, and they have proved it. (However, they have proved it only for a region with a warm climate. Researchers in Vermont have verified that deer chased into the water in winter sometimes contract pneumonia.) The Arkansas biologists did conclude, as many others have, that predation by dogs is of a relatively "sanitary" type, weeding out the sick and unfit, because dogs are not as efficient predators as coyotes, wolves, and cougars.

The dogs used in these experiments were deer hounds that had been trained to follow deer and to bark while tracking so that the hunters would know where the deer were. This meant the deer also knew where the dogs were. The researchers were quick to point out that wild dogs may not bark or betray their presence to the deer. Moreover, I must stress again that dogs used in the experiment were trained *not* to kill deer; they were well-fed; and they were running the deer under conditions not adverse to the deer.

That wild dogs hunt differently, particularly in the North, shows up in the tallying of the kill. In 1969, Minnesota found that dogs killed more than four times as many deer as wolves and coyotes combined. These kills were made in January, February, and March, when snow, ice, and lack of food work against the deer. Conservation officers found that 519 kills were made by dogs, compared to 126 for wolves and coyotes.

In just one month, January of 1962, dogs killed 77 deer in Pennsylvania. Bear in mind that the figure given represents only *located* kills. At least that many must go unreported.

A report from Nova Scotia stated: "An alarming increase this year was noted in the number of dog kills. The known dog kills increased from 15 in 1974 to 53 in 1975."

In one three-year period, Vermont had 4,267 known dog kills. In 1969 there were 1,406; in 1970 there were 1,498; and in 1971 there were 1,363. The dog-kill figures dropped to 631 in 1972, to 541 in 1973, and down to 340 in 1974. Intrigued by the drop in the dog-kill rate, I phoned the Fish and Game Department in Vermont and talked to my friend Bob Candy, head of the Education and Information Division. Bob confirmed what I thought. The years 1971 and 1972 had exceedingly hard winters with up to eight feet of snow. The years 1973, 1974, 1975 had mild winters, easy on the deer.

In the years 1971 and 1972, the Vermont deer herd plummeted through starvation. The weakened survivors were easy prey for the dogs. Bob told me that the state game wardens claimed the kill figures represented only about a tenth of the damage actually done by the dogs. Many deer had been chased and had died of exhaustion, as was proved by the frothy blood filling the lungs. And many deer that were chased into the icy water developed bronchial illnesses such as pneumonia. They were in such poor condition that when they got soaked thoroughly they died. Often, in both cases, the dogs did not actually attack the deer but they had killed them anyway as a result of the chase.

The laws were changed in Vermont in 1970 to allow game wardens and their deputies to shoot dogs seen chasing deer for the period of December 1 through May 31. Prior to 1970, this had been permitted only from February 1 through April 30, so the new law extended control for an additional three months. Dog owners have no recourse to law if their dogs are shot while chasing deer. Many townships are now passing "leash" laws similar to those in New Jersey. This has also helped to curb dogs from running wild.

As Chief Gamekeeper of Conventry Hunt Club, I personally have had dog problems and have witnessed dogs pull down deer. We had too many deer on our club lands for the natural food available, despite wildlife food plantings and brush cutting. At that time we could not harvest the does. When New Jersey finally instituted a doe season, we were able to rectify the situation considerably.

In the 1950s and early 1960s, New Jersey had a lot of snow each winter. In the mid-60s, the jet stream changed our weather pattern. Prior to this, most of our storms came from the west. Now most of the storms swing south through Tennessee and up into Virginia, sweep up across south Jersey, and miss our area. Years ago, 24-inch snows were common. An adult deer is only 20 inches from the ground to its chest and six-month fawns are shorter. The deer could move through this snow depth only by leaping, which was exhausting. While the snow remained powdery, dogs could not move any better, but the weather in New Jersey seldom stayed cold enough to keep the snow powdery. The surface would soften on warm days and then freeze to a crust at night. The deer's sharp hooves would break through a crust that could support a dog, and the slaughter was on.

One family in our club owned big black mongrels that were a cross between a shepherd and black Labrador retriever. These dogs were seen pulling deer down. One day I found them eating the hind leg off a young deer. The deer was still alive, but too weak to get up. It lay there and watched the dogs eat its legs. The dogs ran at my approach but the deer could not be saved. Its anus and the inside part of the ham had been eaten. When I confronted the man who owned the dogs, I told him his dogs would have to be penned up or I

This doomed deer was too weak to rise after part of its hindquarters and one leg had been ripped by free-running pet dogs.

would get authority from the state to shoot them. He never knew how revealing his answer was: "I can't pen them up, they don't even come in to eat anymore."

The dogs were finally "controlled," not because of the deer damage but because they hit the owner where it hurts, in his pocketbook. The dogs were seen killing sheep and a young heifer belonging to a neighboring farmer.

The laws are anachronistic. If a man's prize bull, worth thousands of dollars, gets out and is killed by a car on a highway, the farmer must pay the car's owner for the damages. If a man's dog destroys that same farmer's bull in a pasture, or the public's deer, the dog's owner is not liable for the damages, legally, in most states. In most states, anyone shooting a dog for the destruction of personal property can be sued. These laws need changing.

In 1969 the State Board of Health in Georgia figured there were over three hundred thousand stray dogs in that state. There were several attacks by these wild dogs on people. Robert Nash, vice president of the Georgia Cattlemen's Association, stated that of 11,610 head of cattle destroyed by dogs and other predators in 1967, $888,058 worth of damage was done by dogs. The damage to the swine industry was $238,014 that year, for a total loss of $1,126,072 worth of cattle and hogs. The loss of deer could not be calculated, but Hubert Handy, chief of Georgia's Game Management Division, has said that the state's deer population of a hundred and twenty thousand would be 60 percent larger if it were not for the casualties inflicted on the deer herds by wild dogs.

I want to state here that I am not a hater of dogs. I love dogs. I raised springer spaniels for years. But I also love wildlife.

Throughout most of New Jersey, the dog problem has been alleviated, although not eliminated, by licensing and by prohibiting free-ranging dogs. Almost all townships also have dog wardens to take care of wild dogs. The most effective law is the one prohibiting dogs from running loose, though if dog owners all used good sense, there would be no need for such a law. People who profess to love their dogs should love them enough to want to know that their dogs are safe at home. Since dogs on private land can run loose when accompanied by the owner, there is no very severe restriction placed on either the dogs or their owners. Laws merely help ensure that the dogs are not free to kill deer during the winter, or to kill fawns in the spring. Even the researchers in Georgia, Virginia, and Arkansas had reservations about what the trained dogs, let alone wild dogs, would do to newborn fawns or to the adult does just prior to, during, or immediately after they gave birth.

Deer are quick to recognize when a dog is chained or penned up, and in that situation they are not frightened even if the dog barks.

There are also several records of the tables being turned and the deer attacking the dogs. Charles Laux of Freeport, Pennsylvania, was hunting raccoons one night when his hounds were set upon by a buck. The buck was slashing at the dogs with his feet and the dogs were jumping in and out trying to bite the buck. The fight moved into a small stream, and here the deer really began to work the dogs over. Using a front foot, he pushed one dog underwater. Every time the dog came up, the buck pushed him under again. Laux was afraid the buck would kill his dog, so he hit the buck over the antlers with his cane. The cane bounced back, hitting Laux on the chin and badly bruising him. The buck, tiring of the sport, shook his head and trotted off. Laux and his dogs were glad to see him go.

One of the most unfortunate aspects of the dog problem is that dog owners just can't believe, or don't want to believe, that their dogs would chase deer, let alone kill them. People with this attitude are not likely to cooperate by restraining their dogs unless forced to do so by the law. And then there is also the argumentative individual who feels his "rights" are being violated when his dog is not allowed to roam free to do as it likes. It is most unusual to encounter a person like one dog owner who was confronted by a Pennsylvania

District Game Protector and his deputy. The man's dog had been caught by the deputy running deer. When the conservation officers interviewed the man about his dog's deer-chasing activities, the man picked up his gun, went outside, and eliminated the problem.

One additional item should be mentioned in the relationship between the deer and its predators. The natural predators of the past, and those that still survive today, have been so efficient in controlling deer populations that the deer has never developed the intrinsic population controls exhibited by species such as the lemming, snowshoe hare, gray squirrel, etc. In areas where the natural predators are gone, man, the hunter, has to take up the slack because the deer can be its own worst enemy. Its breeding potential is such that without population control, destruction of the deer's range and habitat is inevitable.

# 15

## Life in Summer

It is summer. It is hot. In the Midwest the golden wheatfields are ripening. In the Corn Country the leaves of the corn are turning slightly upward and inward, thus reducing their exposed surface area in order to cut back the sun's evaporation of vital juices. The leaves will continue their gradual inward curling until the next hard rain makes such conservation measures unnecessary.

In the Southwest, the air is redolent with the odor of pine pitch that is slowly oozing from countless thousands of pines. Even the fragrance of the pine needles is masked by the sharp, raw smell of the pitch.

The temperatures soar in the Southwest until even the lizards do not venture out into the sun. Yet it is not unbearable if one can get in the shade. The rising heat thermals create a breeze, and the rapid evaporation makes sweating cool the body considerably. In the shade of the rim rock the deer are not uncomfortable.

At the higher elevations of the western mountains, the days are hot but the nights are cool. These mountains are probably among the most pleasant places to be at this time of year, and most big-game animals forsake the lowlands for the high country.

In the North Woods, across the continent, in summer, life seems to stand still. The growth taking place on all sides is discernible only in one's mind. The leaves hang apparently listless, yet they are all factories working at top speed and on double shifts in the long summer days. They are converting the sunshine into something wildlife can eat.

The heat makes the living easy. It is the one time of year when deer, even the does with their young, can take their ease. In the noonday heat there are no thoughts of the frigid winter to come, yet all of this growth is in preparation for the long, cold nights that will follow.

Daily, countless millions of living things die so that countless millions can live. The number of living things in the summer is so vast that those eaten are but a fraction of the total. Nature is lavish with seed and young.

## Infancy

Fawns are not ruminants at birth because they are on a milk diet. All that is needed for them to become ruminants is to consume vegetation; the proper symbiotic bacteria are already in their stomachs before they are born.

About ten years ago I was returning to my home from nearby Belvidere, New Jersey. It was about 11:00 a.m. on the last day of May, and the highway traffic was heavy. Four miles out of town, a doe dashed out of a roadside corn-field and tried to cross Route 46. A car ahead of me hit the deer broadside at about 50 miles an hour (80.4 kilom.). Glass and chrome flew and anti-freeze sprayed in all directions as the fan chewed through the radiator. The doe was ricocheted down the highway for perhaps 100 feet (30.5 m.). In my capacity as a deputy game warden, I stopped to be of assistance. Fortunately, the driver was uninjured, though the car was a wreck. The impact not only killed the doe, it burst her abdomen apart, spilling out her paunch, intestines, and two full-term fawns. I was driving a pickup truck, so I put the dead doe in the back. When I gathered up the two fawns, one of them moved. To keep the lit-tle fellow warm until I could dry him off, I put him back into his mother's body cavity. I made a brief stop at a garage to send back help for the motorist, then dashed home to care for the fawn.

When I got home I toweled the fawn dry and got some warm evaporated milk into him. I had always heard that fawns get their needed stomach bacte-ria from their mothers via the milk or by mouth contact. This fawn never saw another deer until long after he was a working ruminant, thriving on natural vegetation. That laid to rest another old myth.

When fawns are about three weeks old, they begin to follow after their

In early summer, fawns begin to amble about with their mothers, sampling vegetation.

mother. At this time they begin to sample all types of vegetation, either as a trial-and-error experiment or in imitation of the doe. At the age of four to five weeks, they are quite selective in what they eat, having already developed taste preferences, and they seek the plants they like. Fawns usually prefer broad-leaved forbs. At the age of three weeks, captive fawns begin, voluntarily, to take dry feed. At four weeks they also begin to drink water, although they still depend on milk for most of their liquid and food requirements. Fawns are usually weaned when they are four to five months old but research has shown that they are dependent on milk until they are least three months old. If fawns in the wild are orphaned after three months of age, they can probably survive. If orphaned before three months, they would undoubtedly die.

The speed of the weaning process depends on the individual doe. I believe most fawns would continue to nurse if their mothers permitted it, and some

Fawns more than one month old drink water, though they still depend on milk for most of their liquid and food requirements.

does do allow the young to continue long after they have lost their spots. I have often seen fawns nursing at six to seven months. Some mothers are simply more indulgent than others.

When a doe is trying to wean her fawn, she allows it to nurse for a short period and then walks off. What probably helps to prompt the weaning process is that the doe's milk production drops after the first two months. A two-month or older fawn has learned to nurse efficiently and it takes but a minute or so to empty the doe's udder. The fawn then butts the udder, trying to get more milk. This butting, combined with the fawn's larger teeth, hurts the doe and she just won't stand still. As the fawn's milk intake diminishes, the consumption of vegetation increases. At ten weeks, signs of wear begin to show on the premolars, indicating that the fawn is now chewing a cud and is a ruminant.

A short time after the doe gives birth to her new fawns, her yearlings rejoin her. If she has a yearling doe that also gave birth, the yearling will bring her fawn along to join the family group. It is not uncommon to see five or six does feeding as a group while their fawns play.

Play is a conditioning for later life. Most mammals engage in it, some more than others. Even if a fawn is by itself, it will suddenly run, buck, kick out, jump, and dash around in circles. Young fawns play tag, run races, and seem to have their own version of "king of the hill." Running and dodging helps to stretch and build muscles, increases lung capacity, develops reflexes, and stimulates the heart. And this is all training that will be used later for escaping

When the time for weaning approaches, does shorten nursing periods by walking off.

Even when the fawn is alone, it will engage in play sessions—jumping, bucking, and running.

from predators or other dangers. It is not done, however, in the manner of a training exercise. It is done with the exuberance and joy of living that accompany youth and well-being. Sometimes the does join in the play. Usually, however, the does watch for danger as the little ones play.

In working with deer—and other animals—throughout the country, I have noticed that when animals are very young, they are trusting. They have not yet learned fear. At two to three months, they become more wary but usually depend on their mothers to warn them of danger. But at four to five months, they are at the "bashful age." Paradoxically, they become wilder than the adults. This is particularly true in national parks or preserves where the animals are semi-tame but not in danger from humans. Time after time, I have noticed that the adults would stand and study me but the young would break and dash off. Whenever the young did this, it galvanized all of the animals into action. In a twinkling they were all gone. This inherent "wildness" is the quality that keeps wild animals wild.

Toward the end of August the fawns begin to lose their spots. Blacktails and mule deer wear their spots off at about eight to ten weeks, while whitetails lose their spots in twelve or more weeks. All of the deer begin to shed their thin, red summer coats in September and acquire their heavy, hollow-haired,

These blacktail fawns are in the process of losing their spots. Blacktails and muleys wear their spots off earlier than whitetails.

grayish-brown winter coats shortly thereafter. The fall molting takes much less time than the shedding of the winter coat in spring. In the fall, as in the spring, the difference in the number of daylight hours is the stimulus to molt — all controlled by the endocrine glandular system.

Deer don't sweat as we do, so they need another method of cooling off. To get rid of excess body heat, they breathe at a much faster rate than usual through their opened mouths, in the manner of a panting dog. The heat exchange takes place in the lungs, with the incoming cool air picking up the heat from the blood and the blood vessels, and the warm air being expelled. A very hot, late summer, after the deer have started to acquire their heavy winter coats, causes them to curtail their activities during the day.

## Foods and Minerals
A deer's home range is no larger than it has to be to meet its requirements for food, water, and shelter. This range is smallest in the summer in most sections of the country because the requirements are more easily met then. A

This blacktail buck is browsing on red alder leaves, a favored summer food. (For a list of preferred foods, see Appendix I.)

A young mule deer buck here eats ferns, a food that is also avidly sought by whitetails in many locales.

This whitetail doe is eating forbs and herbs. All three basic types of deer seek these foods in summer, and they also eat quantities of mushrooms.

deer, at any time of the year, is seldom more than 400 yards (365.8 m.) from cover, and in the summer cover is usually close on every side.

Food is usually extremely plentiful at this time, although the quality of some of the vegetation lessens as the plants mature. Weather is another important factor in the nutrition of plants. If the summer is cloudy or very rainy for long periods, the protein value of the growing plants lessens. Plants growing in woodlands where they become shaded when the leaves come out on the trees also lose protein value. This affects the whitetail deer in the forests but not the mule deer because the muley spends more time in open areas. The food of the blacktail deer of the Northwest is subject to more fog, clouds, and shade than the food of any other deer. A list of common, or preferred, summer foods for the three types of deer appears in Appendix I.

All of the deer, in all sections of the country, avidly eat nonpoisonous mushrooms. It has never been understood how they differentiate between the poisonous and nonpoisonous types. Many other animals, such as horses, also eat many mushrooms and avoid the poisonous ones. Red squirrels pick poisonous mushrooms but hang them up in tree branches until the poison leaches out of them. When mushrooms are available, they often form a high percentage of the deer's diet.

Deer evidently need the trace nutrient of nitrogen as they have a decided preference for nitrogen-fixing legumes such as alfalfa, clover, peas, soybeans and lupines.

I once saw a huge tree that had been struck by lightning; even the radial roots had been exploded and laid bare. Within a couple of days, the deer had eaten all the loosened soil from around the roots, evidently to get the nitrogen that had been concentrated in the roots by the lightning.

There has been much controversy, over the years, about putting out salt blocks for deer. It always smacked of illegality because shooting over salt was a traditional poacher's trick and some states still have laws on the books prohibiting the shooting of deer over salt. On two occasions, I have seen hunters putting out salt that they were going to stand over. One even had a bag of potato peelings mixed with the salt. They evidently thought the deer were all starved for salt and would smell salt and come running.

Deer do eat salt but the latest research shows that the need for it is greatly overrated. Again, it seems to be a taste preference. Deer come to salt, but I cannot say for certain whether they locate it by odor or just come across it while feeding and then remember the place and return for more. I believe they locate it by smell. Their need for it apparently varies with their diet. Most deer have easy access to salt put out for livestock. Few of the farms in northwestern New Jersey are being actively farmed today. The land lies idle or is

All deer seek salt and other minerals. Here a whitetail button buck licks a salt block.

used for horse pasture. New Jersey has more horses today than it had when horses were a major means of transportation. Almost every pasture has a horse in it and a salt block for the horse that is available to the deer.

I have noticed that deer usually do not lick the salt block itself but eat the salt-impregnated soil beneath the block. One summer, a Scout camp where I lived used a burro for pack trips. A salt block remained in the pasture after the burro was gone. The deer ate a hole into the earth that was 21 inches (53 cm.) deep by 24 inches (61 cm.) across. They also licked clean a handful of stones that they could not remove from the hole. The stones had to be pushed aside each time the deer wanted to eat the earth beneath.

In the wild country, all of the hoofed game animals frequent seeps and springs for all sorts of trace minerals in addition to salt.

Years ago, when the D. L. & W. Railroad still had tracks crossing the river at the Delaware Water Gap, railroaders kept a barrel of salt on the trestle to be used to keep a switch from freezing. Some of the salt leaked through the base of the barrel onto the ties. The deer in the area located this salt and would walk out on the open framework of bridge ties to lick the salt. This was very unusual because most hoofed mammals will not walk on anything with openings that their legs could go through. Horses, cattle, and even antelope will not cross the cattle-guards that are used out West instead of gates. Of course, the rails used in the cattle guards are narrower and more difficult to walk on than railroad ties.

A number of years ago a writer, who was not a naturalist or biologist, was researching an article on deer. She came across the fact that deer have been known to eat fish. This was the kind of "revealing" data she was looking for. Evidently interpreting her little discovery as having great significance, she wrote that does take their fawns down to the streams and teach them to kill suckers with their feet. One doe actually was seen catching suckers as described, and there have been additional records of deer eating fish—but fish are novelty items, not a standard bill of fare for deer.

Robert Dailey of Yorkshire, New York, reports a buck and a doe eating bluegills and perch that had been caught by ice fishermen thrown out on the ice. Severinghaus and Cheatum, in *Deer of North America*, tell of five instances of deer eating fish. Photographs are not always proof of something happening but Tom Rogers, Jr., of Altamont, New York, has a movie of a whitetail doe eating fish that he had tossed up on the bank of Lower Sargent Pond in New York.

The oddest example of food intake by a whitetail deer involved a 2½-year-old doe that was killed in Herkimer County, New York, in August, 1969. Pieces in her stomach proved that she had eaten a bird, a rufous-sided towhee. Undoubtedly the bird had just been killed when found by the deer. It was eaten as carrion.

A deer is not able to convert dry food into water (as many rodents do). Deer have a daily requirement of about 1½ quarts (1.4 liters) per hundred pounds (45.4 kg.) of body weight in the winter, and 2 to 3 quarts (1.9 to 2.8 liters) per hundredweight in the summer. Lack of water is definitely a limiting factor to the deer population in the desert areas of the Southwest. To compound the problem, the feral burros and wild horses are constantly increasing in those areas and often drive deer and wild sheep away from the few open waterholes.

Except in winter, much of a deer's water requirement is met by moisture in the vegetation it eats. Additional moisture is obtained from dew or rain water on the vegetation eaten. In winter, deer will eat snow or lick ice, particularly if all the free water is frozen over.

In summer, particularly in the north country, deer often feed in water. They eat a great many types of water plants, such as eel grass, but they particularly like the algae—the pond scum. I have often watched deer eating long strings of this green ooze. The algae is very nutritious, for it is high in protein.

Research in Ohio indicated that some deer may have died of algae poisoning

In summer, deer often feed in water. This whitetail doe is eating algae.

in 1933. I do not know what algae the Ohio deer were eating or if the pond water was contaminated. Deer do not eat the flat, thick sheets of algae floating on the surface. They prefer the gauzy, filamentous type that floats suspended in the water. It is the same algae that beaver and moose eat so readily.

Deer also feed in the water in an attempt to get relief from hordes of stinging, biting, blood-sucking insects that can make much of the forest a nightmare. While the deer may get some relief, they also have a chance to encounter serious trouble as they inadvertently pick up snails in the water. Among the parasites that infect deer, some of the most troublesome are transmitted by snails.

**Parasites**

Deer are infested, and infected, by a great number of parasites. The larger the deer population and the more deer are crowded onto a range, the more parasites are transmitted from one animal to another. On overcrowded ranges, where there is malnutrition, the impact of the parasites on deer herds is greater. Research with domestic livestock, as well as deer, has proved that when animals receive sufficient nutrition parasites are a nuisance but not a decimating factor. Thus, again, proper nutrition is a key to survival.

Deer are subject to all the discomforts imposed upon all wild creatures by deer flies, black flies, midges, and mosquitoes. From personal experience, I know the extreme discomfort and even agony that these insects can inflict. In

Photographed in Alberta at an elevation above 8,000 feet, this muley keeps to higher elevations to escape insects.

the rain forests of southeastern Alaska, or during the fly season in New York's Adirondack Mountains, repellents, headnets, and gloves are survival equipment. The deer have no recourse but to seek relief in water or escape to the highest windswept elevations. George Wright found a buck mule deer on Mount Kaweah in Sequoia National Park, California, at 12,750 feet (3,886 m.). That is the highest recorded elevation for deer that I can find. I have seen mule deer above 8,000 feet (2,438 m.) in the Waterton Mountains of Alberta, Canada.

I will never forget a photograph I saw in *National Geographic* magazine many years ago, in which black flies had eaten away the eyelids of a moose. I have seen large scabs where black flies had eaten large sores on the hind legs of both moose and deer. The deerflies are also very annoying. In the summer almost every whitetail deer that I see has a bloody spot on the bridge of its nose where these flies seem to concentrate their biting. A deer's tail is useless as a fly whisk. The deer have to rub the flies off by scraping against vegetation or by using their feet.

The nose botfly (*Cephenemyia phobifer*) is found in about 10 to 15 percent of all whitetail deer. It is also a parasite of both blacktail and mule deer, but the percentage is not as high. The botfly is a bee-like insect. Female flies lay eggs around a deer's nostrils and they even crawl into the nasal passages. I

This whitetail buck is scratching an irritation caused by flies.

have seen deer try to thwart these flies by snorting wildly, closing the nostrils, or brushing them away with a front foot. When the flies are attacking, the deer will stand with their heads almost touching the ground, snorting and pawing. Then they often dash off at top speed for a hundred feet or so.

When the fly's eggs hatch, the larvae crawl up the nasal passages and into the pouch — the nasopharynx — above the soft palate on the rear of the roof of the deer's mouth. Feeding on the deer's mucus, the larvae develop into yellowish grubs over an inch (25 mm.) in length. In the spring, these worms crawl back out of the nose or are snorted out in irritation by the deer. After about two months, the worms develop into adult flies that mate and go forth to infest other deer. The irritation of dozens upon dozens of these worms crawling around inside a deer's head, where they cannot be reached or scratched, is a torment we can only imagine.

Wood ticks imbed their heads in a deer's skin and become bloated with blood.

Prior to 1958, the screwworm (*Callitroga americana*) took a devastating toll of deer across the southern half of the United States. The screwworm fly lays its eggs in cuts or wounds in warm-blooded creatures. Newborn livestock and deer were particularly susceptible, for these flies would lay eggs in their navels. They also infested sores made by ticks.

It was estimated that in Texas the screwworms wiped out 80 percent of the annual fawn crop. In Florida, the deer herd increased 60 percent after a screwworm-eradication program went into effect.

The U. S. Department of Agriculture and state agricultural and game departments collaborated in a program that raised millions upon millions of infertile screwworm flies. After the captive screwworm eggs hatched, the larvae were exposed to a cobalt treatment that sterilized them. Sterilized adult flies were then released by airplane all over the infested areas. These flies mated with the native flies and, of course, no fertile larvae were produced in the wild. Thankfully, the screwworm has now been brought under control in the United States.

Many kinds of ticks are found throughout the country and they can make life miserable for both man and beast. At times they can kill. In 1968, researchers found that the Lone Star tick was killing an estimated 25 to 50 percent of all whitetail fawns in eastern Oklahoma alone. They found as many as 1,300 ticks on one three-week-old fawn. The ticks usually concentrate around the eyes, ears, and mouth, though they can be found on all parts of the body; 20 percent of the fawns go blind. The fawns' flesh literally dies from a toxin injected by the ticks in their blood-sucking, and this opens the way to more infection.

Whitetail bucks here engage in mutual grooming. Bucks often bite pests off one another.

Cooperation between cattlemen and the game departments has led to better control of ticks. Cattle are dipped in vats of insecticide. Killing the ticks that the cattle pick up reduces the number of ticks available to infest deer. The cattle can be dipped every month or so and, in effect, they serve as sponges to "soak up" the ticks. In addition, treated food is put out. Both cattle and wild deer get food pellets to which a systemic insecticide has been added. This gets into the animals' blood stream and renders their blood toxic to the ticks. Much work remains to be done on this problem, but great strides have been made.

Groups of does are almost always larger than groups of bucks, yet I find less social grooming among the does than among the bucks. Although does are

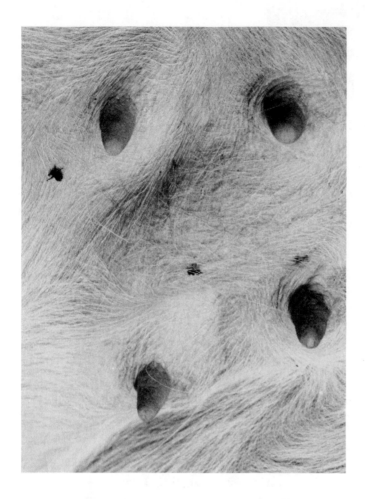

Here are blood-sucking deer-louse flies on a doe's udder.

always cleaning their fawns, adult does seldom tolerate one another's ministrations. I have, on a number of occasions, watched two adult bucks groom each other, concentrating on biting ticks off. It is almost impossible for deer to get ticks off their own necks and heads, generally the areas most heavily infested. The deer often try to dislodge the ticks by scratching them, usually with a hind foot, but the most efficient method is mutual grooming.

The deer-louse flies, *Lipoptena depressa* and *Neolipoptena ferrisi,* are almost universally found on blacktail deer, and often on mule deer and whitetails. These pests seem to cause no real harm but are another blood-sucking annoyance. The adults have wings, which they lose when they are established on a host. From that time on they get around by crawling, and all too frequently a hunter becomes the temporary host when he is dressing or handling a deer.

A California mule deer licks an itch
caused by parasites.

Louse flies do not become established on humans but they can give one a
"crawly" feeling. Some blacktail deer have been known to have as many as
2,000 louse flies on them during the heavy, early-summer infestation.

Lice of various kinds are also found on deer but, again, they seem to be a
nuisance rather than a threat.

Internally, deer are parasitized by a vast array of worms. There are lungworms, brainworms, throat worms, eye worms, foot worms, round worms,
flat worms. There are specialized worms that show up in almost all parts of
the body. Most of these worms are usually of no great importance, but some
are deadly.

The lungworms, *Leptostrongylus alpanae,* are probably the most common to
infest deer. They are very similar to the cattle lungworm, *Dictyocaulus
viviparus,* which the deer may also have. As many as 40 percent of the deer
may be infested. The female lungworms lay hundreds of eggs in the tissues of
the lungs. Heavy infestations create damage to the deer's lungs, causing bronchial infections, often resulting in pneumonia. After hatching, the larvae crawl
up the bronchial tubes to the trachea, where they are swallowed by the deer
and pass out of the body with excrement. The larvae infest snails, which are
afterward eaten by deer, completing the cycle.

Liver flukes, *Fascioloides magna,* are another parasite dependent upon snails as an intermediary host. This is a parasite very often picked up by deer when they are eating waterplants. Needless to say, it is not a parasite of any importance in desert regions, but it is most prevalent in the mountainous or wooded areas of the North. About 65 percent of the northern whitetails are infected.

At one time I thought it odd that deer would be eating so many snails, but that was before I ate a great deal of watercress. In some of the springs where I pick watercress, I have found hundreds of snails fastened on a couple of dozen plants. Although I now carefully clean the watercress, I've probably also swallowed a few snails now and then. After my experience with the snails, I can see how easily the parasites of deer are transmitted via snails.

Liver flukes look very much like fresh-water leeches. Flat and brown, they may be 3½ inches (8.5 cm.) long and 1½ inches (3.7 cm.) wide. They form pockets, or holes, in the liver and are usually discovered when the hunter slices the deer's liver to eat it. At times the liver may be so badly infested that it is mushy. This can cause a deer's death. The eggs of the liver fluke are passed out of the deer's body through the intestinal tract. The eggs hatch in ponds and lakes, and the larvae then infest the water snails. After further development, these larvae pass from the snail's body and attach themselves to the stems of water plants. The larvae develop a protective coating while they wait for the plant to be eaten. When a deer eats the water plants, it ingests the parasites. The protective coating of the larvae dissolves in the deer's stomach, and the larvae make their way to the liver to complete their adult development. Liver flukes are also found in sheep and cattle. Fortunately, they do not infest humans.

The deer brainworm, *Pneumostrongylus tenius,* also uses snails or slugs as an intermediary host. The whitetail deer picks up the worm by ingesting an infected snail or slug along with the grasses it is feeding upon. Once inside the deer's stomach, the worm's larvae leave the snail, go through the stomach wall, and get into the abdominal membranes. Traveling through the tissue, the larvae move up and get into the deer's spinal cord. The worms work their way up the spinal column and continue their development. In about forty days they emerge, as adult worms, in the spaces around the brain. There they breed and lay eggs in the tissue. The eggs and larvae pass into the bloodstream and the lungs. The larvae break through the tissue into the air sacs of the lungs and are coughed up into the deer's mouth. They are then swallowed and pass out of the deer's body with the feces onto vegetation, where they again infest snails to complete the cycle.

Brainworms are not fatal to whitetail deer because whitetails have been exposed to them for eons and have built up a resistance to them. However, it has now been proved that, because of these worms, whitetail deer should not inhabit the same territory as moose. Brainworms are fatal to the moose. This discovery was made in 1963 by a Canadian biologist, Dr. Roy C. Anderson. Elk, caribou, and mule deer may also succumb, but less often than the moose.

Brainworms infest 41 to 81 percent of all whitetail deer. Each female worm produces several thousand first-stage larvae which are passed off through the feces. The moose then eats infested snails, or vegetation upon which snails have deposited these larvae. When the larvae attack the moose's brain, the moose becomes disoriented, loses its fear of humans, aimlessly wanders about, goes blind, loses muscle control, becomes paralyzed, and finally dies.

In area after area, as the whitetail deer increased its range, the moose population crashed. In some areas today there seems to be a lessening of fatalities among moose that have contact with the deer. The moose, in time, may build up a resistance to the brainworms. Fortunately, moose and deer prefer different foods and have different habitat requirements.

In the deer's stomach there are round worms, flat worms, and pin worms. Most of these do little actual harm except in times of stress. Many species have evolved in such a way that they now draw sustenance directly from the deer's own food supply rather than from the deer's tissues or blood. These worms are present in about 81 percent of all deer.

## Diseases

In 1924, infected livestock transmitted hoof and mouth disease to the blacktail deer in Tuolumne County, California. Both the cattle and the deer were shot in an effort to curb this very infectious disease. Of the 22,214 deer that were killed, 10 percent were found to be infected. Thankfully, this disease has not been a problem to deer since then, mainly because of improvement in control of the disease among cattle.

In August, 1955, a highly fatal disease swept through the deer herds in Morris, Essex, and Somerset counties in New Jersey. The deer that had this disease appeared to be in a state of shock, and all of the deer that exhibited symptoms died. They completely lost their fear of man and usually lay on the ground with their necks outstretched and their ears drooping. Their summer coats were very rough. When they got up, they staggered around. They were all running a high fever, and most of the carcasses were found in or near water where the deer had gone to alleviate their heat. So far as was known, this disease had not been encountered before.

Dr. Richard Shope of the Rockefeller Institute for Medical Research led an investigation, aided by Les MacNamara and Bob Mangold. The autopsied deer all exhibited identical symptoms. All of the organs showed evidence of rup-

tured blood vessels and hemorrhaging. Most of the organs were heavily discolored—purplish-black with accumulated blood. There were also accumula-
tions of blood in the groin area and in the intestines. A clear, straw-colored
liquid was present in the abdominal cavity and the heart sac.

An extensive research program was pushed through, combining the forces of
the New Jersey Game Department, Department of Health, Department of Agriculture, and State Police. It was thought at first that the deaths were being
caused by poisonous agricultural sprays.

When several sick deer were kept in a pen with healthy deer, the healthy
ones did not contract the disease and everyone breathed a little easier because
it proved that the disease was not infectious. Injections of ground tissue from
deer that had died of the disease produced illness and death in the experi-
mental deer. It then became known that the disease was transmitted via some
biting vector, such as flies or mosquitoes. Even to this day, the vector has not
been identified. With the first frost, all evidence of the disease vanished.

Continued investigation showed that the illness was caused by a filterable
virus. Research also showed that it could not be transmitted to other animals
or birds, nor could it be transmitted to man. As this was the first time the disease had been encountered, the research team simply named it Epizootic Hemorrhagic disease of deer.

Hundreds of deer died from the disease that year, and many of the carcasses
were not found at the time because of rapid deterioration caused by the summer heat. The disease has since been found in many other states. It is always
connected with an overpopulation of deer. Recently, in James City County in
Virginia, a couple of hundred deer died in one season. Parts of North Carolina
have annual outbreaks in areas restricted to "bucks-only" seasons. States that
have regular doe days, or where a good part of the entire deer population is
harvested, are relatively free of the disease. Dr. Frank Hayes of the College of
Veterinary Medicine, University of Georgia, encourages the hunting of deer
during outbreaks of the disease to lower the deer population to healthy levels.
Since there is no danger to man, Georgia, North Carolina, Arkansas, and
South Carolina regularly conduct normal hunting operations during outbreaks.

The hemorrhagic disease hit New Jersey hard again in August of 1975. A
total of 358 deer are known to have been killed by this disease, and, again,
many carcasses must have gone undetected. The hardest-hit area in the state
was the township where I live. It had not been uncommon to see up to a
hundred deer at a time in some of the fields on neighboring farms. The deer
did not suffer much from starvation because the biggest gun club in the area
had an extensive winter feeding program. So lack of natural food had no
chance to be a population check, but overcrowding, produced by the artificial

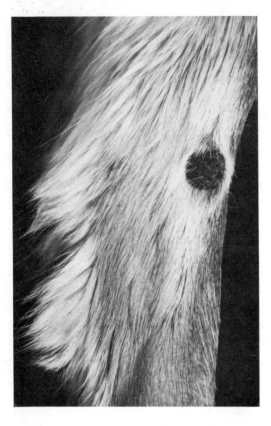

Papilloma is a warty skin growth caused by viral infection.

feeding, was checked by the disease. To compound the problem, the club did not allow hunting in the fall of 1976, which would have brought the herd to a more healthy level. The best and most efficient check on this disease is a greater harvest of deer in areas threatened with the overpopulation that over-protection brings.

In 1960 another new disease — one transmissible to man — was discovered in New York State. The disease produced boils and lesions on deer. Four of the people handling infected deer also developed small boils on their skin. The boils were not painful, and most of them and the resulting scabs disappeared in a week or two. There were no other ill effects to the persons who contracted this disease. Research showed that the causative agent was a *Dermatophilus,* meaning "lover of skin." This disease has been found in both wild and domestic animals in South America, Europe, Africa, Asia, and Australia. It had been encountered only once before in the United States, on domestic animals in Texas. The disease, known as *Streptothricosis,* is not considered a threat.

This is a benign fibroma tumor on a whitetail.

Deer sometimes exhibit benign tumors known as papillomas, fibromas, and lipomas, which are caused by viral infection, cannot be transmitted to man, and are seldom very injurious to the deer. Papillomas are the form most frequently seen and, even so, less than 1 percent of the deer have these tumors. They are hard, warty growths on the skin, ordinarily ranging from one to a dozen or more and from the size of a marble to the size of a golf ball or even a bit larger. Almost every year, newspapers and sporting and conservation magazines carry photographs of deer with encrusted areas of papillomas, but unless the growths become massive they do not incapacitate a deer. When a deer is skinned the growths come off with the hide, and the meat underneath is both safe to eat and as tasty as the rest. Cattle also have papillomas, but of a different type, and the growths are not transmitted from livestock to deer or vice versa.

The fibromas are less often seen. They develop lesions that look as if a scab had been knocked off. Fibromas do not affect a deer's meat. The lipomas are very rare. They are tumors found in the deer's fatty tissues.

Deer, like most animals, are afflicted with many other viral, bacterial, and parasitic ailments, but those I have described are the most important, and they are the ones most likely to be encountered by the layman.

Research has shown that during the period when bucks are becoming sexually mature, at the end of summer, they are more susceptible to disease. The physiological changes taking place within their bodies are somehow connected to a lowering of their resistance.

This whitetail buck has bedded in high grass while he chews his cud. Lush summer growth makes long feeding periods unnecessary, and bucks seldom move about much while the sun is visible.

## Activities

The habits of all deer change because of the heat. Now they feed primarily at night. The does and fawns may come out just before sunset, their shadows covering long distances on the ground. The bucks are seldom seen while the sun is still visible. The deer feed heavily for a couple of hours at dusk. They seldom have to feed long, because this is the season of abundance. They will then probably bed down in the fields or clearings where they have been feeding because the vegetation is high and affords excellent protection. There is a heavy feeding period around midnight to 1:00 a.m., and another that begins just before dawn. The deer will feed until the sun is up, but when the temperature gets above 60°F. they head for shady cover. All of them head for brush but mule deer do not seek out the heavy stands of brush that the blacktail and whitetail favor. Over much of the mule deer's range, such heavy cover is not to be found. I have often watched mule deer, lying under pine trees or in the

Long daylight hours stimulate a hormonal surge. This muley, pictured in midsummer, has fully developed antlers still in velvet.

shadow of upturned rocks, get up and move several times during the day as the sun's progress pulled the shade away.

Comparative inactivity during periods of high temperature lessens the requirements on the deer's body. The does are nursing their fawns, the fawns are converting their food to body growth, and the adult bucks have about completed their antler development.

In midsummer, the buck's antlers have reached their maximum growth. The long daylight hours have spurred the pituitary gland's stimulation of the testicles. As the testicles begin to increase in size and drop down into the scrotum, the male hormone, testosterone, is produced and the first live sperm is formed in the semen. It is this hormone that causes a buck's antlers to harden and causes the velvet to dry up.

The middle of summer causes a tremendous upheaval in the life of the deer in California and Alaska, because the hunting season opens. I have spent four summers in Alaska, where the hunting seasons open early because the summers are so short. I have encountered lots of ice and snow there in August. I was surprised to find that California's season opened in the summer, however, especially in view of the fact that the weather is so hot that keeping the meat from spoiling can be a problem.

The biologists I questioned said that tradition was the main reason for the early California season; the deer have always been hunted there at that time. But there are better reasons. The blacktail deer and many of the mule deer in California are at their greatest body weight in midsummer. The vegetation dries very rapidly in late summer due to the lack of rain. Both the protein content and the digestibility of the vegetation drop, and so does the weight of the deer. And bucks taken prior to the rut do provide better meat. During the rut, the bucks lose a lot of weight and their muscles are tougher because of the constant running after does.

Evidently, California hunters are used to hunting while it is hot, though hunters in most sections of the country associate deer hunting with cold weather. The early season has some disadvantages. If a deer is shot but lives long enough to move a considerable distance, particularly in heavy cover, it may have been dead for hours by the time the hunter finds it. On a very hot day, the meat may be getting "high" by then. Furthermore, I think most hunters would agree that hunting is harder before the rut because the bucks are more cautious, more wary than when they are preoccupied with the urge to mate. The major disadvantage, it seems to me, is that most hunters prefer trophy bucks, the bucks that do most of the breeding. It has to be detrimental to the deer herd to remove the finest bucks from the gene pool prior to the breeding season.

Arizona, Colorado, Nevada, South Carolina, and Utah follow California, opening their hunting seasons during the latter part of the summer.

With his antlers hardened and the testosterone coursing through his body, a buck's maleness asserts itself. The most apparent change is in his increased activity and aggressiveness. All spring and for most of the summer, bucks are shy and retiring because, in effect, they have been neutered by Nature. But now, instead of seeking to avoid hitting the brush with their antlers, the bucks seem bent on subduing all the bushes and saplings in their area.

The velvet is usually (though not always) stripped from the antlers within a twenty-four-hour period, but I have noticed that most of the stripping is not done in a single night. Usually, some of the velvet is peeled off the first night so that the tips of the tines can be seen. Most of this stripping activity must

By summer's end in most latitudes, velvet dries and begins to peel from antlers.

be nocturnal, because I have only been able to get a couple of photos of deer with partially peeled antlers. After the second night, the brown, bloodied antlers are usually fully exposed, although some strips of velvet may still hang from parts of the antlers, usually at the base.

A buck is very thorough in removing the velvet. Picking a resilient sapling, he rubs his antlers lengthwise along the trunk. He does this in between the tines, on the inside of the antler's curve, and on the outside. He even turns his

Like a boxer training, this buck "spars" with a tree as he polishes his antlers.

head sideways, parallel to the ground, to try to get the velvet completely off the antler bases. Frequently, bucks become very excited during this procedure. The more they rub, the more it stimulates them. The rubbing becomes faster, and the pushing harder, and the bucks really start to "work out" on the brush.

Joe Taylor told me of a buck on his preserve that completely removed the velvet from his antlers in about ten minutes. The buck's actions were frenzied. He started to peel the velvet by rubbing against a sapling, then whirled and rubbed against the fence, then back to the sapling again. All of this was done with considerable force and great speed. This animal was the dominant buck on Joe's preserve and in excellent condition, and he peeled early. Joe thought the buck was actually peeling a little *too* early because more blood was visible on the velvet and the antlers than he had ever seen on any other buck. It is usual for the biggest, best-conditioned, dominant bucks to peel first. Joe told me he has also seen a couple of the bucks take three days to get the velvet off.

Some bucks seem to have a favorite rubbing tree, and most of them seem to have a favorite area. This rubbing and fighting with the bushes is done far more often than most people suspect. In a short time, many saplings and bushes in many areas will bear the bright, white scars of buck rubs. People who think that bucks rub trees only to get the velvet off may get an erroneous impression that there are far more bucks in the area than there really are. Most bucks will scar many saplings in the process of getting ready for the rutting season. They attack the trees in much the same way a fighter attacks a punching bag when he goes into training.

246

# 16

## Life in Autumn

The full moon never seems as big, as full, as it does in autumn. Perhaps this is due to the clarity of the night air now that the chill has erased the haze of summer. Perhaps it is because this is the reason for fullness. This is the time when most living creatures enjoy the fullness of life, the season when the growth of most living things in the Northern Hemisphere reaches a climax. The fruit trees have yielded their fruit, although some apples may remain to be picked. The nut-producing trees, if it has been a good mast year, are raining down their seeds. Most of the wild vegetation is slowing its pace, its growth being consolidated.

For the broad-leafed trees, one job remains. They must drain their plumbing system before the winter freeze. Moisture is recalled from each leaf, each twig, each branch, and from the trunk for storage underground. If this moisture were not removed, the trees would freeze and split during cold weather. Residual sugars, or the lack of them, will determine the color of the leaves. The brilliant leaves of the sweet-sap trees set the forest afire in a blaze of color. Even those trees that had bitter or tannic acid in their veins produce a variety of browns to delight the eye with their subdued, somber hues.

While things of the plant world have passed their peak of activity, autumn is a frenetic time for the things of the animal world. Many of the birds have gone south, not in quest of summer warmth but in response to diminishing light, the prod that sends them to southern climes where their stomachs can be filled. Most of those that feed on insects have already left the North. All summer the woodchucks have been feasting, and now, with their days of activity numbered, they compulsively gorge themselves. The woodchucks are not alone. The raccoons and bears cannot escape winter by hibernating, as the woodchuck will, and they frantically consume everything edible in an attempt to layer the fat upon their bodies to sustain them during their periods of inactivity. The raccoon will actually consume a third of its body weight in food each day if it can get it.

Deer are said to be crepuscular creatures, because their periods of greatest activity take place just before and after sunrise and sunset. More deer are active before dawn than after and more are active after sunset than before—particularly the bucks. Their daily activities are greatly influenced, however, by the weather and the phase of the moon. A heavy shower or thunderstorm will cause them to seek temporary shelter, though a protracted rain will not. If you see deer out feeding during a hard shower, you can count on the storm lasting several days. If they are seen feeding much earlier in the afternoon than normal, it is because the night will be dark and stormy. Deer will also feed earlier if the moon is in the new phase and the light at night will be minimal. Deer can see well in the dark but they curtail their activities during the darkest nights. Conversely, they may not come out until after dark on the nights of the full moon, as they can then feed freely all night. A full moon also makes deer more nervous, as it deprives them of their protective cover of darkness.

## Food

I am not sure whether deer feed more compulsively in spring or in autumn. The early spring feeding is an attempt to rebuild the bodies that, in some cases, did little more than harbor the flickering light of life. It is certain that they consume much more food in autumn simply because so much food is available. The bounty of the year is theirs. They eat compulsively because they know instinctively that this period of plenty is brief, and if they do not take advantage of it they may forfeit their chance of survival. It takes so little to blow out the light of life.

I can state unequivocally that, in the northeastern, central, and southern regions of the United States, acorns when available are the number one whitetail food. There are times when acorns comprise 80 percent of the diet. When

This whitetail buck feasts on acorns—a favorite food in autumn and winter.

the acorns drop, deer forsake their regular haunts and most of the other available foods to feast on these succulent brown nuts. Although they will eat all kinds of acorns, the deer of my area have a decided preference for white-oak acorns, which are sweeter than others. White acorns contain the least amount of tannic acid. Time after time, people who were used to seeing deer feeding in old orchards on the dropped apples, or in corn fields, have asked me where the deer had disappeared to. They had not disappeared; they were just concentrating on acorns. When deer feed in the orchards or fields they are easily seen but they are not usually seen while feeding in the woodlands. When the acorns drop, deer stay in the woods and up on the hilltops. They need not travel because the acorns are in their bedding areas.

The whitetail is not alone in this taste preference. Acorns are very important to both the mule deer and blacktail, as well. These nuts are more prominent in the blacktail's diet than in the mule deer's, however, because the muley spends much of its time in areas too high for oaks to grow.

Not all oaks produce a good crop every year and not all of the oaks drop all of their acorns every year. Species belonging to the white-oak group will produce and drop mature nuts each year. Those of the red oak group take two years to produce mature nuts. Quite often some of the "baby acorns" fall off the tree in their first year, but the difference between these and the mature nuts is instantly apparent. An individual white-oak tree seems to produce a heavy mast crop every third year, while some other trees, such as the rock oak, have a more sustained yield. Some trees just seem to be cyclic. Rainfall, heat, and the length of the growing season also affect mast production. Sometimes the quantity of acorns varies greatly in adjoining localities.

I have my own rough way of estimating the relative production of the mast crop. I wear size 11½ boots. When the nuts have fallen, if I put my foot down and cover nine acorns with one shoe, that's a good crop. When I cover a dozen, that's a fantastic crop.

In one area, the Pennsylvania Game Commission found that the 1975 acorn production was 8 pounds per acre, and in 1976 it reached 528 pounds per acre. Wild turkeys have been seen following after the deer to feed on the acorns that are missed when the deer paw down through the snow.

According to old-timers, a heavy nut crop foretells a hard winter. The old-timers may be right. The extremely good crop in 1976 was followed by an extremely cold winter, and I have seen the same thing happen before.

In my area, the deer eat all the acorns they can get, but in a preferred order. White oak acorns are eaten first, then the acorns of the pin, the red and the black, the scrub oak, and finally the large rock oak. Although the rock oak belongs to the white-oak group—and produces the largest acorns—deer simply do not have as great a liking for this species as for the others.

H. R. Gilbert and G. H. Hart tested the chemistry of the acorns eaten by Columbian blacktail deer and found that the preferred acorn, that of the California black oak, has only 1.9 percent tannin; it has 4.3 percent protein and 14.7 percent fat. The interior live-oak acorn has 5 percent tannin, 3.5 percent protein and 17.8 percent fat. In autumn, acorns make up 53 percent of this deer's diet. A surprising discovery was that in the month of May acorns form 83 percent of the blacktail's diet.

The California chaparral has countless thousands of oak trees, but they do not compare in number, size, and productivity with the oaks of the eastern two-thirds of the continent. Competition for acorns is always keen, but more so in California; the dropping of an acorn sets off a race between the deer, the squirrels, and the acorn woodpeckers.

All acorns have a low protein content but they are all high in fats and starches. They also have the advantage of being easily digestible, and their nutrients are readily absorbed. Without loosening a deer's bowels, acorns are processed and passed through the body in a very short time. This allows the deer to consume greater quantities of acorns per day than it would of other foods, which raises the daily protein intake. Conversion of the fats and

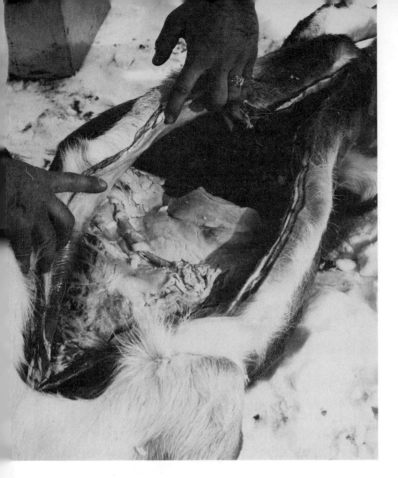

Enormous fat reserves can be seen in the body cavity of this deer, being hog-dressed.

starches to the deer's body fat is very rapid. You can almost see the deer putting on weight. In adults, substantial supplies of body fat are built up in less than two weeks. The first fat is stored beneath the skin, over the back and hams. Then the fat is stored under the belly skin and in the abdominal cavity around the organs. Then skeins of fat, looking like a fish net, envelop the intestines. The deer literally become "hog-fat."

Adult deer, having attained their full body growth, are able to convert to fat all of this high caloric intake that is above the needs of their basic metabolism. Young deer are still producing muscle, bone, and tissue. Their growth rate does not slow down until late in autumn, so they fatten at a much slower rate.

The feeding competition among wildlife is keen. In good mast years, the competition really doesn't matter, but in poor mast years every acorn counts. Poor years may be the limiting factor in the establishment of some wildlife populations, particularly the wild turkey. The turkey population is slowly expanding over much of the United States, but poor mast years and deep snows combined have, on several occasions, wiped out nucleus flocks.

Domestic pigs are allowed to roam free in most of the southern states, and

A whitetail buck here feeds on red maple, a preferred food. Other autumn foods are listed in Appendix I.

in many of these states there are now many herds of feral pigs. North Carolina and Tennessee also have herds of European wild pigs. Since pigs like acorns, pigs are among the deer's main competitors for them.

Squirrels of all kinds, bears, and raccoons all fatten on mast. The death of the American chestnut some fifty years ago robbed all wildlife, as well as humans, of untold thousands of bushels of nuts each fall. Hickory trees are steady producers of mast, but beechnut trees are not. The beechnut is a very sporadic producer, although the nuts are avidly sought by all wildlife because they are so sweet. Pecans are important mast producers in the South. Walnut trees produce abundantly but the deer do not eat the hard-shelled nuts; they are left for the squirrels. Even the squirrels gather and store acorns before they turn to using walnuts. It is as if they know the walnuts will still be around when the acorns are gone. Or perhaps squirrels dislike working that hard to get a little nut meat.

Autumn's bounty includes a great many other foods that are avidly sought by one or more of the three types of deer. These preferred foods are listed in Appendix I.

In addition to the wild foods, the deer in some areas feed heavily on such cultivated crops as alfalfa, clover, soybeans, corn, and apples. Most of the corn and apples are the gleanings—dropped apples and the corn missed by the mechanical pickers. Orchards, at all times of year, are good places to look for deer. Except when the trees are young, deer do not cause much damage by browsing, but the bucks do cause great damage by rubbing the one-inch (2.5 cm.) saplings.

This doe and fawn are gleaning dropped apples, another favorite food.

Just as humans get indigestion from overeating, so do deer. The proper name for it is rumen overload, or rumenitis, or the old farmers' term "bloat." This happens when deer suddenly get too much high-carbohydrate food such as corn, sugar beets, grapes, pears, or wheat. Ordinarily, apples drop from the trees a few at a time and, with a number of deer eating them, not too many are consumed by each deer. Then along comes a high wind and the apples are dashed to the ground by the bushel. The deer then eat far more than is good for them and get indigestion.

When apples and pears drop to the ground, they usually are badly bruised and the skin splits open, allowing air to get inside the fruit. When such fruit

Most fawns are weaned by late summer, but some does are indulgent mothers. This one is allowing her hefty fawn to nurse in midautumn.

lies in the sun, it begins to ferment. Some claim deer become intoxicated on the fermented fruit. I have never seen it happen nor have I read of it, but it is possible. Birds are known to get drunk on fermented berries. Bees, bears, and cows also get drunk on fermented apples. My family once had a Jersey cow that got so drunk she could not stand up.

A very important food, particularly for whitetails in the Northeast, is provided by autumn's falling leaves. The preferred dry leaves are the same kinds that are preferred when green. Maples are among the most important, but dogwood leaves seem to have top priority. Deer will eat the leaves when they are quite dry but prefer those with some moisture still in them and, for that reason, they will eat those leaves that are falling rather than those that dropped off a few days previously. Times without number, I have watched deer walking through the woods in autumn leisurely feeding on the just-dropped leaves, turning aside to eat one that just fell, in preference to one that came down a day before. Red leaves have a high content of residual sugars, and they are most avidly sought. Conversely, the dry leaves of oaks, elms, and hickories are seldom, if ever, eaten because of the tannic acid they contain.

Deer will also eat the leaves as roughage, after they have become totally dry. They instinctively know that roughage is needed for their digestive well-being. Even captive deer, offered all the grain they can eat, will feed on dropped leaves for their roughage.

Most of the fawns have been weaned in late summer, at two to three months of age, although some are still nursing late in autumn, at five months. Most of the does' udders will have dried up prior to the breeding season, although W. T. McKean of South Dakota found that 83 percent of the whitetail does were still lactating in December, and up to 50 percent of them were in January. As a doe's milk production lessens, the milk's protein content continues to creep up. Deer instinctively seek out the high protein they need, and perhaps this is why so many fawns try to nurse for as long as they can.

The average fawns in late autumn are about two-thirds the size of their mothers, and they are perfect little carbon copies. When the fawns have reached this size, they stop growing until the vegetation starts to grow again the following spring. Once their growth stops, their bodies can convert all nutrients, above the needs of their basic metabolism, to fat. And this fat is essential to survival.

## Migration and Dispersal

The habits of all deer change drastically in autumn, the period of greatest daily activity. They feed longer and more often, they move about more within their ranges. And the mule deer and blacktails shift their ranges by migration.

Snow comes early in the mountainous country of the West, and it is the snow that sends the elk and deer down from the high mountain meadows, where they spent the summer, to the lower elevations. Deer and elk don't like the cold or the wind, but it is not until the snow begins to pile up that they start their migrations down. A small snow storm will not start the migration. It takes 8 to 12 inches (20 to 30 cm.) of snow, or the threat of a big storm, to start the animals moving.

Once started, they waste little time. They follow the natural drainages down the mountains, funneling through draws, gaps, passes, and valleys. They

Mule deer migrations are prodded by the first
heavy accumulation of snow.

may not follow the most direct route but it is usually a route of easy traveling. These migration routes are traditional. The fawns follow the doe as she
leads them down trails where she was led by her mother, and where her
mother was led before that. Much of what we think wildlife does instinctively
is actually learned. So long as some members of the herd have been shown the
route by the older animals, that route continues to be used. If ever a break in
the chain of learning occurs, that particular migration route may never be
used again.

Because migration often takes place under cover of darkness, there may be
no deer in a particular area one day and dozens of deer will be found there the
next day. During their fall migration, the deer do not linger to eat, as they did
when they moved upward in the spring; they grab a few mouthfuls of food as
they travel, rest a while during the daytime, then continue their journey.

Some of the mule deer migrations are 90 to 100 miles (144 to 160 kilom.)
long. The herds that winter together may not be the same deer that have spent
the summer together. There is much crisscrossing of migration routes, and
many deer actually travel much farther than they have to. Males tend to travel
slightly greater distances than females because bucks usually spend their summers at higher elevations than does.

There is no migration by those blacktail deer that live in regions where the seasons do not change much—for example, the coastal areas of Oregon and Washington. Most whitetail deer do not migrate today. There is a shifting of the northern whitetails from summer areas to winter yarding areas, but this is usually less than 10 miles (16 kilom.). Some whitetails in Michigan travel about 30 miles (48 kilom.) to get to their yarding areas. Years ago, some of the whitetails in Michigan had much longer migration routes.

George Shiras III recorded the longest regular migration of whitetails as being about 75 miles (120 kilom.). In the mid-1800s, whitetail deer that spent the summer on the western end of Michigan's Upper Peninsula would migrate each winter down into Wisconsin. The migration was due to a lack of winter food. As with most migrating animals, the travel in autumn would be direct and fast, while the return in the spring would be more leisurely and would be led by the does.

This whitetail migration stopped after 1870 because of lumbering operations. As the virgin timber was cut off, the second-growth sprouts provided unlimited year-round deer food. After twenty years, much of this food had grown beyond the deer's reach. But since the migration pattern had been broken, from that time on the deer yarded locally each winter.

Every autumn about 25 percent of yearling whitetail bucks and about 5 percent of the does disperse from the area they were born in. There is some dispersal among mule deer and blacktails, but it is not as noticeable because of their migrations.

A recent research project on the home ranges and dispersal of whitetail deer was conducted by K. E. Kammermeyer and R. L. Marchinton in Floyd County, Georgia, on the Berry College Refuge. The deer population was very high in the summer, with about 78 deer per square kilometer, or 30 per square mile.

Thirteen deer were fitted with radio transmitters and 40 with bright plastic markers. The average summer range of the bucks was 28 acres (11.3 hectares) while that of the does was 18 acres (7.3 ha.). Prior to the rutting season, the bucks began to increase the size of their ranges, to 83.77 acres (34 ha.).

All of the three types of deer have overlapping home ranges; they are not territorial—that is, they do not have inviolate territories. Each buck has a large enough home range so that is overlaps the ranges of a number of does and some other bucks.

Six out of 19 tagged bucks dispersed but only one of the 21 tagged does dispersed. All of the dispersed deer went from areas of high deer concentrations, ample food, and protection from hunters, to areas of lower deer populations, less food, and intensive hunting pressure. The researchers concluded that the dispersal resulted from the breeding competition among the bucks.

I do not doubt the researchers' conclusions, but another aspect of such dispersals should be mentioned. Nature abhors a vacuum. There is always a dispersal from areas of high population concentration to areas of lower population, even if conditions in the low-population areas are less favorable. This is the basic reason for dispersal; it is nature's method of filling every niche that will support a particular species. A low concentration has tremendous survival value because it lessens the chance for disease to spread through the population. It also insures that a localized calamity will not affect the species as a whole.

An intensive five-year study in Texas on whitetail range and dispersal provides some very interesting data. During the five-year period, 204 deer were marked and tagged. Four hundred sight records were made on 68 of the marked deer. It was found that the average doe had a home range of about 93 acres (37.63 ha.). Three does evidently didn't want to be cramped, as two of them had home ranges of 502 acres (203 ha.) and the third had a home range of 690 acres (279 ha.). The bucks had an average home range of 1,079 acres (436 ha.)—more than ten times that used by the does. The average distance moved by does was only about 400 yards (365 m.). The maximum distance moved by a single doe was 2.9 miles (4.6 kilom.). The maximum distance moved by any buck was 4.5 miles (7.24 kilom.), and movements of 2 miles (3.2 kilom.) were common among bucks during the rutting season.

Food was abundant in the spring and summer, when the bucks were growing their antlers and the does were tending their fawns. These factors reduced the deer's range at that time to about 24 acres (9.71 ha.). The bucks were actually utilizing an area of about 13 acres (5.26 ha.). With the advent of cool weather and the breeding season, all of the deer again became very active, and that was when the bucks moved the greatest distances. However, the Texas research agreed with findings in other whitetail states that only a little over 20 percent of the deer population moves more than 1.5 miles (2.41 kilom.) in dispersal.

Although most whitetails are not inclined to travel far, wanderlust seems to claim a few individuals—for instance, two does tagged by researchers in Tennessee. One doe, tagged near the Clarksville military base in 1963, was killed by a car near Kenton when she was eight years old. She had traveled 90 miles (144 kilom.). The other one, killed near Dresden when she was 12½ years old, had traveled over 100 miles (161 km.) from her birthplace. In South Dakota, an archer named Everett Gothier shot a whitetail that had been tagged as a fawn 140 miles (225 kilom.) from where he killed it. Bill Hlavachick, a biologist in Kansas, recorded the longest distance traveled by a whitetail. It was a doe tagged in Sheridan County and shot in Kingman County, Kansas, a distance of 170 miles (273 kilom.).

Bill also tells of a buck mule deer that was tagged on June 8, 1970, in northwestern Kansas and shot on November 13, 1971, near the Platte River in Nebraska, a distance of 65 miles (104 kilom.). If this was a dispersal record, it was a good one for mule deer. If, on the other hand, the deer was migrating, it was not exceptional because many mule deer migrate 100 miles (160.9 kilom.) each spring and autumn.

"Picturebook" bucks like this blacktail are most magnificent at the onset of the rut, when they are still sleek and strong, their antlers polished, their necks swollen. (Photo by Len Rue, Jr.)

Not much research has been done with regard to the homing ability of deer. I know of one buck, trapped by New Jersey wildlife officers, that was removed from land at Belvidere, New Jersey, to reduce a captive herd. The buck was released at Mountain Lake, a distance of 6 miles (9.7 kilom.). The buck returned home, clearing the 9-foot (2.8 m.) fence to get back in. Within a week, the buck was retrapped. This time he was released at Dunfield Creek, a distance of 11 miles (17.7 kilom.). Again he returned home. Finally, he was transported 100 miles (160.9 kilom.) and this time he did not return.

## The Rutting Season

The rutting season is the period of greatest activity for all three types of deer, particularly for the bucks. It is their reason for being.

At this time, the bucks are exactly what we picture a buck to be: strong, sleek, in the best possible condition, virile, the epitome of maleness. They are truly magnificent animals at the time of the rut.

In November and December, a buck's thyroid, adrenal, and testicular glands all reach a peak of activity, weight, and hormone production. (I am speaking here of the northern states; the timing differs somewhat in other latitudes, as mentioned in earlier chapters.) The sperm-laden testicles of a 150-pound (67.9 kg.) buck will measure 3¾ inches (9.5 cm.) in length by 2¼ inches (5.7 cm.) in diameter. The scrotum does not have the tear-top appearance that it has in cattle and sheep. Connective skin and muscle at the rear of the scrotum facilitate a raising and lowering of the testicles in accordance with the temperature.

Live (motile, or active) sperm develop within the testicles in late summer. However, the testicles must be kept cooler than body temperature if the active sperm count is to be high. Heat destroys sperm. As the testicles enlarge, they fill the scrotum; there is no loose, excess skin as in humans. The scrotum has a thin skin, short, thin hair, and some sweat glands to help in cooling. The scrotum drops down, away from the body. The testicles must be kept cool but not cold. Warmth relaxes the muscles, and the scrotum descends to move the testicles farther from the body and allow the circulation of air for cooling. Cold weather reverses the procedure, retracting the scrotum. Cold, dry weather definitely stimulates sexual activity in deer. It is as if they instinctively feel that winter will soon be upon them, that the season of the rut is brief, that they must mate now if the fawns are to be born at the best time.

The bucks are ready sexually long before the does are willing or able to accept them. As their frustration mounts, the bucks become much more aggressive and they begin to travel almost constantly in a search for receptive does. What seems like poor timing—this "ripening" of the bucks before the does are receptive—probably is most efficient. For one thing, mates are available for

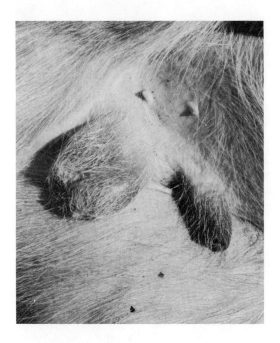

A buck's testes descend and he is ready to mate before most does come into estrus.

any does that come into estrus earlier than usual. For another, by the time most of the does are ready, the bucks have become so enthusiastic, so determined, that a large number of breedings will be assured.

But before that, the bucks take out much of their frustration on saplings and brush, which serve as surrogate opponents. Captive bucks hook the fences viciously. Saplings are attacked with all the strength the bucks can muster, and with movements almost too fast to follow. The fury of attack can be seen where the earth has been torn up by their hooves.

Now the big bucks begin to make scrapes. These are roughly circular patches of earth that have been torn up by bucks pawing with their front feet. Most scrapes are about three feet (.9 m.) across and several inches deep. They are conspicuous, particularly in the forest where the bare, churned earth shows among the leaves. The scraping must be done in a frenzy of pawing, as if the animal had opened a relief valve to let off excess energy. The tracks show that the buck pivots around while making a scrape.

Almost every scrape I have seen was made under a bush or near a tree with limbs hanging low enough—about 4½ to 5 feet (1.4 to 1.5 m.)—so that the buck could reach up and hook them with his antlers. The branches above the scrape are always broken and scarred, showing that the buck put a lot of effort into the hooking. I am convinced that scrapes are made only where such branches are available.

Many people have seen deer scrapes but very few have witnessed a buck actually pawing a scrape, as this buck is doing.

Occasionally a buck will urinate or defecate in these scrapes, but there is usually very little odor to them. Both Joe Taylor and I have carefully sniffed a number of scrapes, and the only odor was that of fresh earth. Wet areas of urine are seldom seen. These scrapes are not to be compared with the wallows of elk. The elk's wallow is a churned-up mud bath, reeking of urine and semen, which the bull elk rolls in, plastering goo all over his body. Only once have I found a deer scrape impacted by the buck's lying in it.

Unlike the buck rubs, which are usually used only once, a scrape is used every time the buck is in the area. Bucks don't have a territory in the usual sense but the scrapes are used to advertise their presence.

This whitetail buck is masturbating. Self-gratification is common among rutting bucks and seems to relieve tension before does become receptive.

Anyone observing wild or domestic animals soon comes to the conclusion that, like humans, they are sexually motivated creatures. And as with humans, masturbation is common in the animal world. Denied sexual release because the does are not yet physiologically capable of copulation, the bucks seek relief by masturbating.

A buck's penis sheath, in the relaxed state, usually hangs straight down and is about 3¾ inches (9.5 cm.) long. When not erected, a retractor muscle pulls the forward part of the penis back into the sheath, causing the penis to fold into an S-curve known as the sigmoid flexure. When stimulated, vesicles in the buck's penis fill with blood under great pressure and, although the penis does not increase very much in thickness or length, the S-curve is straightened out and the penis becomes rigid. There is no bone in the deer's penis, as in some other mammals.

The erected penis points forward and protrudes from its sheath by 8 to 10 inches (20 to 26 cm.). When masturbating, a buck stands with his back humped up and his tail held stiffly erect. With a rhythmic forward thrusting of

With tail up, showing sexual excitement, this whitetail buck is tracking a doe.

the pelvic region, he rubs his extended penis against his abdomen. Just prior to ejaculation he lowers his back, and his final thrustings rub the penis beneath his rib cage. Often the buck will lick his penis sheath prior to masturbation and the penis after ejaculation. The sex drive varies with the individual; some bucks masturbate occasionally, others more frequently.

## The Dangerous Time

About three weeks before the first females come into estrus, the bucks start to really "run" the does. The bucks are now ranging far and wide, constantly searching for a receptive female. Most of the does will not allow a mature buck to get close to them at this stage. The presence of immature bucks is accepted because they do not posture as adult bucks do.

When a mature buck is tracking a doe, he follows along the trail with his head close to the ground and with his tail pointing almost straight up. When the buck locates a doe, he runs toward her with his head held low but ex-

This whitetail buck begins to curl his lip as he scents a doe in estrus.

tended and pointing forward. This posture is similar to the one used in aggression. When the does run from the bucks, they usually clamp their tails down and bend their legs so that their bodies are closer to the ground. They lower their profile as if they hope the buck will ignore them. He doesn't; he will chase after them in an attempt to smell their vaginas. If a doe urinates, the buck will sniff at the urine, then raise his head, and curl his upper lip up. This is called flehmening. The upward curling of the lip concentrates the doe's odor at the entrance to the buck's nostrils, intensifying the scent. The buck can then tell instantly if the doe is in estrus. If she is, he is interested; if not, he dashes off in the hope of finding one that is. Ordinarily, when a group of does and young bucks see a mature buck in the outstretched-neck position, they scatter before him like leaves before a wind.

Wild does are seldom injured by overly amorous bucks because they can run from him, and because other does are available to distract him. Frequently, does in captivity are killed when a frustrated buck flies into a rage. Bucks are much more dangerous just prior to the breeding season than after it starts.

Until they actually experience the release that comes with copulation, they are unstable — mammalian time-bombs ready to explode at any moment. I know of people who have had captive bucks injure or kill the does penned up with them. C. W. Severinghaus reports that six does were killed by bucks in the pens at the Delmar Wildlife Laboratory.

John Madson, in his book *The White-Tailed Deer*, told of a buck that had been raised as a pet on a farm in Michigan. The buck was very docile and was allowed to roam about as he liked. One fall the farmer put the buck in a pen near his rabbit dogs with the idea of saturating the dogs with the deer odor to break them from running deer. One day the buck charged the farmer and knocked him into a snow drift. When the buck attacked again, the farmer caught him by the antlers and held him off by sheer strength. It was fortunate that the farmer was a strong man. Answering the farmer's call for help, two men armed with a pick handle and a wooden beam beat the buck back so that the farmer could escape.

In an attempt to pacify the buck, the farmer put two does in with him. The buck killed one immediately. The second one was injured but was removed in time to save her.

The farmer then put in a spike buck, figuring that the young buck's spikes would slip through the big buck's rack and give the young buck an advantage. The adult buck struck first, disemboweling the spike buck on the first thrust. Not one to give up, the farmer next put in a large buck, the equal of the rogue buck in size and rack. This last buck was also swiftly killed. The "pet" buck had attacked a man, wounded a doe, and killed a doe and two bucks in two days. That probably is some kind of a record.

You may recall my saying earlier that the loss of antlers seems to be an insurmountable psychological shock to a rutting buck. In this case, the farmer sawed the antlers off and the rogue buck became as docile as he had been before the rutting season.

Ordinarily, deer are not dangerous animals, and for nine months out of the year a buck has normal control over his actions — but not during the rut. A buck's actions at this time are triggered by the male hormone testosterone. Being under hormonal influence, a buck cannot be judged by human standards of good and bad. When he does injury to someone or something, he is not being vicious, he is merely being a buck. His actions are not deliberate. *No buck is to be trusted during the rutting season.*

Stories of aggression are common but there is one aspect of the danger that, for the sake of safety, should be given more publicity. This was brought home to me by a letter I received from a young woman whose parents have a farm at New Paltz, New York. Her family had raised a buck fawn as a pet. All went well until the buck was 1½ years old, sexually mature and with antlers that would definitely interest a hunter. This always presents a problem with "pet" deer, for the animals cannot be allowed to run loose during the hunting season. What compounds the problem is that such deer have lost their fear of humans and are very dangerous at this time since they are in the rut. The family wanted to pen the animal until hunting season closed but they discovered that the buck—now fearless—would try to mount any woman who was having her menstrual period. During their menses, women should be extremely cautious about large animals, keeping away from deer, elk, or bears encountered in national parks and refuges where such animals have lost their fear. At least one of the young women killed by a grizzly bear in one of our national parks a couple of years ago was having her menstrual period and may therefore have unwittingly attracted danger.

## Fighting

Bucks seldom fight with the other bucks that belong to their own group. They have associated with one another throughout the rest of the year, and dominance has already been established among such bachelor groups. Each buck already knows where he stands. Occasionally a younger buck may get ambitious and have to be reminded of his standing in the social hierarchy, but posturing and threats by the dominant buck usually suffice. If the dominant buck is an old one, then a younger but fully mature buck may prove to be a serious challenger. In the fight that determines the outcome, the younger buck may be able to displace the old one.

As mentioned earlier, the extensive home ranges of mature bucks will frequently overlap those of other mature bucks. These are the deer most likely to fight. The fights I have seen were not over does, although that is often the cause. The fights I witnessed occurred because of the onset of the breeding season and one buck's invasion of another's turf.

When two unacquainted bucks meet, the first sign of aggression is a stooping or squatting position, assumed by one or both bucks. The hind legs are bent and brought forward so that the hind quarters are lowered and the back slopes below the horizontal.

The buck's head and neck are extended, and the head is held slightly lower than the level of the back. The ears are laid back flat against the neck. The whitetail buck's tail is clamped down at this stage while that of the blacktail buck is held away from the body and often quivers. The bucks of all three types seem to "bunch" their muscles and appear to be under great tension at this point. The head's low, extended position causes the eyes to move to the front of the socket so that the whites are plainly seen at the rear.

Ears on this whitetail buck are laid back, signaling extremely aggressive feelings.

The bucks lick their noses constantly, their tongues flicking in and out. Elk and bison also do this, and a sure sign of extreme aggression in a moose is when its mouth is opened and the tongue is extended.

With a stiff, stilted walk, the bucks may circle each other, or they may approach each other more directly but usually with a sidling walk. This action has always puzzled me and I still cannot give a reason for it. The deer want to protect their bodies from an opponent's antlers, yet they expose their bodies by turning sideways.

While circling or approaching each other, the bucks tuck their chins in so that their antlers are tilted forward. With their ears flattened against their necks and pointing to the rear, and with the whites of their eyes showing, the bucks look "mean as hell," and they are. The hair on their bodies is erect, and this is particularly noticeable along their spines. The erected hair and the

A whitetail buck may approach with a sidling walk, as shown, when other threat displays have failed to intimidate the rival.

bunched muscles make a buck appear even larger than he is, a picture of powerful, controlled fury. The bucks snort or grunt as they are about to do battle.

When the bucks finally lunge, one of them must make the first move, yet the opponents are so keyed to each other's actions that they appear to explode into action simultaneously. The distance between the bucks when the rush is made may be up to 20 feet (6.4 m.) but most often is 6 to 10 feet (2 to 3.1 m.).

The initial impact may be so great that pieces of antlers are broken off. Joe Taylor witnessed a fight in which a buck lost an entire antler from one side.

These are battling whitetails.

This whitetail probably broke the one antler in a fight during the rut.

Life in Autumn

These locked antlers are still attached to decaying skulls—mute evidence of a rare but generally fatal occurrence.

Joe said that the antler went flying up in the air about 20 feet (6 m.) and the two bucks dropped to their knees and spun around in a circle like a top while fighting. In less than a minute, the buck with the broken antler ran off. Joe said the initial charge was so fast that if he had blinked his eyes he would have missed it.

The fights I have seen lasted longer, although none of them lasted more than five minutes. The bucks banged together and then pushed and shoved in an effort to force each other backward or down. In the process, they circled slightly but it was usually almost straight-forward pushing.

As I have stated often, fights occur only between nearly equal animals; lesser animals give way before the big ones. Because of this, the bucks usually do not injure each other although they are trying to. If one of them loses his footing and falls, the rival will try to gore him, but this seldom happens. There are eye-witness reports of rival bucks fighting for 20 to 30 minutes, until each was completely exhausted, but I have not witnessed such a fight. Usually, when one of the bucks tires he breaks off contact and dashes away. The victor seldom chases his rival for more than a few steps. He is not interested in chasing a rival he has beaten.

The literature abounds with reports of bucks locking antlers. Their antlers lock when the force of the initial impact springs the antlers apart so that the tines and beams become enmeshed. This locking happens with deer and moose, less frequently with elk, and I have seen photos of only one occurrence

271

in caribou. Deer do lock antlers, but it is not common. Its rarity is what makes it so newsworthy, which is why it is reported in sporting and conservation magazines. I have seen evidence of it only once. I would be willing to bet that the locking of antlers occurs no more often than a couple of hundred times a year among the millions of deer across the nation. All the reports of locked antlers that I have seen were of bucks with big racks having eight and more commonly ten or more tines.

Orrin Emerson, a veterinarian, and Marley Griffith were called to separate a pair of whitetail bucks that were locked together on Howard Harvey's farm near Humboldt, Iowa. They sawed one antler off the eight-point buck, freeing him. This buck dashed away. The other deer, a ten-point buck, was taken to Emerson's clinic but died three days later of head injuries.

The men were lucky that the eight-point buck ran off. All too often, men have tried to release locked deer only to have a buck turn on them when it was freed.

J. H. Ridley and Dan Bares, of Maida, North Dakota, were hunting pheasants when they discovered two bucks locked together in a stream covered with thin ice. The deer kept fighting as they broke through the ice, trying to reach the far shore. Both bucks were large ones with big racks but one buck was heavier than the other. The lighter one got up on the far bank but the heavier one failed. Eventually his struggles pulled his opponent off the bank and both were drowned.

It is a shame that such magnificent animals had to drown but at least it was a comparatively merciful death. All too often, when two bucks are locked, they suffer a lingering death from exhaustion and thirst. Sometimes one buck will die and the surviving buck may drag him around for several days before he, too, succumbs. I saw one photograph of locked bucks in which dogs had eaten a good part of the dead buck. What a harrowing period that must have been for the surviving buck!

Joseph Bruckac, a taxidermist of Greenfield Center, New York, mounted a trio of locked whitetail bucks from Jamestown, North Dakota. Joe figured that an eight-point buck and a ten-pointer were fighting when another eight-point buck joined the fray by jumping over the back of one of the fighting deer. His rack locked the three sets of antlers together, and as he twisted around, he broke his neck and died. His hanging weight kept all of the antlers locked until the other two bucks died.

## Breeding

During the pre-coital period, the bucks try to smell the hocks and genitals of every doe they encounter, and the action is not entirely one-sided. About two days before a doe comes into estrus, her vulva starts to swell and she may

A whitetail buck here checks a doe to determine whether she is in estrus.

actively seek out a buck. She urinates on her tarsal glands frequently. Many captive does have been reported to pace their pens almost constantly just before coming into estrus. On several occasions I have seen a wild doe attempt to mount another doe, in the same way cows do. As the doe doing the mounting was the aggressor, I assumed she was the one about to come into estrus. The doe being mounted would always scoot out from under, and she usually ran off.

Joe Taylor is sure his captive does have attempted to mount his buck. He bases this assumption on the fact that the hair on the buck's back was all roughed up over the hindquarters just before the does were bred.

Arthur Einarsen reported his observations of two mule deer does and a buck on November 21, 1939, in the Malheur National Forest in Oregon. The does were in estrus but the buck was evidently tired. He was gaunt and his coat was rough. He showed little interest in breeding but he was given no rest by

Having migrated prior to the breeding season, mule deer often concentrate in large groups.

the two does. Einarsen did not describe what the does did but he wrote that they "continually attempted to claim the attention of the buck." After about half an hour, the buck finally mounted and bred one of the does but was evidently unable to breed the second doe. This latter doe continued to pester the buck for twenty minutes more, until they were lost from sight.

There are definite differences in the breeding activities of the three types of deer. As a rule, whitetails are not yet yarded up when the breeding season occurs, so the does are widely scattered in their little matriarchal groups. This forces the whitetail bucks to cover a large area, seeking out does coming into estrus.

Usually, mule deer have migrated prior to the breeding season, so they are concentrated, sometimes into large numbers. The bucks mingle with the herds and stay with them if the deer are in a national park or if the hunting season has not started. If the buck is subjected to hunting pressure, he will seek heavy cover on the fringes of these herds and will join them only under cover of darkness.

Some of the blacktail bucks behave in the same manner, while others attempt to gather a harem of does, as do elk. I have not seen such harems, but a number of authorities have reported their occurrence. They have also reported that while the herd buck is battling a rival, a smaller buck may slip in and service a doe that is in estrus. And occasionally a big buck will share the favors of the does in his harem with a subordinate buck.

There are records of two whitetail bucks breeding one doe without animosity between the bucks. I have never seen this, but Joe Taylor has. Another friend of mine reported that he and several others witnessed a "gang rape" of a whitetail doe by nine bucks near Belvidere, N. J. The incident occurred in a fenced area of several thousand acres, adjacent to a manufacturing plant. An exceedingly large deer herd had built up there. The doe came down off a hill pursued by the bucks. Her mouth was open and her tongue hung out from her exertions. She could not outrun the bucks, and every time she lay down one of the bucks hit her with his antlers or feet and forced her to get up. She got no respite, and in the fifteen or twenty minutes while she was in sight she was mounted by three different bucks. There was no fighting among the bucks.

When a buck finds a doe in estrus, he smells her hocks and licks her vulva. The doe usually urinates immediately. The buck licks the urine and then raises his head and curls his lip, flehmening—breathing the odors in deeply. Even though the doe is ready to be bred, she usually does not stand for the buck the first time or two that he attempts to mount her. His tongue constantly flicks in and out as he licks his lips. He caresses the doe with his tongue about the head and body, and she also caresses him. Sometimes she will rub her body against the buck, further stimulating him. It is well known that the tactile stimulation of pressure or the rubbing of bodies, especially if returned, increases sexual tension. At times the entire body seems to be an erogenous zone.

When the doe finally allows the buck to mount her, intromission is not always accomplished. However, the buck's penis has a very flexible tip and actively seeks out the doe's vagina. As Leonardo da Vinci said, "the penis seems to have a mind of its own, if not a life of its own."

There is no mistaking when copulation is completed. After entering the doe, the buck gives only one or two preparatory thrusts and then lunges, plunges deeply into her and ejaculates. The ejaculatory thrust is so violent that many times the doe is thrown forward to her knees and the buck's hind feet leave the ground. The buck immediately withdraws. The doe then either stands with her back humped up or squats as if to urinate, straining hard with her tail upraised over her body. Although I have never seen evidence of it, some researchers report that the doe discharges a yellowish secretion at this time. If she is a young one that has never been bred before, she may stay in this squatting position for twenty minutes or more. The reason for this behavior is uncertain.

Again I must stress that each animal is an individual and its actions reflect that individuality. After copulation, some bucks pay very little attention to the doe while some I have seen are as attentive to her afterward as they were before copulation. Some bucks may breed a doe only once or twice in the twenty-four hours that she is receptive. I personally know of one buck that bred a doe eight or more times in the daylight hours. Undoubtedly he bred her

A muley buck here covers a doe. (Photo by Len Rue, Jr.)

many more times during the hours of darkness while she was in estrus, but their actions could not be seen. I also saw a buck breed a doe twice in about fifteen minutes.

Most of the breeding is done at night, because that is when deer are most active, particularly if hunted. Where they are not hunted, the bucks are active both day and night during the breeding season.

The tremendous activity of chasing after the does, fighting, and breeding leaves little time for the bucks to eat. The rutting season usually lasts about sixty days. During this time, a mature buck may breed with only four or five does or perhaps as many as twenty. In captivity, bucks have been observed to breed with two does and even three in a single day. Bucks have been known to have their sperm count drop because of overbreeding so that they become temporarily infertile. In the wild, however, bucks are seldom so fortunate as to find two or three receptive does in one day. A buck usually stays with a doe for a day before she comes into estrus, spends a day copulating with her, and then goes off to seek another doe.

If the doe has conceived, she has no further interest in bucks. If she has not conceived, she will come back into estrus twenty-six to twenty-eight days later. She is usually geared to the twenty-eight-day lunar cycle. It is most unusual for a doe not to be bred during her first or second estrus period. If she is not bred or does not conceive in either of these two periods, she will come into estrus a third and perhaps even a fourth time before she goes barren for that year.

The length of the rutting season helps to ensure some fawn survival in the case of a catastrophic happening during the birthing period the following spring. Although the bulk of their breeding takes place during a sixty-day period, the season may extend a hundred and twenty days or more. A study of 894 deer in New York State showed that the earliest breeding date was October 1 and the latest was February 9, with the peak of activity occurring between November 10 and December 15. This length of time is typical of all deer, all species, in all sections of the country, although the dates may differ in particular sections. Some blacktail deer have been seen breeding in July in the southern latitudes, while the northern populations are capable of breeding until April. But these are extremes and are not typical of the species.

Cold weather stimulates the onset of the breeding season but photoperiodism, the response to light, is the primary trigger. Every step is orchestrated— a precise fitting together of season, conditions, responses. A poor diet may cause a late or irregular breeding season. An overabundance of food may also delay the season or delay pregnancy in an individual doe.

Researchers have found that obesity will cause a doe to come into estrus later than normal. Excessive fat retards development of the follicle. Fat in the doe's reproductive tract may prevent a fertilized egg from reaching the uterus or becoming implanted if it does get there. This may be why, after a particularly good autumn with a superabundance of food, many does may not breed during their first estrus period. The colder weather before a doe's second estrus period burns up some of the excess fat so that pregnancy then becomes possible.

The bucks that enter the breeding season as magnificent specimens quickly lose weight and vigor, becoming quite gaunt, and listless, and rough-coated. A weight loss of 25 to 35 percent is not uncommon. As the rut wanes, the buck's swollen neck decreases to its normal size and the buck loses interest in the does. In a short time his antlers will drop off. His main interest now is in eating all the food possible to regain his weight and fat reserves before winter sets in. The depletion of the body reserves is one of the main reasons why the most vigorous bucks (and the largest bull elk, too) are often the ones to die off in an exceedingly hard winter. They have given too much of themselves for

.After the rutting season, whitetail bucks are gaunt, thin-necked, and rough-coated.

the perpetuation of the species. With the next generation assured, nature sacrifices those that made it possible. It was their reason for being.

A fawn's diet determines whether it will breed at six to seven months of age or have to wait until the following year. If the fawn had a 16 to 18 percent protein diet, it will be in condition to breed by the time it is six or seven months old.

Whitetail fawns have a much higher breeding potential than that of mule deer and blacktails because many whitetails have access to a much better food supply. Blacktail deer have the poorest record of all. On some of their poorest ranges they do not breed until they are 2½ years old.

On an average range, about 40 percent of whitetail fawns breed. On the best of ranges, 65 to 74 percent breed. If a fawn can attain a weight of 80 to 90 pounds (36.3 to 40.8 kg.) she usually comes into estrus, though she is likely to do so about a month later than is normal for the mature does. The yearlings that give birth contribute about 30 percent to the annual herd increment. In one recorded instance in British Columbia, a blacktail fawn doe was bred by a fawn buck. This is the only such record I have found for blacktails.

Ordinarily, bucks do not become physically mature until they are 4½ years old. They usually become sexually mature when they are 1½ years old, but many are sexually precocious when only a few months old.

Here a sexually precocious, five-month-old fawn makes advances to his mother.

I have observed hundreds of little bucks attempting to mount other fawn bucks, fawn does, and adult does, including their mothers. When the fawns are young, these actions are part of their play pattern. After four or five months, the advances are made in earnest. Usually the subordinate fawns just run away from the sexual advances of a dominant buck fawn. Even some adult does will run.

When a precocious buck fawn attempts to mount his mother, she usually whirls around and strikes at him with a front foot. Her rebuke does not always have much effect because some of the little bucks just keep trying.

I believe that as more research is done, it will be found that more buck fawns are capable of breeding than previously thought possible. The ones that can breed are those that have advanced enough physically to have polished little antlers at six or seven months, although this is not the only criterion.

## Interbreeding

Ordinarily, in states that have populations of both mule deer and whitetails, the ranges of these two deer don't really overlap. Their food preferences and habitat requirements differ enough so they remain more or less segregated. Where they do encounter one another, the whitetails give way before mule deer, not because of any aggression but simply because the mule deer are larger.

Interbreeding between the mule deer and the blacktail deer is common and widespread, for the blacktail is really a subspecies of mule deer—at least at this stage of the blacktail's evolution. But if, as most experts agree, the blacktail is an emerging species in its own right, interbreeding with the mule deer will probably become less compatible in the distant future. Hybridization between these two deer is evidenced primarily in the size of the offspring and in the color pattern and shape of the tail and rump patch, as noted earlier.

Interbreeding between the mule deer and the whitetail has occurred on a number of occasions, though it is not common. The buck may be a mule deer and the doe a whitetail, or vice versa. Usually, but not always, the offspring will be infertile.

R. Havel, a biologist from Nebraska, reported 10 hybrids out of 17,039 deer that were examined in that state. W. C. Peabody, a biologist from Kansas, found two hybrids among 983 deer that he examined. The highest percentage of hybrids was reported by R. Webb, who found six hybrids out of 1,000 deer that were checked in Alberta. Unfortunately, none of the reports could say whether the hybrids were first- or second-generation hybrids and whether they were fertile.

Jerome J. Pratt reported a number of generations of fertile crosses between the Coues whitetail and the desert mule deer. The original interbreeding occurred in captivity and some of the fertile offspring escaped into the wild. In 1963 the last two hybrid bucks were turned loose. These hybrids were proved fertile.

There are also records of the whitetail and blacktail interbreeding. Most of the offspring of such matings were infertile but a few were not.

The offspring of any of these crosses reveal the hybridization in a number of ways. Most frequently it shows up in the antlers. A hybrid may look like a whitetail but have the bifurcated rack of a mule deer, or vice versa. The size and placement of the metatarsal gland is also different than on either parent. And the tail and rump patches may be confusing.

A final note on the subject of the breeding season comes from a Pennsylvanian named John Miller, who contributed it to the January, 1977, issue of *Pennsylvania Game News.* Some friends were visiting Miller in late October, and en route they had seen a number of deer crossing the roads. One of the visitors, a lady, asked why so many more deer than usual were moving about. Miller told her it was because of the rut. "What do you mean, rut?" the lady asked, John explained that the deer were mating. After a thoughtful pause, the lady said, "If you are going to get into a rut, I think that's the best kind."

## The Hunting Season

Perhaps the greatest disruption in the life of the deer is the opening of the hunting season. In many areas, the small-game hunting season opens first, so the farmland deer and those of the fringe areas are preconditioned to the influx of hunters and the noise of shooting. But nothing quite compares with the opening of the deer season.

People assume because I spend so much time photographing, studying, and working with deer that I can easily go out and shoot a deer as soon as the season opens. Not so. It would be comparatively easy to get a deer any other time of the year, because then the deer are living predictable lives. All of that changes on opening day.

In my area, even though some tracts of land encompass several square miles, there are enough roads so that any area can be approached from all sides. And they are. When the hunters get out of their cars along the perimeter of such an area, they usually push the deer ahead of them to the tops of the small mountains. Then, unless the hunters are willing to climb the ridges, they wonder where all the deer have gone that they had seen so often in the lowland fields. The habits of all of the deer are changed drastically during the hunting season.

Bucks are almost always warier than the does and doubly so in those states that have bucks-only hunting. Adult does are warier than the yearling bucks because, even if not hunted, they have been subjected to more pressure by hunters. The more a deer has been hunted, the greater its flight distance becomes. I have also found that the more a whitetail buck is subjected to hunting pressure, the more it runs with its tail down. The younger bucks make up the greatest proportion of the annual hunters' harvest, not only because they are less wary but also because there are a lot more of them.

Where there is no hunting, the ratio is 100 bucks to 160 does. Where there is hunting of either sex, the ratios do not change greatly as most hunters would rather take a buck than a doe. Where only bucks are hunted, the adult bucks comprise 10 to 15 percent of the herd, adult does about 50 percent, and the fawns 35 to 40 percent.

Though there are fewer bucks than does, a hunter who sees a doe move past should assume that a buck will follow. I am not saying a buck *will* follow, but there is a good chance that one will. Where the hunting season coincides with the rut, the chance is all the better. But even when a buck is not intent on mating, he is likely to bring up the rear while does are likely to take the lead. This is true of many ungulates. Perhaps the male serves as a rear guard, exposing himself to danger more constantly than the female since natural enemies usually catch deer by pursuing them.

More deer escape hunters by merely standing still than by any other means. Deer blend into their backgrounds amazingly well, and most hunters walk right past them. Some hunters don't really see anything in the woods at any time. Others are looking for deer—picture-post-card deer. They are not looking for an ear, an antler, the movement of just a tail that may be all that is visible. At other times the deer are aware of the hunters' locations, and they circle around and come in behind the hunters.

Many states have conducted controlled hunts in fenced areas perhaps a mile square. The number of bucks in the enclosure is known and a specified number of hunters are allowed in at a given time. Then the entire proceedings are watched by biologists from high towers placed at strategic points in the enclosure.

Six hunters at the Cusino Wildlife Experiment Station in Michigan hunted for four days before any of them even saw one of the nine bucks that were enclosed in the mile-square area. On the fifth day one of the hunters did kill a buck. These men were experienced hunters. They were hunting in good weather and had the advantage of a tracking snow. Many people thought that hunting the deer in an enclosed area would be like "shooting fish in a barrel." But deer are elusive animals, and this and other experiments conclusively proved that point (although it needs no proving to anyone who knows deer).

When anti-hunters declare that the deer never have a chance, they just don't know what they are talking about. It is true that our modern weapons give the hunter more clout than in yesteryear, if he sees the deer. Man has weapons and a superior brain. In all other aspects, the deer are far superior to man. Their sense of smell is something of conjecture. The deer's sense of hearing is far keener than man's. Its eyesight is better than ours on moving objects because deer are more alert. They are stronger, faster, have more stamina, know the area better. And I'm not so sure that their innate knowledge, coupled with their learned experience, isn't the equal of man's intelligence in the escape and evasion situation. Deer have the ability to stand still much longer than a man does. Deer are not pressed by time. Deer don't have to be in or out of the woods at a certain hour, they don't have to meet someone at a certain time, they don't have to be in a certain place at a certain time. Today means nothing to them; they don't even have to eat. So when a deer suspects danger from a certain point, it can stand or lie all day in one spot without moving— until the danger betrays its presence or departs.

Biologists report that most of the time the bucks stand still and allow the hunters to walk past. Then they may remain in that spot or sneak off to one they think may be safer. Bucks have been seen to circle behind hunters and follow them at a safe distance. The bucks often crawl into thickets or under

Bedded in high grass, this whitetail buck remains nearly invisible even at a short distance. Deer most often escape detection by remaining immobile.

blowdowns, or get behind or under cover that looks too skimpy to conceal a deer. Unless startled from a hiding place, or shot at, deer almost never run. If they do run, it is only far enough to reach the next piece of cover. Most blacktail and mule deer stop just before plunging into cover. Some whitetails do, others don't.

Deer that know they are being tracked will watch their back trails, sometimes even circling back to watch the trail from the side. The only way a hunter can hope to get a shot at such a deer is to make large circles from the track, arching around where the deer might be in the hope of getting ahead of it.

Windy days are bad for hunting because the deer are as skittish as a panful of Mexican jumping beans. Conditions are ideal after a rain has softened the fallen leaves, or after a light snow. Even then, the still-hunter should do a lot more looking than walking. A light, soft snow is a tremendous advantage to the hunter because it softens the leaves, allows the deer's tracks to be seen and followed, and makes deer stand out from their surroundings. But of course, just as snow makes the deer more visible to a hunter, it also makes the hunter more visible to the deer. Wearing white camouflage clothing is of no help if the hunter moves because a white object walking in front of the black trees is also easily seen. As noted earlier, a certain amount of blaze-orange—"safety-orange"—is required in many states. But if you can sit still, the color of your clothing doesn't matter.

A really cold snow does allow the deer's tracks to be seen but the creak of the sharp edges of snow compressing under a hunter's feet are as noisy as dry leaves. Deer can stand still in cold weather a lot longer than a hunter can, so again the advantage is with the deer.

Many hunting parties conduct deer drives. Drives may be slow and silent or fast and noisy. A slow, silent drive gives the drivers as well as the standers a chance at a shot, while a noisy drive usually provides only the standers with shots. One thing is certain: You don't actually drive deer, you only stir them up; they go where they want to. The most successful drives are generally those that have been held by the same groups on the same territory for a number of years. These groups get to know where the deer prefer to go when stirred up and can place the standers on the productive spots.

In parts of the Southeast where driving deer with dogs is not only legal but a must, it is important to know the natural crossings. Another requirement is that the dogs be "open trailers" so the stander can hear them coming and be prepared. The hunter must also remember that the deer may be quite a distance in front of the dogs. Ordinarily, the cover is so dense that unless the stander knows the dogs are coming in his direction, he may not be alert enough to see a deer go by. Fast-running dogs should not be used because the slower the deer is pushed, the more likely it is to stay in the hunting area instead of hightailing to the next county. A slow-moving deer makes a much better target, too, even though the hunter will probably be using a shotgun instead of a rifle. With the deer quickly ghosting through exceptionally dense cover, a rifle is often useless for such hunting. Moreover, the standers (and occasionally the drivers) in a hunt with dogs may be too close for safety with a rifle.

The hunter who stalks mule deer in the western states will concentrate on the brushy draws and coulees because western deer favor such areas. The deer know every gap in the high country, and they know the shortest way over the ridges. The hunter had better know, too. Mule deer do not "stay put" as tightly as whitetails. There is less cover for them to hide in or behind, and they are accustomed to moving out in front of danger.

A lone hunter can often flush a mule deer out of a patch of cover if he makes noise while approaching the cover and then stands motionless. Mule deer cannot take much of this kind of "war of nerves." If a buck knows he is in danger but can't smell the hunter—doesn't know where he is or what he is doing—it won't be long before that buck seeks shelter elsewhere.

Mule deer can usually be driven from their beds in the thickets below the rim rock if a hunter up on the ridge chucks small stones down into the brush as he walks along. Without the disturbing sound of the stones coming through the brush, a buck would probably lie still and let the hunter walk by. The buck would feel safe because of the distance to the ridge. Small stones should be used, because large ones will frighten the buck badly and drive him out at full speed, whereas he will probably try to sneak out if only disturbed. From a vantage point on the ridge, the hunter will probably be able to spot the deer before he gets out of range.

Lone hunters who prefer to stand have to know the deer's trails in the particular area and the times when the trails may be used. The lone stander is also in position to take advantage of deer stirred up by other hunters. He should also realize that, during periods of intense hunting pressure, the normal trails may not be used at all. And the direction of the wind is of vital importance to the still-hunter who attempts to stalk or follow a deer and to the lone stander who hopes to ambush one.

Most of the deer that are taken in any particular area are killed during the first two days of the hunting season. Each Saturday is also a big day, because most of the hunters don't have to work that day. The deer's habits and patterns, completely disrupted by intensive hunting pressure, revert to normal when the woods quiet down for even a couple of days. Normal areas for feeding will again be used, although most of the feeding will be done after dark. Deer may be almost anywhere and may go almost anywhere, but they use their established trails whenever possible. These deer trails are not the result of random wanderings but are the easiest way for the deer to reach a given destination. Depending on where a trail goes, or why it was used, it may not be used today or even for some time. However, the main trails will be used by the deer that made them for as long as the deer live, or as long as the trails continue to serve their purpose.

The noise made by two bucks fighting attracts any other buck that hears the sound. Sometimes the third buck will join in the battle; at other times he is just curious. Some hunters take advantage of this by rattling deer antlers together, slashing at the brush, and raking the ground to simulate the sound of bucks fighting. I have tried this on numerous occasions and have never had any luck. Nor do many of the hunters in the Northeast. This ruse does work in the Southwest, and seems to work equally well there on both whitetails and muleys. It is effective only during the rut but most states' hunting seasons correspond to the rutting season.

We can only speculate as to why the rattling technique works so well in the Southwest and not elsewhere. A friend of mine, who has hunted deer both in the Northeast and in Texas, believes it is because of the southwestern terrain and vegetation. Much of the southwestern deer habitat is relatively flat, and the brush, though it may be thick, is not very high. Sound carries far and there is no mistaking the direction of its source. In such habitat, deer must frequently hear fights during the rut. The rattling of antlers is a sound they recognize and react to. Amid the rolling ridges and taller timber of the Northeast, sound is often blocked or has an echoing, ventriloquial quality, so that even an animal with a deer's keen hearing might not hear the rattling of embattled bucks very often, or might not be able to pinpoint the direction of the sound. Therefore, my friend theorizes, northeastern deer are not conditioned to respond to the rattling unless the sound happens to be very close. They do sometimes respond to loud noises, in contradiction to the normally valid rule that a hunter ought to be silent.

Once I got a nice buck that came up to see what was making all that noise. I was. I hadn't planned on hunting that particular day but a friend came by before dawn, so I agreed to go out with him for a couple of hours. We got into the woods while it was still dark. When the morning mist dissipated, I did not like the spot I had chosen because there were no "alleys" where I could shoot through the dense rhododendron. So I moved to a spot that looked better. Since I had already made some noise walking on the leaves and forest duff, I figured a little more wouldn't matter. I didn't really expect much action anyway until after 9:00 a.m., when most of the hunters would get cold and tired of sitting and start to move around.

Wanting to be comfortable, I knocked down an old dead chestnut tree. I propped this up against another tree and used it for a seat. I made no attempt to be quiet. I was seated for about two minutes when, to my surprise, I saw a young buck walking through the brush toward me. Evidently he was drawn to the spot by the racket I had made. He was equally surprised to see me but I recovered and moved faster and was done hunting for that season.

This was not an isolated instance. I have talked with many hunters and have read many accounts of deer walking up to investigate loud or strange noises. Deer are very curious creatures. I don't recommend banging on the bushes to attract deer, but at times it has worked.

Many times deer have been attracted by the smoke of a campfire. Ordinarily, smoke must be an alien odor that spells danger to deer, yet at times it attracts them. There are rural areas where most of the homes (as well as deer camps and vacation cabins) have wood stoves or fireplaces, and perhaps in these regions the smell of wood smoke is so constant that deer lose any fear of it. Sometimes, there is no accounting for what wildlife is likely to do.

Though deer are normally wary — especially in locales where they are subjected to heavy hunting pressure — their curiosity occasionally prompts them to approach humans. This wide-racked buck approaches to investigate noises from a photographic blind.

People often ask me if the deer scents that are sold for hunting really attract deer. Some of the scents are made from fruit products, such as apples, while the best ones are made from the deer's glands or other attractants. Deer scents usually do two things. Some of them attract deer, and most of them mask the human odor. Do they work? Yes, they do. There is no point in using scents on a deer drive. Driven deer have no time to be attracted by the scents. Scents work best for the lone stander, and those I have used do attract deer.

There are also a number of commercial deer calls. Most of them imitate the low, raspy, reedy, blatting call of a buck. Some are higher-pitched and sound like a fawn. I have not been able to call in a buck with any of these during the hunting season, but I have called in both does and a couple of bucks when I tried the calls prior to the hunting season. The one thing I don't like about them is that the sound does not travel very far — and if used when the deer is close, a call helps the deer to pinpoint you.

This spike blacktail, still in velvet, is hiding in dense thicket while observing the photographer. Blacktails are subjected to considerable hunting pressure and they inhabit heavy cover where they have become as elusive as whitetails.

### "Smartness"

There is often a great deal of discussion about the relative "smartness" of the three types of deer. The whitetail is undoubtedly the smartest, mainly because of the areas where it lives. The proximity of man has forced the whitetail to become more wary. The fact that this deer is also found in or near heavy cover means that it has a better chance to hide and stay hidden.

Mule deer are usually found in more open country where they can be seen for greater distances and where there may be far less cover to screen them. The human population puts far less pressure on the mule deer, and when this deer is high in the mountains, it may not even see a human for months on end. Furthermore, the mule deer has had only about half the number of years of association with Europeans and their descendants and their firearms. Mule deer subjected to increased hunting pressure have proved that they can "smarten up."

The blacktail receives more hunting pressure than the muley and lives in closer proximity to larger human populations. The blacktail inhabits some of the densest cover of any of the deer and is as elusive as the whitetail. He has had the opportunity to become "smarter" than his cousin, the mule deer.

**The Wounded Deer**

A fact of life that we all have to live with is that there are "slob" hunters in the woods as well as genuine hunters. Nonhunters and anti-hunters don't realize that the genuine hunter—the sportsman—is as much against the slobs as they are. The slob is the one who blazes away at anything, at any time, at any distance. He also has many other unsavory characteristics, such as disregard of private property, littering, and so on, but we are concerned here with another issue: decency toward wildlife. Anyone who hunts has a moral obligation to thoroughly know his quarry, his weapon, himself, and his limitations. A decent hunter will not try for a "pot" or "luck" shot but will be sure that both he and his weapon can kill the game cleanly and quickly if he shoots.

Unfortunately, not all shots are killing shots. This is true for the best of hunters. Every hunter must check to make sure whether the deer he fired at was missed completely or wounded. If the animal was wounded, the hunter should spare no effort to follow, locate, and dispatch it.

There are no hard rules about a deer's reaction to being hit. There are differences in bullet and arrow weights and the speed and shocking power with which they are delivered. The actions of the deer before being hit also have a tremendous bearing on its reactions. A deer that is shot while standing and not alarmed can be dropped in its tracks much more easily than a deer that is excited and has been running. An excited deer has adrenaline pumping through its system and may run hundreds of yards with its heart shot out. All the same, most deer will react in the manner that I will describe.

Brain, neck vertebrae, and spine vertebrae are the surest, fastest-killing shots when it is possible to get them. When hit in any of these three spots a deer will drop instantly, although it may not die instantly. Unfortunately, these are also three of the most difficult shots to make. And if a hunter feels that the deer in his sights is worth mounting as a trophy, he is unlikely to shoot at its head.

A shot in the lung-heart area is almost always fatal, but the deer probably will not be killed instantly. When hit in the heart, the deer may hunch up and kick out with its hind feet. The blood from a heart wound will be a deep red, and the hair that may be cut off by the bullet will be the regular long guard hair. Sometimes a heart or lung shot will knock a deer off its feet, and occasionally a lung shot will cause a deer to rear up. Blood from a lung shot will be bright red and often frothy. Deer shot in these areas should be followed immediately because they are not going to go far.

A paunch-shot deer usually hunches its back and clamps its tail down. Clamping the tail down is not a sure sign of a hit, because scared deer often do this, too. The blood will be dark in color, with a greenish or brownish tinge from the stomach contents. This is an unfortunate area in which to hit a deer, and it is one that no hunter ever tries for deliberately. A shot through the entrails creates more shock, as it severs more of the deer than does a paunch shot. Deer shot in these areas should not be followed at once. If pressed, such a deer may keep moving for a long time and for a long distance — traveling on adrenaline, so to speak. It is better to wait awhile before following the blood trail, thus giving the deer time to find cover, lie down, and "stiffen up." I put quotation marks around that last phrase because the phenomenon is called stiffening up but, on the basis of my own experience as well as research, I am not sure the term is accurate. A wounded deer does not really seem very stiff before death but it does have more and more difficulty moving. The explanation probably lies in the effects of shock. Unfortunately, the advice to let a wounded deer stiffen is impractical in heavily hunted regions like my own, because if a hunter does not immediately follow his deer, someone else will collect it.

Shots that go through the shoulders usually hit either the lungs or the spine. Shots in the hams may sever the femoral artery. If so, deer will soon bleed to death. Deer that are shot in the lower legs often escape. If only one leg is hit, the deer may bleed but it can run almost as fast on three legs as on all four. Deer that lose a leg are crippled when they walk, but the limp is seldom noticeable when they run.

Deer that are wounded will seek the nearest heavy cover they can find. If you cannot find your deer the first day, perhaps because of darkness coming on, look the next day along the nearest water. The fever that is created by the wound will cause most deer to seek water. Usually a wounded deer will go downhill, simply because it is easier for it to do so. A deer with a broken front leg will try to keep on level ground as it has trouble going downhill.

In trailing a wounded deer, walk to one side of the track, and try not to disturb the trail you are following. If possible, walk on the opposite side of the trail from the sun. Tracks and disturbances of the leaves show up much better against the sun. If you are following a blood trail and you suddenly lose it, tie your handkerchief to a branch as a marker. Then make ever widening circles until you find another sign. If you fail to find a new sign, you have your marker to tell you where the last sign was. If no more blood or tracks can be found, the best bet is to go in the same general direction as the trail had been going and check all possible pieces of cover.

I hope that any deer you shoot drops in its tracks. But make sure your deer is dead and not only stunned or wounded before you attempt to dress it out. Many "dead" bucks have recovered and dashed away. Many have attacked the hunter. Always approach a downed deer ready to shoot again. If the deer starts to get up, shoot. An extra shot is as nothing compared to the trouble a wounded deer can cause. To make sure a deer is dead, touch its eye, with a long branch. If there is no involuntary response, it is safe to commence dressing it out. A dead deer's eye turns greenish, but not until about half an hour after death.

# 17

## Life in Winter

$S$nowstorms take a variety of forms. Some are herded in by a "Norther"—their flakes slanting in, almost horizontal. The wind presses the attack from all sides, and wind-driven snow is capricious. A field may be swept almost bare, while beyond the fence rows the drifts are piled like frozen ocean breakers. Such storms shriek as if consciously intent on locking half a continent once again in the grip of an Ice Age. The cold penetrates. It is driven through all living creatures, for the wind-chill makes a mockery of thermometer readings.

Other snowstorms look like storybook pictures, blanketing everything in deep, white silence. The fenceposts stand like soldiers at attention under their shakos of snow. The evergreens are transformed into tipis, their snow-laden branches bent to the ground. The world looks like a fairyland, but it can be a deadly fairyland. Some creatures reap a benefit from it; for others it wreaks havoc.

The meadow mice love snow. Under its protective white shield, they link the area together with networks of tunnels through the grass. They are safe

Here are deer tracks through winter's first heavy snow.

from the prying eyes of hawks in the daytime and owls at night. The mammalian predators take a toll, but it is only a fraction of what it was before the earth was mantled.

The smaller predators, deprived of such fare as meadow mice, intensify their pressure on rabbits, hares, and grouse. The rabbits are eager to share a woodchuck's den, and the hibernating woodchuck will not even realize that it has a tenant. As soon as the storm ends, the hares will be as busy as a state road crew tramping out their highways and byways. A grouse may seek shelter under the tipi evergreens, or it may plunge completely beneath the insulating blanket of snow.

To the deer, snow may be many things. It can force deer to move or it may keep them from moving at all. Deep snow can be a trap or a blanket. It can provide the deer with food by bending down the branches of trees and bushes, or it can deprive them of food by burying it.

It was the threat of deep snow that forced the migration of the mule deer and blacktails down from the high country in autumn. It was the cold wind before the coming of the deep snow that forced many of the whitetails to abandon their regular haunts and seek shelter in the swamps and in the gulleys and draws along watercourses.

Yarding areas are not chosen because they provide food. They are used despite the fact that often little food is available there. The main requirement of a yarding area is protection from the wind. Cover is more important than food in areas of cold weather and deep snow, even though the nutrition of the food available is low.

Not all whitetails yard up every winter. It depends upon the winter. My area of New Jersey is on a dividing line. Deer in the areas south of here almost never yard up. The winter of 1960-1961 was exceptionally cold, with deep snow, and the New Jersey deer yarded up for most of the winter. We have had comparatively mild winters since that time, with only a couple of years when the deer retreated temporarily to sheltered areas. Our deer were yarded up in the winter of 1976-1977 because of the extreme cold and strong winds, although we had only a moderate amount of snow. Fortunately, our deer were able to move out to seek food as soon as the weather moderated. In New York and upper New England, extreme cold and wind, coupled with deep snow, took a terrible toll of the deer. Thousands upon thousands perished.

In most warm blooded creatures, man included, the basic metabolism rate speeds up as the temperature drops. Basic metabolism is a measure of energy requirements since, if a creature's body temperature is to be maintained, heat production must equal heat loss. It is like running a furnace under forced draft. You can raise the temperature, but this requires extra fuel. This is why it is vital for anyone who expects to be out in cold weather to carry emergency food to prevent hypothermia. A few years ago, biologists discovered to their great surprise that a deer does not respond to cold in this manner.

It had been known that young animals of all species have a higher basic metabolic rate than adult animals, and that the larger species have a lower basic metabolic rate, in proportion to their body size, than the smaller species. This is another reason why the northern members of a single species are larger than are their southern counterparts.

Males of many species—including deer—are larger than the females, and yet they have a higher basic metabolic rate. Bucks are usually larger, grow faster, and are more active, curious, and independent than does. They leave their dam sooner than the females, and they get into more trouble through their curiosity and independence. Owing to all these factors, bucks burn up their body reserves faster. Most adult bucks do not go into the winter season with as good body reserves as the females, unless they have access to almost unlimited food after the rutting season. Unfortunately, this is seldom the case, and

Good habitat gives deer the tremendous advantage of being in top condition as winter descends. This buck should survive deep snows and food shortages easily.

This is a typical bed. Unlike moose, which envelop themselves in insulating snow, deer scrape snow away so they can lie on leaves.

winter mortality is therefore usually higher among adult bucks than does. Nature seems to have foreseen this situation and counteracted it to some degree by providing for the birth of more male than female fawns.

The basic metabolic rate for a deer requires about 1,140 calories per day for each 100 pounds (45.4 kg.) of body weight, if the air temperature is 32° F. (0° C.) or higher. This metabolic rate *drops* instead of speeding up when the temperature gets below the freezing level. Because of their lowered metabolic rate, deer will lose 12 to 15 percent of their body weight in cold weather even if they have an abundance of food. They simply do not take in as much food, nor could they utilize more even if it were available in the winter. And an abundance of deer food is seldom, if ever, available in the winter.

The glands of the deer's endocrine system—the adrenals, pituitary, and thyroid—are at their smallest and are mostly inactive during January and February, the period of the coldest weather. When winter begins, the deer have not adjusted physiologically to withstand the severe weather, and they respond by heavy feeding. If the temperature drop is slow and steady, the deer adjust to the slowing down of their endocrine system and become adapted to the cold. If the temperature drop is very sudden, severe, and prolonged, they may go into shock and die. Once the physiological adjustments to the stress of winter's cold are made, the deer voluntarily fast, seek cover, and hold their daily activities to a minimum. After the endocrine adjustments have been made, they can then withstand a sudden and severe drop in temperature without dying.

Bedded comfortably in snow, this buck maintains his vigil.

During a heavy snowstorm, deer will lie down and not get up, unless disturbed, until the storm passes, even if it is of several days' duration. They literally become buried in the snow. The insulating qualities of their coats are so efficient that the snow won't even melt. And the covering of snow itself also acts as insulation, giving the deer additional protection from the cold.

It has been found that deep, soft snow is important to the survival of moose. They lie down in it so that the snow actually envelops their bodies. Deer don't do this. Deer paw down through the snow to the leaves below, if possible, before lying down. Moose will not use their snow beds a second time, whereas deer use the same beds again and again. On numerous occasions I have seen a large buck and even an adult doe drive another deer out of its bed and then lie down in the same spot. This habit of pawing out a hole in the snow costs the deer vital calories, because the snow would be a more effective blanket if it enveloped the animal's body. Deer do not take advantage of the snow, as some other species do. This supports the theory that the deer living in the North today got there through range expansion, an expansion that is still going on. They did not evolve in the north.

Their habits change drastically in the winter; most of their activities are now during daylight hours. They remain bedded through the long, cold nights. They do not bestir themselves even at dawn. About 8:00 a.m., as the sun comes up, they begin to feed if any food is available. Lying still at night conserves energy, and feeding during the daylight hours also helps. Even on days

Deep snow provides insulation and wind shelter for this bedded doe.

that are clouded, the air temperature generally rises so that less calories are burned for heat during the periods of activity.

The deer will avoid windy areas wherever possible. They like to feed on steep mountain slopes that face south, southeast, or west. They will sometimes utilize almost vertical slopes. The snow is usually lighter on these slopes, and here it usually melts off faster and vegetation is usually heavier. Deer will also choose these areas as bedding sites to take advantage of the sun. However, if the temperature rises above 40° F. (5° C.), they will seek shade, even in winter, because they become uncomfortably warm in their winter coats.

**Winter Food**

The fantastic growth of summer vegetation gives a false impression that deer food must be very plentiful. This vegetation is important but the critical vegetation is that which is available during winter, particularly that which is available in the yarding areas for the deer that are forced to yard up.

In the winter most deer revert almost entirely to browse because they are forced to. Most of the other herbaceous food is just not available. Protein is high during the plant's growing season, highest in late spring and early summer and tapering off in the fall. The protein content drops as the plants begin to dry up, at the time when deer need it most.

Not only does the protein level of the plants drop as much as 25 to 40 percent, but their digestibility also lessens. In the springtime the deer may be able to digest about 70 percent of the plants consumed. The digestibility ratio may drop to 45 or 50 percent in August and as low as 12 percent in the winter. Low digestibility means that even less of the protein content can be utilized. If deer could eat more vegetation, they could obtain more protein, but there is even less food to eat in the winter.

Until snow depth inhibits movement, deer continue to walk about in search of small, nutritious twigs on which to browse.

However, the protein content remains proportionately higher in the dormant browse than in the herbaceous plants and forbs. Deer are selective feeders, and research has proved that they instinctively select the food with the highest protein.

Many states have performed research operations on deer whereby tubes, bags, or openings were placed in the animals' throats or stomachs so that food could be removed for testing. In this way it was proved that the deer instinctively ate more nutritious food than what the researchers selected for them. When allowed to feed freely on research plots, they selected a 17 percent protein diet, compared to a 7 percent protein diet collected by the researchers from the same vegetation on the same plots. There is also the possibility, however, that the acids and the fermentation in a deer's digestive processes add to the protein content of the food eaten.

Deer need a mixture of forage types. It has been proved that the very best of foods will sustain them for only about two weeks without ill effects if it is fed as a single-item diet. In the wild, deer always eat a mixed diet if at all possible.

There are other very important factors besides the protein content of a food. White cedar is lower in protein than balsam fir, yet deer prefer the cedar and will thrive on it, while balsam is a starvation food. White cedar has only 2.7 percent protein while aspen has 5 percent protein, yet deer can eat three times

Red maple sprouts are excellent deer food and can withstand heavy browsing.

as much white cedar as aspen and will thrive on it while starving on aspen. This is because cedar is much more digestible than the aspen.

The same is true of bitterbrush and sagebrush. Bitterbrush is lower in protein than sagebrush but mule deer much prefer it. Sagebrush is an important winter food, but deer that are fed sage exclusively soon stop eating, as it decreases their appetite. It is also known that the aromatic, volatile oils of the sage, which impart its distinctive odor, are antibacterial and therefore inhibit the microflora and bacteria of the deer's digestive system. The more volatile oils a plant contains, the less it is favored by deer.

My area has a tremendous amount of spice bush that is highly aromatic. Deer can eat it, but they don't. Although I have never seen any test results, I would bet that the disfavor is because of the oils.

Deer are forced to do more browsing in the winter. Fortunately, winter browsing, while the plant is dormant, does less damage to the plant than browsing during the growing period. Various types of plants have different degrees of tolerance to browsing. Many plants die if they are 30 percent browsed, while others are actually stimulated by the same degree of browsing. Mountain maple is an excellent deer food, and it can withstand 80 percent browsing each year. White cedar and yew, both favored deer foods in parts of the North, are severely damaged by even moderate browsing. Browsing is a form of pruning, and as gardeners and orchardists know, each variety of plant must be pruned differently. In the wild there is no such control, so the most highly favored plants will usually be overbrowsed and may even be killed off. Then the deer are forced to feed on less beneficial plants. Where the deer population is high, the best food plants are soon eaten or killed off. And as long as the population remains high, there is no way for the favored plants to come back.

Here blacktails feed in a livestock pasture.

Deer seem to prefer sprouts that grow directly from the stumps of trees over those that grow up from old root systems. Probably the protein content is higher or the taste is better. But the reasons are not known for certain. Sprouts of either type grow much faster than seedlings because they have the old tree's entire root system to utilize. Before the tree was cut, the roots had to gather enough nutrients to provide for an entire tree, whereas now all the nutrients go into a few sprouts. The sprouts compensate by growing fantastically large leaves—four to eight times larger than normal. Unless browsed heavily, in just a few short years the sprouts will grow beyond a deer's reach and the deer will then be forced to feed on seedlings.

In Wisconsin it was calculated that the whitetail deer were crippling or eliminating over 600-million tree seedlings every year. Where the deer populations are high, neither natural nor artificial reforestation is possible. The deer have the capability of changing the entire composition of the forest areas they inhabit.

It is during the winter that competition between deer and domestic livestock becomes most acute. Northern whitetail deer are seldom affected because most livestock in their range are kept in barns during the winter. The blacktail and particularly the mule deer have to compete with range cattle, sheep, and, in the Southwest, goats.

Goats especially are competitors of the deer all year because browse makes up over 50 percent of their annual diet. The competition is highest in autumn, when both sheep and deer are feeding heavily on forbs. Deer and cattle com-

Overbrowsing of this live oak by blacktails has resulted in "teepeeing"—natural topiary art.

Young Douglas firs like this one are a major western deer food.

pete mainly in the spring, when both are feeding on newly sprouted grasses. In the other three seasons of the year there is minimal competition, but in the winter on overgrazed ranges even cattle are often forced to feed on browse. At such times livestock may prevent deer from occupying the same ranges. Since more and more beef cattle are now being raised in the southern states, this problem is also found east of the Mississippi River. In some regions it is acute. The problem does not occur where the range is not overstocked.

It is at this time of year that blacktail deer feed most heavily on the seedlings of the Douglas fir and western red cedar, much to the consternation of lumber companies that are trying to reseed huge tracts of land where they have cut the timber. In some areas, the deer actually prevent the reforestation that is essential to sustained timber yields. For a list of such plants—the common winter foods preferred by the three types of deer—see Appendix I. When possible, whitetails will pick up whatever corn has been lost to the picker, and they also feed on rye grass, alfalfa, and winter wheat. Dry leaves, when available, are eaten by all three deer in the winter even though they are low in protein and digestibility.

A whitetail reaches high for oak leaves and begins to create a distinct browse line.

In my home area, red cedar is browsed as high as the deer can reach, yet red cedar is only a "stuffer"—starvation food. I have heard countless deer hunters refer to rhododendron and mountain laurel as good deer food. These plants, too, are "stuffer" foods. Deer are able to eat these evergreens, even though the leaves contain a poison known as andrometatoxin, which is deadly to livestock. But the fact that deer can eat something—and may eat great quantities of it when other forage is unavailable—does not make it good deer food. I have opened the stomachs of countless deer that had died of starvation and found them stuffed with red cedar and rhododendron. Unfortunately, these plants, as well as mountain laurel, are low in nutrients. Deer often fill their paunches with these plants for lack of better food and then slowly starve.

Harley Shaw of Idaho reported that on five different occasions during the winter of 1961-1962 he found where whitetail deer had pawed down through 3 to 6 inches (75 to 150 mm.) of snow to eat wintering colonies of ladybug beetles. There were no food plants in the deer-scraped areas, and the rumens of three out of eight deer collected had large quantities of beetles in them, proving that the deer had actively sought out the beetles as food. This is the only instance of insect-eating that has come to my attention, but it is not totally surprising since insects are virtual reservoirs of protein.

303

Red cedar is a poor deer food, yet these cedars show a browse line because better forage was inaccessible to yarded deer.

## Deer Yards, Dominance, and Aggression

Deer yards are usually in dense evergreen swamps, draws, gulleys, or along brushy watercourses. The deer's main objective is to get out of the wind. Snow depth is usually less in these sheltered areas because a lot of the snow remains on the tree branches. Often, more than half the snow depth is held aloft. And when the snow starts to melt, the area under the trees will be bare long before the surrounding area is free of snow.

These spots are always warmer because they trap whatever warmth the sun gives. The dark trunks of the trees absorb and hold the warmth instead of reflecting it away as do snow areas. The branches also provide a protective umbrella that prevents a rapid heat loss at night. You may have noticed how much faster the temperature drops on a clear winter night than when there is cloud cover. Even in winter, some heat is given off by the trees in the form of thermal radiation. In effect, the trees create a microcosm that works to the deer's advantage.

Although the wind and cold cause the deer to yard up, it is snow depth that determines how long they remain yarded. They will stay in the yard area until the snow melts sufficiently, and once they leave it they will not gather there again until forced to do so the following year.

They do not deliberately tramp out a network of trails through their yarding areas; the trails are a result of their search for food. There is almost always a food shortage in the winter yard areas, and this creates belligerence as the deer respond to the most important life-governing force—the survival instinct. Not only is there a food shortage and physical stress from the cold, but also the

This is a deer trail with droppings in an over-browsed yard.

psychological stress of crowding. Whitetails, unlike blacktails and mule deer, are not herd animals; they gather into large groups only when forced to.

Aggression is very common in the deer yards. Bucks turn on does, and does even turn on their own fawns, and fawns turn on other fawns. Dominance in a deer yard is in a constant state of flux. It is readily achieved but has to be re-established at almost every contact because of the desperate need for food.

Bucks usually dominate the does simply because they are larger and heavier. However, some of the large adult does are so used to being leaders that they will not give way before the bucks. The matriarchal does will drive subordinate does away from food. Fawns of the dominant does are dominant over fawns of subordinate does. It is much like human society. The children of the rich and powerful tend to be dominant over the other children even though they have done nothing on their own to warrant this rating. An often overlooked factor in this social standing is that dominant parents, in both human and animal populations, can more easily provide what the young need, so these young have an early advantage that they tend to maintain all of their lives. The condition in which a fawn enters the winter is very important. Its condition and size will play an important role in establishing its rank on the dominance scale.

Another interesting fact about dominance is that when a subordinate is not

A six-month-old fawn of a dominant doe, already shows his own dominance by kicking out.

a threat it will be tolerated and granted more privileges than a more aggressive deer that is higher up in the social standing. I have seen a big buck tolerate a yearling buck and allow it to eat, though the big buck would drive off all other large or older bucks. New deer moving into an area are usually dominated regardless of their sex, age, or size. After they become established as residents, they may fight their way up the social ladder, but once dominance has been established in a yarding area the status quo is usually maintained for that winter. Dominance is not a leadership trait but merely "might making right" and "survival of the fittest."

The dominance of adult bucks sometimes shows up in strange ways. The New Jersey Game Department found that in any live-trapping program bucks constituted 80 percent of the catch for the first week or so. Live-trapping is most successful when natural food is scarce. The deer can then be lured into the traps with food. The adult bucks showed their dominance by driving other deer away from the traps. Their dominance gave them the first chance at food and the chance to be trapped first.

The fact that the bucks lose their antlers prior to or during the winter months of hardship proves that the antlers are sexual weapons. If they were to be used for protection, they would be retained until spring at least. With his antlers gone, a buck fights or achieves dominance by striking out with his front feet, just as the does will at all times of the year.

In achieving dominance, all deer of either sex usually follow the same pat-

Button bucks display aggression in an effort to achieve dominance.

terns. In threatening another deer, the aggressor usually drops its ears down and back until they lie against its neck. Then the aggressor stares at the other deer. If the aggressor decides it needs to carry the action further, it sidles up toward the lesser deer. This is usually followed by rushing and snorting. Then the front foot is raised and used to strike out and down. If the lesser deer does not give way, the aggressor will stand on its hind feet and flail out, alternately striking with both front feet. Most often the objective is achieved by just a single strike, and sometimes the aggressor will skip the preliminary steps and just rush at its opponent and strike out. At times the attack will come from the side or from the rear with no warning at all, and often patches of hair are knocked out in these encounters. Sometimes both deer rise up and flail away. The larger, heavier deer wins out.

It is hard for the fawns to understand why the mother that has taken such good care of them now drives them away from what little food is available. The doe cannot understand it, either; she is just instinctively responding to the necessity of obtaining food for herself. Intolerance increases as the winter goes on and the food supply decreases. It is from the fawns that nature extracts the greatest toll.

In deep snow deer must bound rather than walk, as evidenced in these tracks.

The legs of an average deer are 18 to 22 inches (46 to 56 cm.) long. The legs of a seven- or eight-month-old fawn are only 16 to 18 inches (41 to 46 cm.) long. If the snow is 18 inches deep, the adults can walk through it even though it is hard going. The fawn's chest drags, and walking through snow of that depth is almost impossible for it. Its only means of moving about is to jump over the snow, and this is exhausting. Even the adult deer can move only with great difficulty when the snow reaches 24 inches (61 cm.). Snow above that depth imprisons them.

Researchers have concocted a descriptive formulation of conditions. They use the term "severe winter" to mean 60 days with a 15-inch (38 cm.) depth of accumulated snow or 50 days with a 24-inch (61 cm.) depth of snow. A "moderate winter" is 60 days with 12 inches (30 cm.) of snow. I can understand their trying to work out a common denominator, but their two categories for a "severe winter" are not the same thing. A deer can walk in 15 inches (38 cm.) of snow and it cannot in 24 inches (61 cm.). That's a tremendous difference.

The deer are usually forced into their yarding areas before the snow becomes too deep for them to get there. Most whitetails travel no more than 2 or 3 miles (3.2 to 4.8 kilom.) to yard up. The maximum distance is about 15 miles (24.1 kilom.). In their quest for food, a network of trails is soon established but only within the sheltered area. Food can be available a ¼-mile away but once the deer yard up, that food might just as well be on the moon.

This pronounced browse line marks an overbrowsed wintering area.

They will not go out into the exposed areas to eat. Depending on the size of the yard and the number of deer in it, all food that is easily reached may soon be consumed.

### Starvation

When the easily reached food is gone, deer stand on their hind legs to reach overhead branches. A seven-month-old fawn, standing on its hind legs, can reach up about 5 feet (1.5 m.). An adult doe can reach up about 6 feet (1.8 m.), an adult buck about 7 feet (2.1 m.). Naturally, the fawns get the least food. When all the available food is eaten up to the 7-foot height, a "browse line" is apparent. This is also called "high lining," but it really means starvation.

It has always been a puzzle to me why deer have not developed the habit of "riding down" browse as moose do. When a moose wants to reach the uppermost branches of a sapling, it will stand on its hind feet and put its chest against the sapling. With its body weight, the moose then pushes the sapling over so that it can easily feed on the upper branches. This often kills the sapling by breaking it, but it helps the moose now and in the future because it

Even when there is no snow in an impoverished habitat, deer may be forced to reach high for browse.

creates holes in otherwise dense stands of same-age saplings that would otherwise grow too large for the moose to push over or to reach the lower branches. New saplings soon grow in the holes thus created.

I have often watched deer balance on their hind legs to get a few mouthfuls of food, but I have never seen them even attempt to put their feet against the trunks of saplings as domesticated goats and some African antelopes do. Many of the saplings a deer browses could be pushed over, yet deer have not developed this behavior.

310

This doe ate pencil-thick twigs after smaller, far more beneficial browse was depleted.

They prefer browse that is no thicker than a wooden matchstick. A study showed that they prefer red maple twigs up to 4.17 mm. in diameter, quaking aspen up to 3.84 mm., northern red oak up to 3.47 mm., black cherry up to 2.95 mm., and gray birch up to 1.26 mm. When hunger is severe, they will eat browse up to the size of a wooden pencil.

But eating browse of this larger diameter is a losing battle for several reasons. First there is the fact that the smaller twigs are the newest growth and their bark has the highest protein content. The older bark of the larger twigs not only has less protein but is less digestible. A deer gets its nutrition out of the bark and not out of the cellulose of the wood.

Then there is the fact that larger twigs have less bark in proportion to their volume. The amount of bark on a twig can be calculated by multiplying the diameter of the twig by 3.14 to find its circumference, and then multiplying the circumference by the length of the twig. A matchstick-sized twig of 3 mm. diameter and 100 mm. length has 942 square mm. of bark. A pencil-sized twig of 8 mm. diameter and 100 mm. length has about 2500 square mm. of bark, or a little less than three times as much bark.

To find the volume of the twig, you multiply 3.14 by the radius of the twig, then multiply the resulting product by the radius again, then multiply that product by the length. Thus a twig of 3 mm. diameter and 100 mm. length has a volume of about 707 cubic mm., while a twig of 8 mm. diameter and 100 mm. length has a volume of 5,024 cubic mm., or about seven times as much bulk. In other words, the larger twig has seven times as much volume for less than three times as much nutritious bark. What it means is that when a deer is forced to eat the large twigs, it is actually getting less than half of the nutrients out of each paunchful of browse because it has to consume so much more bulk for the amount of life-giving bark. And this is *if* the deer can find enough of even the larger twigs to fill its paunch.

To compound the problem of volume, the bark of the larger twigs has less protein and is less digestible than the bark of small twigs, and that cuts the amount of available nutrients even further.

There is one last problem, and this is often the one that pushes deer over the brink of starvation. When a deer eats any browse during bitterly cold weather, it must produce extra body heat to thaw out the frozen twigs in its paunch before they can be utilized. When the deer is eating the large twigs, the body heat and energy lost in coverting this food to assimilable nutrients may be greater than the benefits gained.

The same thing happens when the deer eats snow while in a weakened condition. Water is imperative, because much of starvation weight loss is actually caused by dehydration. The drain on a creature's body to thaw the snow and convert it into water is tremendous. It is for this reason that a person who is tired and cold should not eat snow to alleviate thirst. Doing so can bring on hypothermia and under some conditions cause death. Young mammals require a higher percentage of water per body weight than do adults. Because of all of these factors, fawns comprise about 60 to 80 percent of the deer that die of starvation.

It is normal and expected that deer, like range cattle, will lose 12 to 15 percent of their body weight due to the cold winter weather even if they have all the nutritious food they can eat. A deer can lose up to 30 percent of its body weight and survive. The critical point lies between 30 and 33 percent. A loss of a full third of its total body weight is almost always fatal.

Most deer, in most areas, go into the winter with some fat on their bodies. The amount of fat is determined by the quantity and quality of the food available before the onset of winter. The amount of fat, the amount of winter food available, and the severity of the winter are the three crucial factors determining survival. A deer with poor fat deposits may survive a mild winter because it will be able to move about more freely and have access to more food. A deer with poor fat deposits cannot survive a protracted and severe winter.

As the temperature drops and the food intake is lessened, the fat deposits are utilized. The fat surrounding the back and hams is the first to go, and then that of the abdominal cavity. Essential fatty acids (aceto-acetate and hydroxybutyrate) are derived by the oxidation of these body fats.

A deer with any fat on its body will have a very high fat content in the marrow of its bones. The marrow of a deer in good condition is white and contains about 95 percent fat. This fat looks like suet. After the body fat has been utilized, this marrow fat will be withdrawn. The color of the marrow changes in accordance with the percentage of fat that is left—from white to yellow to pink, and finally to bright red. The bright red color has the look and the consistency of cranberry sauce and denotes a fat content of about 1½ percent. A deer with marrow like this is dying or already dead. To find out for certain whether a deer has died of starvation, one has only to check the marrow of the upper leg bones. Break the leg bone and if the marrow is red, no further research is needed. The carcass need not be fresh to prove this point. Even in late spring or summer, when nothing is left but scattered bones, starvation can be proved by this method. The marrow will have dehydrated but the remaining dried shreds will still show the red color.

At the same time that the fat is being withdrawn from the marrow, the body is also forced to "cannibalize" its own muscle protein. As starvation continues, the deer's liver is also affected. Ordinarily the liver produces glycogen from glucose and proteins and stores it to be released to the muscles as energy when needed. Without glucose or glycogen, the deer develops hypoglycemia—an abnormally low level of blood sugar. A deer with severe hypoglycemia is subject to trembling and may become too weak to stand. This condition almost always foretells death. Deer in such a weakened state become increasingly susceptible to pneumonia and other diseases, and to predation. They also lose all fear of man, mainly because they just don't have the strength to escape. This loss of fear may also be attributable in part to brain dysfunction, since the brain is starved along with the rest of the body.

Starvation of deer is extremely common, and in many areas it is growing worse each year. Those states that allow does to be hunted and are harvesting a greater percentage of their deer herds are reducing the losses due to starvation. In states that still have a bucks-only law, the situation is becoming increasingly bad. A. Starker Leopold, a zoologist at the University of California, has estimated that in a severe winter as many as two million deer die in the United States from starvation.

We are learning that one of the most important things we can do for deer faced with starvation is to leave them alone and make sure everything else leaves them alone, if possible. It has been proved that, except where highly nutritious natural food is abundant, deer usually lose more by active foraging

This deer is in good enough condition to move through snow without undue harm.

than they gain, because of the energy expended. We also have learned that, where the deer's endocrine system has had a chance to adapt to the cold, the animals are geared to be sedentary. The key to their survival is their inactivity. Any activity burns up calories, which when not replaced by food, have to be taken from the body tissue. Strenuous activity burns up much larger numbers of calories and also produces stress.

For a variety of reasons—which will be discussed in the section on management—even artificial feeding can lead to undue activity and stress. Moreover, it can maintain an unhealthy overpopulation which will cause greater starvation problems later on. Such feeding should be restricted to real emergency situations. For a fuller discussion of this topic, see Chapter 23.

Some fawns have been known to go more than a month without food and still survive. Some adult does have been known to go over two months without a mouthful of food and still live. So long as the weather stays extremely cold, a deer will not move any more than it is forced to. It is, in effect, idling its engine so that fewer calories are consumed. Any kind of disturbance that forces the deer to move out of their beds during severe weather lessens their chance of survival. For this reason, the disturbances sometimes caused by snowmobiles can be extremely detrimental.

There is nothing wrong with using snowmobiles, provided people don't misuse them. Snowmobiles provide great sport when used in open fields or on woodland trails designated for them. They should not be run all through the old woods roads that lead back into the swamps and other deer yarding areas.

This emaciated deer cannot move about in snow without sacrificing crucial energy reserves. In this case, winter may mean death.

Thankfully, there are not many irresponsible snowmobilers who actually run deer with their machines. But unfortunately, there are some. Many snowmobilers have harmed deer inadvertently by just disturbing them, causing the animals to leave their beds and try to move out of the area. Such people would not dream of harming the deer, they merely want to see them. Many snow-mobilers have only realized the harm done after I have explained to them how important it is for the deer to remain as inactive as possible. There are times when just the noise of the snowmobiles is enough to disturb the deer. Research has shown that deer that are forced out of an area on weekends by snowmobiles will usually return after a day of quiet. It is unfortunate that the deer have to expend the energy to leave any area and then return to it at a time when they are fighting for survival.

Helenette Silver, a New Hampshire Game Department biologist, determined in 1959 that a 112-pound (51.2 kg.) deer at rest needs 1,323 calories in a 24-hour period. Arthur C. Guyton calculated that a 154-pound (69.9 kg.) man at rest needs 1,850 calories. Using this basis, Severinghaus and Tullar, of New York State, figured that a man and a deer of equal weight would need about the same number of calories if both were at rest. Carrying this supposition further, they calculated that a deer and a man engaged in the same type of motion would expend similar amounts of energy and require the same number of calories.

A mule deer suns himself in a bed sheltered from the wind. If he were moving at a fast walk, he would be burning up six times more calories. (Photo by Len Rue, Jr.)

Charts prepared by Guyton indicate that a man walking very fast requires over six times more calories than when resting. If he walks up steps he will burn up eleven times more calories than at rest. The researchers figured if a deer was panicked and ran from a snowmobile, it would burn up six to eleven times more energy than while at rest. The running deer would burn up about 900 calories per hour.

Snowmobiles are used most extensively on weekends. On weekdays the deer may spend 12 hours bedded down, for a cost of 1,200 calories; 6 hours of standing relaxed, for a cost of 630 calories; 4 hours of light exercise such as feeding, for a cost of 680 calories; two hours of running, for a cost of 1,140 calories—for a total of 3,650 calories. Severinghaus and Tullar calculated that if snowmobiles went into the deer yard for four hours on any day, the deer's energy expenditure would skyrocket to 6,830 calories per day. This is almost double the normal daily expenditure.

If deer were disturbed by snowmobiles on the weekends during December, January, February, and March, those weekends would cost each deer as many extra calories as would ordinarily be used in one month of normal living. In effect, it would subject each deer to one additional month of winter. We are losing countless thousands of deer to starvation because, with the food available, they cannot produce enough calories to survive a normal winter. A winter of weekend snowmobile harassment, which burns up an additional 100,000 calories, means that more deer are going to die needlessly.

Dogs are another menace and particularly so during the period of deep snow and cold. Although there are wild dogs that live on deer year-round, in the winter most of the dogs chasing deer are somebody's well-fed pets. Two collies and an Irish setter, wearing collars and tags, have just come running through my land searching the bottomlands for deer. Such dogs are just out for a romp. They may not even be interested in killing the deer; they just enjoy the chase. And it is the chasing of weakened deer that hastens their death.

The stress of fear alone would surely be detrimental, even if the deer were not run hard. When they run, their mouths gape, their tongues often protrude, and they breathe heavily. Sometimes these same symptoms are visible when they are frightened but not running. The surge of adrenaline entering the nervous system during stress may produce the symptoms of a hard run.

When the snow is deep and fluffy, hungry wild dogs are at as much of a disadvantage as the deer, but well-fed dogs have a distinct advantage. All dogs have the deer at a tremendous disadvantage when the snow forms a crust hard enough to support a dog's weight but not a deer's. Dogs, for their body weight, have a much larger foot surface than deer, and the deer's sharp, pointed hooves break through all but the strongest snow crust. Under these conditions, the dogs or other predators wreak havoc on the deer.

Yet another major fault of snowmobiles is that the dogs follow in the packed-down tracks the machines make in soft snow, and are thus enabled to get back into areas they otherwise could not penetrate. Dogs, snow, and deer are always a bad combination; when these components are coupled with severe cold they are most lethal. Deer movements are not as devastating if the weather is moderate.

The weather may give the deer a respite. Even the most severe winter usually includes one major period and two lesser times when the weather moderates. The January, or mid-winter, thaw usually occurs around the third week of that month. This break may be no more than a day or two or possibly three

Whitetails begin to move about during thaws.

days long, but it usually sends the thermometer up above the freezing mark.

As soon as this happens the deer start to move about, and if there is any food available they will feed all day long. Usually, February also has a couple of short periods of moderating weather. Every moderate spell, no matter how brief, gives the deer a new lease on life.

The Indians called February the "Starvation Moon," as it was thought to be the month of the greatest winter hardship. There is no doubt about it, February can be brutal. It is usually the month of greatest snow accumulation. January is usually the coldest month, and the snows that have fallen have little chance of melting. February is a snow month and its snows pile up on top of the base laid down in January. But most of the deer that die of starvation do so in the last part of February and the first half of March. March is a month of promises seldom delivered.

In southeastern Alaska, the Sitka blacktail deer are forced from the steep mountainsides by the deep snows of a hard winter down to the sea beaches—and to their death. The beach areas are the only space where the snow is shallow enough to allow the deer to move. The deer feed on the remnants of the western red cedar and the hemlock and then are forced to feed on the kelp and seaweed washed up on the beaches. Except for the latter stuffer foods, the beaches are bare and, soon, so are the bones of the deer, bleaching whiter than the driftwood they are scattered among. Along the Nakwasina Passage and Deadman's Beach, the remains of as many as ten to twelve deer per mile are commonly found each spring following a hard winter.

A whitetail buck comes to water during a temporary moderation of winter weather.

The Gunnison mule deer herd in south-central Colorado has probably been studied as extensively as any herd in the country. All kinds of management practices have been tried there. Overpopulation and range destruction were major causes for the deer population to decline. In one canyon, in one spring, after a severe winter, biologists found 253 carcasses of mule deer that had died of starvation.

The literature on the whitetail deer abounds with records of thousands dying of starvation. The spring of 1977 added pages of statistics. Although the winter of 1976-1977 was the coldest on record, in my area of northwestern New Jersey, we did not have a great snow depth. Our deer were fortunate. They did seek out the sheltered draws during the prolonged periods of cold, but they were able to move out as soon as the weather moderated. Our deer also had the advantage of going into the winter hog-fat from a fantastic acorn crop. They were still feeding on acorns in mid-February.

The winter of 1960-1961 caused the greatest die-off from starvation that I have ever personally seen. The 63 inches (160 cm.) of snowfall compacted to about 4 feet (1.2 m.) and that depth remained for most of the winter and late

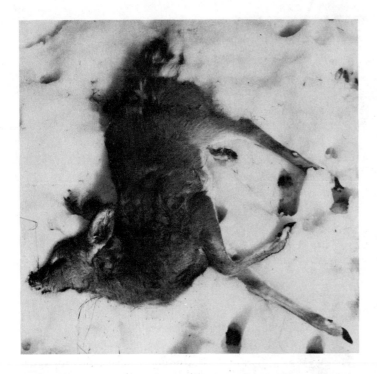

This young victim of starvation is just another number in the astronomical winterkill statistics.

into the spring because of the cold weather. Many of our deer wintered in the red-cedar-covered lowlands, which became death traps for many of them but allowed a viable nucleus to survive. When spring finally melted the snow, I found 27 dead deer in one square mile.

When you hear preservationists talk about "letting nature take care of its own," you know they have never witnessed deer dying of starvation by the dozens, by the hundreds, by the thousands. They have not seen a beautiful deer turn into a dull-eyed, listless rack of bones, wrapped in a rough coat, stoically awaiting death. The deer don't comprehend what is happening to them. There is nothing they can do about what is happening, so they only attempt to endure.

The preservationists have not seen the accidents that happen to starvation-weakened deer. Fences that the deer once cleared with ease become insurmountable obstacles. Many deer catch their feet in the top strands of fence wire, and they hang and struggle until death releases them from shock and cold. In the mule deer country, hundreds of skeletons are hung up on the fences each winter like laundry bleaching in the sun. In the early spring, trout fishermen find the rotting carcasses of deer that tried to get some of the new vegetation growing along the streamsides. The deer that slipped into the water are the ones that left their carcasses there.

Weak with hunger, this deer failed to clear a fence, was caught in top strands, and struggled there until it died.

The preservationists have not seen the deer being eaten by dogs while still alive but too weak to offer any resistance. They have not seen the deer try to arise, only to fall at once, too weak to really struggle. They have not seen these things, or they would not be preservationists but conservationists. They would realize that deer are a crop that must be managed, harvested, and utilized. The deer are better served by biologists with facts than by people who act only from emotion and sentiment.

The number of fetuses a doe is carrying depends on her age and her general health, as previously discussed. When a doe is subjected to starvation, several things may happen. During the first four months of a fetus's life, nature is interested in saving the life of the doe if a choice has to be made. If she is carrying twins, one of the fetuses will die and the nutrients that were the fetus will be absorbed into her body and utilized. Occasionally the dead fetus will be aborted, but this is a waste of nutrients and seldom happens. The remaining fetus will continue to live, growing very slowly. Before the critical point in an extended period of starvation is reached, the remaining fetus will also be sacrificed and absorbed. The doe will be barren for just that year. Barren does

This whitetail fawn stands in the characteristic, humped starvation position.

are a rarity, and are usually the result of starvation and not of old age or lack of impregnation. A fetus that is carried four months usually survives because by that time the new sprouts of spring are available. In March the deer's endocrine system reverses itself and the basic metabolism speeds up, forcing the doe to be more active and to feed more to secure the nourishment that is now needed by the fetus as its growth speeds up. From the age of four months on, the demands of the fetuses take priority over the bodily needs of the doe.

Deer that are in the last stages of starvation stand with their backs humped up against the cold. Their hair stands on end in a futile effort to increase the depth of insulation. The fawns are short-faced, because they have not reached their full growth, and with their hair standing on end this shortness is emphasized. The eyes of a starved fawn appear to bulge out of their sockets. The deer stand until they are too weak, and then they collapse.

One fawn that I found during a severe winter was so weak that he staggered as he walked. His chest was skinned and cut from falling on ice and rocks. He had been trying to get some food from the few blades of grass that grew in the warmth of a spring hole. When the fawn staggered off into the deep snow, he fell and could not get up. As I walked toward him, he struggled to get to his feet and bawled loudly. I picked him up and he lay in my arms without a struggle.

The little buck was between eight and nine months old. On good food, he should have weighed about 80 to 90 pounds (36.2 to 40.7 kg.). Good food was

The fawn here is so weakened by starvation that it cannot stand.

something he did not have, and he weighed 34 pounds (15.4 kg.). His skin hung in loose folds; his backbone protruded so sharply that every segment could be felt. He had the typical winter-starved look, with the hair of his head on end, giving him the typical fuzzy appearance.

I took the little buck home and put him in a sheltered pen. He could not or would not eat any of the good maple sprouts and browse that I brought him. I tried soft commercial feeds and even tried to feed him warm milk concentrates, but to no avail. Too much had been taken out of his body, he had been pushed beyond the point of no return. He died five days later.

I thought the reason was that, through starvation, the microflora and bacteria in his paunch had died, and without them he could no longer digest food. This was the common belief held by the biologists until 1971. Reports and scientific papers in the most prestigious wildlife journals lent credence to this theory. It was believed that a starved deer could reintroduce these symbiotic organisms by direct mouth-to-mouth contact or mouth-to-anus contact with a healthy deer—by eating browse that another deer had chewed or by eating the feces of a healthy deer. Deer do exchange their stomach organisms in these ways but we now know that this is not needed.

In 1971 David DeCalesta, Julius Nagy, and James Bailey, all from the Department of Fishery and Wildlife Biology at Colorado State University, shattered that myth for all time. These researchers starved nine penned mule deer under controlled conditions. After the deer died, fluid from their rumen was compared with the fluid taken from non-starved deer. Naturally, the microorganisms in the rumen fluid of the starved deer were lower than in the non-starved deer. But there were still more than a billion viable organisms in the rumen of the starved deer. The starved deer had maintained viable bacteria in their digestive system without having to reintroduce any from outside sources. This proved that starved deer would be capable of digesting food if they had access to it.

In another experiment, the researchers starved 26 mule deer fawns and does. Four fawns died after having no food for 33 and 34 days but the other nine lived after being starved for 36 days. One doe died after being starved for 54 days, but all of the other does lived, including one starved for 64 days. The main purpose was to observe and record the effect of the reintroduction of food. The researchers had already proved that the deer had the organisms in their stomach to digest food but tests were needed to prove that the starved deer could actually handle it. Equally important, the tests proved the deer did not suffer from digestive problems such as bloat after they again had access to food. The crucial factor was that deer that had lost less than 30 percent of their total body weight could survive, but a loss of more than 30 percent doomed them. They were not doomed because they could not handle the food but because with a 30 percent weight loss too much had been taken out of their systems to allow survival.

These two experiments have begun to change many concepts of deer management because, for the first time, biologists can calculate the deer's chances of winter survival. Given the known factors of the condition of the deer going into winter, the amount of winter food available, the weather and snow conditions, and the estimated days of starvation, biologists can more readily estimate deer survival and herd population. This information is vital in setting long-range plans for the harvesting and the management of deer.

Those surviving deer that have lost the greatest amount of body weight make the greatest weight gains in the spring when food is again available. Deer have a tremendous tenacity for life; they are tough. Although many will die, more will live, and it has always been so. Individual areas may be hit very hard but this has little effect on the total population of deer. They have lived with adversity for many millions of years, and have evolved with it and because of it.

# III

## Toward Sound Deer Management

# 18

# A Brief
# Historical View
# of Management Problems

The easiest part of wildlife management is managing the wildlife; the hardest part is educating the public so that the wildlife can be managed.

Before World War I, most Americans lived in rural areas; they had their roots in the soil and they knew about the relationships that living things have with the soil. Today most Americans live in urban areas and many have no roots at all. When we were a farm-based people, we understood that all living things were products of the land or the water. We knew that the number of living things such areas could support was directly related to the food available and to the protective shelter provided for each species. We understood the meaning of the word habitat before that word became fashionable.

We find it humorous when we hear of city children who think that milk comes from cartons and can't imagine taking it from a cow. We don't find it humorous when these same city children become voting adults who make decisions concerning wildlife and our natural resources, for they make those decisions with no more information than they had about the source of milk.

Rocky Mountain mule deer, like this one, inhabit northern Arizona's Kaibab Plateau. Decades ago predators and hunting were eliminated. Subsequently, overpopulation victimized the herd.

Some of Walt Disney's nature movies are excellent educational films. But Disney was also responsible for the creation of the "Bambi syndrome" that pervades the thinking of millions of our citizens who grew up with the utopian view of deer promulgated by the movie "Bambi." That classic children's movie, which endowed wildlife with human emotions and intelligence, was intended to be a beautiful, sentimental fairy tale, involving cartoon characters no more true to life than the "Big Bad Wolf" that Disney created to go with his "Three Little Pigs" or the three bears encountered by Goldilocks. Unfortunately (and incredibly to those of us who have spent any time observing wildlife) a large segment of the public actually sees wild creatures through the sentimental haze of a cinematic fairy tale. This works to the great detriment of wildlife rather than to its benefit.

The most important reason for deer management is that "the deer is its own worst enemy." The deer is an exceedingly adaptable creature, one that can thrive almost anywhere in the United States. Deer populations are limited only by the availability of food, water, and cover. If these three requirements

Although the Kaibab deer herd had flourished despite predation, 4,889 coyotes were killed when the area was made a preserve. Cougars, bobcats, and wolves were also virtually exterminated—to the detriment of the deer.

can be met, deer have the reproductive capability of increasing their numbers to the point where they will destroy their range and devastate their own numbers. Given good habitat and a lack of predators, a deer herd will almost double its numbers every year. And this has happened time after time.

The classic example of deer mismanagement, and the proved destructiveness of overpopulation, has to be the Kaibab Plateau in northern Arizona. The Rocky Mountain mule deer that inhabited the Kaibab were magnificent animals with exceptionally large antlers. The Navajo and Piute Indians came into the area to hunt the deer each fall but they did not live there. The plateau, which covers about a million acres, is bordered on the southeast and south by the Grand and Marble canyons, on the west by Kanab Canyon, and on the north and northeast by a belt of semi-desert and open plains providing very little water. Thus, the deer were effectively fenced in.

The area had been leased to ranchers for grazing since 1893, and as many as 200,000 sheep, 20,000 head of cattle, and large numbers of horses were pastured there. There were between 3,000 and 4,000 mule deer on the plateau when it was made into a preserve by President Theodore Roosevelt in 1906. It was designated as the Grand Canyon National Game Preserve.

With the creation of the preserve, all hunting was forbidden. The Forest Service, which administered the preserve, established game patrols and employed trappers and hunters to eliminate predators. With guns, traps, and poison they killed 4,889 coyotes, 781 cougars, 554 bobcats, 20 wolves, and a few bears. Gradually the sheep were prohibited from grazing there, although cattle and horses continued to be pastured in the area.

With the elimination of all natural predators and with no hunters harvesting any of the surplus animals, an eruption of the deer population occurred by 1923. Although the official government estimate of the population was a conservative 30,000, other estimates put the population at over 100,000. The experts could not agree on the population figures, but one thing that was apparent to all was the tremendous destruction being done to the vegetation. And it was not just the damage done by the deer. Overgrazing by cattle and horses had destroyed most of the native grasses and forced the cattle to feed on browse in direct competition with the deer. The overgrazing by livestock denuded the soil of its protective vegetation, and thousands upon thousands of tons of top soil were lost through erosion.

In 1919, Edward Goldman, one of the top biologists with the Bureau of Biological Survey, was sent to the area to study the deer problem. His reports were filled with warnings of imminent starvation of the deer. Goldman's concern was echoed and supported by George Shiras III, on the basis of his personal investigations of the Kaibab.

To complicate the problem, in 1919 part of the plateau had been made into the Grand Canyon National Park and was now under the jurisdiction of the Park Service and not of the Forest Service. When the Forest Service suggested that the deer herd be thinned out by shooting, stiff opposition came from the Park Service, which would not tolerate any shooting on its land. Further opposition came from Arizona's Governor, George Hunt, who was opposed to any federal control as a violation of states' rights. When the Forest Service wanted some of the deer hunted, the Governor threatened to have his game wardens arrest any man who came off the plateau with a deer. While the squabbling raged on, the deer population skyrocketed—and, like a skyrocket, it was about to explode.

Zane Grey evidently believed that cowboys could do everything in real life that he could have them do in his novels. He gathered forty cowboys and seventy Navajo Indians to herd the deer off the plateau and across the Colorado River in an effort to thin out the herd. Two futile attempts in 1924 proved once again that you don't drive deer. Not a single deer was herded off the plateau.

That winter, the deer died by the thousands. Goldman, in the spring of 1925, figured that between 30,000 and 60,000 deer had died in the previous two winters. Subsequently, limited shooting was approved. Between 1925 and 1930, 1,124 deer were killed by federal employees, 2,652 were live-trapped and removed, and 11,641 were killed by sportsmen under special federal permits. This total of 15,417 deer taken in five years did not even keep up with the annual herd increment. The range destruction continued at an accelerated pace.

330

The program to reduce the Kaibab deer herd and restore range succeeded, though some habitat scars still show. The area is again producing muleys like this one. (Photo by Len Rue, Jr.)

In 1930, a panel of experts in forestry, livestock, and wildlife toured the area on behalf of the federal government. This panel recommended that the war on predators be stopped, that all wild horses be removed from the plateau, and that live-trapping, regulated hunting by sportsmen, and controlled shooting of the deer by federal authorities be increased.

Hunters had taken deer in 1929, and in 1930 over 5,000 were harvested. Through the combination of starvation, disease, lowered birth rates due to malnutrition, and shooting, the deer herd was finally reduced to less than 20,000 by 1931. At last the range began to show signs of recovering. And so did the deer. The management program that had begun through trial and error eventually evolved into the proper game and range management, brought about by application of scientific research. The Kaibab Plateau, when I visited it a couple of years ago, still showed some scars of the range devastation that was once so common. But today, trophy heads are again being taken from the Kaibab.

This starving whitetail doe, her ribs showing through her hide, stands on her hind legs to reach remaining browse. Her condition typifies the result of ultra-protectionist laws.

Let me cite a few more examples of the deer's breeding potential. George Shiras III, in a letter to Ernest Thompson Seton, told how his family stocked Grand Isle, Michigan, in Lake Superior, with game during the late 1800s. By 1920 there were between 3,000 and 4,000 whitetails, as well as 250 elk and moose. The island has 14,000 acres, or less than 22 square miles. Each winter the Shiras family carried on an extensive feeding program, but even so the numbers of animals far outstripped the carrying capacity of the range. Before the crash there were about 160 deer to the square mile. With the range destroyed, all of the moose and elk died as well as more than half of the deer.

Some of the remaining deer were live-trapped and moved to other areas. Two adult bucks and four adult does were placed in a fenced enclosure of 1,200 acres in southern Michigan. In just five years those six deer multiplied to about 160, and the range destruction started there too.

In 1962, the Michigan Game Division put six bucks and eleven does on South Fox Island, an island of 3,000 acres, or about five square miles. This island lies about seventeen miles from the mainland in Lake Michigan. Although there had been deer on the island previously, they had all been killed off. Logging had taken most of the big timber, but the second growth that covered most of the island provided excellent habitat.

Two of the deer died from unknown causes that first winter, so fifteen deer were the nucleus of the population explosion that followed. Some of the landowners shot a few deer each year, but by 1969 only about forty had been taken. In 1969 it was figured that there were at least 500 deer on the island, and the range showed signs of deterioration. To alleviate these conditions, a special hunting season was held and the hunters took 188 deer.

As the breeding potential was still too high, a concentrated hunting effort was made in 1970, and 382 deer of all ages and both sexes were taken. A population count the following spring showed that there were still 194 deer on the island, and the population level the following fall would be back up around 400. It has been calculated that the deer harvest every year will have to be heavy enough to maintain that number as a peak population or else the range destruction will continue and the island's carrying capacity will deteriorate further.

The Llano Basin of the Edwards Plateau in central Texas provides another example of the reproductive capabilities of deer. The eradication of the screwworm was one of the leading factors that permitted this deer eruption. There are approximately 525,000 acres in the basin. From 1954 to 1961 there was an average density of 14.4 deer per 100 acres, or 75,600 deer. That is 92.1 deer per square mile. By 1961 the deer had increased to 18.9 per hundred acres, or 99,750 in the basin. That is 121 deer to the square mile—one of the heaviest deer concentrations in the nation. This fantastic population took its toll, as the deer became smaller each year because of malnutrition. The average field-dressed whitetail buck in 1961 weighed only 72 pounds (32.6 kg.), while an average doe, field-dressed, weighed 55 pounds (24.9 kg.).

Such increased density breeds stress as competition for food and cover increases. The friction generated between the deer usually lowers the reproductive rate. Although the herd population increased, the reproductive capability of each doe decreased.

The drastic overpopulation of deer was an impossibility before man eliminated the large predators. When nature was in balance, as the prey species increased the predators increased, and the localized decrease of both creatures was also almost simultaneous. Deer do not have the built-in control mechanisms that keep the populations of lemmings, varying hares, grouse, gray

The most destructive force against deer and other wildlife is symbolized by the bulldozer at work on the outskirts of a town. Here good edge habitat has been replaced by dumps, houses, industry, and landfills that allow additional "land development."

squirrels, some voles and mice, and other cyclic creatures under control. Cyclic animals attain a peak population density within a predictable period, after which the population is abruptly self-thinned by a combination of such factors as massive dispersion, decreased reproduction, and ailments closely related to population density. A new cycle then begins. Deer are not cyclic, and although they are self-destructive in that they create the conditions of their own starvation, these conditions do not materialize within a self-regulating cycle. The cyclic creatures do not destroy their range on a large scale, as deer do, before their populations are reduced. Deer populations can be kept under control only by eliminating the annual increment. This can no longer be done by predators, so the surplus must be harvested by man. And the most efficient and practical method is by regulated sport hunting.

When anti-hunting groups and preservationists voice such platitudes as "let Nature take care of its own," "get Nature back in balance," and "let's bring the big predators back," they are also proclaiming that they have lost touch with reality. Everyone would like to see nature more in balance, but to achieve this we would have to wipe out most of our human population and destroy most of our civilization.

The single most destructive force in the world is our own burgeoning human population with its resultant habitat destruction. We are currently losing a million acres of habitat to development each year. As our population increases, we need more homes, schools, factories, roads, etc. These areas can only be taken from wildlife habitat of some kind. With its habitat gone, the wildlife that formerly lived there is also gone — gone as effectively as if it were killed at the moment the development started. This concept is hard for many people to accept.

Many people prefer to think the wildlife just moves out of the area before it is built on. It does move out, but in most cases it really has no place to go. If the habitat into which the wildlife is forced to move could support more wildlife of that type, such animals would already be there. Nature abhors a vacuum and almost every niche is already filled at all times.

Although the human population growth in the United States has been drastically reduced, all demographic projections show that the population will rise tremendously from our present 216,000,000. The destruction of habitat will continue apace, and the numbers and types of our wild creatures will continue to decline. There is nothing game managers can do about this. It is a matter of personal concern for everyone. Unless we can control our own population, most of the wild creatures and the wild places will be lost, and with them the quality of our own lives.

The experiences on the Kaibab, Grand Isle, South Fox Island, and others all provided a fantastic education for wildlife managers and biologists throughout the world. The price was high but, as with any good education, it was worth the price. We have learned our lesson. Or have we?

The game managers, the biologists, and many hunters have learned from the devastation that the deer bring on themselves. But most of the general public, especially the preservationists, have not. They react out of emotionalism and ignorance — by-products of the Bambi syndrome. Such emotionalism stopped New Jersey's first proposed "doe day" back in 1958, when most of the opponents were deer hunters who knew very little about deer. Such emotionalism caused a "pocket-sized Kaibab" in New Jersey from 1970 to 1974 when such preservationist groups as Fund for Animals, Friends of Animals, Society for Animal Rights, and others stopped a hunt for deer in New Jersey's Great Swamp.

The Great Swamp National Wildlife Refuge is an area of some 6,000 acres in Morris County, New Jersey. Biologists on the refuge proposed a limited hunt in 1970 to reduce the rapidly expanding deer herd. For four years, legal action by preservationist groups stopped any hunting in the area. The herd continued to increase and the destruction of the range was severe. Damage to the shrubbery of homes in the area surrounding the Great Swamp was also severe. And the deer began to die of starvation. Ten cases of confirmed starvation occurred in the spring of 1974, and the biologists estimated that at least four times as many cases of starvation had occurred that winter.

New Jersey's Great Swamp National Wildlife Refuge has been the scene of a great controversy concerning the harvest of overabundant deer. This habitat is a mixture of wetland, grassland, and woodland. Its 6,000 acres can healthfully support about 250 deer, but in recent years the herd has been more then twice that number. Disease and starvation have resulted.

The first hunt in the Great Swamp took place in December, 1974. Busloads of protesters from the preservationist groups picketed the area, carrying placards charging collusion between the hunters, the National Rifle Association, the arms industry, and the wildlife biologists. One young woman carried a sign proclaiming that the hunters should prove their masculinity in the bedrooms and not with a gun. I don't know if she had any takers.

An interesting footnote to these demonstrations has been turned up by Dr. James Appelgate, working with polling experts from Rutgers' Eagleton Institute of Politics. He found that "the greatest opposition to hunting comes from college age females living in urban areas." One has to wonder how many hunting opponents have had an opportunity to observe or study wildlife. In fact, one has to wonder how many of them know anything at all about this subject.

It was estimated that there were 554 deer in the Great Swamp area, or about 55 deer to the square mile. That is more than twice the average population usually found on good range. And the habitat in the Great Swamp was in very poor condition. A hundred and six hunters hunted each day for the six days and harvested 127 deer.

One of the bucks taken had seven pounds (3.17 kg.) of papilloma tumors on his head and neck. The tumors covered one eye and had destroyed the cornea of

Although this buck appears to be in good condition—so far—he is licking at an itch caused by parasites. Heavy parasite loads and skin infections are widespread in overcrowded habitat.

the other, resulting in blindness. Two other deer also had crippling tumors. Many of the deer had heavy loads of parasites, and most were below the weight and size for the average New Jersey deer. Several deer died the spring following the hunt from a bacterial skin infection known as dermatophilosis. This was only the second known time that deer had died of this disease. In 1975 a parasite was found on the deer that had never been found on deer before. None of these tumors, parasites, or diseases had ever been found on the Great Swamp deer until overcrowding and starvation became rampant. It is a well-known biological fact that the incidence of disease and parasites increases as the health of the deer declines due to overcrowding and the resultant decrease in available food.

Hunting has continued at the Great Swamp each year, with a goal of bringing the herd down and keeping it down to about 250 animals, the carrying capacity of the land.

The biologists and wildlife managers have the hard facts on deer management. But facts do not sway the preservationists from their continued plotting of a collision course for the deer on the shoals of disease and starvation.

Fanatic preservationists are a tremendous threat to the future of most wildlife. Their "no-hunting" attitude, if allowed to prevail, would guarantee that

The anti-hunting preservationists have advocated the re-establishment of the wolf in eastern states to control deer herds without hunting. But astronomical numbers of wolves would be needed and—understandably—dairy and beef cattlemen would surely try to eradicate them.

wildlife populations in the future will be only a fraction of what they are now. The wildlife would not only diminish in numbers but also in physical size and health, as their ranges would be devastated. Under natural conditions, most species produce more young each year than their habitat can support. Unless something is done to increase the carrying capacity of a species' habitat, the yearly surplus of that species, whether it be made up of old or young specimens, must die. There is absolutely no biological argument about that incontestable fact; the surplus must die. The only question is how. It can be through starvation, predation, disease, or hunting by man. It is this surplus that sport hunting takes, and sport hunting thereby serves as a tool of proper game management. Not a single species of animal has been put on the endangered list by sport hunting. And the success stories of the management of deer, antelope, Canada geese, most ducks, and so on have been made possible by money provided by the sport-hunting fraternity.

Preservationists are motivated by a sincere belief in their cause. But sincerity does not necessarily make a belief right. Preservationists just don't know the facts. If they did, they would not be preservationists. The facts prove that most game species are, like deer, their own worst enemies; that if allowed to reproduce unchecked, they would destroy their food, their habitat, and ultimately themselves.

A favorite preservationist theme is that "if we bring back the wolf and the cougar—the big predators—we won't need to hunt the deer." I was lecturing

This cougar is caching a deer it killed. Cougars are efficient predators, but in New York State alone, 750 cougars and at least 3,500 wolves would be needed to maintain the population control achieved by hunters. In New York, herd control by predators might work on a limited basis, but only in Adirondack wilderness areas.

on deer in March, 1977, before a nature club in Westchester County, New York. It is amazing how many deer inhabit the little wooded enclaves of that county, just 30 miles (48.3 km.) north of New York City. Sure enough, a club member advocated the proposal of bringing back the predators to do away with hunting. The facts will reveal the impracticality of this motion.

In 1975, licensed hunters took 103,225 deer in New York. Biological research has proved that a cougar eats, on the average, a deer a week or fifty per year. It has been proved that a pack of eight wolves will kill 29 deer every 63 days. To equal the number of deer legally harvested by the hunters, New York would need a fantastic supply of predators.

Cougars never were as plentiful as wolves but are much more efficient predators, so we can allot them 37,500 deer per year even if New York has "only" 750 cougars. To kill the remaining 65,725 deer would take 438 packs of eight wolves each—3,504 wolves. New York is one of the chief milk-producing states. How do the preservationists propose keeping these 750 cougars and 3,504 wolves from killing the dairy cows and beef cattle, which are so much larger, "dumber," and easier to kill than the deer? How many people in urban Westchester County, just north of New York City, are going to want their share of the cougars and wolves? In 1975, the controversy over reducing the wolves in three of Alaska's game-management areas reached incendiary levels. Governor Jay Hammond offered to ship some of the live wolves down to any of the states that wanted them. There were no takers.

As much as I thrill to the sight of a deer, I thrill even more to the far rarer sight of a cougar or wolf. And, yes, I would like to see these predators returned to appropriate wilderness areas in the eastern United States. There are true wilderness areas in New York's Adirondack Mountains, for example, where relatively few people hunt. The Adirondacks have a high loss of deer due to starvation, and I believe these predators could help to alleviate the loss there. As both the wolf and the cougar are wilderness animals, they would be unlikely to leave the wilderness. They could help to keep the deer herd in balance with the range, and without reducing the game available to hunters.

Nor would man have anything to fear from either predator. In North America, there is only one authenticated record of a wolf attacking a man. The wolf was rabid. It was killed, and the man was not. Cougar attacks on humans have been authenticated, but they are extremely rare. The farmers adjoining the wilderness areas would probably lose some livestock, for which they would have to be compensated. I do not believe the losses would be frequent enough to make the cost of compensation prohibitive. In a few cases, where livestock predation continued, an individual predator would have to be eliminated.

In some regions, the numbers of predators must be controlled for the sake of deer and other wildlife whose habitat man has altered and diminished. In other regions, predators need all the protection they can be given, and they should be re-established in true wilderness areas where they have been extirpated. But the problem of too high a deer population for the carrying capacity of the habitat will not be solved by substituting predation for sport hunting. Facetiously, I sometimes recommend providing every American family with three automobiles in order to reduce the human population, and perhaps the deer population as well, in areas that are too densely occupied. But I hardly think any preservationist group will adopt my recommendation.

# 19

## Automobile Fatalities
## and Other Accidents

According to figures released by the American Automobile Association—figures gathered from all the states' game and highway departments—over a million wild creatures are killed on the nation's highways every day. That total of over 365 million wildlife deaths each year is a shocker.

A comprehensive listing of road-killed deer was published by the Fred Bear Sports Club for the year 1974. In that year, the number of deer actually picked up by wardens and other officials amounted to 146,229. That figure is the only one that can be substantiated but, having worked as a deputy warden for many years, I personally know that the figures reflect only a part of the kill.

For one thing, many deer that are struck by automobiles are not killed on the road but run, walk, or stagger out of sight and die. I tracked one young injured buck by following the toboggan-like trail it made in the snow with its chest. Both of the buck's front legs had been broken and it was traveling by sliding on its chest, pushing with its hind legs. I dispatched this buck, but many deer that are fatally injured are never found.

The author followed a strange, toboggan-like trail and found this doomed young buck. Both front legs had been broken in an automobile collision. Many such kills are never found and reported.

Nor do the statistics reveal the many road-killed deer that are removed by motorists or local residents for meat. In a few states this is legal, but in most states picking up a road-killed deer amounts to illegal possession of deer and is as much of a crime as poaching. Although I hate to see good venison wasted, it is easy to understand the states' position about the removal of road-killed deer by other than authorized personnel. There are just too many unscrupulous people who would deliberately kill deer by one means or another, then break a few bones and claim the animals were road-kills. Based on my personal experiences and years of research, I would say that at least a third of the deer that are killed on the roads do not appear on the fatality lists. The figure of 146,229 road-killed deer may be official but it is far too low. I would be willing to bet that a more realistic figure would be over 200,000.

Pennsylvania leads the entire nation in the number of road-killed deer. In 1974 it had 26,445 deer killed on its roads. The year 1975 was a record-breaker with 29,914. As the Pennsylvania report emphasizes, "those figures include only those deer which are physically removed from the state's highways by Game Commission personnel." The report also points out that the number of deer killed by vehicles in Pennsylvania exceeds the number of whitetails harvested by hunters in each of thirty-five other states.

In springtime auto accidents, what appears to be one kill may be two or three. This doe was carrying two full-term fawns when she was struck by a car.

The highest number of road kills usually occur during the rutting season, in October and November. More deer are killed on weekends than on weekdays because the traffic is heavier, and the peak hours are about sunrise and sunset to two hours later because this coincides with the peak of the deer's daily movements. Weather, temperature, and moon phase seem to make no appreciable difference.

A smaller peak period of road kills occurs in April and May, because this is the time that the first new sprouts of grass are shooting up. The grass along the highway edges is always up and green sooner than the grasses in the nearby fields or woodlands. Most new highway shoulders are fertilized to get them established, and deer prefer to feed on fertilized ground or rich soil. Most established roadways are mowed regularly, and those in the East never have the cut material gathered. This green mulch makes excellent fertilizer. The

This whitetail doe dashed across the road just ahead of an oncoming automobile.

absorption of the heat and its reflection by concrete or macadam creates a thermal strip providing a greenhouse effect, and this stimulates the grass to grow earlier. Much of the rain that falls on a highway is sprayed back on the shoulders by the automotive traffic, so the vegetation gets more than its normal share of moisture.

Pennsylvania currently estimates its deer herd at 600,000 animals. A known road-kill of nearly 30,000 means one out of every twenty deer in Pennsylvania will be killed by an automobile. New Jersey's deer herd is estimated at about 75,000 and we lose over 2,500 deer per year, or one out of every thirty. New York loses about 17 percent of its deer to road kills. These states have much higher percentages than most other states because of the tremendous volume of traffic on high-speed roads through the heart of good deer country.

Surprisingly, I can find no comprehensive, nationwide compilation of human deaths caused by collisions with deer on the highways. But in 1969 in Michigan alone, nine persons were killed in deer-car collisions. Nationwide, the number of fatalities must be considerable. A great many vehicles are involved, and well over sixty million dollars' worth of damage is done to vehicles annually in accidents with deer. A friend of mine was hospitalized after a deer attempted to avoid being hit by leaping over the hood. The animal crashed through the windshield, and my friend was lucky to come out of the accident alive. I have seen numerous cars wrecked when the drivers, in a desperate attempt to avoid hitting deer, went off the road.

For years, Pennsylvania had an excellent driving slogan: "Give wildlife a brake." My advice is always to drive defensively and be particularly alert in areas of high deer concentration. Most public highways have road signs warning motorists of deer-crossing areas.

During the periods of darkness, drive with your high beams on unless another car is coming toward you. This will allow you to see a deer at a greater distance. Watch for deer and also for the eyeshine of deer along the side of the

Driving defensively can reduce road kills. When driving through deer habitat at night, watch for eyeshine of deer near the road.

Here a herd of mule deer jump a fence and bound across the road.

road. When a deer crosses a road ahead of you, slow down and watch for more deer that may be following. If the deer that crossed was a doe, you can almost bet that her two young are just a few jumps behind. Apply your brakes to avoid hitting a deer, if possible, but don't jeopardize your vehicle or your own life by sudden braking if traffic is close behind you. Nor should you violently swerve to avoid hitting a deer.

Many ideas have been tried to lessen the carnage on the highways. New Jersey borrowed an idea that originated in Holland. The Dutch found that by using stainless steel mirrors to reflect the lights of automobiles into the woods they cut their deer kill to zero. New Jersey installed the mirrors on 5.4 miles of the Garden State Parkway. The three sections that had the heaviest deer kill were chosen. The mirrors were mounted 36 inches (.91 m.) off the ground, with 160 to 200 mirrors to the mile. Success has been only minimal, perhaps due to the fact that the light intensity of the mirrors is cut down by their distance from the center of the road. The New Jersey mirrors had to be placed much farther from the road than those in Holland because space had to be left for disabled cars and for snow removal. The use of mirrors by New Jersey has been discontinued. Maine has had better results with the mirrors and continues to use them.

Pennsylvania did considerable experimenting with deer-proof fences on stretches of Interstate Route 80, where the road kill was highest. The highest number of kills occurred where the highway had been carved through the forest with no grassland or fields to act as buffer zones. One-way gates were installed so that if a deer did get onto the highway by coming around the end of a fence or jumping over it, the animal could get back off the road. The gates worked, and the fences drastically reduced the highway kills.

In 1974 the last strip of Interstate 80 in New Jersey was opened, just a few miles from my home. This section of the highway, between the Hackettstown exchange and the Blairstown exchange, runs through some of our very finest deer territory. When the highway opened, carnage resulted. As many as four deer in one night were killed on this 8-mile (12.8 kilom.) stretch, and hardly a day went by without at least one deer being killed. In 1976 the highway department started to install chain-link fence the entire length of Route 80 through New Jersey. The idiotic aspect of this measure is that the fence is 5 feet (1.5 m.) high in some sections and even lower in others. This is no hindrance to a deer.

Interstate 70, near Mud Springs, Colorado, intersected a major migration route of the mule deer of that area. When the state built that section of highway, it installed an underpass for the deer. For a considerable distance on each side of the underpass, the highway was equipped with deer-proof fencing, which was 14 feet high, 14 feet wide, 99 feet long (4.27 m. × 4.27 m. × 30.48 m.). The tunnel had a concrete floor and low-wattage lights in the ceiling. Deer passage through the underpass was monitored by an electric-eye counter, by track counts in the raked dirt on either side, and by visual observations. About 60 percent of the deer used the underpass, although it took up to three days for some of them to work up courage to do so. Observers believe that a dirt floor and no lights would make the underpass more acceptable.

Utah is experimenting with a wide dirt-covered highway overpass on a major mule deer migration route at Beaver. As this has just been completed, no results are available yet, but it should be successful.

In 1974 New Jersey built its first deer underpass beneath Route 15 near Sparta. The area was equipped with deer-proof fence on each side of the underpass. Studies are being made of the deer's usage of the underpass, but the results have not been made public yet.

Fences figure importantly in connection with deer and deer damage. There are areas where some crops have to be fenced to prevent deer damage, but there are also areas where fencing is impractical. There are areas where certain crops cannot be raised because of deer damage, and there are others where deer damage precludes planting any crops at all. Back home on my family's farm we could not plant soy beans because the deer ate every sprout as soon as it broke through the earth.

Electric fences are seldom practical because deer jump over them. Some farmers have tried three-strand electric fences and the deer either jumped over the low ones or through the strands if they were widely spaced. A deer that touches a single strand of electrified fence is not grounded and therefore feels nothing at all. Areas subjected to prolonged dry spells cannot use electric fences, either, because there is not enough moisture in the dried soil to make a good ground.

Cyclone-type fences are best, but the cost is usually prohibitive. Most farmers use hog-wire fencing with 6- to 8-inch (15 cm. to 20 cm.) mesh. Whereas a 4-foot (1.2 m.) fence is high enough to keep in livestock, a deer fence should be at least 6 feet (1.8 m.) high. A 7-foot (2.2 m.) fence is much better. A deer can, but rarely will, jump an 8-foot (2.4 m.) fence. Various designs have been tried in which the top strands have been made of barbed wire, some with the tops inclined inward, others with the tops inclined outward. None of the designs or types of wire make much difference to the deer. The major deterrent is the height of the fence.

The statistics on road-killed deer can also be used as a game management tool. Over a period of time, they can tell of the deer herd's age and sex composition, shifts in ranges, dispersal of tagged deer, general health, and much

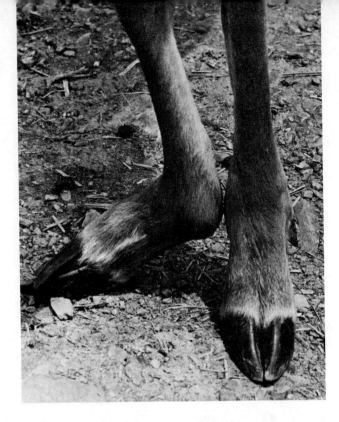

The right front hoof is deformed, the result of a break.

more. James Durell, Assistant Director of Game Management in Kentucky, deplored the increase in the number of road-killed deer in his state, yet he was not entirely unhappy about the statistics. He declared that as long as the road-kill was increasing steadily, it meant the deer population was also increasing steadily.

Automobiles are not the only vehicles that kill deer. Railroad trains and airplanes also kill them, though not in such great numbers. During the winter, when snow is on the ground, deer that are not yarded up will frequently walk along railroad tracks because the passage of trains keeps these lines of travel open. In 1970 a railroad that was relocated because of the Libby Dam on Montana's Kootenai River started operating in the midst of some of that state's best winter whitetail range. A survey of the carcasses along the railroad was made each spring to tabulate the damage. As many as 37 deer to the mile were killed by the trains in some of the best wintering areas.

In 1976 in Clearfield County, Pennsylvania, a deer crossing the runway at the local airport was struck by an airplane. Pilots from different parts of the country have told me that they often have to "buzz" the grass airstrips at some of the little rural airports to chase deer off the runways before attempting to land. Many of these back-country strips are hewn out of wilderness, and the runways may provide the only grass available in otherwise wooded areas. Even in open country, the grass on the runways is more tender and contains

These three-legged deer were probably born in a hayfield and injured by a mowing machine.

more nutrients because it is constantly being mowed and the grass is always comparatively new growth.

Deer can also get into trouble in their own habitat and without man's help. Bounding through the woods, they sometimes impale themselves on unyielding snags or branches. One deer, killed by a hunter, was found to contain a dead stick that had punctured a lung long before he was shot. The wound had healed, the lung had inflated itself again, and the stick had acquired a gristle-like covering that prevented it from further damaging the lung.

A deputy game warden in Williamsport, Pennsylvania, killed a nice buck one hunting season. The warden had the heart cooked for his supper, and as he was slicing it his knife hit something hard. Imbedded in the heart was a piece of bone 1 inch (25 mm.) long by ½-inch (13 mm.) thick. This bone, too, was completely surrounded by gristle, proving it had been in the deer's heart for a considerable period of time. How it penetrated the deer's body—and eventually pierced the heart without killing the animal—can only be conjectured.

District Game Protector H. P. Goedeke of New Alexandria, Pennsylvania, while on patrol, got a radio call from his wife. He wasn't sure she had the story straight but he finally decided to go check out the reports of a deer up on a roof. The deer had run up a ramp from the ground and fallen onto a roof 30 feet (9 m.) below. It had then jumped down to a lower roof, where the warden found it. When chased, the deer jumped off that roof to the ground 10 feet (3 m.) below and dashed away.

John Doebling and Lincoln Lang, game protectors in Monroe County, Pennsylvania, had to rescue a deer that had run up a trestle and fallen into a commercial coal bin. The wardens fastened a syringe to a pole and climbed into the bin to give the deer a tranquilizing injection. The deer, thrashing around in the bin, discouraged that idea. Finally, the men succeeded in lassoing the deer and then giving it the injection. Once the deer was drugged, they managed to truss it up and remove it to wild country where it was released.

Game Protector H. T. Nolf of Fort Washington, Pennsylvania, had to remove a deer that had crashed into a supermarket. While he was subduing that deer, he got a call about a deer that was in a local bowling alley. That one, too, was safely removed. That was the second deer that he had removed from a bowling alley. He has also had to remove deer from a grocery store and a local bank.

The president of a Freeport, Maine, bank came back empty-handed from a deer hunt in that state. He had just returned to his office when a six-point buck came crashing through the plate-glass window. The buck evidently had noticed an error in his balance because he dashed right into the bookkeeping department. From there he went down to the basement to sulk. He was removed by the local game warden.

Deer have fallen down wells and into swimming pools, broken through thin ice on ponds and rivers, become mired in mud, and fallen over cliffs. One in Oak Dale, Long Island, New York, ran head-on into a concrete wall and broke its neck.

In June 1963, near Kaibab, Arizona, a muley doe and her two fawns were electrocuted when lightning hit a huge ponderosa pine under which they were standing.

Near Erie, Pennsylvania, a high-voltage line broke loose from its insulator and fell to within a foot of the ground without interrupting electrical service in the area. Three deer, a buck and two does, touched the wire and were in-

Found on a Texas ranch, this mule deer skull has 20 pounds of fence wire tangled around one antler.

This is a skeleton of a muley fawn caught on a fence.

This whitetail doe recently broke her jaw. Unable to eat, she now will starve to death. This injury probably was caused by a fence wire.

stantly electrocuted. Two red foxes that came to eat the deer were also electrocuted. Two mongrel dogs made the same mistake and were also electrocuted.

On Cherry Creek, in Montana, two mule deer bucks were slugging it out during the breeding season. As they shoved each other around, one of the bucks' antlers got twisted up in a strand of barbed-wire fence. As the bucks continued to twist and turn, their antlers were thoroughly and fatally tied together by the wire. Eventually, one buck was strangled by a piece of the wire twisted around his neck. When the two deer were found by James R. Martin, the live one was so close to death that he had to be dispatched, too. In the course of the fight, the deer had pulled loose yards and yards of wire and had broken off thirteen fence posts.

When I visited the Gage Holland Ranch near Big Bend, Texas, in 1967, I was given a mule deer skull that had about twenty pounds of fencing wire wrapped around his antlers. Evidently the buck had run into the fence and torn loose hundreds of feet of wire. As he turned around and around, the wires were twisted into a cable. Not being able to free himself, the buck died.

Wire and deer are a bad combination. I have found deer twisted up in woven-wire as well as barbed-wire fences in both winter and summer. I have seen them break their antlers, their jaws, and their legs on cyclone fences. And there really isn't much we can do about it. It's just one more hazard of civilization that deer have to contend with.

I have a number of records of deer that have been caught in tree crotches that they had tried to jump through. Some were caught by the feet and several were caught around their middles. Near Ludington, Michigan, a six-point buck reached up to get some apples that had lodged in a large hollow in the crotch of an old apple tree. When he tried to drop back to the ground, his antlers got caught in the hollow. The harder the buck tried to pull away, the more pressure he put on his neck. At least in this case death must have been quick, for the area was not torn up by the deer's hooves.

# 20

## Reducing Crop
## and Landscape Damage

As noted in the last chapter, deer are seldom deterred from "trespassing" by any but the highest (and thus most expensive) fences. A number of other means have therefore been tried. Deer repellents have been used with varying (and limited) success. Some areas have used propane-gas cannons or carbide flash guns to fire loud blasts at timed intervals. These can be used only away from all human habitation because the periodic explosions would not be tolerated by residents. Unfortunately, deer become accustomed to the noise and the cannons lose their effectiveness. In California in 1976, I heard devices used to keep deer and birds out of vineyards by periodically emitting high-pitched shrieks and perhaps even ultra-sonic noise. These seemed to be effective, for I saw no depredation from any wildlife. The deer probably find the high-pitched sound painful.

Lights have been placed in fields to ward off deer but, if anything, the illumination helped the animals to see better what they were eating. Repellents consisting of dried fish meal and the blood of cattle from slaughter houses have been tried, again with very limited success. The first rain usually nulli-

This is the special planting tube used by Weyerhaeuser to prevent deer from eating seedlings.

fies their effectiveness. Creasote oil and naphthalene flakes give some protection but for a limited time only.

"Goodrite Zip" is a chemical deer repellent, made by the Goodrich Chemical Company, that has proved to be one of the best commercial deterrents available. Researchers are now testing other compounds that seem to be effective repellents for use on plants during the fall, winter, and early spring—the times when deer do most of their browsing.

Any company that comes up with an effective long-range deer repellent is going to make its shareholders rich. Repellents are of great value to orchardists and inestimable value to home-owners. As more and more people from cities come out to the suburban areas to build their homes, the destruction of deer habitat increases apace. The owners landscape their property with expensive ornamental shrubbery that the deer promptly eat because their normal browse has been reduced and they have probably fed in that same area before the houses were built. Deer particularly love yews—those nice big $35 yews—and it takes about three to four yews to feed one deer for one night. No one has tabulated the cost of the destruction of ornamental shrubbery by deer, but it has to run into millions of dollars yearly.

Diversionary foods, such as dry corn left standing in autumn, can reduce damage to valuable crops and ornamental vegetation. These plantings benefit landowners as well as deer and other wildlife.

I am sometimes called in to appraise deer damage and offer solutions, especially on large estates. Repellents are one answer for some situations, some of the time. Fencing would do the job but many estate owners feel that fences would detract from the beauty of their estates, and they are right. Often, there is no easy or complete solution. I find many of these large estates closed to hunting. Many sportsmen would love to hunt on the estates, and each deer taken would lessen the problem. When the estate owners post their land against hunting, they are actively working against the most logical solution to their problem — that of reducing the deer population.

Diversionary foods are sometimes helpful, although not practical for every landowner. Good plantings include plots of corn left standing unhusked in the fall, an alfalfa or clover patch left unmowed, rye grass seeded as a winter cover crop after the harvest, and buckwheat left unharvested. These foods will temporarily alleviate the damage, but they do not solve the problem and may in the long run contribute to it by attracting deer if the deer herd remains unharvested.

The same problem exists with the use of deer attractants. Tests in California have proved that spraying mixtures of molasses, salt, and trace minerals in a water base on plants will attract deer to eat foods that they might otherwise find unpalatable. As a boy on the family farm, I had the job of running the dry corn stalks through a chopper and then sprinkling a molasses solution on the fodder to make it attractive to the cows. It is the same idea. In the California tests, the deer stripped the sweetened foliage from the undesirable plants and left the conifer seedlings alone. The major drawbacks are that the mixture itself and the spraying are quite expensive, the success of the diversion depends on how much brush is available to be sprayed, and the fact that it may attract additional deer to the area. Moreover, the sprayed vegetation may sometimes be less nutritive than what the deer would normally eat, so this method could occasionally lead to management problems.

Another recourse for homeowners is to plant shrubs and flowers that are relatively deer-resistant—or unattractive to deer. It must be borne in mind that under normal conditions a deer may not eat a plant that it will feed upon when forage is scarce in the winter. Some of the shrubs and flowers that are highly unpalatable to deer are lilac, boxwood, jasmine, china-berry tree, hercules club, century plant, persimmon, sea buckthorn, holly, smoke tree, butterfly bush, black locust, pepper tree, wax myrtle, narcissus, daffodil, jonquil, aloe, columbine, clematis, iris, larkspur, foxglove, and English ivy.

Some apple orchardists I know lessen the damage of deer, mice, and rabbits by piling all the yearly pruned branches in low piles around the perimeter of their orchards. The bark and the tips of these twigs are more nutritious and more palatable than anything these creatures could reach in the orchards. The twigs have to be pruned anyway, so both the orchardists and the wildlife benefit. Of course, most orchardists welcome hunters, in order to reduce the deer herd. In most cases, the deer in their area cannot be overhunted, and they are drawn to apple trees like iron filings to a magnet.

# 21

## Cutting Timber to Improve Habitat

Most of the large lumber companies do everything possible to attract hunters to their lands, even providing maps and maintaining the back-country roads so that the hunters can get into as many sections as possible. This practice is good public relations and good business.

Clear-cutting large blocks of timber or pulp is the most practical method of harvesting the wood that grows there, and it creates excellent wildlife habitat. Many people oppose clear-cutting because it denudes large areas of trees all at one time, and on steep slopes it can cause erosion due to fast water run-off. I decry the erosion and the temporary silting of streams as much as anyone, but the timber and pulp must be harvested if we are to continue to live in wooden houses and use paper and countless wood by-products.

I'll never forget when I first saw the vast clear-cutting operations of the pulp companies in Canada, where I guided wilderness canoe trips for many summers. When the huge tracts of virgin spruce went down before the saws and

This clear-cut tract of western forest shows excellent deer food sprouting.

machines I was appalled. The land looked like photographs I had seen of "no-man's land" taken during World War I. I thought the practice of clear-cutting was criminal negligence.

But the following year, the entire area was clothed in the greenery of bracken ferns and berry bushes. Within two years, the spruce seedlings were starting to show, if you looked carefully. The logging roads that had been bulldozed were soon covered with white pine seedlings. The seeds of the white pine are so large that the tree cannot reseed itself through the duff and debris of a forest floor; they must fall on bare earth. Only when these areas were "logged off" was the pine able to come back. Within five years a new forest was well on its way.

Those virgin spruce forests had held little wildlife; the newly emerging forests abounded with wildlife, and the deer expanded its range northward. And so it is with many clear-cut areas in our country.

When the mature forests go and the second growth sprouts, the wildlife populations explode. Therein lies a problem for many of the lumber companies. The Douglas fir is probably the most important tree to the lumber companies of Washington and Oregon. The Douglas fir is also one of the most important

Pulp was harvested from this tract in Quebec. Such operations need not be wasteful or destructive. Forests can be managed for sustained yields of deer and other wildlife as well as wood.

A California mule deer feeds on lush vegetation of cut-over land that was formerly climax forest.

Where mature forest is cut away, plant succession begins anew and clearings fill with browse. In this instance, a whitetail is feeding on sumac.

foods of the mule deer and blacktail deer. It is easy to see why the lumber companies woo the hunters. They need them in order to harvest as many deer as possible.

One of the greatest problems facing the whitetail deer today is that over much of its range very little, if any, lumbering or timber cutting is being done. The conditions that allowed the fantastic explosion of whitetails in the early 1900s no longer exist, nor are they apt to be duplicated again on this continent. The whitetail population is continuing to increase, on the whole, because the deer are still being introduced to areas from which they had been wiped out.

The whitetail population was not high in the early colonial days in those sections of the East that were heavily forested. When the virgin timber was taken out by the settlers, the deer population increased but so did the hunting pressure. That pressure was eventually reduced, mainly because the deer's very existence was threatened during the last of the 1800s. At that time we were still a nation of woodburners, and forest growth was constantly being stimulated by the felling and regrowth of the trees. When I was a boy, my family had three wood stoves. All the farm families of my area constantly harvested the firewood from their fencerows and woodlots. Where wood was taken out, more was constantly growing back in, and the deer benefited from the abundance of browse.

Woods in much of the whitetail's range have grown into mature forests. In this part of the forest deer have little reachable winter browse.

Today, I live in an all-electric house, and the wood I cut for my fireplace is done by thinning my woods or cutting up the blowdowns. Even if I clear-cut my land I could not get new growth started, because the local deer population is too high to allow forest regeneration. The mountains behind my home have thousands upon thousands of acres of trees that are about thirty to forty years old. And thousands of these acres are old, abandoned farm fields or woodlots that are no longer cut. This is the basic cause of the chronic food shortage for the deer in my area. The trees have grown beyond the deer's reach, and this climax forest will remain useless to them until it is cut again, or burned over, or until disease wipes out enough trees to open the forest canopy.

"Bean-pole" woods may look more bountiful than stands of huge trees, but tracts like this lack edge and low brush. Deer will find scant food here.

The problem of the forests growing beyond the reach of the deer is widespread and will become increasingly so. The deer are faced with the dual calamity of losing habitat to urbanization and losing the use of much remaining habitat because of a lack of food. One of the basic tenets of wildlife management is that mature forests and wildlife do not go together. Where you have mature forests there is very little wildlife of any kind because of a lack of food. This principle is as hard for many hunters to grasp as it is for non-hunters. Many hunters go up to the North Woods or other forested areas to hunt deer, but they find very few deer in extensive areas of mature forests.

The early Indians were efficient hunters, and they were the first to practice game management in this country. The colonists found extensive burned-over areas in the midst of the virgin forests. Some of these fires had been set by the Indians. The Indians knew that the number of deer and other animals in an area increased in direct proportion to the food available. Deer might run through the mature forests and would go there in the autumn to feed on the mast crops, but they didn't live there. They were and are creatures of the "edge."

Where second-growth forests begin to reclaim old fields or clearings, good edge-type wildlife habitat is created. Deer will eat well here.

*Edge* is one of the most important words to describe excellent wildlife habitat. Edge is where grassland or an open area meets or abuts a forested area. Edge usually means both food and shelter, and that is what habitat is all about.

Wild turkeys need mature forests for the mast but they also need open grassland where their poults can feed on insects. About 80 percent of all ruffed grouse nests are located along old wood roads or along the edges of the woodland. A single wood road creates edge through a forest by allowing sunlight to reach the forest floor. Pheasants and quail venture into croplands and open areas but they nest in the edge. Every brush row is an edge favored by cottontail rabbits.

The game birds and animals, and most of the nongame species, will be found in the transitional stage where grassland or old farmland is being reclaimed by the forest. This stage of plant succession is edge on a grand scale—until the forest matures. Where we have edge, wc have wildlife. One of our major problems is that we are running out of edge because we are no longer creating any. We are not cutting wood in the eastern forests as we once did, we are not clearing homesteads, we are not cutting woodlot roads through our forests. Often, where new suburban enclaves or industrial developments rise, the manicured lawns and asphalt strips and blankets end abruptly where the mature forest is left standing—without any real edge. Even in some of our most important farming country, much of the edge has been removed. The small, traditional "patchwork" farms have given way in many regions to huge "agribusiness" corporations that practice modern "clean" farming—enormous single-crop tracts unbroken by woodlots, windbreaks, or natural fencerows of shrubs, small trees, brush.

A muley doe and her three-month-old fawns amble through edge habitat where food is plentiful and where higher, denser cover is close.

"Clean" farming such as this destroys great expanses of wildlife habitat. This landscape includes no food or shelter.

Here is a blacktail doe in a rain forest where trees grow to tremendous size. Under ideal conditions there will be an understory and sufficient brush, but some forests of this type can be improved for wildlife by selective cutting. (Photo by Len Rue, Jr.)

Today, we are aware of the importance of wilderness, not only to wildlife but to our own physical and mental well-being. Many of us are better able to cope with the stresses of civilization if we can escape periodically to some of the wild spaces. Many people benefit just by knowing that there are some wild places to escape to, even if they never actually get to them. I, for one, could not live if all the "wildness" were taken out of life.

A major problem, however, is that today many people have a reverence for trees that is not necessarily good for the forest or for wildlife. Most people are against cutting trees. In the western states this is not a problem because most of the forested tracts are owned by lumber companies or are on National Forest land. Multiple land use is the major theme of our National Forests.

There have been and continue to be abuses in the application of multiple-land-use programs. Most of the abuses stem from overgrazing, and some are created by poor timber-cutting practices. However, the multiple-use idea is a sound one and the hunting and lumbering must be continued. It is the abuses that must be corrected. Our forests must be managed to provide the greatest benefits to the largest number of people. This means that the bulk of our forests should be thinned or cut off systematically, by sections, at a prescribed rate, for a sustained yield. When this is done, both wood and wildlife are renewable resources.

In the eastern states, most of the timbered land is in forest preserves, state parks, or private ownership, so multiple-use management—including timber cutting—is often opposed. Where the land is in forest preserves or state parks, a legislative act is frequently required before any cutting can be done. It is vital that our state foresters and game departments work in closer harmony, getting together to inventory the forest land, the trees growing thereon, the game, the habitat. Then decisions can be based on facts about which lands to hold inviolate, which can be managed, and when and how to manage them. A united front must be presented by these two divisions because their decisions are inseparable. They ought never again to act independently, as they so often did in the past. The soil, the water, the vegetation, and the wildlife are not separate entities but integral parts of a whole. Only when a united front is maintained can a legislative body be approached with reasonable hope that our lands and wildlife can be properly managed for the best interests of all.

The woodlands that are in the private sector are another situation. Many of the old mountain woodlots are held by absentee owners who don't know what they own. Most of these people could be persuaded to have at least some of the timber on their land cut if they knew that their interests would be protected and that wildlife would benefit. This, too, requires a sales job by a team of foresters and game biologists. In my lecture appearances, I have found that many people will abandon misguided preservationist attitudes if the biological facts are presented to them. More timber must be harvested and more forests opened up if we are to maintain healthy deer and halt the diminishing of deer populations—for although we have a high overall deer population, the herds are suffering needless privation and reduction in many regions.

The Pennsylvania Game Commission, a leader in deer research and management, had the foresight to provide a place for the deer to live and a place for the hunters to hunt the deer. Over a period of many years, the commission acquired State Game Lands, millions of acres held in perpetuity for wildlife of all kinds and outdoor recreation of all kinds. These lands—and the taxes paid on the lands—all come from hunters' license fees, permits, and game-violation fines.

Some habitat is better than it appears to laymen. Very little browse appears here, but deer have been pawing through the snow for acorns, and there is brush nearby.

The hunting seasons in Pennsylvania are carefully tailored to keep the deer herd in balance with the land and food available. The herd is stabilized at about 600,000, with an annual harvest of about 140,000. In 1976, to provide better habitat and more winter food, the commission sold the commercial timber on 8,300 acres. This timber must be cut in the winter so that the tree tops can be used as deer food. In addition, the commission has crews cutting brush on 2,800 acres where there is no timber that can be commercially harvested. These brush-cutting operations slow down the forest's race to maturity and improve the habitat enormously for many kinds of wildlife.

Over the years, much of Maine's wintering deer areas were growing up into even-age stands of trees that were beyond the reach of deer. In the 1950s the Department of Inland Fisheries and Wildlife devised a cooperative, voluntary, winter-habitat management program between the state and some private land-owners. Although the program was sound, it was not done on a scale large enough to really benefit enough of the state's deer.

To expand the program, the state made aerial surveys of all major deer wintering areas. Maine has over ten million acres of unorganized township land that comes under the jurisdiction of the Land Use Regulation Commission. On that land, 903 wintering areas were located. A law was passed requiring private owners of such land to obtain a permit before harvesting any of their timber. The idea was to get the owner, the forestry department, and the game department together before any cutting was done, thus ensuring that the interests of all three would be served.

Blocks of trees are being cut on a fifteen-year basis. This maintains mature tree stands which serve as winter shelter for the deer, while the cut areas provide the sprouts needed for food. And the blocks that are cut systematically provide a sustained yield of timber. Through such cooperation, everyone benefits, especially the deer.

Deer are quick to take advantage of the tops of trees felled in winter unless deep snow prevents the animals from moving about. Frank Brochu, supervisor of a hardwood-cutting operation at Bingham, Maine, reported that 11 deer came out of the woods and began to feed on the tree tops while the cutters were still working. The next day all 11 of the deer were bedded down in the immediate area, waiting for the saws to start up. Deer have learned that chain saws mean food. In the Upper Peninsula, the Cusino deer herd is often subjected to starvation. While the lumbermen there cut up the felled trees, the deer often feed on the tops.

I saw the same thing happen in my own area when large-scale timbering was done for the first time in many years. Fortunately, the year of the largest operations coincided with the year of the deepest snow. The deer had become accustomed to feeding on downed tree tops even before the snow came. The dense forest and the numerous gulleys gave good protection from the wind, so the deer did not have to yard up. Over fifty spent the winter in the immediate vicinity. The sound of a chain saw was like the gong of a dinner bell. This is the most practical way of providing supplemental winter food. Feed the deer with a saw and an axe.

# 22

## Controlled Burns, Rights of Way, Browseways, and Other Habitat Boosts

Smokey the Bear died in late 1976. For a quarter of a century he was a very successful symbol for forest-fire prevention. The message that he conveyed reached untold millions. But even before Smokey died, a lot of what he stood for also died. There is still no excuse for the negligence that could start a forest fire. Fire prevention is still of tremendous importance in most areas in most situations—but not in all of them. Fire is now gaining acceptance as a tool of forestry and wildlife management.

Game managers and foresters have long understood that some forested areas are scrub-covered and their trees, grown too high to provide food for the hooved big-game animals, will not yield harvestable timber. Much of this scrub would be too expensive to cut. Fire is the logical answer. Fire has always been one of nature's ways of keeping the woodlands under control. The fires that used to sweep across the prairies kept the trees from invading the grasslands. The fires that swept through much of the forests were even more beneficial because they opened the solid forest canopy to sunshine and started anew the cycle of subclimax, or transitional, plant succession.

Ground fires like this do not benefit wildlife because they do not open up the forest canopy.

Before the 1900s, forest-fire control was almost unheard of. Huge, destructive fires ravaged miles and miles of timber throughout the last century. These fires, coupled with the timber harvesting, set the stage for the eruption of the deer population that took place in the early 1900s. Since then, the control of forest fires has become almost a science, and this control has coincided with the decline of lumbering. The combination of fire control and reduced lumbering contributed to the chronic food shortages that plague our deer herds in many sections of the country, particularly in the Northeast, by allowing forest vegetation to grow beyond the reach of the deer.

Of course, accidental fires still occur. In 1975 a forest fire burned almost 2,000 acres of Worthington State Park in New Jersey. All of the local fire companies and hundreds of volunteers fought the fire for days before bringing it under control. These fire fighters performed heroic work. Yet I wish the fire had covered more area and had been hotter. There was very little harvestable timber in the burned area, and no homes or personal property were threatened. On almost half the burn, the blaze was only a ground fire that consumed the dead leaves and downed wood, and killed off some underbrush. It did not kill most of the trees or open up the forest canopy, so as wildlife habitat the forest is in worse condition now than it was before. The trees continue to shade out the understory and there is almost no regenerative browse coming on.

In the areas that *were* burned clean, the trees that were killed were primarily scrub oak and rock oak. It is true that in good mast years these trees might produce 200 to 400 pounds (90.6 to 181.2 kg.) of acorns per acre. In poor

The circular spot on the head of this whitetail buck is a pedicel, having begun to heal after the antler was shed.

years they might produce only 10 to 50 pounds (4.5 to 22.6 kg.). The first year after the burn, I observed that such an area grew up with snakeroot, berry bushes, ferns, and many forbs and grasses. That fall many of the deer did not come down off the ridges at all but stayed up in the burn area and fed on the new growth. Within two more years, the new sprouts that are shooting up all over the area will produce up to a ton (906 kg.) or more of browse per acre and will do so every year for the next 10 to 15 years.

The situation there for the deer is ideal. Worthington State Park is one of New Jersey's public hunting areas and is subjected to intensive deer-hunting pressure. The number of deer there is low for the amount of land, not only because of the hunting pressure but because the area was a mature forest. With the population low and a superabundance of food coming on, this area is set for a localized deer-population explosion. When a species' population is below the carrying capacity of the land, the population grows at the highest rate possible for that species. This is known as the law of inversity. The more dense a population becomes, the more the reproduction rate declines. Because of the hunting pressure, the population will be kept in line with its food supply. Hunting in the area should be excellent for the next couple of decades. The grouse population, which has steadily declined in that area, should also make a strong comeback. This is also about the only area in New Jersey where the snowshoe hare has a chance of being re-established. At different times the

Efforts to re-establish the snowshoe hare may succeed on burned land of New Jersey's Worthington State Park, even though such efforts have failed elsewhere in the state, because the burn now is producing enough food for both hares and deer.

The site of the Tillamook burn in Oregon is shown here blanketed with exceptionally fine food and cover for many kinds of wildlife.

New Jersey Game Department has tried to restock the extirpated snowshoe hare. These stockings were doomed because of competition with the deer for the available food. The burned area will produce food enough for both species. Even more good would have resulted had the fire been hotter and more extensive.

That big burns have been exceedingly beneficial to most types of wildlife has been proved time after time by such examples as the previously mentioned Tillamook burn in Oregon, which resulted in more and bigger blacktail deer in the area, and the Kenai burn in Alaska, which benefited moose. Management plans in both areas call for the continued use of fire, on a rotating basis, to keep the habitat productive.

To my knowledge, the largest controlled burn in which the federal government has recently participated was the fire in Grand Teton National Park in 1975. Thousands of acres of scrub were allowed to burn to improve the browse for elk and mule deer. After years of publicizing the evil of all forest fires, the government was the target of tremendous criticism. There is a compulsion in man to put out a fire. Most of the time that compulsion is laudable, but we now know that a *controlled* fire can yield marvelous benefits. Knowing it, we now have the job of convincing the general public.

The greatest benefits could be gained from controlled burns in mature forests by burning swaths no more than ½-mile (804.5 m.) wide. Deer do not like to be more than 400 yards (365.8 m.) from cover at any time.

Ideally, the forest managed for the maximum benefits to all would be divided into strips of thirds. The mature, harvestable timber would be cut and removed from one third of the land. The deer could feed on the tops that winter. The following spring that third would be burned, providing good deer food for about twenty years. At the start of the second twenty-year period, the next third would have the timber harvested and then would be burned. At the start of the third twenty-year span, the last third would be harvested and then burned. In the northern sections of the country it takes about sixty years to produce good, harvestable timber. In the South, where timber grows faster, the time span could be shortened to twelve or fifteen years or whatever is required to grow harvestable timber. On this rotating basis, we would produce a maximum population of many kinds of wildlife and a sustained yield of lumber.

The deer could feed on the new sprouts that come in after a burn. And because of the profusion of sprouts, the foresters would have a better chance of growing the type of trees they wanted on these tracts. In some areas, the destruction of seedlings by deer is so great that for every five hundred seedlings planted to the acre, no more than eight grow to be harvestable trees. The ma-

Greenbrier thickets interspersed with taller vegetation provide excellent food and shelter for deer, rabbits, and other wildlife. Mixed vegetation is far better than solid woods.

turing strips of trees would provide excellent cover for the deer as well as acorns and other types of mast crops.

This plan would benefit the forests as well as the wildlife because all too frequently nonproductive trees are allowed to grow on unmanaged lands. Although we do need some large, dead trees to provide homes for cavity-nesting birds, unmanaged forests have too high a percentage of trees that are crooked, deformed, or rotten on the inside and that benefit nothing.

Do I expect this plan to be adopted? No. At least not until all of the departments concerned can devote the necessary years to educating the public.

A mixture of browse plants is always desirable. Deer do not feed on any single plant species exclusively, no matter how nutritious it happens to be. For a deer's rumen to function properly, the animal must use a variety of foods whenever possible. A mixed stand of vegetation offers more in the way of food and shelter than a solid stand of any species. In the northern states it is common to find unbroken stands of hardwoods, especially in areas that at one time were farm fields. These hardwoods offer food but no shelter. Where possible, blocks of conifer trees (up to an acre) should be interspersed throughout the hardwood trees. This would greatly benefit the deer because it would break up the wintering concentrations. On level terrain, it does not matter where these blocks are planted. Where the terrain is hilly or rolling, the blocks of evergreens should be planted on the south or southeast slopes or down in the hollows. These are the areas favored by the deer in winter.

Powerline rights of way create long, wide, food-rich strips of edge through forests.

As a naturalist and conservationist, I am often asked by ecology groups to endorse some project or program. I often do, but not until I have satisfied myself as to the merits of each endeavor. One program I will not endorse—in fact, I fight against it—is the underground installation of high-tension power-lines.

To some people the towers and their sweeping wires are esthetically offensive. Personally, I am often fascinated by the form and composition of the towers, but I will admit that in some areas the proliferation of these towers is an eyesore. In urban areas, underground installation may be a good idea, but I don't want to see it happen out in the country. Where the big powerlines run through a forested tract, as they do in my area, the swaths cut through the woods are often the only unending source of good, nutritious deer food. Like the back-country roads I mentioned earlier, they provide excellent edge-type habitat.

The right of way beneath the power lines is usually 250 to 300 feet (76 to 91 m.) wide. Periodically, the brush on the right of way is cut to prevent it from growing into trees that could interfere with the power lines. The new brush that is constantly sprouting up makes excellent deer food. The brush that is cut and piled along the edge of the right of ways creates fantastic habitat for cottontail rabbits and nesting birds. The electric companies do this cutting in their own interest but inadvertently they create miles and miles of edge and excellent wildlife habitat.

376

California chaparral provides the scene of continuing experiments in range improvement. Mature stands of this brush offer only cover, no food. But controlled burning, crushing, and creation of browseways can result in excellent forage.

In September of 1976 I visited the University of California's Hopland Field Station, operated by the university's Division of Agriculture. The director, A. H. Murphy, provided me with a knowledgeable guide, a young graduate student named Mike Frey. I was interested in the work being done to improve conditions for the blacktail deer in the dense stands of chaparral. Much of the chaparral country is on rolling hillsides that are too steep for crops. Erosion is a problem, too. This area was formerly used very heavily for sheep ranching, but sheep in California have been reduced from over three million head to about a million. Many of the areas are blanketed with the high bushes of chamise, manzanita, madrone, and the like that make up the chaparral. These dense stands are so extensive in some areas that there would be no food for the sheep, which prefer grasses and forbs. Many of the ranchers are now engaged in game ranching—managing their land as hunting clubs and charging the hunters a fee. The dense stands of chaparral brush have to be managed for the deer because as mature, unmanaged stands all they offer is cover. Most of the brush has grown beyond a deer's reach.

Controlled burning is one of the best methods of opening up the chaparral brush. Studies show that perhaps 100 pounds (45.3 kg.) of browse per acre, per

At left, after a controlled burn in California chaparral, the chamise looks desolated, but soon afterward, as seen at right, dense new clumps of chamise sprout up.

year, may be all that is available to the deer in the mature stands. After a fire there is far more browse per acre on the same land. I saw an area that had been burned about a month earlier. The bases of the mature brush had already begun to put out millions of sprouts. After a burn, the deer will often feed on some of the new sprouts of brush types that they ordinarily find unpalatable.

Crushing is another method of opening up the chaparral where the hillsides are not so steep that they preclude the use of the heavy equipment needed to do the job. Crushing, used alone, also allows the deer to feed on the flattened tops of the chaparral. Frequently, brush that has been crushed is later burned. In this fashion, the deer gain the greatest benefits from the existing plants, because fire not only opens up space for new sprouts but also revives the soil —literally fertilizes it.

The crush-burn areas are often planted with grass seed and then, two years later, are crush-burned again. This second burning in two years usually kills the chaparral brush and keeps the opened areas in grass. This benefits the sheep as well as the deer. The deer perhaps benefit most because the second burn gives them access to grasses and forbs as well as the new brush sprouts. These grassy areas create lots of edge.

A California mule deer browses amid luxuriant growth. A tractor with a flailing instrument can be used to create browseways where low vegetation soon proliferates like that shown here.

The main drawback to controlled burning in the chaparral is that California is so often a tinder box. The regulations now require such an outlay of equipment and manpower, to make sure the fire remains under control, that the cost is becoming prohibitive.

The creation of browseways is also gaining in popularity. This approach is less efficient than the controlled burn, but the cost is far less. A huge heavy-duty tractor is used in conjunction with a heavy-chain flailing instrument. This is used to beat or cut the shrubs off about 6 to 12 inches (15 to 31 cm.) above the ground. The advantage is that it creates no fire hazard nor does it cause any erosion since the soil is not disturbed. Browseways facilitate both the deer's and the hunter's movements through the chaparral, while providing new brush sprouts in all the areas that have been cut. Some browseways still provide good browse fifteen years after their creation. I am sure this method of producing browse will continue to grow in popularity.

Here a whitetail doe nibbles on sedges in early spring. Open, sufficiently moist spaces are needed for this sort of vegetation.

California has also experimented with chemical sprays to kill brush. If there are no long-lasting effects of the herbicides and they are not harmful to wildlife, this may prove to be the most inexpensive method of all. Such sprayings will be of greater benefit to agriculture than to wildlife unless only small areas of brush are opened up to create edge and to plant limited amounts of grasses. Whereas burning, crushing, and flailing do not kill the brush—and the deer benefit from the new sprouts—the chemicals do kill the brush.

Minnesota has been using a phytocide (2,4 dichlorophenoxyacetic acid) as an aerial spray in a mixture of 2 pounds of acid to 3½ gallons of water. This spray is used on areas where the existing vegetation is not used by the deer. In a very short time grasses, forbs, and herbs grow profusely on the sprayed areas, providing excellent deer food.

Here a whitetail doe feeds on dogwood. New York studies have proven that deer feed more heavily on shrubs of nitrogen-fertilized land than on untreated plots.

Maine has been experimenting with nitrogen fertilizer to increase the growth of brush and to boost the protein rate. Investigations have shown that, on the areas tested, the normal protein content of browse such as aspen, sarsaparilla, and bracken fern is about $7\frac{1}{2}$ percent in April, 10 percent in early summer, and down to $6\frac{3}{4}$ percent in December. When nitrogen was applied to this browse, the protein content shot up to 15 or 16 percent, which botanists feel is about optimum for the plants. Nitrogen fertilizer is expensive, however, and will probably never be applied on a large scale. The use of the fertilizer did double the benefits of this browse to the deer.

Studies in New York showed that on plots heavily fertilized with nitrogen the deer browsed 80 percent of the flowering dogwood shrubs. On untreated plots, they ate only 3.6 percent of the same shrubs.

This blacktail buck browses on thimbleberry leaves. On new burns, this and other favored foods have a heightened protein content.

Studies in Oregon and New York showed that the chemical composition of soils changed dramatically after fires. Nitrogen, which had been converted from an inorganic substance to an organic one after being assimilated by the plants, was once again available to the new forest growth. Potash from the burned wood produced enormous amounts of potassium. These two fertilizer components greatly enriched the soil and the plants that grew upon it. Deer will feed even more avidly on the new sprouts that spring up after a burn than on those that follow a lumbering operation.

Arthur Einarsen, in his work on blacktail deer, found that not only did the chemical composition of the soil change on burned-over land but so did the protein content of the plants. An analysis of the blacktails' favorite foods, such as vine maple, thimbleberry, blackberry, and salmonberry, showed an average protein rate of 12 percent on a new burn. The same plants on a six-year-old burn showed only 6.8 percent protein. This is to be expected because with time the chemicals in the soil are leached out by rain and sun. The chemicals are also removed by the deer that eat the plants that had assimilated the chemicals from the soil.

Eventually the chemical value of the soil on burned-over land drops below that of cut-over land. Fire makes the chemicals available immediately, whereas the decomposing tops of vegetation release the same chemicals at a slower rate, making them available for a much longer period.

# 23

## The Problems of Artificial Feeding

Whenever we have a winter with deep snow and cold weather, the concern about the deer's well-being mounts. Game departments brace themselves for a flood of letters and telephone calls. Concerned citizens suggest (or demand) that the deer be fed at once. These people always seem very sure that supplemental feeding will solve the starvation problem.

There are many reasons why the artificial feeding of deer doesn't work. The main one is that instead of solving the deer problem, it compounds it. The second major drawback is that the cost of a feeding program is prohibitive. Feeding deer during emergencies does far more for the human psyche than it does for the deer. In times of emergencies people feel they should do *something* for wildlife.

When the number of deer in a given area does not exceed the carrying capacity of that land there is no need for supplemental feeding. However, given the breeding potential of deer, this utopian situation does not exist except where 35 to 40 percent of the deer herd is harvested each year. As most deer harvests are far lower than this, the deer population soon exceeds the carrying capacity of the land, and starvation is imminent. Where deer overpopulate their range, a herd reduction of at least half is needed to bring the balance back. If overpopulation becomes a long-term proposition, a 50 percent reduction may not be enough. It depends on the damage to the range. *But artificially feeding the deer is never the answer.*

Such feeding permits the survival of more starving deer. The food may mean that a starving doe not only will survive but bear young. If she is well fed, she may bear the normal set of twins instead of being barren or having a single fawn. Unless that doe or her young can be harvested, there will then be three deer struggling to survive on land that did not have food enough to support one deer. Now three times as much supplemental feeding is needed, and the problem grows progressively worse. Experimentally, an anti-fertility drug has been tried on deer, the objective being to lower the birth rate where such overpopulation developed. Unfortunately, it did not work.

I am not suggesting that the deer be allowed to starve. I am stating that the wildlife managers and the biologists should be allowed to manage the deer. They should be allowed to regulate the proper harvesting of the deer so that starvation is not a problem and supplemental feeding is not needed.

Feeding deer on an individual basis or in special situations is not wrong. What is wrong is to allow a situation to develop in which large part of a state's deer population is threatened, and then to expect the game department to feed the deer. In the past, some game departments have attempted to feed deer on a large scale. No state has the manpower or the money needed for the job, nor have the results ever been truly beneficial.

For a feeding program to be successful, it must be started *before* there is snow, so that the deer are freely moving—coming to the food. This has the drawback of concentrating the deer. High concentrations intensify the problem and increase the danger of disease and the spread of parasites. If the deer are getting sufficient food, they can withstand the cold, and if there is heavy cover such as a stand of conifer trees nearby, they will not be forced to leave the food to yard up elsewhere. Most feeding programs are started only after the deer are on the verge of starvation and then they may be getting too little too late. After deer are yarded up, the food has to be delivered to the yard because the deer will not leave the protected area. Studies in Maine have shown that deer food, either natural or artificial, that is 100 yards (92 m.) away from the yard will be left untouched.

A major drawback to feeding deer in their yards is that unless the food is dropped in by helicopter, its delivery produces compacted trails to the yards. Dogs and other predators then follow the trails right to the deer.

This deer was found dead of starvation in spring, even though food was brought to the vicinity of its winter yard. Studies have shown that food must be brought right into a yard because deer will not move out even 300 feet to get it.

This deer was killed and eaten by dogs. Delivery of food to yarded deer — unless it is dropped by helicopter — produces compacted trails that lead predators to the weakened deer.

Here volunteers make an emergency delivery of alfalfa and corn, both good winter foods deer will seek on their own in farming areas. Unless deep snows prevent deer from feeding outside yarding areas, starving deer mean overpopulation. In this case, winter feeding programs allow more deer to survive, further inflating the population beyond the land's carrying capacity.

When the snows pile up, many sportsmen's clubs and other groups and individuals attempt to feed the deer in their areas. They often go to the local supermarkets and get stale bread and discarded greens—lettuce, cabbage and the like. This is hauled out into the woods for the deer. Tame deer will eat bread. Wild deer will not. If the greens are placed where the deer can get to them, they may be eaten, but the small amount of nutrition in these discards is worthless.

People often ask me what *is* good food for the deer. I repeat that the best way to feed them is with saws and axes. Cut good nutritious browse for the deer. However, you are not legally free to cut browse except on your own land.

Alfalfa or clover hay is also good food, and most deer will readily eat it. Timothy hay is not good deer food, although the deer will pick through it to eat the dried weeds and forbs mixed in it. Deer that have access to corn in the fall can be fed corn in the winter. This is an excellent deer food because it is high in carbohydrates, which produce body heat. Wilderness deer are not likely to eat corn, however. They don't seem to know what it is. Commercial deer pellets, manufactured by many of the large milling companies, are excellent deer food and are usually readily eaten. In emergencies, the pellets fed to goats or rabbits also make good deer food.

For years, hundreds of acres of corn were raised near my home. That corn helped to create a deer problem. When the farming was discontinued, the deer herd was much too large to be supported by the natural food available. We lost a great many deer to starvation because at that time we could not harvest does.

When enough time had passed, our deer no longer knew what corn was. Each fall they came to feed on the dropped apples in an orchard near my home. One year the apple crop was exceedingly poor. Because I like to watch the deer, I put corn out for them. But no corn had been grown in the valley for about five years. The deer did not know what it was. They smelled it and were not afraid of any odors on the corn, but they would not eat it. None of the deer that came in had been alive when corn was a mainstay; the link was broken and the corn remained untouched.

Whether a private feeding program is good or harmful depends on the situation. My friend Helen Whittemore loves to watch deer, and she has fed them regularly for many years. Helen feeds several hundred pounds of cracked corn each day, as well as dropped apples and apple pumice when it is available. I have seen over fifty deer at her feeding station at one time. Although they are fully protected on her land, they are hunted when they leave. So, although the deer do come in to feed, they remain healthy and wild and they do not build up an excessive population. In Helen's case, the feeding is therefore beneficial.

A number of the neighboring farms here in Hardwick Township have banded together and control perhaps a thousand acres. Their hunting club usually takes more than two dozen bucks during the first two days of the season and they also harvest some of the does, but their limited membership takes far less than the annual increment of deer. In the past I have seen as many as a hundred deer in some of their fields. They have long had an efficient winter feeding program. They take good care of their deer, but they have just too many.

Their deer do not die of starvation, but the feeding concentrates them and thereby makes them vulnerable in other ways. Two years ago the deer in New Jersey were hit by Epizootic Hemorrhagic disease (described in Chapter 15). Almost every occurrence of disease is the result of overpopulation. One of the hardest-hit areas was that of the neighboring farms—the scene of the feeding program.

There are times, of course, when feeding may be necessary for the deer's survival. When the winter is excessively severe, or if it is essential to preserve the nucleus of a deer herd, then feeding may be the only solution. To be brutally practical, under such circumstances it is cheaper to feed the deer—and risk any later consequences—than to restock the deer if they are wiped out.

# 24

## Restocking and the Techniques of Live-Trapping

Restocking was the salvation of the North American whitetail herds. This is the only way to get deer back into an area where they have been wiped out. Deer populations swing like a pendulum between boom and bust. The goal of deer management is to shorten the swing, and if possible, stabilize it in the center of its arc. In most areas, the pendulum is still swinging toward the boom for whitetails.

Today, there are not many areas in the United States that are actually in need of restocking. Most of the good deer country already has deer. In 1966, Roy Anderson, Chief of Game Management for the Tennessee Game and Fish Commission, imported twenty-seven young blacktail deer from Oregon. The deer were released on the grounds of the Volunteer Army Ammunition Plant, on the outskirts of Chattanooga. In 1967, three dozen more blacktails were brought in to bolster the new herd. Free-running dogs killed six of the deer and automobiles killed eleven. But the herd thrived, and by 1971 it numbered a hundred and fifteen. These deer have grown larger in size than their western counterparts because of the abundance of food. A 3½-year-old blacktail buck

Oregon blacktails have now been stocked in Tennessee, where they are growing very large and developing outstanding racks. This photo shows a button buck. (Photo by Len Rue, Jr.)

Restocking saved America's whitetail herds. Ten-point bucks like this now inhabit woods where deer had been virtually wiped out at the turn of the century.

may weigh 140 to 170 pounds (63.4 to 77 kg.) and have racks that sport eight or ten points. If all goes as planned, some of the surplus will eventually be released into the wilds of Tennessee.

One of the major problems of live-trapping and removing surplus deer from an area is that there are so few places that need to be restocked. Several states estimate that it costs about $75.00 per deer in materials, time, equipment, and manpower to live-trap and relocate one deer. Generally speaking, live-trapping is successful only in times of food shortages because the deer must be baited into the traps with food. (Where the traps are to be used in one area over a long period, they are frequently baited with salt instead of food. This often works when natural food is plentiful.) Most live-trapping projects are carried out during the winter, when hunger lures the deer. A drawback is that the cold and snow may force the deer to yard up, and most deer yards are not accessible to roads. The snow makes it difficult to get trucks into the areas where the deer are located.

Public ignorance and vandalism also cause problems. There are some people who inadvertently trip a trap while they are just looking at it, and there are others who trip it "just for the heck of it." There are also misinformed people who trip the traps to prevent deer from getting caught and release those that are caught. Sometimes these people even include misinformed hunters who don't want any of "their" deer taken away.

Almost all deer that are live-trapped are tagged. Metal or plastic tags or streamers are placed in their ears. Some are prepared for monitoring by placing transistorized radio transmitters around their necks. They are also aged and weighed. By the use of the numbered and coded tags, biologists can obtain ready information on a deer's age, travels, and so on. The radios allow the biologists to locate the deer at any time of day or night and to study their daily activity patterns and the areas they frequent, their escape routes, dispersal, etc. This radio monitoring is relatively new. It is a valuable tool for biologists and wildlife managers.

The trapping of deer has its lighter side, too. Biologists near Ashland, Maine, caught one adult doe eight times in one year, in the same trap. A puzzle to the biologists is that, although she has been caught so often and is conspicuously marked with ear tags, she has never been seen except when she has been caught in the trap. With regard to the number of times she was caught, the Ashland doe set no record. One state live-trapped a whitetail doe fifty times in three months.

Deer can become so used to being trapped that they practically take up residence in the trap. A few years ago, when New Jersey was trapping and tagging deer in the mountains above my home, one trap became the exclusive prop-

Biologist Mike Frey stands with a lightweight live-trap used in California.

erty of one doe. She was so eager to get the apples used for bait that she ran right in every time the trap was set. She finally had to be removed from the area.

The traps most commonly used are modified versions of the venerable box trap with dropping end doors, tripped by a treadle. New Jersey uses the old-style all-wooden trap. Some states are using wooden traps with metal doors and guides because they don't warp and jam when wet. Some of the newest traps are made of aluminum. Their advantage is lightness. They weigh about 180 pounds (81.5 kg.), whereas wooden traps weigh about double that.

In California I saw the lightest type of all. The framework was made of pipe, and the sides, top, and even the gates were made of heavy fish netting. There was no bottom to the trap. The four guide pipes for the gates were driven into the earth to give the trap extra rigidity and prevent its being knocked over. The entire trap weighed about 35 pounds (15.9 kg.).

The Pisgah live-trap has an added chute at the end to facilitate boxing the deer for transportation. Most deer-transport boxes are made of plywood and designed to keep the deer in as near-total darkness as possible. Almost all wildlife remains much calmer if it cannot see what is going on.

Live-traps provide researchers with obvious advantages, since the deer can be handled, aged, sexed, weighed, tagged, marked, and examined, blood samples can be taken, and the animals can be moved to other areas if need be. The major drawback is cost. Modified snares are more economical if tagging is the main intent.

Several types of collar snares have been developed. These snares, placed in deer runways, allow the deer to tag themselves. When a deer puts its head into the snare, it pulls the collar about its neck to a predetermined size and locks it. As the deer continues to pull, the collar snaps free from the snare wire. Biologists have found that the snares are about 50 percent effective, allowing them to collar and tag large numbers of deer at a fraction of the cost of other methods.

The use of immobilizing drugs, delivered by the use of an arrow or a dart gun, has gained wide acceptance but is used mainly on animals in holding pens. The range and accuracy of the darts leave much to be desired.

# 25

## Taking the Census

Knowing the number of deer in given areas in each state is of the utmost importance to biologists, wildlife managers, game departments, and the general public. Management requires a knowledge of how many deer are in a herd, the age-and-sex composition of the herd, and the quantity and quality of the range.

Live-trapping allows the biologists to check on individual deer, but live-traps catch only a fraction of the animals. Radio transmitters pinpoint the exact whereabouts of a particular deer, thus accumulating much data on daily activities and travels. Tagging provides a basis for long-range records on weights, ages, and dispersal. Still, when we want to know how many deer are using any given area, we have to count them by some means. The most effective and accurate method is by large-scale drives. This can be prohibitively costly because of the manpower involved. However, most gun clubs are more than willing to volunteer the help of their members for such undertakings.

The areas to be driven must be tracts that can be thoroughly and completely surrounded by the number of men involved. Those who are designated as

When a large-scale drive is used for census-taking, each counter watches for deer passing on his right. He must be very alert to avoid missing deer like this one, quietly sneaking through cover.

counters are placed in the position first, downwind where possible. Each of them must be able to see the counter on either side of him. If they are placed on a road, they can be as far apart as such sightings allow. Since each counter only counts the deer that pass on his right side, there is no duplication. The drivers must be close enough together to move all the deer within the area. The drivers move slowly and with a minimum of noise. It is of the greatest importance that the drivers' line be kept as straight as possible and that each driver be able to see the driver on either side. The drivers count only the deer that run back through their line, and each of these men, too, counts only the animals on his right side. This is the most accurate method of censusing deer in a specific area.

We once took a census of the deer on Coventry Hunt Club land by going out at night and driving along, or through, all of the fields adjoining the woodlands to count the deer with the aid of automobile headlights and spotlights. When this was done for four consecutive nights, we had a good estimate of how many deer were on that land. Because I knew the areas intimately, I did not need to drive each one. Instead, I could do sample areas and then make projections. This method works well on appropriate terrain and is comparatively inexpensive.

The auther has successfully conducted counts at night, with teams in automobiles using headlights and spotlights. A deer's eyeshine eases the job of spotting, but the method works only where roads border fields used by feeding deer.

On Coventry Hunt Club land, nighttime censuses have been made with automobiles. Note that deer are concentrated in fields adjoining woodlands.

Track counts can be made most
easily and accurately after snow or
heavy rain.

By doing it in late summer or early fall, we obtained not only a total count
but the sex ratio and an accounting of the fawn crop. So long as the ratio of
fawns to does was high, we knew the range was still adequate and the herd
was increasing. When the deer had reached the carrying capacity of the range,
our fawn count dropped.

Mule deer are usually tallied when they are concentrated in February or
March. A count is made by two persons, walking on opposite ridge tops of
each drainage. As each person walks along, he counts only the deer he sees on
the opposite slope. This is much more effective than for each man to try to
count the deer on his own slope. The number of deer seen are tallied against
the estimated acreage covered, to give a count per square mile. This figure,
calculated against the total square miles of the mule deer's winter range, gives
an estimated herd population.

Where a crew of census-takers is unavailable, there are methods that require
only one or two men if the area to be covered is not too large. One such
method is a track count, which is best made after a rain or snow. Old tracks
can be raked over. If the tracks are to be counted on a dirt road, dragging
heavy brush or a piece of chain-link fence behind a car will usually wipe the
old tracks out.

These are fresh, sharp-edged blacktail tracks. If a track count is to be made on a dirt road, brush or a chain-link fence is first dragged to wipe out the old tracks.

Counts of droppings are also made. Deer defecate an average of 13 times each 24 hours. Some researchers advocate picking up all old pellets before counting the new ones. That's too time-consuming. I have found it much faster to mix up some bright water-paint and use a pump oil can to spray a few drops of paint on the old defecations. In a short time you complete your counting of the heaps of new pellets, and the water-paint has washed away. This method, like the track count, is useful because it requires no crew of census-takers.

In areas that have snow, the easiest way is to count the defecations on top of the snow. The number of heaps of pellets divided by the number of days since the snow fell, divided by 13, gives you the number of deer using the area censused.

Counting deer by airplane has never been very accurate because even the smallest planes fly too fast and the counters miss too many deer. The use of helicopters is far more accurate since they can hover in one spot to check out cover thoroughly, and they can be lowered over dense conifer cover to flush the deer out. New Jersey makes extensive use of helicopters to census the deer

The deer population can also be estimated by counting droppings in a specified area. Deer average 13 defecations in 24 hours. Before counting, old droppings can be sprayed with water-paint to prevent double counting.

when there is snow on the ground. Elsewhere, too, helicopters are being used increasingly.

Infra-red photography is also gaining wider usage in censusing wildlife. The heat of an animal's body affects the film and shows up as white spots. For deer, this method has been more efficient in summer than winter because a deer's winter coat is such an effective barrier to heat loss that the body heat fails to register on the film.

In addition to these methods, statistical analysis and computers make use of the data gathered from the return of the hunter-kill cards. This data would be even more accurate if all hunters, *whether successful or not,* were required to turn in a report card at the end of each license year. Human nature being what it is, I suppose this is an impossibility. Even states that require the cards to be sent in have a large percentage of hunters who just don't bother. More data could be gathered if each hunter were required to fill out a report card when he got his new license. Unfortunately, many hunters don't buy their licenses until just prior to the hunting season, so the data would be over a year late and of no use in setting seasons and limits for the current year. Another drawback is that many states do not require landowners to have a license while hunting on their own lands.

New Jersey, like a number of other states, requires that every deer killed be presented at a checking station within a day. This very effective regulation gives the state the opportunity to gather and tabulate a wealth of data very soon after the season ends. It is an inconvenience to the hunters, but some inconveniences are necessary.

New Jersey's deer-management program was computerized in 1974. The state was divided into thirty-six management zones. This new system divided the state by prominent boundaries such as major highways. Most of our major highways follow natural geographical divisions—for instance, through the valleys between mountain ranges. Prior to this, information was gathered by counties—along political lines that were not recognized by the deer and couldn't be recognized by most humans, either. The new system allows data to be collected from smaller units, where the deer and range characteristics are similar. Data about the number of deer inhabiting each zone, their reproductive rate, age, sex and weight classes, and general condition, as well as the range conditions, are tabulated and fed into a computer at Rutgers University.

The seventy-two mandatory checking stations provide a wealth of information on about eleven thousand deer in the one week of the hunting season. Analyzing this data manually had been costly and time-consuming. Using the computer, the deer managers now have an overall view of most aspects of New Jersey's deer herd and are better able to manage the deer by increasing or decreasing the hunting pressure in each of the deer-management zones.

# 26

---

# Poachers

Wherever there is illegal money to be made, somebody is always ready to make it. Just as organized crime has invaded legitimate business, the poachers have stepped up their operations against legal hunting.

A recent and comprehensive survey on the poaching situation in the United States was conducted by John Cartier, a field editor for *Outdoor Life* Magazine. He divided the continent into seven major sections. Questionnaires that he sent to all of the states provided his statistics. Cartier found that deer poaching, over the past decade, has increased by 19.5 percent in the Prairie States, 34.3 percent in the Southeast, 59 percent in the South Central region, 60.6 percent in the Northeast, 88 percent in the Inter-Mountain States, 99.1 percent in the North Central region, and 112.1 percent in the Far West. The major increase in deer poaching is due to the increasing disregard on the part of the general public for all law and order. Another important factor is that the explosion of the deer population in most parts of the continent coincided with the human population explosion. There are more people to shoot the deer and

In some parts of the mule deer's range, poaching has increased greatly. Most professional poachers shoot bucks, does, and fawns indiscriminately.

more deer for people to shoot. The rise in deer poaching is also the result of a decline in most areas of small and upland game and in the waterfowl populations, with a resultant decline in the poaching of these species. Then, too, the poaching of deer gives a much greater return for the time and effort expended. One average 125-pound (57.8 kg.) deer yields the poacher as much edible meat as 50 rabbits or ducks.

During the Great Depression, many backwoods people and farmers took a deer now and then to feed their families. Many of these people still take a deer for the same reason, even though their financial situation may be vastly improved today. Some farmers feel that, although the deer belong to the state, the crops the deer eat and the land the deer live on belong to the landowners. I'm not about to argue the merits or morality of that issue because the landowners and farmers have a good point. In any event, these people do only a small fraction of the poaching.

It is the professional poacher, the outlaw, shooting the deer to sell the meat, who makes the heavy inroads on deer herds. Many such poachers conduct their operations with the precision of military maneuvers. Many use scope-sighted high-power rifles and are equipped with four-wheel-drive vehicles that

In some locales, poaching specialists concentrate on trophy bucks like this whitetail for sale to unsuccessful hunters.

can negotiate the roughest terrain. Some are even equipped with C.B. radios with which they keep in touch with cohorts to help to spot game and with lookouts who watch out for conservation officers. Such organized groups move into a back area, kill all the game possible, and are on their way in a couple of hours.

While hunting with a friend in Wyoming, John Cartier discovered thirteen dressed-out antelope and mule deer hung up in an old shack on the friend's ranch. By the time the friend and Cartier got back with a conservation officer, the shack was empty.

A couple of years ago, four professional poachers from Rhode Island were arrested and convicted of shooting twenty-five deer near Chelsea, Vermont. When that many animals are involved, there can be no doubt that the poachers are professionals, engaged in selling meat and skins, and sometimes trophy heads.

A friend of mine told me that on several occasions, while hunting in Maine, he had been approached by poachers who offered him a buck with a rack of whatever size he could pay for. The larger the rack, the higher the price. The bucks had been shot before the season opened. My friend was a real sportsman who wouldn't dream of buying his deer—and wouldn't need to. Many hunters, after hunting all week without shooting a deer, will buy deer from poachers rather than go home empty-handed. The hunters who patronize these poachers evidently lack the intelligence to realize that they would have a better chance to take their own deer if the poachers hadn't "skimmed off the cream" before the legal season. The easiest prey for these poachers is the non-resident hunter who happens to be an urbanite, has not done much hunting, knows little about it, is easily discouraged, and—to borrow a phrase of current jargon—is more interested in an "ego trip" than a real hunting trip.

The practice of selling trophies has been common in many states, including my own. Today New Jersey has sharply curtailed this practice by requiring that no deer be moved without being tagged by the hunter and that every deer killed be taken to a checking station within twenty-four hours. A number of other states now employ similar means to combat this type of poaching.

A deer's eyes turn green half an hour after death, rigor mortis sets in about three to four hours, and it takes at least ten or twelve hours for a carcass to freeze solid, even where the weather is extremely cold. The inside of the body cavity turns dark as the meat is exposed and tends to dry out. With all of these clues, it is fairly easy to tell how long ago the deer was killed. Trophy deer can still be sold, but the deer cannot be stockpiled before the season. Trophy poachers are most apt to be local professionals.

Most commercial poachers concentrate on taking deer out of season and selling the venison—mainly to individuals and to a lesser extent to restaurants. They care little about trophies. They find it much more profitable to shoot any deer they can get in their sights.

The greatest difficulty in stopping all this is apprehending the violators. Having worked as a deputy conservation officer, I can attest to the fantastic number of hours of waiting or patrolling that it takes to catch a single poacher. And sometimes those hours turn out to be fruitless; that poacher escapes. Conservation officers have to be at about the top of the list of unappreciated heroes. This situation is changing and will continue to change as more

Poachers often shoot deer at night, using spotlights, and kill great numbers out of season. A buck like this whitetail in velvet may be killed in spring, thus reducing the herd's breeding potential. A doe killed in spring may be carrying fawns, or may have given birth to fawns that will be doomed.

hunters and the general public come to realize that the deer the poachers take are *their* deer. The active cooperation of indignant citizens is at last beginning to make life harder for the poachers.

No state has enough conservation officers to do the job properly, although these men try hard. Minnesota, for example, has about 84,000 square miles. To patrol that area, the state has 129 conservation officers, or one to every 650 square miles. Minnesota had 359,432 licensed hunters in 1975, or one officer to every 2,786 hunters. New Jersey has 35 conservation officers, or one to every 229 square miles. We had 159,475 licensed hunters in 1975, or one officer to about 4,555 hunters. Deputies help, and the conservation officers are now also getting help from the Game Protective Association. This association is made up of members of organized gun clubs who volunteer their time to assist the conservation officers whenever needed. They are entitled by state law to carry badges and make arrests. The results have been very good, and other states would find it advantageous to establish similar organizations.

Unfortunately, conservation officers can devote only a portion of their time to apprehending deer poachers. The officers in most states have to enforce all of the game laws, help with game releases, enforce the fishing laws, help with fish stocking, give protection to all protected non-game species, appear in court to prosecute cases, write up reports, and do public relations work for the division. It is a wonder that any deer poacher is ever caught.

How many deer are poached? How many poachers are caught? Naturally, there are no concrete statistics to answer the first question, but many of the states report some astonishing figures.

One state estimated that 41,000 deer were poached each year in just that state. A state in the Northeast calculated that the illegal deer kill equaled 95 percent of the legal hunter kill. A north-central state reported a 400 percent increase in deer poaching in the past decade. Most states require that a poacher be caught in the act or be found in possession of illegal game. The odds are definitely in favor of the poacher.

George Dahl, Chief of Michigan's Department of Natural Resources Law Enforcement Division, stated that in the 1973-1974 big-game season 2,763 violators were arrested. But according to Michigan statistics, 181,183 violations were probably committed, which means that arrests were made for only 1.53 percent of the violations.

To compound the problem, after a poacher is apprehended, too many lenient judges make a mockery of the laws. Unless the fines are mandated by law and are high enough to be a deterrent, being arrested is merely an inconvenience for a poacher and the fine is just part of his cost of doing business. At one time, Pennsylvania confiscated any vehicle involved in poaching. *That* was a deterrent. Most states confiscate the poachers' guns, but some do not. Some states revoke the poachers' hunting privileges, but some do not. Revocation of hunting privileges is a very important deterrent and should be more widely applied, although I realize that this will not stop professional poachers any more than the registration of guns would stop professional criminals from possessing them.

Many of the older, rural judges, who remember the Depression years, are inclined to be lenient and seldom impose more than the minimum fine. As these older judges retire and younger, more conservation-minded judges are presiding at the courts, the fines are mounting. Judges who are elected locally are also reluctant to impose stiff fines on local poachers. Petitions have been circulated and publicity given to many unfair decisions of these judges. The public that elected lenient judges can vote them out of office again — if public apathy to deer poaching can be overcome. State-mandated fines now take most of this power of decision away from local judges, so the proper action should be instigated by the hunters and general public at the state level.

It is no coincidence that the states with the highest fines have the lowest rate of increase in poaching. The north-central state that had a 400 percent increase has an average $69.00 cost for illegally killing a deer. New Jersey has a minimum $200.00 fine, and deer poaching has not increased in proportion to the population.

Missouri has one of the lowest rates of poaching increase in the nation, a mere 15 percent in the past decade. It imposes an average fine of $300.00 per deer.

A few years ago, during a meat shortage, Missouri had an outbreak of cattle rustling as well as deer poaching. All of the Missouri law-enforcement agencies cooperated in their expenditures of money and manpower to blanket the state with posters and with notices in the papers and over the airwaves, alerting the public to this illegal killing. The public responded enthusiastically by refusing to buy illegal meat and by reporting the sellers to the authorities. The outbreak was stopped and the trend even reversed.

You can't appeal to a poacher's heart or sense of honesty, but you can hit him where it hurts — in his pocketbook. Stiffer fines, confiscation of weapons, loss of hunting privileges, and public cooperation can and will reduce the poaching of deer.

The National Rifle Association supplies free wallet-sized cards that can be carried and should be filled out by any one witnessing a game violation and then forwarded to the proper state authorities. All bona fide hunters are eager to rid their woods and fields of the unsavory characters who kill game illegally, and increasing cooperation is being shown. Through the education of all hunters and the general public, the poachers can be deprived of a market. If a poacher can't sell the deer he shoots, he will soon stop shooting deer.

# 27

## Wildlife Management and Politics

$O$ne of the foremost needs of the majority of fish and game departments is to be completely severed from all political connections. I do not have statistics on how many states fill the top jobs in their conservation and fish and game departments with political appointees, but the number is far too large. Many of the departments cannot manage their game properly because the major decisions are not made by game biologists but by the state legislatures. Many of the legislators have little or no knowledge of the basics of wildlife management, and without this knowledge they are vulnerable to the politics of pressure groups.

When the top jobs in the department are filled by political appointment, the qualified, competent biologists, trained in game management, are thwarted in their advance to positions of authority where their knowledge could be put to the best use. Instead, the qualified men are relegated to lesser jobs. Chafing under the impossibility of advancement, they often quit working for the state, and for wildlife, to seek jobs in the private sector.

Wildlife-management policies must be flexible because many variables, such as weather, often change the conditions affecting the wildlife, and decisions must be made at once. Often there is no time to wait for these decisions to arrive by the slow route of legislative procedure. There are times when bad weather prevents a deer kill large enough to harvest the proper number of animals. A quick decision to extend the season will allow for this contingency. Some game departments, such as Pennsylvania's, having no political strings pulling them, are able to manage their wildlife for the benefit of the wildlife, the hunters, and the general public. But many other states are not so fortunate.

Let me quote a few examples of how politics can thwart wildlife management. The first quotation is from the August, 1976, issue of *Michigan Out-of-Doors:*

" 'Bio-politics' killed a proposed antlerless deer hunting season in a sizable portion of the eastern Upper Peninsula this year. Biologists had recommended issuing 8,930 permits to take antlerless deer in a large area in the eastern Upper Peninsula, a proposal that would have sparked vitriolic charges at the commission meeting by doe hunting foes. The issue was defused, however, by Department of Natural Resources Director Howard Tanner's recommendation that the Commission reject the biologists' proposal.

" 'The eastern Upper Peninsula biological recommendation is based on a harvestable surplus of 2,000 animals,' Tanner said, 'but we as a department have paid a tremendous price for pushing for antlerless seasons in the face of stiff opposition there. A harvest or not of 2,000 animals cannot be that important biologically.' "

Here is one from *Deer Production in the United States, 1969-1973,* by Professor Sidney Wilcox:

"In 1969-1970, Wisconsin lost fifty to sixty thousand deer from starvation and Michigan lost 25,000 because recommendations for more [hunting] permits went unheeded by the legislatures."

In *Illinois Wildlife* for November 17, 1976, an article entitled "Capers in Conservation," by John Warren, had this to say:

"As this installment was written before the November 2nd election, no conclusion can be given herein as to the course conservation may take in Illinois during the next two years.

"One thing is certain, however, Illinois will very shortly have its seventh conservation director in eight years.

"With this kind of political maneuvering, any real advance in resource preservation is impossible—which is exactly what those who plunder and despoil the resources for personal or corporate gain wish.

This is a small whitetail doe in the North Country, where game managers cite "bio-politics" as the cause of overcrowded habitat, stunting, poor reproduction, and exceptionally high winter-kill statistics.

"Conservation administration in Illinois has finally now sunk so low that the top executive no longer need know anything at all about fish, wildlife, forestry, law enforcement, parks, outdoor recreation, nature preserves, etc. All he need be, is a product of the Governor's office, with no background in natural resources either from an educational or an experience standpoint."

Michigan, Wisconsin, and Illinois are by no means the only states where wildlife and wildlife biologists have been victimized by politics. Observers have frequently cited Vermont as a classic, and tragic, example. In 1968, *Vermont's Big Game and Waterfowl Review and Forecast* tersely declared that "the waste continues under legislative control." Two years later *Vermont's Game Annual* reported that "in most sections of the state, the 1970 fall deer population will exceed the size of the 1969 fall population. . . . Physical deterioration of bucks and does will certainly continue with further reductions in the already sharply retarded reproductive rate." In 1971, *Vermont's Game Annual* reviewed what had happened in the previous five years—and was continuing to happen:

"In the Review of the 1966 Big Game Seasons, Fish and Game Department Commissioner Edward F. Kehoe stated that it was 'obvious' our deer herd was at a 'turning point.' No matter how obvious the situation was at that time, perhaps no one really knew how swiftly that point turned and how disastrous and far-reaching the results would be.

"That a turning point was unavoidable should have been no surprise to Vermonters. In 1963, the 'crash' of the deer herd was predicted by the Department as an absolute certainty if immediate steps were not taken to correct the situation. In each of the subsequent three years, the warning was repeated in many Department publications, at hundreds of speaking engagements and through all of the news media. . . .

"By March of 1966, the newly reapportioned Vermont Legislature felt it was time to do something about the increasing crop and forest damage complaints and to lessen the incredible numbers of deer being wasted on the highways, to free running pet dogs and to illegal hunting. The resulting bill, effective until March 31, 1971, created an advisory Interim Committee (consisting of the Chairman and Vice Chairman of both the House and Senate Fish and Game Committees) and directed the Fish and Game Board to hold public hearings in those sections of Vermont which were overpopulated with deer. Further limitations, not included in the bill but mutually agreed upon between the Committee and the Fish and Game Board, restricted antlerless deer removal to no more than eight percent of the available antlerless population and required that proof of a seriously depraved situation must exist before such token controls could be applied.

"By November of 1966, Vermont had crowded more deer per square mile within its borders than had ever before been recorded by any state. The saturation point had been achieved. . . .

"An average December, followed by a mild January, lulled most of us into thinking that the winter of 1966-67 was to be another mild one. But February brought us some of the most bitter winter temperatures ever recorded in Vermont. These extremely low temperatures, coupled with deep snows, caused winter mortality to rise sharply. March dumped more than normal amounts of snow on southern Vermont and continuing sub-normal temperatures brought further statewide hardship to our deer herd. In March of 1967, as Commissioner Kehoe was issuing his 'turning point' statement to Vermonters, the inevitable had begun.

"From March of 1967 to March of 1971, the Vermont white-tailed deer herd suffered winter mortality that, in all likelihood, exceeds any ever documented in any other state or province, or for that matter any similar land mass in the world.

"Losses during a single winter in some yarding areas exceeded 200 carcasses counted per square mile and this does not include fall illegal or crippling losses. . . .

"The decline of the deer herd beginning in February and March of 1967 has continued to the present day. Depending on winter severity, it could continue downward for several more years.

"Some people blame the demise of the herd on 'shooting does and fawns.' The fact is that we have never taken more than eight percent of the antlerless herd by lawful hunting while the harvest level to stabilize herd size should be about 20 percent. . . .

"Over widespread areas of Vermont, 50 percent of all fawns entering the winter yards never live to see spring. Damage in three out of four winter yards is so severe on all species of palatable and nutritious deer food that at least a decade will pass before meaningful improvements in food availability could possibly be seen. . . .

"Vermont's buck kill has declined sharply since 1966, but the Department has never had control of the deer herd in Vermont.

"All of the deer harvested during antlerless seasons held from 1966 to 1970 were only slightly more than the number of deer killed on the highways over the same period. Another comparison to keep things in perspective is that the deer killed by dogs during the past *two* winters of 1969-70 and 1970-71 exceeded the total antlerless harvest for the *five-year* period between 1966 and 1970. This statement is not a reflection of the effectiveness of the Department's enforcement efforts on free running pet dogs. It is the inevitable result of carrying too many half starved wintering deer that are unable to escape from this unfortunate and wasteful form of predation.

"The only real argument that opponents to herd management have is the decline in buck kill. True, the buck kill did go down, but a closer examination of this decline will reveal that *the decline was greatest in areas where antlerless deer have not been harvested for 50 years.* . . .

"Even with mild winters, the buck kill may never recover to levels enjoyed during the middle sixties. A return to higher harvest levels of deer can only be attained after a recovery in the quality of the habitat. Recovery of the habitat will take several years of intensive herd management. . . .

"The Vermont Legislature now bears absolute responsibility for the future of Vermont's white-tailed deer herd. Legal authority for the Vermont Fish and Game Department to declare even token antlerless seasons has expired. . . .

"Unfortunately, our deer herd will continue to suffer until we all decide to face the distasteful facts. Our overbrowsed winter yards continue to decline and will not support the numbers of deer we have known in the past. Man has removed Nature's large deer predators and *he* must assume their role in checking and balancing Vermont's deer population. . . ."

Still the warnings went unheeded, and in 1972 the same publication characterized Vermont's whitetails as "one of the most underharvested and poorly managed deer herds in the country." The reason was beginning to sound like an old refrain:

> "Sincere Department efforts to correct the problems and meet its objectives of perpetuating a healthy deer herd met with a number of obstacles. Limited public appreciation of the situation and public acceptance of the recommended corrective measures certainly were major obstacles. The Legislature has not been willing to support the Department to the extent necessary to implement sound management practices. . . . Legislators should be asked to justify their decisions and supply evidence supporting their actions."

Did the legislators at last do so? The answer can be found in the 1975 edition of *Vermont's Game Annual:*

> Findings of the spring dead deer surveys coupled with all the other studies of the Deer Project continue to dramatically point up the need for well-regulated, antlerless deer harvests in most sections of the state. The deer herd and the hunter are both getting short-changed by a lack of proper management.

Need anything more be said on the subject of politics in wildlife management?

# 28

## The Value of America's Deer

The estimated population of whitetail deer in the United States in 1975 was 12,728,910. This overall population is steadily increasing, even though herds are declining in many of the states and the extremely severe winter of 1976-1977 brought an additional decline in some states. There are about a million whitetails in the Canadian provinces.

The mule deer and possibly the blacktail populations are declining. The estimates show 2,778,120 mule deer and 960,190 blacktail deer in the United States. There are perhaps a million mule and blacktail deer in the Canadian provinces. British Columbia has an estimated 500,000 blacktails and 100,000 mule deer. While whitetails are increasing in Manitoba, the mule deer there have just about disappeared. The estimated totals for North America, then, are 13,728,910 whitetails and 4,738,310 mule and blacktail deer—that is, 18,467,220 deer of all three varieties.

What are those deer worth? There is no way to put a value on them that would be accepted by everyone, or even by most people. Deer mean many things to many people.

Here is a superb, high-racked whitetail buck in autumn. There is no way to assign a monetary value to the joy of seeing or photographing such animals in the wild.

To people like me, their value is immense. In practical terms, they are a big part of my "bread and butter." As a wildlife photographer, I make a good part of my living from the sale of photographs of deer. I sell at least a hundred deer photos for every photo of an African lion or elephant. As a lecturer, I find that deer are one of my most popular subjects. As an author, I have chosen to make deer one of the main topics I write about.

More than my livelihood is involved. I have taken over 25,000 photos of deer, and I am just as thrilled and anxious to take my next as I was my first. I started taking photographs of deer as a hobby, just because I loved to watch and study deer. Gradually my hobby became my profession. If, for some reason, I never sold another deer photo, I would go right on taking pictures of deer.

The greatest financial support for wildlife conservation comes from hunters. One study estimated the average expenditure at $40.00 per hunter per recreational day.

What is the esthetic value of deer to people who just want to watch them? It is beyond calculation. There are no records of the number of people who go out for a drive on a Sunday afternoon, chiefly in the hope of seeing deer. Some of the back roads in my area on Sundays—and on evenings throughout the week—are crowded with cars carrying people who are looking for deer. Six times more people visit wildlife refuges to merely watch the wildlife than to hunt in those areas.

Professor Sidney Wilcox's study at Arizona State University has given the value of $40.00 per day for the recreational value of hunting. This is what a man would be willing to pay. This is not the actual cost to the man per day because in some cases the figure would be high and in others far too low. The states reported that each firearm hunter averaged 5.41 days of hunting and each bow hunter averaged 8.75 days of hunting. Multiplying 9,098,771 licensed gun hunters (in 1975) by 5.41, we can calculate 49,224,351 man/days of hunting. The man/days times $40.00 per day comes to $1,968,974,040. The 1,186,049 bow hunters (in 1975) multiplied by 8.75 equals 10,377,928 man/days of hunting. That, at $40.00 per day, comes to $415,117,120 worth of recreation. The two figures give us a total of $2,384,091,160 of recreational value for the year 1975, if we consider only hunting in the estimate.

I realize that not all of these licensees hunted for deer. Many hunted for other game. But I also realize that there are no statistics on the numbers of unlicensed landowners who hunt deer. We know that 21.4 percent of those who hunt do so legally without licenses. If we trade off the unlicensed hunters for the licensed hunters who don't hunt deer, we might well come up with approximately the same statistics just given. There is no way of ever finding out, but the estimates we do have are impressive.

Taking the known figures a step further, it can be theorized that if six times as many nonhunters as hunters use the refuges and other wild areas, not counting national parks, the total is about 62,000,000 nonhunters. There is no season on hiking, bird-watching, nature study, nature photography, or similar activities, and these people spend more days engaged in their hobbies than do hunters. If we allot only 10 days afield to each nonhunting participant in outdoor recreation (an extremely conservative estimate since a government survey indicates that the actual figure may triple that) we can safely calculate at least 620,000,000 man/days of nonhunting outdoor recreation—plus a total of 59,602,279 man/days spent afield by hunters using both firearms and bows. If we allow the same value of $40.00 a day for the 620,000,000 man/days, the total value is astronomical.

I have been quoting sport-hunting statistics from only one source—the 1975 Arizona State University study—and readers may wonder if the figures are inflated. On the contrary, they are extremely conservative. At the end of 1977, the Fish and Wildlife Service of the U. S. Department of the Interior released an analysis of its own 1975 survey. In that year, according to the government survey, more than 20 million Americans hunted. Over 13 million were big-game hunters who spent over 126 million man/days engaged in their sport, and most of those people—more than 12 million—hunted deer whether or not they hunted any other game. *Of more than 2½ billion dollars spent by big-game hunters on equipment, transportation, food, and lodging, the deer hunters contributed over a billion.* And this does not include expenditures for licenses and other hunting fees.

Of course, those hunters who bring home venison get food as well as sport for the money spent, though in dollars and cents the food procured does not compare with the outlay. The ratio of successful to unsuccessful hunters varies widely with locale, but on a nationwide basis perhaps two hunters out of ten will harvest a deer in any given year. Professor Wilcox's tabulations showed that 2,269,848 mule deer were harvested in the United States in 1975. He figured that an average mule deer or whitetail would yield about 56 to 57 pounds (25.3 to 25.8 kg.) of boneless meat, while an average blacktail would yield about 42 pounds (19 kg.). The total harvest in boneless meat came to

A whitetail doe suspiciously observes her photographer. A question of paramount importance to conservationists is whether the nonhunting public can be persuaded to support wildlife by paying their share for the privilege of witnessing sights like this.

122,816,330 pounds (55,709,487 kg.). Premium-grade ground beef was then averaging $1.15 per pound. Using that price, the total value of the harvested deer meat was calculated at $133,846,931.

As to the skins, many are wasted, many are used by the hunters themselves, and many are sold. Since the average sale price is $2.00 a skin, we can add something in the vicinity of $4,500,000 for deer hides. However, the total meat and skin values are irrelevant to the esthetic and recreational value of deer. Even in purely practical terms, a better indication of the true value of the resource is the willingness of hunters to pay $40.00 per man/day.

But let's look again at Professor Wilcox's $40.00-a-day estimate. Would the *non*hunting public be equally willing to pay $40.00 a day for wildlife-related recreation. I hope so but I doubt it. Up to now they certainly have not paid their way in supporting wildlife. They have taken a free ride, paid for by hunters in license fees, excise taxes on hunting equipment, special-permit fees, and so on.

A major difference between European and American game conservation is that in Europe the game belongs to the landowner, while in the United States it belongs to each of the states—that is, to the public. Although it belongs to the general public, the game departments that administer the protection and harvest of the game are not supported by tax dollars from the general public. Most of the wildlife refuges, most of the state game lands, most of the wildlife research and management, and most of the protection provided for any wildlife, both game and non-game species, come from the hunters' license fees. It is true that *commercial* hunting came close to pushing some of our species over the brink to oblivion, but that was not due to *sport* hunting. It was the sport hunters who brought back the deer, the ducks, the wild turkey, the pronghorn antelope, and other creatures. It was also the hunter who introduced the ringneck pheasant, chukkar, gray partridge, and other foreign species that have now become part of our native fauna.

According to Lynn Greenwalt, Director of the U. S. Fish and Wildlife Service, American hunters paid $154,919,581.69 for hunting licenses in 1975. They paid an additional $51,100,000 in excise taxes on guns and ammunition. This excise is a self-imposed tax put on these items at the request of the hunters, who actively lobbied—both privately and through their various organizations—for the passage of the federal law requiring the tax. All the money thus derived goes to the individual states for wildlife work.

The hunters also paid $11,800,000 in taxes on handguns and archery equipment, of which 70 percent went to the states for research and other wildlife purposes. The remaining 30 percent went to the states for hunter-education programs.

Since 1935, when the "duck-stamp" program was first instituted, hunters have bought over $150,000,000 worth of federal migratory-waterfowl stamps. All of this money has gone into the purchase, rental, and maintenance of refuge lands for the ducks, geese, and swans of North America, as well as countless other game and non-game species that utilize the refuges.

In 1975 alone, hunters contributed more than $228,000,000 for wildlife restoration. Since 1923, they have donated more than $2.1 billion for wildlife.

When preservationists advocate bringing back the predators to control the game so that hunting will no longer be needed, they overlook the crucial fact that predators don't buy licenses, pay taxes, or make charitable donations. Without the revenue from the hunters, most of the state conservation departments would be out of business. There would be no wildlife protection, no wildlife research, no wildlife refuges—and in a short time there would not be much wildlife.

Customarily, the states' fish and game boards, who govern the direction of the fish and game departments, have been made up of officials elected by farmers and other landowners, sportsmen's clubs, and conservation groups. These were the people who were sufficiently interested in wildlife to "put their money where their mouth was." They are the ones who have always picked up the tab. Today the preservationists are demanding a voice in the affairs of wildlife and a seat on the governing boards, and they are getting what they want. That is democracy at work, but why not let them pay for the privilege? A rallying point before the American Revolution was the issue of "taxation without representation." Today the preservationists are trying to perpetrate another injustice: "representation without taxation."

Several states today are experimenting with the sale of *non*hunting wildlife stamps. So far, the results have been somewhat disappointing, because more of the stamps are bought by hunters than by nonhunters. Now several states are contemplating the sale of nonhunting licenses or permits for wildlife-related recreation. The money thus derived, like the hunters' money, would be used to benefit wildlife. Let the hikers, campers, birdwatchers, and all others who are interested in wildlife share in the support of that wildlife.

The preservationists, and many misguided individuals in the general public, do contribute money to the preservationist organizations. Lest they boast about how much money they donate for wildlife, we should scrutinize the activities of some of these groups.

For example, the *Los Angeles Times* exposed the activities of Belton P. Mouras, founder and president of the Animal Protection Institute. Mouras's organization is the one that for a number of years flooded newspapers and magazines with photos of the worst examples of trapped animals that he could locate. The ads stated that tax-free contributions would put a stop to wildlife's suffering. According to the *Times,* the main beneficiary of the contributions was Belton P. Mouras.

In 1974, he collected about $100,000 in salary, fees, and expenses from his protection group. According to the *Times,* "The Animal Protection Institute provides no direct relief to animals and does relatively little lobbying of Congress to enact animal protection laws."

In 1971, during the period when Friends of Animals stopped the deer hunting in the New Jersey Great Swamp, that tax-free organization collected $468,166. Alice Herrington, the driving force behind F.O.A., got a salary of nearly $20,000, while administration and general expenses ran about $80,000. The bulk of the money—$330,604—went to veterinarians for spaying cats and dogs. Friends of Animals did do a lot of lobbying, and ran many advertisements about wildlife, but I can find no record of direct contributions for the purchase or maintenance of wildlife refuges or anything else of that sort.

I was hired by a group of wealthy people who had banded together in a group called the Deer Protection Association. I went to their meeting prepared to lecture on basic deer biology and management. No! That's not what they wanted. They wanted to know how they could get rid of the deer! The deer were eating the expensive shrubbery on their estates. They didn't want to put up fences because fences were unsightly. They wouldn't allow hunters to come in to reduce the tremendous deer herd because they didn't want anyone on their property. No, I didn't have the answers to their problems. And no, I didn't have any sympathy for them, either.

# 29

## Public Education and the Outlook for America's Deer

The greatest and most difficult task still confronting wildlife managers is that of educating the general public, hunters included. The state game departments have to develop better public-relations departments. The general public is not being reached; the reports and recommendations of the game biologists are not being read and understood.

To keep hunters and the general public informed, most of the game departments publish state game magazines. In many states these magazines are now combined with the conservation magazines of the natural resources division, and this is a step in the right direction since the combined magazines reach a much wider audience. The sorry situation is that not enough hunters and far too few other people get their states' magazines. Every game department should see that its publications get into every school in its state. The school children must be reached.

More game departments should develop interesting programs and lectures that can be given in the schools and to church groups, women's clubs, garden clubs, service clubs, and fraternal organizations. Such groups always need

The author here measures a whitetail doe. In his natural-history lectures before all audiences, the author has found that the public hungers for information on wildlife.

speakers and they are the groups that must be reached because, on their own, they probably would not seek out programs on wildlife. These are the people who are constantly bombarded by preservationist groups, some of which do more harm than good, as I have pointed out. The preservationist groups are, for the most part, adept fund-raisers, and they make far better use of television, radio, magazines, and newspapers than do any of the game departments.

Spokesmen for the game departments often speak at meetings of sportsmen's clubs. That's fine. The sportsmen need to be informed too, but for the game departments to speak only to sportsmen's groups is like having Democrats speak only to Democrats. Far greater results can be obtained by talking to people who may not share the same viewpoint. The object of talking to more diverse groups is to expose them to information that they did not have before. I know from personal experience that these groups can be reached, that they are interested in wildlife, that they can be taught the genuine concepts of wildlife management. I know it can be done because I make a good part of my living doing it. I deliver an average of two hundred lectures a year and conduct about two months of outdoor-education classes, mostly for school groups of all age levels. Our country's young people, in particular, love these programs; they literally soak up all the facts about wildlife that I can give them. I never try to make a hunter out of anyone, for that is a personal decision. But I do get students and others to understand that hunting is a most important wildlife-management tool. After all, the youth of today are the adults of tomorrow — the taxpayers and policy-makers of tomorrow. It is up to everyone interested in wildlife to see that the public gets the facts about wildlife. Only when the public has the facts and understands them will wildlife be managed for its own best interest and that of the general public.

Many wildlife agencies send out newsletters to all members of the Outdoor Writers Association of America and to all the newspapers within their states. But more game-department bulletins should be distributed to all the radio stations in each state. Almost all radio stations have a "Community Bulletin Board" for free public-service announcement. I have never heard a game-department announcement in any state, and the game departments are missing out on a vast audience. Most states also have public-education television. This network always needs new material, just as the game departments need more media outlets. Cooperation could be mutually beneficial. The killing of wildlife does not have to be presented. Most hunters themselves find the killing of game the least of the reasons for hunting, contrary to preservationist accusations of bloodthirstiness. Certainly the kill is necessary. It is how we harvest the game. But there is no reason to emphasize it dramatically. I think that the "American Sportsman" television series did sportsmen a disservice by sometimes emphasizing this aspect of hunting. Television programs should be factual, basic, life-history studies of wildlife and wildlife problems — and the game managers' solutions to those problems. Hunting, though not featured, should be shown because hunting is one of the most important tools a game manager has.

The prestigious National Wildlife Federation has published a leaflet entitled *Should We Hunt?* in which the question is asked, "What is the role of hunting?" And it is answered:

"Thinning out of game populations has been accomplished for years by hunting.

Prospects are bright for America's deer, and particularly for whitetails such as this healthy specimen. There are probably more whitetails now than when North America was first explored, and
they are steadily expanding their range.

"Why hunting?

"Because the federal government, all 50 state governments, all of the nation's major conservation organizations and reputable wildlife biologists recognize regulated hunting as an efficient means of reducing surplus wildlife populations. As the United States Council on Environmental Quality stated in its *Fifth Annual Report,* 'Under American law and custom, sport hunting—properly regulated and based on scientific principles—is considered a legitimate management technique as well as a form of recreation.'"

This is the kind of basic message that must be broadcast and elucidated so that the game departments can get on with their job of managing deer and other wildlife.

In several of the previous chapters, and again in this one, I have stressed the problems of game management. Yet it would be misleading—and certainly not my intention—to leave you with the impression that America's deer are in a sorry plight. They are, in general, better off than they have ever been. As I stated much earlier, we probably have at least as many deer now as were present when this continent was first explored. And we certainly have more, far more, than we had in the supposedly "good old days" of the nineteenth century. My reasons for stressing the problems are, first, to present an accurate picture and, second, to do what I can to encourage the solution of those problems. Having done that to the best of my ability, I want to end by summarizing the prospects—the future—of America's deer.

I believe it is a bright future. Management problems notwithstanding, deer are America's most managed, and most manageable, big-game animals. They are also our most common, most widely distributed, most adaptable, most hunted, most loved, best known, and perhaps most fascinating animal. The strong universal interest in deer assures that their well-being will always be accorded a top priority.

Of course, there are and will continue to be both localized and regional setbacks. In my own area of New Jersey, a tremendous influx of new homes, with the resultant destruction of habitat, will certainly diminish the local deer population. Yet my state—whose whitetail population was once little more than a memory—has just recorded its largest deer harvest in history. And like most whitetail states, it should continue to support a large, healthy herd in spite of any localized setbacks.

Prospects for our mule deer are not quite so bright as for whitetails and blacktails. The muley populations are declining in many regions. In Canada's Prairie Provinces mule deer have been nearly wiped out. A major part of the trouble lies in the expansion of the whitetail's domain. This is not a matter of

A young buck, somewhat less curious about humans than human are about him, makes his exit.

competition only but of accompanying problems—for example, the scourge of brainworms brought by whitetails. Mule deer have not developed sufficient tolerance of these devastating parasites, as whitetails have. In addition, the mule deer herds are affected by changing habitat as well as sharply increased hunting pressure in much of the West. These problems are compounded by permissive public-land policies that condone the overgrazing of public lands by domestic livestock. But mule deer are becoming much more wary animals than they once were, and are gradually evolving more adaptable traits. Through it all, they are surviving and will continue to. Moreover, as the public becomes better educated and the game departments are enabled to carry out their duties more effectively, muleys will probably increase once again in some areas and be re-established in others.

Blacktails are already showing signs of increasing. Since the number of hunters is at an all-time high, these deer furnish proof that properly regulated sport hunting is a help rather than a hindrance to healthy deer herds. In Alaska, the blacktails are not only increasing their numbers but are also slowly expanding their range.

Since whitetails are far more widespread, they are hunted by far more sportsmen. Whitetails, too, are increasing their numbers. They are doing so in almost all parts of their range, and that range is steadily growing. I am sure that at no time have America's deer been more numerous or healthy, and at no times have their prospects been brighter.

# Appendix I

## Favored Foods

In Part II of this book, describing the life cycle and habits of deer, I discussed browsing and grazing behavior as well as some pronounced food preferences during each season. This appendix presents fuller lists of preferred foods, although no such enumeration can be truly complete. A particular species of plant may be abundant and strongly preferred in a particular locale, yet the same plant may be scarce or absent in some or most other locales. If a plant suddenly proliferated in a new locale, it might or might not quickly achieve favored status. For example, in wilderness areas where the animals have never learned what corn is, even very hungry deer tend to ignore corn if it is put out for them. But in farm country, corn is a favorite deer food. I have tried to list the foods in an order of preference, but the order is very rough indeed since food preferences vary so sharply from one locale to another. A number of foods, such as cottonwood, mesquite, and Douglas fir, obviously have only a regional availability, though they are extremely important where abundant. You will also note that certain plants are favorable in all seasons while others are not. In some cases (particularly with regard to mule deer, which migrate seasonally between the high country and the lowlands) this may reflect the elevations at which a plant grows. In other cases, a plant may be dormant or absent during the colder part of the year. And in some cases, though a plant is available throughout the year, it is more nutritious or tastier to deer at one stage of growth than at another.

## COMMON SPRING FOODS

| Whitetail | Mule Deer | Blacktail |
|---|---|---|
| May hawthorn | sunflower | grasses |
| clover | fescuegrass | sedges |
| alfalfa | bluegrass | horsetail |
| cinquefoil | bromegrass | bracken |
| crabapple | ragweed | trailing blackberry |
| teaberry | kohleria | fireweed |
| trailing arbutus | needlegrass | red clder |
| greenbrier | wheatgrass | thimbleberry |
| dandelion | ricegrass | salmonberry |
| plantain | goldeneye | salal |
| corn | mountain mahogany | willow |
| wild strawberry | silktassel | cedar |
| trefoils | oak | deerbrush |
| lespedeza | manzanita | chamise |
| aster | wild oats | live oak |
| sunflower | dogwood | scrub oak |
| pokeweed | | mountain mahogany |
| jewelweed | | Douglas fir |
| poison ivy | | |
| New Jersey tea | | |
| bitterbush | | |
| serviceberry | | |
| red maple | | |
| Japanese honeysuckle | | |
| sassafras | | |
| willow | | |
| speedwell | | |
| blueberry | | |
| big and little bluestem | | |
| curly mesquite | | |
| tall dropseed | | |
| magnolia | | |
| Yaupon holly | | |
| bigleaf gallberry | | |

# COMMON SUMMER FOODS

| Whitetail | Mule Deer | Blacktail |
|---|---|---|
| red maple | deerwitch | salal |
| striped maple | fescuegrass | black raspberry |
| blueberry | pine | red alder leaves |
| blackberry | eriogonum | willow |
| greenbrier | serviceberry | bracken |
| alfalfa | oak | grasses |
| corn | bluegrass | sedges |
| dogwood | kohleria | thimbleberry |
| swamp ironwood | needlegrass | vine maple |
| ferns | wheatgrass | salmonberry |
| wild rose | ricegrass | fireweed |
| mushrooms | wild cherry | red elder |
| bluegrass | mountain mahogany | sow thistle |
| bearberry | silktassel | figwort |
| wheatgrass | gramagrass | mushrooms |
| sassafras | mushrooms | trailing blackberry |
| wild grape | lupine | huckleberry |
| chestnut oak | knotweed | plantain |
| pokeweed | thimbleberry | clover |
| sunflower | elderberry | pearly everlasting |
| blackeyed Susan | dogwood | yarrow |
| crabapple | mesquite | rose |
| soybean | | interior live oak |
| wild hydrangea | | buckeye |
| elderberry | | chokecherry |
| jewelweed | | chamise |
| aster | | honeysuckle |
| sumac | | poison oak |
| cabbage palm | | foothill ash |

## COMMON AUTUMN FOODS

| Whitetail | Mule deer | Blacktail |
|---|---|---|
| acorns | creeping barberry | acorns |
| oxalis | bearberry | filaree |
| plains lovegrass | snowberry | bromegrass |
| whorled nodviolet | snowbush | manzanita |
| mat euphorbia | jack pine | chamise |
| arrowleaf sida | sunflower | scrub oak |
| maple | sagebrush | deer brush |
| sweetfern | pine | wavyleaf ceanothus |
| willow | cedar | buckeye |
| wintergreen | mountain mahogany | wild grape |
| grasses | cliffrose | ferns |
| oak | poplar | toyon |
| wild cherry | needlegrass | poison oak |
| lespedeza | gramagrass | western chokecherry |
| snowberry | paintbrush | chaparral pea |
| greenbrier | bitterbush | wormwood |
| blackgum | rabbitbrush | trailing blackberry |
| creeping blueberry | wild cherry | plantain |
| holly | fescuegrass | vine maple |
| live oak | manzanita | annual agoseries |
| persimmon | eriogonum | red alder |
| snakeweed | quaking aspen | huckleberry |
| wheatgrass | sedge | salmonberry |
| honeysuckle | serviceberry | clover |
| aster | hackberry | |
| goldenrod | arrowleaf sida | |
| pussytoes | acorns | |
| palmetto berries | | |
| mushrooms | | |
| teaberry | | |
| sumac | | |
| blueberry | | |
| coralberry | | |
| sassafras | | |
| witch hazel | | |
| crabapple | | |
| dogwood | | |
| wild rose | | |
| wild grape | | |
| clover | | |
| elderberry | | |
| bittersweet | | |
| red raspberry | | |

# COMMON WINTER FOODS

| Whitetail | | Mule Deer | Blacktail |
|---|---|---|---|
| red maple | bearberry | creeping barberry | Douglas fir |
| striped maple | wild rose | bearberry | trailing blackberry |
| witch hazel | aspen | snowberry | red huckleberry |
| sumac | Oregon grape | ceanothus | yew |
| blueberry | spruce | sagebrush | madrone |
| hemlock | white birch | jack pine | salal |
| willow | sassafras | Douglas fir | sword fern |
| white pine | crabapple | rabbitbrush | vine maple |
| viburnums | Japanese honeysuckle | cedar | manzanita |
| yellow birch | apple | mountain mahogany | chamise |
| ash | coralberry | bitterbrush | red cedar |
| wintergreen | honey locust | fendlera | usnea |
| fir | lady's-tobacco | Sierra juniper | moss |
| white cedar | plantain | scrub oak | bracken |
| poplar | strawberry | fescuegrass | yerba santa |
| oaks | speedwell | sedge | scrub oak |
| lespedeza | hawthorn | wild oats | buckbrush |
| snowberry | poison ivy | bromegrass | toyon |
| blackgum | mints | creek dogwood | chaparral pea |
| greenbrier | goldenrod | mesquite | California laurel |
| dogwood | pussytoes | cliffrose | live oak |
| swamp ironwood | aster | holly-leaf buckthorn | coffeeberry |
| live oak | teaberry | turbinella oak | filaree |
| persimmon | acorns | mountain misery | acorns |
| snakeweed | | stonecrop | wavyleaf ceanothus |
| | | elderberry | |
| | | redberry | |
| | | California buckeye | |
| | | antelope brush | |
| | | black oak | |
| | | Pacific serviceberry | |
| | | bitter cherry | |
| | | western chokecherry | |
| | | tesota | |
| | | velvet elder | |
| | | sunflower | |
| | | cottonwood | |

# Appendix II

## Deer Populations and Harvests in the United States and Canada

The following tables—representing populations and harvests as of the 1975-1977 hunting seasons—have been compiled from 1975 surveys by Professor Sidney Wilcox of Arizona State University, from the 1977 Game Survey of the National Rifle Association, and from correspondence with the many game departments. Asterisks denote combined figures. Blank spaces indicate instances in which no figures were available.

| State or Province | Species | Estimated Population | Hunting Bow | Licenses Gun | Estimated Harvest | Percent Hunter Success |
|---|---|---|---|---|---|---|
| Alabama | whitetail | 1,000,000 | 5,000 | 196,000 | 120,727 | 6 |
| Alaska | blacktail | 100,000 | | | 8-10,000 | 60-70 |
| Arizona | whitetail | 32,000 | 7,200 | 69,262 | 2,870 | |
| | mule | 150,000 | | | 13,384 | *22.9 |
| Arkansas | whitetail | 500,000 | 12,500 | 250,700 | 30,000 | 10 |
| California | mule | | | 307,500 | | |
| | blacktail | | | | *86,300 | *22 |

*Indicates combined figures*

| State or Province | Species | Estimated Population | Hunting Bow | Licenses Gun | Estimated Harvest | Percent Hunter Success |
|---|---|---|---|---|---|---|
| Colorado | whitetail | | 9,966 | 138,886 | | |
| | mule | 375,000 | | | *40,449 | *29 |
| Connecticut | whitetail | 19,000 | 5,000 | 8,497 | 758 | 4.6 |
| Delaware | whitetail | 7,500 | 3,000 | 16,000 | 1,808 | 10 |
| Florida | whitetail | 550,000 | | 170,000 | 55,000 | 33 |
| Georgia | whitetail | 350,000 | 28,981 | 218,000 | 60,000 | 18 |
| Idaho | whitetail | 36,600 | 7,011 | 125,709 | 7,390 | 30 |
| | mule | 180,000 | | | 34,086 | 30 |
| Illinois | whitetail | | 26,042 | 74,902 | 16,000 | 5 |
| Indiana | whitetail | 65,000 | 26,491 | 74,043 | 11,000 | 12 |
| Iowa | whitetail | 50,000 | 13,000 | 68,000 | 21,000 | 34 |
| Kansas | whitetail | 30,800 | 5,043 | 10,442 | 4,373 | *40 |
| | mule | 7,700 | | | 1,115 | |
| Kentucky | whitetail | 100,000 | 3,165 | 61,305 | 10,000 | 15 |
| Louisiana | whitetail | 375,000 | 12,808 | 158,046 | 76,769 | 26.6 |
| Maine | whitetail | 225,000 | 2,621 | 216,157 | 34,675 | 19 |
| Maryland | whitetail | 65,000 | 25,000 | 90,000 | 9,737 | 12 |
| Massachusetts | whitetail | 13,000 | 5,000 | 55,000 | 2,525 | |
| Michigan | whitetail | 1,000,000 | 120,700 | 768,080 | 115,590 | 14 |
| Minnesota | whitetail | 400,000 | 31,836 | 327,596 | 66,000 | 21 |
| Mississippi | whitetail | 410,000 | 11,294 | 198,397 | 37,000 | 33 |
| Missouri | whitetail | | 29,974 | 234,471 | 54,048 | 20 |
| Montana | whitetail | | 7,203 | 148,103 | 28,358 | 44 |
| | mule | | | | 49,138 | |
| Nebraska | whitetail | 60,000 | 9,103 | 27,673 | 9,569 | *53 |
| | mule | 37,000 | | | 8,073 | |
| Nevada | mule | 122,000 | 882 | 35,530 | 7,253 | 21 |
| New Hampshire | whitetail | 40,000 | 2,900 | 91,250 | 8,500 | 9 |
| New Jersey | whitetail | 75,000 | 34,208 | 125,267 | 12,688 | 10 |
| New Mexico | whitetail | 18,000 | 9,189 | 177,204 | | |
| | mule | 289,000 | | | *21,425 | |
| New York | whitetail | 426,000 | 95,114 | 665,570 | 103,225 | 9 |
| North Carolina | whitetail | 500,000 | 45,000 | 162,000 | 53,000 | 33 |
| North Dakota | whitetail | 80,000 | 7,043 | 42,379 | 20,666 | 55 |
| | mule | 20,000 | | | 3,961 | 75 |
| Ohio | whitetail | 90,000 | 30,000 | 90,000 | 14,978 | 12 |
| Oklahoma | whitetail | 94,000 | 16,500 | 97,642 | 9,677 | 9 |
| Oregon | mule | 342,000 | 19,840 | 251,930 | 23,620 | 20 |
| | blacktail | 635,000 | | | 31,360 | 20 |
| Pennsylvania | whitetail | 600,000 | 203,000 | 850,000 | 140,000 | |
| Rhode Island | whitetail | 2,000 | 643 | 2,440 | 120 | 3 |
| South Carolina | whitetail | 215,000 | 5,500 | 125,000 | 46,000 | 25 |

*Indicates combined figures*

| State or Province | Species | Estimated Population | Hunting Bow | Licenses Gun | Estimated Harvest | Percent Hunter Success |
|---|---|---|---|---|---|---|
| South Dakota | whitetail | 160,000 | 7,486 | 59,517 | 23,630 | 60 |
| | mule | 90,000 | | | 12,600 | 60 |
| Tennessee | whitetail | 160,000 | 26,526 | 121,880 | 14,890 | 12 |
| Texas | whitetail | 3,100,000 | 20,000 | 565,000 | 349,000 | 42 |
| | mule | 135,000 | | | 11,000 | 47 |
| Utah | mule | | 17,626 | 177,056 | 45,401 | 23.4 |
| Vermont | whitetail | 160,00 | 26,435 | 138,009 | 9,939 | 7.5 |
| Virginia | whitetail | 356,000 | 48,888 | 319,289 | 63,443 | 17 |
| Washington | whitetail | 80,000 | 13,000 | 206,650 | 6,000 | |
| | mule | 150,000 | | | 32,300 | |
| | blacktail | 240,000 | | | 20,400 | *26 |
| West Virginia | whitetail | 288,00 | 24,000 | 185,000 | 35,336 | 25 |
| Wisconsin | whitetail | 725,000 | 120,000 | 560,000 | 130,966 | 20 |
| Wyoming | whitetail | 65,000 | 4,321 | 95,704 | 14,001 | |
| | mule | 355,400 | | | 61,428 | *73 |
| Hawaii | blacktail | 600 | | 1,685 | 11 | 3 |
| Alberta | whitetail | | | | | |
| British Columbia | whitetail | 30,000 | | | | |
| | mule | 100,000 | | | | |
| | blacktail | 500,000 | | | *36,700 | 26.2 |
| Manitoba | whitetail | 55,000 | | | | |
| | mule | 50+/− | | | | |
| New Brunswick | whitetail | 50,000 | | | 5,700 | 24 |
| Nova Scotia | whitetail | 75,000 | | | 72,000 | 50 |
| Ontario | whitetail | 140,000 | | | 13,400 | 15 |
| Quebec | whitetail | | | | 1,220 | |
| Saskatchewan | whitetail | 200,000 | | | 29,924 | 48.1 |
| | mule | 15,000 | | | 2,358 | 80 |

*Indicates combined figures*

# Bibliography

Abell, David H., and Frederick F. Gilbert. "Nutrient Content of Fertilized Deer Browse in Maine," *Journal of Wildlife Management,* vol. 38, no. 3, p. 517, 1974.

Alcock, John. *Animal Behavior.* Sunderland, Massachusetts: Sinauer Association, Inc., 1975.

Alexander, Bobby G. "Movements of Deer in Northeast Texas," *Journal of Mammalogy,* vol. 32, no. 3, p. 618, 1968.

Allen, Ross E., and Dale R. McCullough. "Deer-Car Accidents in Southern Michigan," *Journal of Wildlife Management,* vol. 40, no. 2, p. 317, 1976.

Arizona Fish and Game Department. *Arizona Deer Management Information Performance Reports,* June 30, 1975.

Armstrong, Ruth Allison. "Fetal Development of the Northern White-tailed Deer," *The American Midland Naturalist,* vol. 43, no. 3, p. 650, May 1950.

Bailey, Jr., William, George Schildmam, and Phillip Agee. *Nebraska Deer.* Lincoln, Nebraska: Nebraska Game, Forestation and Parks Commission, 1957.

Behrend, Donald F., and Robert A. Lubeck. "Summer Flight Behavior of White-tailed Deer in Two

Adirondack Forests," *Journal of Wildlife Management,* vol. 32, no. 3, July 1968.

Bellis, E.D., and H.B. Graves. "Deer Mortality on a Pennsylvania Interstate Highway," *Journal of Mammalogy,* vol. 35, no. 2, p. 232, 1971.

Bersing, Otis S. *A Century of Wisconsin Deer.* Madison, Wisconsin: Wisconsin Conservation Department, 1956.

Biehn, Earl R. *Crop Damage by Wildlife in California.* Sacramento, California: California Department of Fish and Game, 1951.

Bolte, John R., Jakie A. Hair, and Joe Fletcher. "White-tailed Deer Mortality Following Tissue Destruction Induced by Lone Star Ticks," *Journal of Wildlife Management,* vol. 34, no. 3, p. 546, 1970.

Boone and Crockett Club and the National Rifle Association of America, *North American Big Game* (7th Edition), Washington D.C., 1977.

Brokx, P.A. "The Superior Canines of Odocoileus and Other Deer," *Journal of Mammalogy,* vol. 53, no. 2, p. 359, 1972.

Brown, Ellsworth Reade. "The Black-tailed Deer in Western Washington," *Biological Bulletin #13,* Washington State Game Department, 1961.

Burkhardt, Dietrich, Wolfgang Schleidt, and Helmut Altner. *Signals in the Animal World.* New York:

McGraw-Hill Book Company, 1966.

Calhoun, John. *Prairie Whitetails.* Springfield, Illinois: Illinois Department of Conservation, 1974.

Carbaugh, B., J.P. Vaughan, E.D. Bellis, and H.B. Graves. "Distribution and Activity of White-tailed Deer Along an Interstate Highway," *Journal of Wildlife Management,* vol. 39, no. 3, p. 570, 1975.

Cartier, John O. "How Poachers Make a Fool of You," *Outdoor Life Magazine,* New York, December 1975.

Caton, John Dean. *The Antelope and Deer of America.* New York: Hurd and Houghton, 1877.

Cheatum, E.L., and Glenn H. Morton. "Breeding Season of White-tailed Deer in New York," *Journal of Mammalogy,* vol. 10, no. 3, p. 249, 1946.

Cook, R.S., Marshall White, D.O. Trainer, and W.C. Glazner. "Mortality of Young White-tailed Deer Fawns in South Texas," *Journal of Wildlife Management,* vol. 35, no. 1, p. 47, 1971.

Cowan, I. McT., and Valerius Geist. "Aggressive Behavior in Deer of the Genus Odocoileus," *Journal of Mammalogy,* vol. 42, no. 4, p. 523, 1961.

———. "Hybridization Between the Black-tailed Deer and the White-tailed Deer," *Journal of Mammalogy,* vol. 43, no. 4, p. 539, 1962.

Dahlberg, Burton L., and Ralph C.

Guettinger. "The White-tailed Deer in Wisconsin," *Technical Wildlife Bulletin #14*, Wisconsin Conservation Department, 1956.

Daniel, Walton S. "Travels of Post Oak Whitetails," *Texas Parks and Wildlife Magazine*, Austin, Texas, October 1973.

Dasmann, William. *If Deer Are to Survive.* (Wildlife Management Institute Book), Harrisburg, Pennsylvania: Stackpole Books, 1971.

Davis, Jerry W. "Deer Ked Infestation on White-tailed Deer in East Texas," *Journal of Wildlife Management*, vol. 37, no. 2, p. 183, 1973.

Dean, Donald J. "Streptothricosis—A New Deer Disease Transmissible to Man," *New York Conservationist*, Albany, New York, p. 15, October-November 1961.

Dean, R.E., M.D. Strickland, J.L. Newman, E.T. Thorne, and W.C. Hepworth. "Reticulo-Rumen Characteristics of Malnourished Mule Deer," *Journal of Wildlife Management*, vol. 39, no. 3, p. 601, 1975.

DeCalesta, David S., Julius G. Nagy, and James A. Bailey. "Some Effects of Starvation on Mule Deer Rumen Bacteria," *Journal of Wildlife Management*, vol. 38, no. 4, p. 815, 1974.

———. "Starving and Refeeding Mule Deer," *Journal of Wildlife Management*, vol. 39, no. 4, p. 663, 1975.

Denahlik, A. J. *Wild Deer.* London: Faber and Faber, Ltd., 1959.

Dickinson, Nathaniel R. "Observations on Steep-Slope Deer Wintering Areas in New York and Vermont," *New York Fish and Game Journal*, vol. 23, no. 1, 1976.

Dickson, III, John D. "An Ecological Study of the Key Deer," *Technical Bulletin #3*, Florida Game and Fresh Water Fish Commission, 1955.

Dietz, Donald R., and James R. Tigner. "Evaluation of Two Mammal Repellents Applied to Browse Species in the Black Hills," *Journal of Wildlife Management*, vol. 32, no. 1, p. 109, 1968.

Doutt, J. Kenneth, and John C. Donaldson. "Antlered Doe Study," *Pennsylvania Game News*, Harrisburg, Pennsylvania, p. 23, Nov. 1961.

Duvendeck, Jerry P. "The Value of Acorns in the Diet of Michigan Deer," *Journal of Wildlife Management*, vol. 26, no. 4, p. 371, 1962.

Ellisor, John E. "Mobility of White-tailed Deer in South Texas," *Journal of Mammalogy*, vol. 33, no. 1, p. 220, 1969.

Elman, Robert. *All About Deer Hunting in America.* New York: Winchester Press, 1976.

———. *The Hunter's Field Guide to the Game Birds and Animals of North America*, New York: Alfred A. Knopf, Inc., 1974.

Fay, L.D. "A Two-Headed White-tailed Deer Fetus," *Journal of Mammalogy,* vol. 41, no. 3, p. 41, 1960.

Forbes, Stanley E. "Diseases and Parasites of the Pennsylvania White-tailed Deer," *Pennsylvania Game News,* Harrisburg, Pennsylvania, December 1961.

————, Lincoln M. Lang, Stephen A. Liscinsky, and Harvey A. Roberts. *The White-tailed Deer in Pennsylvania.* Harrisburg, Pennsylvania: Pennsylvania Game Commission, 1971.

French, C.E., L.C. McEwen, N.D. Magruder, T. Rader, T.A. Long, and R.W. Swift. "Responses of White-tailed Bucks to Added Artificial Light," *Journal of Mammalogy,* vol. 41, no. 1, p. 23, 1960.

Garland, Lawrence E. *A Summary of Known Deer Losses to Causes Other Than Legal Hunting in Vermont 1938-1974.* Montpelier, Vermont: Vermont Department of Fish and Game, 1975.

Gill, Gerald B. *Montana Deer Nutrition Report Study Number 48.02.* Helena, Montana: Montana Fish and Game Department, 1972.

Glazener, W.C. "An Unusual Antler-Drop Schedule in the White-tailed Deer," *Journal of Mammalogy,* vol. 50, no. 1, p. 156, 1969.

Golley, Frank B. "Gestation Period, Breeding and Fawning Behavior of Columbian Black-tailed Deer," *Journal of Mammalogy,* vol. 38, no. 1, p. 116, 1957.

Gray, James. *Animal Locomotion.* New York: Norton, 1968.

Gruell, George E., and Nick J. Papez. "Movements of Mule Deer in Northeastern Nevada," *Journal of Wildlife Management,* vol. 27, no. 3, p. 414, 1963.

Gunderson, Harvey L. *Mammalogy.* New York: McGraw-Hill Book Company, 1976.

Hair, J. Alexander. "Ticks Can Kill," *Outdoor Oklahoma,* vol. XXIV, no. 11, Oklahoma City, December 1968.

Hall, E. Raymond. "The Deer of California," *California Fish and Game,* vol. 13, no. 4, October 1927.

Harder, John D., and Tony J. Peterle. "Effect of Diethylstilbestrol on Reproductive Performance of White-tailed Deer," *Journal of Wildlife Management,* vol. 38, no. 2, p. 183, 1974.

Hartman, Fred E. "Hunting is Big Business," *Pennsylvania Game News,* Harrisburg, Pennsylvania, February 1976.

Haugen, Arnold O., and L.S. Davenport. "Breeding Records of White-tailed Deer in the Upper Peninsula of Michigan," *Journal of Wildlife Management,* vol. 14, no. 3, p. 290, 1950.

Haugen, Arnold O. "Reproductive Performance of White-tailed Deer in Iowa," *Journal of Mammalogy*, vol. 56, no. 11, p. 151, 1975.

Hawkins, R.E., and W.D. Klimstra. "A Preliminary Study of the Social Organization of White-tailed Deer," *Journal of Wildlife Management*, vol. 34, no. 2, p. 407, 1970.

Healy, William M. "Forage Preferences of Tame Deer in a Northwest Pennsylvania Clear-cutting," *Journal of Wildlife Management*, vol. 35, no. 4, p. 717, 1971.

Hesselton, William. "A Wooly-coated White-tailed Deer from New York State," *Journal of Mammalogy*, vol. 47, no. 1, p. 154, 1966.

————. "The Incredible White Deer Herd," *The Conservationist*, Albany New York, October-November 1969.

Hickman, Sr., Cleveland P., Cleveland P. Hickman, Jr., and Frances M. Hickman. *Integrate Principles of Zoology*, 5th edition. St. Louis, Missouri: C.V. Mosby Company, 1974.

Hlavachich Bill. "Wanderlust," *Kansas Fish and Game Magazine*, vol. 29, no. 3, p. 8, 1972.

Hoff, G.L., S.H. Richards and D.O. Trainer. "Epizootic of Hemorrhaging Disease in North Dakota Deer," *Journal of Wildlife Management*, vol. 37, no. 3, p. 331, 1973.

Hoffman, Roger A., and Paul F. Robinson. "Changes in Some Endocrine Glands of White-tailed Deer as Affected by Season, Sex and Age," *Journal of Mammalogy*, vol. 47, no. 2, p. 266, 1966.

Hudson, Paul, and Ludvig G. Browmam. "Embryonic and Fetal Development of the Mule Deer," *Journal of Wildlife Management*, vol. 23, no. 3, p. 295, 1959.

Jackson, Lawrence W., and William T. Hesselton. "Breeding and Parturition Dates of White-tailed Deer in New York," *New York Fish and Game Journal*, vol. 20, no. 1, January 1973.

Jenkins, David H., and Ilo H. Bartlett. *Michigan Whitetails.* Lansing, Michigan: Michigan Department of Conservation, 1959.

Kammermeyer, K.E., and R.L. Marchinton. "Notes on Dispersal of Male White-tailed Deer," *Journal of Mammalogy*, vol. 57, no. 4, p. 776, November 1976.

Karns, Patrick D. "Pneumostrongylus Tenuis in Deer in Minnesota and Implications for Moose," *Journal of Wildlife Management*, vol. 31, no. 2, p. 295, 1967.

Klein, David R., and Sigurd T. Olson. "Natural Mortality Patterns of Deer in Southeast Alaska," *Journal of Wildlife Management*, vol. 24, no. 1, p. 80, 1960.

Knowlton, Frederick F., and W.G. Glazener. "Incidence of Maxillary

Canine Teeth in White-tailed Deer from San Patricio County, Texas," *Journal of Mammalogy,* vol. 46, no. 2, p. 352, 1965.

Korschgen, Leroy J. "Foods of Missouri Deer with Some Management Implications," *Journal of Wildlife Management,* vol. 26, no. 2, p. 164, 1962.

Kramer, August. "Interspecific Behavior and Dispersion of Two Sympatric Deer Species," *Journal of Wildlife Management,* vol. 37, no. 3, p. 288, 1973.

Krefting, Lauritsu, and Henry L. Hansen. "Increasing Browse for Deer by Aerial Applications of 2,4-D," *Journal of Wildlife Management,* vol. 33, no. 4, p. 784, 1969.

Lambiase, Jr., J.T., R.P. Altmann, and J.S. Lindzez. "Aspects of Reproductive Physiology of Male White-tailed Deer," *Journal of Wildlife Management,* vol. 36, no. 3, p. 868, 1972.

Lay, Daniel W. *The Importance of Variety to Southern Deer.* Nacogdoches, Texas: Texas Park and Wildlife Divison, 1964.

Leopold, A. Starker, Thane Riney, Randal McCain, and Lloyd Tevis, Jr., "The Jawbone Deer Herd," *Game Bulletin #4,* California Division of Fish and Game, 1951.

Linsdale, Jean M., and P. Quentin Tomich. *A Herd of Mule Deer.* Berkeley and Los Angeles: University of California Press, 1953.

Liscinsky, Stephen A., Charles T. Cushwa, Michael J. Puglisi, and Michael Ondik. "What Do Deer Eat?" *Pennsylvania Game News,* Harrisburg, Pennsylvania, May 1973.

Lolenosky, George B. "Wolf Predation on Wintering Deer in East-Central Ontario," *Journal of Wildlife Management,* vol. 36, no. 2, p. 357, 1972.

Loveless, Charles M. "The Everglades Deer Herd Life, History and Management," *Technical Bulletin #6,* Florida Game and Fresh Water Fish Commission, 1959.

Madson, John. *The White-tailed Deer.* East Alton, Illinois: Olin Mathieson Chemical Corporation, 1961.

Maguire, H.F., and C.W. Severinghaus. "Wariness as an Influence on Age Composition of White-tailed Deer Killed by Hunters," *New York Fish and Game Journal,* p. 98, January 1954.

Mangold, Robert. *Analysis of Reproductive Data From Does Collected During Hunter's Choice Deer Season.* Trenton, New Jersey: New Jersey Bureau of Wildlife Management, January 31, 1962.

Martin, Alexander C., Herbert S. Zim, and Arnold L. Nelson. *American Wildlife and Plants.* New York: McGraw-Hill Book Company, 1951.

Martinka, C.J. "Habitat Relationships of White-tailed and Mule Deer in Northern Montana," *Journal of Wildlife Management,* vol. 32, no. 3, p. 558, 1968.

Matschke, George H. "Microincapsulated Diethylstilbestrol as an Oral Contraceptive in White-tailed Deer," *Journal of Wildlife Management,* vol. 41, no. 1, p. 87.

McCulloch, Clay Y., and Philip J. Urness. "Deer Nutrition in Arizona Chaparral and Desert Habitats," *Special Report #3,* Arizona Game and Fish Department, 1973.

McCullough, Dale R. "Sex Characteristics of Black-tailed Deer Hooves," *Journal of Wildlife Management,* vol. 29, no. 1, p. 210, 1965.

McDowell, Robert (Editor). "New Jersey's White-tailed Deer," *Report #3,* New Jersey Division of Fish, Game and Shell Fisheries, 1976.

McLean, Donald D. "The Deer of California, with Particular Reference to the Rocky Mountain Mule Deer," *California Fish and Game,* vol. 26, no. 2. Sacramento, California: California Fish and Game, 1940.

Menzel, Karl. *The Deer of Nebraska.* Lincoln, Nebraska: Nebraska Game and Parks Commission, 1975.

Michael, Edwin D. "Birth of White-tail Deer Fawns," *Journal of Wildlife Management,* vol. 28, no. 1, p. 171, 1964.

Miller, Frank L. "Distribution Patterns of Black-tailed Deer in Relation to Environment," *Journal of Mammalogy,* vol. 51, no. 2, p. 248, 1970.

Miller, Gerrit S., and Remington Kellogg. *List of North American Recent Mammals.* Washington, D.C.: Smithsonian Institution, 1955.

Milne, Lorus J., and Margery. *The Senses of Animals and Men.* New York: Atheneum, 1962.

Mireau, Gary W. "Studies on the Biology of an Antlered Female Mule Deer," *Journal of Mammalogy,* vol. 53, no. 2, p. 403, 1972.

Missouri Department of Conservation Newsletter. *Missouri's Biggest Whitetails.* Jefferson City, Missouri: Missouri Department of Conservation, December 1975.

Montgomery, G.G. "Nocturnal Movements and Activity Rhythms of White-tailed Deer," *Journal of Wildlife Management,* vol. 27, no. 3, p. 442, 1963.

Mosby, Henry S. (Editor). *Wildlife Investigational Techniques.* Washington, D.C.: The Wildlife Society, 1963.

Muller-Schwarze, Dietland. "Responses of Young Black-tailed Deer to Predator Odors," *Journal of Mammalogy,* vol. 53, no. 2, p. 393, 1972.

Murphy, Dean A. "Deer Range Appraisal in the Midwest," *White-*

*tailed Deer in the Midwest Symposium,* Columbus, Ohio, 1968.

—— and Hewlette S. Crawford. *Wildlife Foods and Understory Vegetation in Missouri's National Forests.* Missouri Department of Conservation, 1970.

Mustard, Eldie W., and Veron Wright. *Food Habits of Iowa Deer.* Des Moines, Iowa: State Conservation Commission, 1964.

Nagy, Julius G., Harold W. Steinhoff, and Gerald M. Ward. "Effects of Essential Oils of Sagebrush on Deer Rumen Microbial Function," *Journal of Wildlife Management,* vol. 28, no. 4, p. 785, 1964.

——, G. Vidacs, and G.M. Ward. "Previous Diet of Deer, Cattle and Sheep and Ability to Digest Alfalfa Hay," *Journal of Wildlife Management,* vol. 31, no. 3, p. 443, 1967.

Neff, Don J. "Forage Preferences of Trained Mule Deer on the Beaver Creek Watersheds," *Special Report #4,* Arizona Game and Fish Department, 1974.

Nellis, Carl H. "Antler from Right Zygomatic Arch of White-tailed Deer," *Journal of Mammalogy,* vol. 46, no. 1, p. 108, 1965.

New Jersey Division of Fish, Game and Shellfish. "New Jersey's White-tailed Deer," *Deer Report #3,* 1976.

Newson, William Monypeny. *White-tailed Deer.* New York: Charles Scribner's Sons, 1926.

Nixon, Charles M., Milford W. McClain, and Kenneth R. Russell. "Deer Food Habits and Range Characteristics in Ohio," *Journal of Wildlife Management,* vol. 34, no. 4, p. 870, 1970.

Owen, Jr., Wilbur B. *A Survey of the Helminth Parasites of White-tailed Deer in Five Regions of Arkansas.* Fayetteville, Arkansas: University of Arkansas, 1974.

Ozoga, John J. "Some Longevity Records for Female White-tailed Deer in Northern Michigan," *Journal of Wildlife Management,* vol. 33, no. 4, p. 1027, 1969.

—— and Louis J. Verme. "Winter Feeding Patterns of Penned White-tailed Deer," *Journal of Wildlife Management,* vol. 34, no. 2, p. 431, 1970.

——. "Aggressive Behavior of White-tailed Deer at Winter Cuttings," *Journal of Wildlife Management,* vol. 36, no. 3, p. 861, 1972.

—— and Louis J. Verme. "Activity Patterns of White-tailed Deer During Estrus," *Journal of Wildlife Management,* vol. 39, no. 4, p. 679, 1975.

Patton, Art. *1975 Deer Mortality Report.* Truro, Nova Scotia: Nova Scotia Department of Lands and Forests, 1975.

Peabody, Bill. "Of Teeth and Time," *Kansas Fish and Game Magazine,* vol. 29, no. 5, p. 23, 1975.

Pearson, Henry A. "Rumen Organism in White-tailed Deer from South Texas," *Journal of Wildlife Management*, vol. 29, no. 3, p. 493, 1965.

Petraborg, W.H., and V.E. Gunvalson. "Observations of Bobcat Mortality and Bobcat Predation on Deer," *Journal of Mammalogy*, vol. 43, no. 3, p. 430, 1962.

Pratt, Jerome J. *White Flags of Apacheland.* New York: Vantage Press, 1966.

Pruitt, Jr., William O. "Behavior of the Barren-ground Caribou," *Biological Papers of the University of Alaska, #3.* Fairbanks, Alaska, 1960.

Quay, W.B., and Dietland Muller-Schwarze. "Functional Histology of Integumentary Glandular Regions in Black-tailed Deer," *Journal of Mammalogy*, vol. 51, no. 4, p. 675, 1970.

———. "Geographic Variation in the Metatarsal Gland of the White-tailed Deer," *Journal of Mammalogy*, vol. 52, no. 1, p. 1, 1971.

Reed, Dale F., Thomas N. Woodard, and Thomas M. Pojar. "Behavioral Response of Mule Deer to a Highway Underpass," *Journal of Wildlife Management*, vol. 39, no. 2, p. 361, 1975.

Rees, John W., Robert A. Kainer, and Robert W. Davis. "Histology, Embryology and Gross Morphology of the Mandibular Dentition in Mule Deer," *Journal of Mammalogy*, vol. 27, no. 4, p. 640, 1966.

Reynolds, Hudson G. "Mule Deer Killed by Lightning," *Journal of Mammalogy*, vol. 46, no. 4, p. 676, 1965.

Roberts, Harvey A. "Why Check the Deer Kill?" *Pennsylvania Game News*, Harrisburg Pennsylvania, December 1966.

Robinette, W. Leslie, and Dale A. Jones. "Antler Anomalies of Mule Deer," *Journal of Mammalogy*, vol. 40, no. 7, p. 96, 1959.

———, C. Harold Baer, R.E. Pillmore, and C.E. Knittle. "Effects of Nutritional Change on Captive Mule Deer," *Journal of Wildlife Management*, vol. 37, no. 3, p. 312, 1973.

Robinson, William L. "Social Dominance and Physical Condition Among Penned White-tailed Deer Fawns," *Journal of Mammalogy*, vol. 43, no. 4, p. 462, 1962.

Roosevelt, Theodore, et al. *The Deer Family.* New York: The Macmillan Company, 1902.

Rue III, Leonard Lee. *The World of the White-tailed Deer.* Philadelphia and New York: J.B. Lippincott Company, 1962.

———. *Sportsman's Guide to Game Animals.* New York: Outdoor Life Books—Harper and Row, 1968.

Russo, John P. "The Kaibab North Deer Herd," *Wildlife Bulletin #7,*

Arizona Game and Fish Department, 1964.

Samuel, William M. "Parasites of Pennsylvania Deer," *Pennsylvania Game News*, Harrisburg, Pennsylvania, November 1967.

Sauer, Peggy R., John W. Tanck, and C.W. Severinghaus. "Herbaceous Food Preferences of White-tailed Deer," *New York Fish and Game Journal*, vol. 16, #2, July 1969.

Saunders, Barry P. "Meningeal Worm in White-tailed Deer in Northwestern Ontario and Moose Population Densities," *Journal of Wildlife Management*, vol. 37, no. 3, p. 327, 1973.

Schemnitz, Sanford D. "Maine-Island-Mainland Movement of White-tailed Deer," *Journal of Mammalogy*, vol. 56, no. 2, p. 535, 1975.

Sealander, John A., Philip S. Gipson, Michael Cartwright, and James M. Pledger. *Behavioral and Physiological Studies of Relationships Between White-tailed Deer and Dogs in Arkansas.* Fayetteville: University of Arkansas, Department of Zoology, 1975.

Seton, Ernest Thompson. *Lives of Game Animals.* Boston: Charles T. Branford Company, 1953.

Severinghaus, C.W. "Some Observations on the Breeding Behavior of Deer," *New York Fish and Game Journal*, July, 1955.

———. "Deer Weights as an Index of Range Conditions on Two Wilderness Areas in the Adirondack Region," *New York Fish and Game Journal*, July 1955.

——— and Benjamin F. Tullar. "Wintering Deer vs. Snowmobiles," *The Conservationist*, Albany, New York, June-July 1975.

Shafer, Elwood L., Jr. "The Twig-Count Method for Measuring Hardwood Deer Browse," *Journal of Wildlife Management*, vol. 28, no. 3, p. 428, 1963.

Shaw, Harley. "Insectivorous White-tailed Deer," *Journal of Mammalogy*, vol. 44, no. 2, p. 284, 1963.

Shoener, Tom. "Fifteen Years of Big Bucks," *Maine Fish and Game*, Augusta, Maine, Fall 1973.

Shope, Richard E., L.G. Macnamara, and Robert Mangold. "Epizootic Hemorrhagic Disease of Deer," *New Jersey Outdoors Magazine*, Trenton, New Jersey, November 1955.

Short, Cathleen. "Morphological Development and Aging of Mule and White-Tailed Deer Fetuses," *Journal of Wildlife Management*, vol. 34, no. 2, p. 383, 1970.

Short, Henry L. "Rumen Fermentations and Energy Relationships in White-tailed Deer," *Journal of Wildlife Management*, vol. 27, no. 2, p. 184, 1963.

———. "Postnatal Stomach Development of White-tailed Deer," *Journal of Wildlife Management,* vol. 28, no. 3, p. 445, 1964.

Siegler, Hilbert R., Helenette Silver, David L. White, and Henry A. Laramie, Jr. "The White-tailed Deer of New Hampshire," *Survey Report #10,* New Hampshire Fish and Game Department, 1968.

Silver, Helenette. "Deer Milk Compared with Substitute Milk for Fawns," *Journal of Wildlife Management,* vol. 25, no. 1, p. 666, 1961.

————. "An Instance of Fertility in a White-tailed Buck Fawn," *Journal of Wildlife Management,* vol. 29, no. 3, p. 634, 1965.

————, N.F. Colovos, J.B. Holter, and H.H. Hayes. "Fasting Metabolism of White-tailed Deer," *Journal of Wildlife Management,* vol. 33, no. 3, p. 490, 1969.

Smith, Robert Leo. *Ecology and Field Biology,* 2nd edition. New York: Harper and Row, 1974.

Snider, Carl C., and J. Malcolm Asplund. "Invitro Digestibility of Deer Foods from the Missouri Ozarks," *Journal of Wildlife Management,* vol. 38, no. 1, p. 20, 1974.

Stadtfeld, Curtis K. *Whitetail Deer, A Year's Cycle.* New York: Dial Press, 1975.

Stone, Ward B., and Stuart L. Free, William T. Hesselton, and Lawrence W. Jackson. "Polydactylism in a White-tailed Deer from New York," *New York Fish and Game Journal,* vol. 17, no. 2, July 1970.

Stone, Ward B., and John R. Palmateer. "A Bird Ingested by a White-tailed Deer," *New York Fish and Game Journal,* January 1970.

Strung, Norman. *Deer Hunting.* Philadelphia and New York: J.B. Lippincott Company, 1973.

Swank, Wendell G. "The Mule Deer in Arizona Chaparral," *Wildlife Bulletin #3,* Arizona Game and Fish Department, 1958.

Sweeney, J.R., R.L. Marchinton, and J.M. Sweeney. "Responses of Radio-Monitored White-tailed Deer Chased by Dogs," *Journal of Wildlife Management,* vol. 35, no. 4, p. 707, 1971.

Taber, Richard D., and Raymond F. Dasmann. "The Black-tailed Deer of the Chaparral," *Game Bulletin #8,* California Department of Fish and Game, 1958.

Taft, Edgar B., Thomas C. Hall, and Joseph Aub. "The Growth of the Deer Antler," *The New York State Conservationist,* Albany, New York, February-March 1956.

Taylor, Walter P. (Editor). *The Deer of North America.* (Wildlife Management Institute.) Harrisburg, Pennsylvania: The Stackpole Company, 1956.

Teer, James G., Jack Thomas, and Eugene Walker. "Ecology and Management of White-tailed Deer in Llano Basin of Texas," *Journal of Wildlife Management* (Monograph #15), October 1965.

Thomas, D.C., and I.D. Smith. "Reproduction in a Wild Black-tailed Deer Fawn," *Journal of Mammalogy*, vol. 54, no. 1, p. 302, 1973.

Torgerson, Oliver, and William H. Pfander. "Cellulose Digestibility and Chemical Composition of Missouri Deer Foods," *Journal of Wildlife Management*, vol. 35, no. 2, p. 221, 1971.

Trefethen, James B. *An American Crusade for Wildlife.* New York: Winchester Press and Boone and Crockett Club, 1975.

Trodd, L.L. "Quadruplet Fetuses in a White-tailed Deer from Espanola, Ontario," *Journal of Mammalogy*, vol. 43, no. 3, p. 414, 1962.

Ullrey, D.E., W.G. Youatt, H.E. Johnson, P.K. Fu, and L.D. Fay. "Digestibility of Cedar and Aspen Browse for the White-tailed Deer," *Journal of Wildlife Management*, vol. 28, no. 4, p. 791, 1964.

Ullrey, D.E., W.G. Youatt, H.E. Johnson, L.D. Fay, and B.L. Bradley. "Protein Requirement of White-tailed Deer Fawns," *Journal of Wildlife Management*, vol. 31, no. 1, p. 679, 1967.

Ullrey, D.E., H.E. Johnson, W.G.

Youatt, L.D. Fay, B.L. Schdepke, and W.T. Magee. "A Basal Diet for Deer Nutrition Research," *Journal of Wildlife Management*, vol. 35, no. 1, p. 57, 1971.

United States Fish and Wildlife Service, U.S. Department of the Interior. *1975 National Survey of Hunting, Fishing and Wildlife-Associated Recreation.* Washington, D.C.: U.S. Fish and Wildlife Service, 1977.

Verme, Louis J. "Fecundity in a Michigan White-tailed Deer," *Journal of Mammalogy*, vol. 43, no. 1, p. 112, 1962.

————. "Reproduction Studies on Penned White-tailed Deer," *Journal of Wildlife Management*, vol. 29, no. 1, p. 74, 1965.

White, David L. *Deer Kill Summary: Losses to Cars and Dogs, 1947-1976,* New Hampshire Fish and Game Department, 1976.

White, Marshall, Frederick F. Knowlton, and W.C. Glazener. "Effects of Dam-Newborn Fawn Behavior on Capture and Mortality," *Journal of Wildlife Management*, vol. 36, no. 3, p. 897, 1972.

White, Marshall. "Description of Remains of Fawn Killed by Coyote," *Journal of Mammalogy*, vol. 54, no. 1, p. 291, 1973.

Wildlife and Fisheries Commission. "How Much Did that Deer Weigh on the Hoof?" *Bulletin*, Wildlife and Fisheries Commission, 1976.

Winter, Ruth. *The Smell Book: Scents, Sex and Society.* Philadelphia and New York: J.B. Lippincott Company, 1976.

Wobeser, G., and W. Runge. "Rumen Overload and Rumenitis in White-tailed Deer," *Journal of Wildlife Management,* vol. 39, no. 3, p. 596, 1975.

Young, Stanley P., and Edward A. Goldman. *The Puma, Mysterious American Cat.* Washington, D.C.: American Wildlife Institute, 1946.

Zagata, Michael, and Aaron N. Moen. "Antler Shedding by White-tailed Deer in Midwest," *Journal of Mammalogy,* vol. 55, no. 3, p. 656, 1974.

——— and Arnold O. Haugen. "Influence of Light and Weather on Observability of Iowa Deer," *Journal of Wildlife Management,* vol. 38, no. 2, p. 220, 1974.

# Index